# William Walton

*His Life and Music*

*By the same author*

The Unknown Country: A Life of Igor Stravinsky

# William Walton

*His Life and Music*

Neil Tierney

ROBERT HALE · LONDON

*First published in Great Britain 1984*

*Robert Hale Limited*
*Clerkenwell House*
*Clerkenwell Green*
*London EC1R 0HT*

*British Library Cataloguing in Publication Data*

*Tierney, Neil*
*William Walton.*
*1. Walton, William, 1902_1983  2. Composers*
*—Great Britain—Biography*
*I. Title*
*780′.92′4*  M.410.W292

ISBN 0–7090–1784–7

Photoset in Ehrhardt by
Kelly Typesetting Limited
Bradford-on-Avon, Wiltshire
Printed in Great Britain by
St Edmundsbury Press
Bury St Edmunds, Suffolk
Bound by Hunter & Foulis Limited

# Contents

# Illustrations

Sir William with Elisabeth Schwarzkopf and Walter Legge (*Erich Auerbach*)

With Sir John Pritchard who conducted the first performance of his Second Symphony (*Liverpool Daily Post & Echo Ltd, and the Royal Liverpool Philharmonic Society*)

Alan Frank with the Waltons at the first performance of the Second Symphony (*Edinburgh Evening News/Oxford University Press*)

Discussing his Second Symphony with George Szell (*Particam/Oxford University Press*)

'La Mortella' (*Lady Walton*)

Sir William and Lady Walton on Ischia (*Lady Walton*)

Congratulated by Asa Briggs (*The Times*)

An ovation from an audience at the Leningrad Philharmonic Hall (*Lady Walton*)

With Kyung Wha Chung (*Clive Barda*)

With Dame Janet Baker and Christopher Morris (*Oxford University Press*)

With his brothers Noel and Alec, a rare meeting in Manchester during his seventieth birthday celebrations (*Oldham Chronicle*)

Sir William and Lady Walton in London shortly before the celebration of the composer's seventieth birthday (*Sefton Photo Library*)

The 'Grand Old Man of Music' smoking his favourite pipe (*Erich Auerbach*)

Sir William at the Royal Festival Hall in 1982 during a rehearsal of his *Prologo e Fantasia* (*Christina Burton/Oxford University Press*)

# Acknowledgements

Readers of biography have a right to know whether they are being given a reliable account of a life as it was lived, or whether, in presenting that life to the public, the author has distorted and falsified the image. I can only say, firstly that there is enough drama, pathos, humanity and splendour in the life of Sir William Walton to require no artifice, and secondly that my book derives its validity from a mass of published reports, letters and memoirs, and certain unique and revealing documents in my possession, as well as from the unimpeachable reminiscences of persons who knew this great man intimately. No invented speeches or opinions have been put into the mouths of those who jostle in the cavalcade of history that stretches from Oldham to Ischia, and in mentioning that enchanted island, where the composer spent the happiest years of his life, I must acknowledge my indebtedness to Lady Walton for her kindness in reading the typescript of my book, granting me permission to quote passages from letters written by her husband, and supplying me with additional facts which I have incorporated into the relevant chapters.

As regards the research material used, I cannot too warmly express my thanks to Dr Stewart Craggs, the brilliant Sunderland librarian who wrote that now indispensable source of information for musicologists, *William Walton: A Thematic Catalogue*. For his unfailing kindness and cooperation, which have included the placing at my disposal of documents and other papers resulting from his own considerable study of Walton's life and music, I am profoundly grateful. It was because of the recording which Dr Craggs made of Walton's ill-fated *Battle of Britain* music, and because of his own ebullient enthusiasm, that arrangements were made to record a full performance for the first time, and if other forgotten works by the composer are brought out from obscurity it will doubtless be due to his efforts. We can also thank Dr Craggs for having, during research for his own book, discovered the score which Sir William wrote in 1941 for Gielgud's stage production of *Macbeth*. He has become for Walton what

Beecham was for Delius: a respected champion and advocate. We who love the composer's rich and elevated music are indebted to him,—none more so than I.

An important source of information to which I have had access has been the revelatory correspondence exchanged by Walton and his generous, loyal, infinitely compassionate friend Siegfried Sassoon over many years. My research material has included letters written by the Baroness Imma Doernberg and Lady Alice Wimborne: two beautiful, extremely intelligent women for whom, before his marriage to Susana Gil, the composer had loving, passionate relationships. I have also gleaned illuminating facts from letters penned by a host of people who, themselves prominent in public life, played significant parts in Sir William's long and illustrious career; among them the following: Lady Christabel Aberconway, Professor William Alwyn, Mr Ronald Kinlock Anderson, Dr Malcolm Arnold, Mr W. H. Auden, Mr Richard Rodney Bennett, Sir Lennox Berkeley, Sir Arthur Bliss, Mr Dallas Bower, Miss Harriet Cohen, Sir Basil Dean, Professor Thorold Dickinson, Dr Ralph Dorfman, Mr Hubert Foss, Professor Roy Fuller, Mr David Gentleman, Sir John Gielgud, Miss Beryl Grey, Mr Ron Goodwin, Mr Christopher Hassall, Mr Gordon Jackson, Miss Lina Lalandi, Mr Walter Legge, Miss Elizabeth Lutyens, Mr George Malcolm, Sir William McKie, Mr Gerald Moore, Mr Angus Morrison, Mr Boyd Neel, Mr Peter Quennell, Sir Michael Redgrave, Dr Leslie Russell, Miss Moira Shearer, Mr Michael Somes, Mr Vilem Tausky, the Hon. Stephen Tennant, Mr Noel Walton and Mr John Warrack.

Here I must record my appreciation of the invaluable assistance given to me by the British Broadcasting Corporation, with a special word of thanks to the producer Mr Rodney Greenberg of the Music and Arts Department, and Miss Gwyniver Jones of the Written Archives Centre at Caversham Park, Reading. My thanks are also extended to London Weekend Television for kindly allowing me to use quotations from the *South Bank Show*.

I am indebted to Mr Colin Graham, the Artistic Director of the London Coliseum; Sir Charles Groves; Dr Elisabeth Schwarzkopf; the Royal Liverpool Philharmonic Society; the Archives Office of the English Music Theatre Company; Mrs Joan Lane of the Crompton Public Library, Shaw, Oldham; Mrs C. E. Walton; Mr Spencer W. Freeman and Novello and Company; Queen's University, Belfast and its Senior Sub-Librarian Mr W. G. Wheeler; the Royal Opera House, Covent Garden and Miss Francesca Franchi of the Archives Office; Mr Alan Whiteley, music master of New Heys Comprehensive School, Liverpool; the staff of the Music Library, Liverpool City Libraries; Mrs Anne Sykes, the former

Editorial Librarian of the *Oldham Evening Chronicle*; Miss Margaret Higham of the Library Department of the Local Interest Centre, Oldham; the much revered photographer and connoisseur of life, Mr Chambré Hardman; and that other Liverpool master of the camera, Mr Peter Kaye, whose patient, highly skilled restoration of two early Walton photographs can be described only as miraculous. Finally, I express my thanks to Miss Marjorie C. Hill, Miss Christina Clarke and Mr Dennis Moir for their steadfast, always invigorating friendship and encouragement.

# Foreword

I was delighted when Neil Tierney sent me the manuscript of his biography of William. He has researched William's life with care and accuracy and made it a labour of love.

It is my great sadness that he didn't talk to William about this project as it would have made him immensely happy to know that he was sympathetically being brought to life.

It would also have been a joy for Neil Tierney to have met the adorable man and great artist that he has so aptly described—difficult and humble about his achievements and at the same time fiercely protective of his works.

William's friends may have been puzzled by his decision to live the last 35 years cut off from the brilliant and amusing London scene and for his preference for an almost monastic existence in Ischia, and this book highlights the determination and strength that guided William throughout his life, that made this step possible, so that the artist could express with integrity, in peace and at his own pace, his thoughts.

Thank you Neil Tierney.

Susana Walton
May 1984

# Preface

I had originally given the title *Orb and Sceptre* to my book because these emblems of sovereignty seemed in a way to fit the status and dignity of the late Sir William Walton, who did, of course, compose a Coronation March so named; but I felt on reflection that his name should be pre-eminent. Certainly much of his music has a royal or ceremonial flavour: such works as the *Te Deum, Crown Imperial*, the *Gloria, In Honour of the City of London*, the *Queen's Fanfare* and even *Belshazzar's Feast*, which glows with a kingly, though baleful light.

In the quotation from Shakespeare which serves as the epigraph for this book the final couplet has, I believe, some relevance, for so often in the past the 'muddy vesture of decay'—or neglect—prevented the music-loving public from hearing live performances of some of his most inspired pieces. Walton was criticized for failing to explore new horizons, for remaining placidly in the lush green pastures of the post-war years in which, incidentally, he wrote some of his noblest works. It is true that he refused to be swayed by the 'new music' of the '50s, when the cult of serialism spread like the craze for hoola-hoop all over Britain; but the reason was far removed from complacency or cowardice. The profound and many-sided nature of Walton's music powerfully refutes the feeble charges levelled by his denigrators, and affirms that here was a man who found a universal language, a style that raised itself above the fast-flowing stream of musical fashion that changes course from day to day. And there is no law of aesthetics which measures the value of a composer in direct ratio to his pursuit and acceptance of avant-garde trends. Walton, in refusing to conform to the non-conformists, endured a certain degree of disdain, even of contempt and hostility, from those note-spinning modernists who have seemed to regard music as nothing more than a mathematical formula involving a few vertical chord-clusters, reinforced by brief, Webern-like sounds, dramatic timpani rolls and, to use a hackneyed phrase, 'many a pregnant silence'.

Walton's musical style is diverse: there is the Walton of the brittle, biting rhythms, and there is the romantic of the Viola Concerto, in which for the first time he achieved an impressive balance between melodic warmth and pungent wit. He had an acute sense of orchestral colour, matched only among contemporary British composers by Britten and Malcolm Arnold. A slow and thoughtful worker, he was exacting about the dynamic requirements of his scores, with a profusion of expression marks, bowings and the like. Much of the music's impact depends upon precise observance of these directions. About his own value as a composer, Walton was always extremely modest, scorning those fogged, verbose analyses which lesser men foist upon a dazed, uncomprehending public to explain their own musical indiscretions. The note which he penned for the first performance of his *Partita* reads: 'My *Partita* poses no problems, has no ulterior motive or meaning behind it, and makes no attempt to ponder the imponderables. I have written it in the hope that it may be enjoyed straight off without any preliminary probing into the score.'

There are four works which may be regarded as landmarks in his creative life: *Façade* (1926), the Viola Concerto (1929), *Belshazzar's Feast* (1931) and the First Symphony (1934–5). It is clear that *Façade*, which startled the musical world of its day by expressing the jazz idioms of the '20s in terms of specialized orchestral technique, is Walton's most remarkable, though not his most important, achievement. Although it gave brilliant voice to the skittish, dilettante young people of the period and, in so doing, 'dated' itself, the work, strangely enough, has never become cobwebbed and effete but continues to delight audiences, young and old. The second major composition mentioned above, the Viola Concerto, is one of the most satisfying works, in any form, for solo viola in the repertoire, and at a time when critics and public alike regarded the instrument merely as third string voice in the orchestra, it brought a new solo 'star' to the concert platform. Walton's many tongues speak most eloquently, however, in *Belshazzar's Feast*, whose amazing barbarity—as well as pity—still excites the listener and, I believe, will long do so. For sheer physical energy, this monumental piece, with its outbursts of brilliant orchestral frenzy, its sombre opening that indicates a large-scale undertaking, like the beginning of Beethoven's *Choral* Symphony, and its electrifying use of brass bands, must be seen not only as a dramatic tour-de-force but as one which dealt a mortal blow to the old British concept of oratorio. *Belshazzar's Feast* looks back, through its deployment of huge choral and instrumental forces, to the Berlioz of the Requiem Mass. From the first resplendent trombone summons to the final, prolonged bar at the end of the savage, *Elektra*—like dance and song of triumph, one is swept along on the full flood of a story whose archaic flavour is redeemed by a score of indisputable mastery. As for the remaining landmark in Walton's career, the First Symphony, I am as thrilled and engrossed by the drive of the music as I was when I first heard it about forty years ago. Three movements were completed in 1934, the year in which Hitler sprang to power and, alas, the year also in which Holst, Elgar and Delius died, carrying a whole musical chapter and an age into the grave. The symphony is a powerful, aggressive piece whose anger develops at times into a conflict of almost unparalleled ferocity. In the first movement the influence of Sibelius manifests itself in the building-up of tensions by *ostinato* rhythms; in the *Scherzo* a vein of malice and wit enhances the bitter-sweet melodic beauty of the slow movement which follows; and the finale, full of triumphant, glittering sonorities, as well as unpredictable outbursts of violence, concludes the work convincingly.

Walton was never a prolific composer, but his versatility, his fastidious musicianship and his capacity for harnessing to his own use and betterment the friendly services of experts in composition and orchestration, raised him to a high peak of eminence. Standing precariously between the generation of Vaughan Williams and that of Benjamin Britten, he soon made his own personal impact with music carrying a rich vein of satirical gaiety. In the early phase, which included *Façade*, the *Sinfonia Concertante* and the overture *Portsmouth Point*, his attitude to music, like that of Stravinsky, was markedly anti-romantic; but, with the Viola Concerto, there came a striking change. Flinging aside the mask of irony and sophistication, Walton took a deep breath and sang like a nightingale for the first time. The discovery that he had a natural gift for pure, intoxicating melody influenced all the music which he composed from that point onwards, although, influenced also by a fear of being thought old-fashioned, of being regarded as a charming relic from the sweetly diatonic period of musical taste, his temperament hovered uneasily between the extreme poles of poetic soliloquy and aggressive high spirits. Out of this huge, incessant conflict, flowed, over several decades, a procession of vivid, highly individualistic works; some of them, like the First Symphony, *Belshazzar's Feast* and the Violin Concerto, racked by strange alternations of violence and lyrical nostalgia; others, like the *Gloria*, the opera *Troilus and Cressida*, the *Coronation Te Deum* and *Orb and Sceptre*, providing, through raptly expressive or ceremonial music, a passionate and adoring view of life.

A sense of conflict is inseparable from any true appraisal of Walton's life and music. He fought and won more battles than any other composer of his time. In the early 1920s he tilted a brave lance against the too inward-looking crusaders of the old British Music Society, whose narrow parochialism injured their cause more effectively than did the 'invading' foreign music they sought to repel. Under the fustian banner of these zealots British music became synonymous with a kind of narcissistic, village-green outlook, with excessive idolatry, over-praise and boredom. Walton scattered the prim crusaders with his *Façade*, at the same time helping to guide Britain back into Europe's main cultural stream. He took up his lance again with *Belshazzar's Feast*, whose musical idioms troubled and irritated the choral singers who performed it, just as its use of a scriptural text shocked the free-thinking extremists who regarded all oratorios or cantatas as old-fashioned sentiment and claptrap.

Yet the man behind these conquests was no Samurai warrior of music, using a sword of intolerance to cut down those who opposed or differed from him, though admittedly his temper seemed occasionally to have a very short fuse and to ignite all too rapidly. Many people blessed with percipience and understanding regarded him not as an ogre but as a shrewd, tough Englishman with, at times, a Rabelaisian humour; a simple, uncomplicated man behind whose rather austere manner were immense kindness and consideration for others. A careful, fastidious craftsman with complete honesty of purpose and perspective, Sir William had not a vestige of arrogance or pomposity in his character. If any composer deserves the tribute of a biographical study which conforms to the same principle, it is surely he. I sincerely hope that this book provides one.

This book is dedicated
with admiration and esteem to
LADY WALTON
and with undying love and gratitude to
JOAN AND KATHY
my wife and daughter

How sweet the moonlight sleeps upon this bank!
Here will we sit, and let the sounds of music
Creep in our ears: soft stillness and the night
Become the touches of sweet harmony.
Sit Jessica: look, how the floor of heaven
Is thick inlaid with pattines of bright gold:
There's not the smallest orb which thou behold'st
But in his motion like an angel sings,
Still quiring to the young-eyed cherubins;
Such harmony is in immortal souls;
But, whilst this muddy vesture of decay
Doth grossly close it in, we cannot hear it.

From Shakespeare's *The Merchant of Venice*

*The Life*

# 1

# In the Beginning

In the realm of music Sir William Walton has been, as far as Britain is concerned, the Unofficial Laureate of his day, to whose marching music Queen Elizabeth II was borne in majesty through her Coronation, as was her father, King George VI, in 1936. He has also been the Great Enigma, a shy, uncommunicative man with a bee-sting sense of humour, whose career has consistently followed a tortuous, ill-defined path. There is scarcely anything more astonishing about his life than the way in which he suddenly rocketed to fame at the age of twenty with the dazzlingly precocious *Façade*. His musical training in the years of preparation for this lightning, though at first much reviled, achievement seems, indeed, to have been pathetically inadequate, but then genius often has a tendency to proliferate best in stony ground.

William Turner Walton was born on 29 March 1902, at 93 Werneth Hall Road, Oldham, Lancashire. His parents, both singing teachers, instructed pupils in the front room of their terrace house. When Professor Roy Fuller's mother was a girl, she took singing lessons there and recalls a grubby infant, 'Willie', playing happily on the pavement outside the house. Charles Walton, the boy's father, the son of an Inland Revenue official, had been one of the first enrolments at the Royal Manchester College of Music when it opened in 1894 under the principalship of Sir Charles Hallé. He had married Louisa Maria Turner, the daughter of an upholsterer, who subsequently gained renown as a singer in Manchester, using her maiden name, and the ceremony took place on 10 August 1898 at the Macfadyen Memorial Congregational Church, Chorlton-cum-Hardy. She also presented Charles with three other children: Charles Noel, born in 1899, Nora, born in 1908, and Alexander, born in 1910. According to Noel, who died in 1979, his father was not unlike Mr Barrett of Wimpole Street—a man of rigid views with a regal bearing and temper who, resorting to violent forms of discipline, ruled and subjugated his family, compelling the children, as a kind of ritualistic duty, to attend church services and rehearsals. Noel revealed these facets of his father's character in a letter to Hugh Ottoway dated 11 April 1970.[1] Seven years before his death, Noel also remarked that, although his brother William had become a public figure, he 'had not the temperament to enjoy it'.[2] He described him as basically shy, with a combination of reserve and impatience—'a very bad pianist, thumping out Stravinsky scores and that sort of thing'.[3]

Music reigned supreme in the typically post-Victorian Walton ménage, and its titular head, himself a bass-baritone trained by Andrew Black, doubtless rejoiced when William revealed a gift for, and love of, singing, so much so that on one occasion, at the age of six, he shed tears and made a scene because he was not allowed to deliver a solo in the local church choir. The boy, using a Smallwood Tutor, learnt the piano and also took violin lessons from a local man, but his father stopped these when he failed to practise properly. Charles Walton was a capable, highly intelligent man and while at the College had not only sung oratorio but also appeared as Papageno in *Die Zauberflöte* and Mephistopheles in *Faust*. As the much respected organist and choirmaster at St John's, Werneth, he conducted his excellent group of singers, which included both Noel and William, in such notable works as Haydn's *Creation*, Mendelssohn's *Hymn of Praise*, Handel's *Messiah* and Gounod's *Messe Solonnelle*, complete with its beautiful harp effects. One day, browsing through the *Daily Telegraph*, he spotted an advertisement for a voice test for probationer choristers at Christ Church Cathedral Choir School, Oxford, and promptly applied for William to be heard. There was a minor setback when Mrs Walton and her son, finding they had insufficient money for the fares, had to miss their train; but resourcefully she borrowed some from her grocer, and they sped towards Oxford (the boy, full of apprehension, was sick on the way) only to discover on arrival that the examinations had finished. The indefatigable lady pleaded for her son to be given a chance and, suddenly relenting, the twenty-five-year-old organist, Dr Henry Ley, listened while William sang Marcello's '*O Lord Our Governor*', a fine example of quiet, yet intense feeling, then, as an ear test, asked him to sing the middle note of a five-note chord; but his fluent sight-reading and general musical aptitude also impressed the doctor. He was accepted and, leaving Oldham, became a boarder at Oxford, where, during a difficult first term, made traumatic by his inability to 'talk like the others', he finally succeeded in shedding most of his Lancashire accent.

William remained at the choir school for the next six years (1912–18), experiencing delight and pride as a regular treble soloist in the anthems. The outbreak of war in 1914 nearly ruined his father, drastically reducing the number of his pupils and, at one point, making it expedient to bring his son home. Happily, Dr Thomas Strong, the kindly Dean of Christ Church, paid the balance of the school fees, already met in part by the scholarship, and William escaped the rather mundane fate of his brother Noel, who, at the age of fourteen, was packed off to work in a cotton mill office. On reflection, it seems extremely odd that Charles Walton, soured by his own misfortunes as a musician and bitterly asserting that his sons would never follow the same ill-fated profession, should have taken up the *Daily Telegraph* choir school advertisement; but the astute Noel put the matter into perspective:

> The only reason why my parents sent Willie to Oxford was the opportunity to give him a superior education (not all that 'superior' according to W.!) at a comparatively low price, which at that time they could just afford, the fees being £30 per annum, plus extras. The trouble came later—my father's earnings decreased as the Oxford expenses became heavier; also there were the younger children, my brother Alec and sister Nora on the way up. It is my definite opinion that my parents were unaware of Willie's musical talent. I think my father heard one or two of Willie's compositions by 'Cat's Whisker' radio. Yet I think he was incredulous to the end.[4]

Dr Strong took a constructive, fatherly interest in the boy, just as Rimsky-Korsakov did with Stravinsky. He used to have Walton and a few other students to the Deanery after Sunday morning service for religious instruction, and the droll remark 'Do you like your T. Strong?' was usually bandied about by boys immediately prior to these occasions. Sometimes, by way of recompense, he would play such modern pieces as the Schoenberg Op. 11 and Op. 15, or music by Leo Ornstein, who was the John Cage of his day and had composed numerous pieces, including a symphonic poem, *The Fog*, an orchestral suite, *The Life of Man, Impressions of the Thames, Burlesques on Richard Strauss, Three Russian Choruses* and a piano concerto.

Strong, a Doctor not only of Music but of Divinity, and a brilliant pianist with a wide and progressive repertoire, almost vibrated with excitement whenever an unfamiliar piece of music, especially one by Debussy, came his way. Affectionate and kindly in manner and speech, he treated the choristers as if they were his own children, walking with them in the garden of the Deanery, chatting about music or life in general as he entertained them to tea, generously placing his valuable and extensive library at their disposal, or playing to them on the splendid piano in his study and sometimes allowing them to play on it themselves.

One Sunday, when Strong was in the choir, Walton, then aged fifteen, brought with him a bundle of music-paper bearing his compositions and, dropping them on the table, begged the doctor to look at them. Hubert

Parry, always a diligent scout for native genius, happened to be staying with Strong at the time, partly because the music examinations were in progress, and, after studying some of the manuscripts, he expressed his pleasure and surprise, urging his colleague to give special attention to so gifted a pupil—'There's a lot in this chap, you must keep your eye on him.' Walton had, in fact, tried his hand at composition when he was only twelve years old. Writing to his publisher, Hubert Foss, in 1932, he mentioned a set of 'Variations for violin and pf. on a chorale by J.S.B.', which proved, after a dozen bars, to be 'not very interesting' and came to a full stop.[5] The manuscripts of two particularly notable pieces, *Tell me where is fancy bred* and a choral prelude on *Wheatley* which he produced in July and August 1916, at the age of thirteen, are in the British Library. Another fluently scored choral work, *The Litany*, a setting of Phineas Fletcher's *Drop, drop slow tears*, had its genesis in Easter of that year. He wrote a *Choral Fantasia* which greatly impressed not only Dr Ley, who played it after a service, but also the congregation who heard it. His youthful output included what in later years he described as 'about 30 very bad works of various species, songs, motets, magnificats, etc'.[6]

Dr Leslie Russell, who, during his adolescent days at Oxford, flourished as a soloist in the Decani and subsequently became head boy, remembers young Walton as 'uninteresting, quiet, unathletic . . . with a *poor* voice'.[7] Be that as it may, the future recipient of the Royal Philharmonic Society's coveted Gold Medal presented Dr Ley with a procession of church music of high quality, rapidly asserting not only his own fledgling genius but also the determination, independence of thought and flashpoint temperament so characteristic of his maturity. On one occasion the boy handed the manuscript of a choral work to Dr Ley, requesting him to try it over on the piano. While playing the piece, the worthy Doctor spotted some chords of a type frowned upon by conventional musicians and, wishing to help Walton, altered them so that they 'sounded more normal'. His well-meaning interference drew a reproachful glare from the boy, who remarked: '. . . but, sir, that is not what I wrote'.

Russell described Dr Ley as 'far and away the finest organist I have ever heard: the colour, rhythm and dexterity of his playing were unbelievable . . . he often "blew up," but was immensely kind and cheerful and adored by everyone'.[8] One of the Doctor's peccadillos, it seems, was to stop the choir practice abruptly, glance at his watch and say, 'Driver Jones in a Castle Class is at this moment passing through Oxford on the 3.40 from Paddington to Worcester.'

While an undergraduate at Christ Church, young Walton, greatly encouraged by Dr Ley's assistant Basil Allchin, received instruction in such musical subjects as harmony and fugue in preparation for the Mus. Bac. examinations, and, by the age of sixteen, he had learned all about Handelian 'drops' and other facets of the art. His studies in Latin, Greek and algebra suffered badly because he spent many hours in the Ellis Library in the Radcliffe Camera, immersed in scores by Stravinsky, Debussy, Ravel and other composers. Sir Hugh Allen, then Professor of Music at Oxford and his chief mentor, expounded the mysteries of the orchestra to him so cogently that he found he could bring whole complex masterpieces to life by playing them on the organ. A fierce man of dynamic energy, renowned and adored for his rudeness to players and singers at rehearsal, Allen would fling everything off except his trousers and shirt, before taking up his baton. On the occasion of his being appointed to New College, he already enjoyed an *enfant terrible* reputation. Dr Strong brought him back in a car and during the journey regaled him with titbits of College news. 'We did Stainer's *Crucifixion* last term,' he remarked. 'Believe me, sir, it is for the last time!' came the ominous reply. Nevertheless, Allen had rare qualities of compassion and kindness, spiritual strength and leadership, with the capacity to shape the lives and destinies of others. When Douglas Fox (later Director of Music at Clifton College) returned from World War I in a distressed neurotic condition, having suffered the amputation of an arm, Sir Hugh, in a sense, 'raised him from the dead', as Lazarus was raised, giving him new hope and courage. This remarkable man had one of his own hands tied behind his back and, thus handicapped, played Evensong in New College Chapel, demonstrating to Fox that, to those who believe, all things are possible.

Exhilarated as he was by the treasure-house of culture, opportunity and self-discovery which he explored again and again in the 'City of Dreaming Spires', the boy, filled with gratitude and affection, did not forget the parents whose love and sacrifices had made all this possible. He wrote many letters to his mother and in one of them gave a reassuring account of his progress:

> I finished my lectures with Dr [Ernest] Walker [celebrated Oxford musician, pianist, composer, historian, critic and teacher of harmony and composition]. Dr [Frederick] Iliffe [Organist to the University] says I have done wonderfully at my counterpoint and thinks I shall easily be able to get through my 1st Mus. Bac. in May. H. G. Ley came back on Thursday. I showed him my six-part Motet. He said it had wonderful ideas in it. I showed him the others. Those were quite excellent, especially the Fantasia. A new Choral Prelude and two others didn't sound well on the organ, but were fairly respectable on the piano. He is teaching me harmony free and is going over the motets.[9]

Walker, who greatly resembled Brahms in appearance—intentionally, so it was said—was nicknamed 'Pip Squeak' by the students because of his high-pitched voice. When asked for an opinion of the merits of some composition by one of his flock which he had just heard performed, he would trot out his favourite *bon mot*: 'It's bad, but I like it.' Another scholastic celebrity gifted with a humorous serendipity was William Archibald Spooner, Warden of New College, who, after hearing a piece by Delius, declared that he also liked *On cooking the first hero in Spring*. He, of course, was famed for such lapses of tongue, many of which, like the propensity of Beecham for ripe wit and repartee, have suffered exaggeration by repute.

In some letters Walton mentioned the sending of various compositions to Sir Hubert Parry; how, after morning service, Dr Ley had played his *Choral Fantasia*, which many people had warmly praised; and how the Dean had discussed with him the Royal College of Music, remarking: '. . . it is unpatriotic of England to let slip such a musical brain'. In others he revealed a growing and rewarding friendship with Parry—'an awfully jolly old person'. At Brasenose College in 1918 Walton was organist for three services until the regular organist returned from the Army, and on one occasion, as he recollected years later, he 'played half a page at the beginning of *Gerontius* because it was in the manuals, so I hadn't to use the pedals'.[10]

The boy had a splendid Bechstein upright piano in his room at the University, and on this, in 1918, he began to compose his first major work, the Piano Quartet, which he dedicated to Dr Strong and which he wrote to emulate Herbert Howells, 'because he'd had a great success with his . . . and I thought I'd have a go'.[11] It received the Carnegie Award and in 1924 was published by the Carnegie Trust, who rightly spoke of its clear texture, restraint and fine craftsmanship rising to peaks of great beauty and nobility.

Walton, at the tender age of sixteen years and two months, passed the first part of his Bachelor of Music examination on 11 June 1918, at New College. Thanks to the influence and patronage of Strong, the governing body of Christ Church, on 13 November that year, granted the boy, who retained the formal status of Commoner, an in-College Exhibition of £85 a year for two years. Throughout that period, according to Walton, there was little serious music-making at Oxford,—'only the Bach choir and a miserable orchestra'—but during term breaks his father (who must have been a gentler, more considerate man than Noel implied) took him to Hallé concerts in Manchester's Free Trade Hall, where the first orchestral work he heard, Tchaikovsky's *Casse-Noisette* Suite, filled him with rapture. 'I have never lost my affection for it,' he declared nearly twenty years later.[12] He was also dazzled by Beecham's Manchester opera seasons of 1916 and 1917, especially by the exotic, intensely gripping productions of *Boris Godunov* and *Le Coq d'Or*. He attended, for the first time, performances by the Carl Rosa of *Madama Butterfly*, *Faust* and *Mignon*, informing his mother, with a flavour of adult patronage, that 'they were done very well for a travelling company.'[13] Nourished by so much cultural provenance, the boy, in 1918, wrote many songs, one of which, *The Winds*, a setting of words by Swinburne, has survived. Although Walton had passed the first part of the Bachelor of Music examinations, he failed Responsions—the official matriculation examination—and after a final unsuccessful attempt in December 1919 he was sent down for a couple of terms (Hilary and Trinity 1920), a catastrophe made more palatable by the fatherly kindness of Dr Strong, who gave him £50 to go to Italy for a month with some friends.[14] But in June 1920 he redeemed himself by passing the second part of the Bachelor of Music examination, presided over by Sir Hugh Allen, Percy Buck and Ralph Vaughan Williams. It was a harrowing time of alternating hope, frustration, doubt and ultimate resurgence, yet a time blessed by the formation and growth of some enduring friendships—with the poets Siegfried Sassoon (1886–1967) and Roy Campbell (1901–57) and the novelist Ronald Firbank (1886–1926).

Campbell, possibly the most flamboyant and capricious member of this illustrious group of friends—soon to include the Sitwells—had gained distinction not only as a poet but as a professional jouster and bullfighter in Spain and Provence. He fought for Franco in the Spanish Civil War and with the Commonwealth Forces in the Second World War. Campbell wrote assiduously, gaining poetic renown in 1924 with his highly individualistic poem 'The Flaming Terrapin'. So when, after meeting Walton for the first time, this vibrant, singularly gifted youth (as he was then) described him in a letter[15] as both 'a real genius' and 'one of the finest fellows I have ever met', the praise can be regarded as outstandingly sincere and meaningful. The two young men walked out with two girls who were employed as waitresses, one of whom (she remains anonymous) subsequently became a Countess—'something magical seems to happen to everything he touches . . .' remarked Campbell, who also confessed that Walton gave him 'a sense of vocation, of how a man can live for his art'.

Other celebrities whom Walton met included John Masefield, who impressed him as 'a great man', and Wyndham Lewis, the British author and artist who pioneered the new spirit of art which his friend Ezra Pound called 'Vorticism', editing the magazine *Blast*, which proclaimed its extremely daring principles.

Walton's association with those proud, fleet-footed and rapacious tigers, the Sitwells, began in the Oxford University spring term of 1919, when Sacheverell, suffering intense cold, execrable food and almost unrelieved intellectual boredom at his father's old college, Christ Church, was introduced to him by Siegfried Sassoon. Osbert Sitwell had joined Sacheverell at the college, and, accompanied by Sassoon, they went to see Walton in his room there and to hear him play part of the Piano Quartet. The dark, blue-papered room, containing a piano opposite the window and in the middle a table prepared for tea and dominated by a huge plate of bananas—a touch of ostentatious luxury, according to Osbert—must have seemed humdrum to the fastidious, opulent-minded Sitwells, but they found nothing mediocre about their host, despite his excessive shyness. Osbert noted with approval the refinement of the long, narrow, delicately shaped head, the bird-like profile showing the so-called 'bar of Michelangelo', which, according to phrenologists, denotes a musician, and the slight, almost fragile build of the seventeen-year-old prodigy who, with his pale skin and blond hair, looked like a Dane or Norwegian. After a strained, uneasy period, filled with desultory talk punctuated by sudden bursts of amiable, well-intentioned chatter from the guests, Walton sat down at the piano and commenced to play the slow movement from his Piano Quartet, followed by excerpts from some of his other compositions. Despite a painfully unprofessional performance, he impressed the Sitwells, who considered that he had a spark of genius.

Other influential people at Oxford shared this conviction. They included Dr Strong and Dr Ley, who were trying hard to induce Walton to continue studying composition in London at the Royal College of Music. With the singularly high-minded and regal magnanimity for which his family were noted, Sacheverell disagreed with the musical oligarchy and promptly persuaded his brother Osbert that they must support young Walton, if only to shelter the tender, swelling bud of his genius from the blight of academic teaching. In particular, it must be protected from the debilitating influence of Sir Charles Villiers Stanford, the father of the English musical renaissance and a lecturer at the college. This witty Irishman was himself a prolific composer, but his rigidly conservative cast of mind, steeped in the traditionalism of Bach, Beethoven, Brahms and Wagner, posed a kind of drawing-room respectability unacceptable to any warm-blooded spirit of enterprise. To allow the precocious boy to develop as his genius dictated, the Sitwell brothers, with impulsive generosity, proposed to adopt him, take him to live with them at Swan Walk, Chelsea, and later at Osbert's House, 2 Carlyle Square, and, in effect, to make him another member of the family.

Walton soon found himself the subject of a prolonged and vigorous battle to possess him, the protagonists being his father on one side and his new, altruistic friends on the other. It was resolved when Walton senior finally decided that his gifted offspring must settle the issue for himself. William chose the Sitwells, not realizing that he would share their lives for the next seventeen years. 'If it hadn't been for them,' he remarked in later life, 'I'd either have ended up like Stanford, or would have been a clerk in some Midlands bank with an interest in music. Life would have been a great deal duller'.

Osbert summed up the battle and the outcome in these words:

> In the end, perhaps, all that we were able to accomplish directly for him was to have prevented his being sent to one of the English musical academies and to have lent him, as a musician, what prestige we ourselves possessed in the world of art and writing at a time when he lacked supporters, and when, in consequence of our attitude, we incurred a certain amount of odium, both from those who did not believe in him and from those who did. Especially were we blamed by these last—and rightly—for being responsible for his not attending in London one of the two or three colleges officially provided for an academic training in music. These people worked in different ways, but united in tormenting about it Walton's father, a well-known teacher of singing in Lancashire, and fortunately a man of character. On one occasion they so well succeeded in their efforts that Mr Walton, very busy though he always was, came up to London especially to investigate, and failing to find my brother or myself, instead called on my aged Aunt Blanche, then rising eighty, who was speedily able to reassure him. The relationship between William and his father and mother, both of whom were fine musicians, was unusually happy, and it was said that almost the last words of his father were "Let William have his own way; he knows what he is doing. . . ."[16]

If one may, paradoxically, look ahead and then, putting everything into perspective, look back, it is to realize that the fruits of Walton's 'adoption' by the Sitwells were twofold: firstly, the dauntless trio, although at that time renowned only in a small, exclusive circle, widened his cultural and social horizons immeasurably, keeping him in touch with the vital creative works of the age and some of the illustrious people who had fashioned them; secondly, they freed him from the narrow deprivation, the depressing bleakness, of the kind of poverty-stricken environment which can impose a strait-jacket of discontent on many a sensitive artist, inhibiting or preventing full and true self-expression. They made it possible for him to attend concerts of contemporary music and, in so doing, to familiarize himself with new avant-garde trends and developments. These generous, high-minded friends combined with Dr Strong, Lord Berners and Siegfried Sassoon in guaranteeing Walton an income of £250 a year, in those days an appreciable sum and one that enabled him to spend his life composing, untroubled by the need to earn his living through some uncongenial job.

Osbert, who liked to pose as a kind of twentieth-century Prince Esterhazy, directing his lofty intelligence and patronage at any new prodigy or existing *Wunderkind* who seemed to merit such favours, was at that time much preoccupied with the music and personality of the greatly neglected Dutch composer Bernard van Dieren, whose tortuousness and obscuranticism of thought made some of his compositions difficult to assess. In due course, Walton, through his association with the Sitwells, became friendly not only with van Dieren but also with Cecil Gray and Peter Warlock, who interested him in the music of Delius, Bartók and Gesualdo. He had a special regard for the Dutchman and, in later years, told Murray Schafer: 'The works of Bernard van Dieren deserve to be resurrected. He is never performed today, but he developed a style of free dissonance altogether his own, contemporary with Schoenberg's early work. I have only heard his *Chinese Symphony* once and it struck me as being very rich and profound. I should like to hear it again and I am sure many others would, too.'[17]

Walton's letters to his mother fairly crackled with his enthusiasm for the diverse interests and activities which, arising from his relationship with the Sitwells, had fallen like treasure-trove into his outstretched hands. He mentions his part in arranging concerts for the presentation of music by van Dieren, Delius and—most wonderful of all—himself. 'Some of my songs,' wrote the boy, 'are going to be sung at Lady Glenconner's concert in London on Friday. Also, I shall be conducting two pieces for orchestra at the Russian Ballet.'[18] It should be explained, in passing, that Lady Glenconner was the mother of Stephen Tennant, the dedicatee of Walton's *Siesta*. One letter described a recital by Cortot which he attended: 'He is simply magnificent,' wrote Walton, adding, as further proof of his social emancipation: 'Lady Ottoline Morrell asked me over to her house last Sunday. It was very entertaining. I went to London yesterday for the afternoon and saw the new ballet *Parade*. It was very marvellous, especially the scenery. The music is by Erik Satie, a Frenchman. I am to meet Stravinsky next month or perhaps before, so that will be too exciting for words. . . .'[19]

Walton, in June 1919, took up residence at Swan Walk, Chelsea, the London home of Osbert Sitwell, where his host found him more shy and silent than he had seemed previously. He would vanish, like an introvert child, into his room at the top of the house, where, sitting morosely by the open window, he stuffed himself with black-heart cherries from a paper bag, shying the stones through the window, to fall with a dry staccato rattle on the brown-tiled pavement outside the front door. Mrs Powell, the housekeeper, kept a proud, watchful eye on him, popping in every so often to see if he needed anything. When a piano was hired for him, he seldom ventured outside the room, remaining affectionately and possessively close to the instrument and sometimes attacking it with more vigour than virtuosity. Osbert, anxious to help, advised Walton to practise on a dumb keyboard but promptly retreated before a fusillade of indignation. Walton had remarkably sensitive, tactile fingers and when a door-key was lost Osbert did not hesitate to ask him to pick the lock, which he did with a Raffles-like efficiency; but, as he himself confessed in later years, he gained very little mastery over a piano, no matter how hard he tried.

It was not until Walton had travelled with the Sitwells to Sicily and Italy in the spring of 1920 that Osbert was able to grasp his very definite but perplexing character. At first mistaking his protégé's taciturnity, his apparent inability to communicate with others, as mere shyness, he soon realized that behind this curious mixture of strength and delicacy was an iron will, a temperament not easily swayed by flattery or indulgence. Walton, teasingly referred to by the others as 'Osbert's fag', regarded the older man as 'part elder brother, part father-figure',[20] and, remarkably self-possessed for one so new to life in the *haute monde*, appeared to take no offence when Osbert, trading a little on his dependence on favours, uttered such remarks as 'Willie, do fetch that book for me.' Indeed, according to Peter Quennell,[21] he was made to feel that he occupied a very inferior position in the household. On one occasion someone knocked a tin of biscuits onto the floor and one of the Sitwells rapped, 'Pick 'em up, Willie, pick 'em up, pick 'em up!' Quennell described his inauguration into the Sitwellian way of life as 'like being ushered into a cage at the zoo, full of furious, but friendly animals'. Walton, he said, reacted by putting his hands into his pockets, popping a cigarette into a corner of his mouth, and going his own way.

Italy, with its warm, intoxicating atmosphere, its exotic landscapes and its glorious heritage of Renaissance art, must have been a revelation to the young composer, especially Amalfi, that panorama of almost flawless beauty. He and his companions stayed there at a hotel that had once been a monastery and was owned by Don Alfredo Vozzi, an aristocrat with shrewd, penetrating eyes and a black, pointed beard, who understood the peculiarities of British tourists. Don Alfredo occupied a cell in the precise centre of the hotel and warmed throughout the winter days by a large brass bowl of red-hot ashes standing on the cement floor, eking out a monk-like existence. He was a gentle, melancholy man, but with the natural authority of a *grand seigneur* which, spreading outwards into every part of the hotel, brought housemaids, porters, cooks and valets scurrying to obey his every command.

All around the hotel, an old white building with simple lines that stood on a narrow ledge overlooking the Gulf of Salerno, Walton could see a fantastic landscape of sea and mountains, with pretty villages, toy-like in their bright paint, poised on soaring crags, with immense castles of stone, huge grotto-impregnated limestone cliffs, and a whole range of distant green hills fringed by impenetrable rocks. Perhaps the local wine, as well as the clear Italian light, unlocked the door of his imagination. Fired with ambition, he spent most of his time by himself in a room which contained what Osbert described as 'a typical South Italian piano-similar to those upon which, as you pass beneath in the street of a southern Catholic city, you hear young girls practising, high up, from iron-barred convent windows'. Walton, fortified by Tuscany cigars which he cut into halves with a razor-blade, sat composing and copying out music at a large window in the cloister, feeling, for perhaps the first time in his life, happy and fulfilled.

He and his friends returned to Italy many times during the ensuing years, sometimes taking up residence at the huge castle at Montegufoni, the property of Sir George Sitwell. The castle contained a beautiful, though simple, chapel and a splendid Cardinal's Garden beneath whose massive walls, in a small hamlet, was another chapel, presided over by Osbert Sitwell's father-confessor, '*Il Priore*', a slightly unreal cleric with an exuberant, rather incongruous passion for amateur theatricals. On one occasion the tranquillity of the midnight hour was shattered, as far as the inhabitants of the castle were concerned, by a ferocious roaring like that of doomed souls being roasted in the flames of Hell. It turned out that the impresario-priest was preparing a production of *Quo Vadis* and that, deeming midnight to be a suitable time for rehearsal, he had gathered together all the peasants who were to play the lions and was energetically teaching them how to roar. It was all very strange and picturesque for young William Walton after the homespun charms of his birthplace, Oldham, and the cloistered restrictions of academic life.

In September or early October, peasants moved with stately ease through the leafy corridors of the vineyards, picking the ripe grapes, while the strong odour of must from the vats mingled with the scent of blossoms from the castle gardens. Some of the grapes and part of the fig-harvest were carried on oval rushwork platters into the Great Court, on whose crumbling, olive-green stone walls grey, white or tawny pigeons, perched on cornices, drowsed in the blinding sunlight or took off, with a sudden flapping and whirring of wings, in eccentric arcs of flight. In the village streets women with placid, friendly smiles sat in doorways, plaiting straw hats or floppy baskets, their honest faces warmed and browned by a sun that glowed white-hot until, with the sleepy sound of the Angelus, the light darkened a little and the air, filled with fireflies and huge russet moths, became noticeably cooler. Then, at least in the earlier part of the year, silence yielded to the singing of nightingales and the rattling of innumerable cicadas. With its atmosphere of faded grandeur, of a hieratic pomp and majesty proudly challenging the fast-moving, often vulgar sophistication of the big modern cities, with their shining new cars and prissy penthouse dwellings, their concrete apartment blocks and garbage-littered alleys, the castle stood there like an inspiring dream-fantasy, reminding Walton, perhaps, that the age of romance—in music as well as architecture—was not yet dead. He undoubtedly loved Montegufoni, but it was Amalfi, with its gentler, more refined character, that first dazzled and seduced him. The cicadas shuffled and rattled their love-emotions just as blithely, the nightingales fluted no less exquisitely, and after a day of work, perched in front of that 'typical South Italian piano', shaping his own 'song of destiny', Walton could always enjoy a pleasant, illuminating after-dinner conversation with his kindly, if austere host, Osbert Sitwell.

Behind that rather abrasive face, Osbert, the polished and sophisticated man of letters, harboured a keen sense of humour. He found much to amuse him in various incidents that arose from his protégé's youth and inexperience. On one occasion, when he and Walton were at Scarborough in 1921, William, suddenly taken ill, had to be removed to a nursing-home. Osbert, at the time, was Liberal candidate for that division, and one of his constituents, a middle-aged lady of prim outlook and ecclesiastical demeanour, offered to sit with Walton and read aloud. The offer, after being accepted, was not repeated, since the invalid, innocent of face and pure of spirit, handed her, open at a particularly ripe passage, Urquhart's translation of Rabelais! While the composer, who genuinely saw no harm in this rollicking piece of prose, clearly revelled in what he heard, the poor woman, blushing to the roots of her hair and gasping for breath, galloped headlong to a full stop, then, much wiser in the frailties of the human race, gathered up her skirts and departed. At least Walton, who, according to his mother, could sing bits from the *Messiah* before he could talk, showed great catholicity of taste.

His combination of taciturnity and mischief could be extremely irritating, as Osbert recalled in his autobiography.[22] When the young composer, some years after he had settled at Swan Walk, visited Sacheverell to stay for a short period in his home, he found to his dismay that the old rickety staircase leading to his own room was much too narrow for a piano to be carried up, although six stalwarts from the warehouse supplying it spent a whole morning attempting the impossible. The piano was left on the first-floor landing at the foot of the stairs, and the disgruntled Walton—grieving for lost opportunity—was informed that, two days hence, the muscular stalwarts would return with a trolley and crane and hoist the instrument into his room through the window. In the afternoon the Sitwells went for a motor drive; they returned a few hours later to find the massive instrument safely installed in Walton's bedroom. How, single-handed, had he accomplished this fantastic feat of skill and strength? 'I did it with a bit of string,' explained the composer with that slightly provocative brevity and irony of speech that, over the years, infuriated or captivated listeners. Often and persistently did the Sitwells implore him, in the days that followed, to reveal the secret of his necromancy, but Walton maintained his usual Sphinx-like impassivity, declining to comment further.

Apart from a few unidentifiable songs, very little remains of the music he created in 1919–20, one survivor from 1920 being *Tritons*, a setting of words by William Drummond. Another rather flimsy relic from the same period is *The Passionate Shepherd*, the text of which comes from Marlowe's famous poem. Walton showed some of his works to Ferruccio Busoni, but the Italian-German pianist, composer and conductor was not impressed, as he told his wife:

> The young man Walton (who was at the Spanish Restaurant) sent me some manuscript music. He has a little gift for counterpoint. In other respects, they all write according to a formula: notes, notes, notes, all 'hither and yon,' without imagination or feeling. Taste in connection with the conception of *beauty* is certainly changeable. Wagner's music, for instance, is often 'beautiful'; he knew very well that this too belongs to the craft. Talent is really at the root of the matter and is the deciding factor.[23]

Walton, partly through the Sitwell patronage and influence, partly through his own remarkable, if rather dour, personality and brilliance, attracted a coterie of distinguished friends, one being Lord Gerald Berners, who stood out among the great eccentrics of his day. Ballet dancer and choreographer Robert Helpmann, who in 1972 played the Mad Hatter in the film *Alice in Wonderland*, once visited the peer's mansion near Oxford and, when ushered into the drawing-room, found him with an elegant silver tea service and a mettlesome horse. His host greeted him, asked him if he took cream and sugar, poured out two cups of tea, then fed buttered scones to the horse. He proffered no explanation but presently told the horse that it had eaten enough, and the animal was led out through the french windows. When Helpmann, doubtless feeling that he had strayed into Mad Hatter fantasy land, asked about the horse's presence, Lord Berners remarked 'When people see the horse, they become as nervous as I am, so that after a while I get over it. Then we can have a normal conversation.'[24] Berners had a companion, a huge, beefy man known, significantly, as 'The Mad Boy', who kept him amused with bizarre, surrealistic pranks. Once he painted himself green all over and drove the noble lord's Rolls-Royce up the front steps of the house. On another occasion Berners climbed into the car and found that a clavichord had been installed on the back seat, then, returning home, discovered that 'The Mad Boy' had painted his white doves pink and blue.

During those exciting, formative years the young Walton, in the Café Royal and the 'Six Bells' in London, had also met and charmed those picturesque Bohemian giants Walter Sickert, Augustus John and Percy Wyndham Lewis, as well as Ernest Ansermet, the great Swiss conductor and a pre-eminent interpreter of Stravinsky's music. Another illustrious, if eccentric, personality joined the circle in 1922—Constant Lambert, whose death in 1951, at the age of forty-six was a major loss to British music. His most famous composition was *The Rio Grande*, a setting for choir, piano and orchestra of a poem by Sacheverell Sitwell, a beautiful and enlivening piece which evokes the blazing sun and the exotic atmosphere of Brazil. His witty and aggressive book *Music Ho! A study of Music in Decline* epitomized the critical climate of British music in his day. Lambert's father was a portrait-painter; his brother, Manuel, a sculptor. He suffered from deafness, the result of a serious illness—probably septicaemia—which had struck him down at school, and, in consequence, used to stare, with a pathetically intense, anxious look, at anyone who spoke to him at any length. His illness had left him with a limp and, suffering acute pain, he sought solace in the alcoholism that helped to destroy him. Because of drink and diabetes, Lambert was somewhat unreliable as a conductor. Two days before his forty-sixth birthday, he died of broncho-pneumonia and delirium tremens, his will to fight sapped by the savage critical broadsides that had raked his final ballet, *Teiresias*.

At Renishaw, the Sitwell family home, he and Walton, invited there as almost permanent friends and guests, spent most of their time playing on two pianos—one an enormous, obsolete Bechstein of antique vintage, the other a more up-to-date instrument hired from Sheffield—and the sound of their keyboard skirmishes filled the house. Renishaw, a huge, rambling place, with endless corridors and big, draughty rooms, was a house to remember, with a special kind of magic. Set in a great park, it had splendid views of the Derbyshire countryside, of distant green hills and far-off towns like Bolsover and Hardwick glimpsed faintly through the shimmering summer heat haze or the soft glow of autumn. In a county famous for its legends and folk-tales, the house, lit in earlier days by flickering oil-lamps and candles, was filled with mystery and enchantment. At the time of Sacheverell's birth, 1897, twelve ghosts haunted Renishaw, one of them being an acrobatic wraith who hung above the main front door and frightened the postman nearly out of his mind, and another the spectre of a young eighteenth-century Sacheverell Sitwell who kissed beautiful women while they slept and met his death by drowning in the river.[25]

Untroubled by any psychic ruminations and striving to subjugate his own neuroses, Lambert, blessed with a flashpoint sense of humour, made a perfect companion for the gifted young composer from Oldham, who had his own formidable battery of mischief and irony. Other visitors to Renishaw, and friends of Walton, included Edmund Dulac, the renowned caricaturist in three dimensions who played the nose-flute, and Sir Edmund Davis, a flamboyant, likeable character who bought a village near Zanzibar because he admired its Moorish tiles.

# 2

# The Man on Horseback

It was towards the end of 1921 that Edith Sitwell, dismayed by the rhythmic flaccidity and verbal deadness of so much published verse, realized that a change in method and direction had become necessary. Accordingly, she wrote *Façade*, treating the poems as Liszt-like studies in transcendental technique; they have a strange magic utterly disproportionate to their content or length. Effects of rhythm and speed are conjured up by the careful, sometimes complex positioning of rhymes, assonances and dissonances. In one verse the use of two rhymes placed immediately together at the end of each of two lines makes the sound leap into the air. The following example, the product of a highly developed onomatopoeic sense, brilliantly conveys the soft gleam of silver and the sound of waves breaking on fine shingle—or perhaps of a windswept cornfield:

*Thetis wrote a treatise noting wheat is*
*silver like the sea; the lovely cheat is sweet as*
*foam; Erotis notices that she. . . .*

Some of the poems have a haunting sadness; others radiate the capricious gaiety and lightness of a butterfly on the wing. The idea of presenting them as a stage or concert-hall entertainment originated with Osbert and Sacheverell, who, warmly supported by Edith, invited Walton to set the verses to music. At first he rejected what seemed to him a rather odd commission, whereupon the dauntless trio cunningly replied that they would ask Constant Lambert to provide the music. Walton capitulated. 'Of course I couldn't possibly let that occur,' he remarked some years later. Doubtless the young composer, now complacently entrenched in the precarious maturity of his nineteen years, regarded Lambert as a dangerous rival in a musical firmament increasingly lit by new fashion-constellations, and certainly *The Rio Grande* had been highly praised, one critic, Edwin Evans, describing it as 'a blend of the nostalgia of Baudelaire with the festive glamour of Debussy's *Fêtes*'.

Of the poems to be set to music by Walton, a few had been written several years before, as Sacheverell Sitwell subsequently revealed.[1] 'Mariner Man' appeared in his sister's book *Clown's Houses* in June 1918, shortly before World War I ended; 'En Famille' in *The Chapbook* in July 1920; 'Aubade' and 'Long Steel Grass' in the *Saturday Westminster Gazette* for, respectively, 2 October 1920 and 3 September 1921. She had published one or two other poems earlier, but it was in 'Long Steel Grass' that her very distinctive streak of genius first showed. Osbert considered that the pure, undiluted magic of the stage entertainment planned by Edith and Walton could be found in 'Through Gilded Trellises', 'Four in the Morning', 'Black Mrs Behemoth' and 'Long Steel Grass' ('Trio for Two Cats and a Trombone'), poems whose rhythmic and melodic provenance derived from Stravinsky's *Pribaoutki* and the Russian ballet *Parade*, with music by Satie and a magnificent curtain by Picasso. He did not regard Walton as a fervent lover of poetry, but admitted that his protégé understood, and responded with sensitive rapport to, Edith's verses, making his music inseparable from some of the imagery.

Stimulated by Lambert's rivalry, Walton, who at that time had left Swan Walk and shared a house with the Sitwells in Carlyle Square, commenced work on the *Façade* project, which, in the early stages, he regarded as just one big experiment. Mrs Powell, the housekeeper, mothered him and darned his socks; the Sitwells, undemanding and generous, accepted him as a kind of co-opted, free-board member of the family. He had a room with a piano at the top of the house; there, undisturbed by domestic responsibilities, he wrote music which marvellously complemented the sparkling wit and rhythms of Edith's poems.

It was Sacheverell who, probably recalling that Cocteau had used a similar device in the ballet *Parade*, suggested that the poems should be declaimed through a megaphone, in fact, one constructed of papier mâché and invented by Herr Senger, a Swiss operatic baritone who, at Bayreuth, used it to sing the part of Fafner the dragon with a greater force and resonance, filling the Festspielhaus with a booming like a blow-hole about to erupt. Dazzled by its amplifying wizardry, the Admiralty subsequently took up the Sengerphone and used it successfully during both wars and in particularly violent storms at sea when the captain, his voice tossed about and blunted by a howling wind, had to shout orders from the bridge. The instrument chosen for *Façade* had a mouthpiece covering the lower part of the face and was, according to Walton, 'a lovely instrument'. Sacheverell considered that the Sengerphone, the speaker and the chamber orchestra should be hidden from the audience behind a painted curtain. He and Walton travelled by bus to Hampstead and interviewed

Senger, who gave permission for his dragon trumpet to be used. In matters concerning opera and singing he was a fanatic whose flashpan temper might easily be sparked off by some innocent remark or failure to conform to his wishes. Once, as Osbert Sitwell recalled[2], he attended a rehearsal of *Façade* and heard Edith practising the most difficult of her poems through the megaphone. Suddenly he sprang to his feet and, with eyes bulging, hurled himself at her throat. 'You are using your voice the wrong way!' he bellowed, and twisted her glottis so fiercely that he nearly throttled her.

Despite the oddity of her appearance and, sometimes, her behaviour, Edith Sitwell was a deeply sensitive, highly intelligent woman of outstanding kindness and sincerity. Many people regarded her as a remote, formidable figure who, with her grand, very gothic manner, heavy medieval brocade dresses and theatrical gestures, radiated a discomforting aura of eccentricity. An awe-inspiring personage in her long gowns and trailing Tudor hats, she was six feet tall, had beautiful hands and wore extravagant aquamarine and cornelian rings. What her denigrators failed to glimpse behind the masquerade was the generous, childlike and rather insecure woman who longed for friendship and understanding. Malcolm Williamson once disagreed with her violently about a certain novelist whose work she detested, and he expected never to hear from her again, but the following day her secretary telephoned and said: 'Dr Sitwell was so pleased with the way you stood up to her'. Almost paranoiac in her response to adverse criticism or unkindness, Edith reacted swiftly to a scarifying review in the *Reynolds News* in 1940 with a successful libel action. Utterly fastidious herself, she loathed the soiled journalistic personality of the newspaper columnist Hannen Swaffer as ardently as she disliked his writing. He invariably dressed like a broken-down Bohemian poet of the 1890s and, commenting to Walter Allen about his unscrubbed appearance, she said, 'I've discovered Hannen Swaffer's secret—he cleans his nails with a lead pencil.' She could, paradoxically, be extremely tolerant of faults in others, accepting, for example, the homosexuality of Pavel Tchelitchew, the artist with whom she fell in love; and nobody could have been more gentle and patient than Edith Sitwell when she nursed her governess through a cruelly devouring cancer. She supported many of her friends with gifts of money, and even knitted pullovers for Marilyn Monroe, the tragic child-goddess in the twentieth-century temple of cinematic deification.

Walton, in his collaboration with Edith, found no insurmountable obstacle, and the long periods they spent together, usually of three hours, during which they read, then accented, the text, seem to have passed in a friendly, harmonious atmosphere. The grip of winter reduced that atmosphere to freezing-point, despite the warmth generated by two huge, blazing fires of Derbyshire coal; but Mrs Powell provided a constant supply of inner heat by ferrying trays bearing large Chianti-flasks filled with a marvellously thermal home-made sloe-gin, which she handed round in generous potions to the company. Osbert glowed inside, not so much from the housekeeper's libations but because, as he listened to the music, he was acutely conscious of the bright flame of Walton's genius. For him this music suggested a kind of vertiginous fermentation, with crude birdsong and the growth of animals; it conveyed the pulsating breath of a world of truth sadly forfeited, of intermingled sorrow and gaiety.[3]

At first, the players who rehearsed for the private première, given on 24 January 1922 in the pink, blue, white and violet drawing-room of the Sitwell house at 2 Carlyle Square, reacted with some asperity not only to the strange new sounds which they snatched from the score but also to the rather cocky, self-assured young conductor-composer who, standing there with poised baton, looked, according to Osbert, like an elegant and handsome snipe, although, when some difficulty required a pause in the music, he saw him rather as the human embodiment of a popular animal music-hall star of the period, the Boxing Kangaroo. Undeterred by their manifestations of irritability or anger, Walton safely guided his little chamber group through the reefs and cross-currents of *Façade*; so that, as hostility and bewilderment slowly changed into delighted approval, they became quite friendly and, at one rehearsal, a clarinettist teasingly asked him, 'Excuse me, Mr Walton, has a clarinet player ever done you an injury?'[4]

At the performance itself the room was packed with slim, opulent gold chairs on which sat a carefully selected audience consisting of painters, musicians and poets, reinforced by a few more orthodox friends of the Sitwells. The sheer volume of sound in the little drawing-room nearly deafened the listeners, and although the artistic coterie applauded enthusiastically, their conventional neighbours hardly knew what to say, or where to look. Happily, the sponsors of this unusual event had guilefully arranged a supply of special hot rum punch, brewed from an old recipe among whose ingredients were green tea, sherry, China tea and fresh pineapple juice. No doubt this diplomatic restorative revived those who, concussed or disorientated by what they had heard, needed a really potent morale-booster. The late Mrs Robert Mathias, patron of the Russian Ballet, was so captivated by the entertainment that, rejecting the advice of more prudent friends, she begged Osbert Sitwell to organize another private presentation of *Façade*, and this was given on 7 February 1922 at her house in Montagu Square.[5]

No potions of rum punch or other tonics were available on 12 June 1923 when the première of *Façade* took place at the Aeolian Hall, where, as on the previous occasion, Edith Sitwell recited the poems and Walton conducted a chamber orchestra. Osbert subsequently wrote with razor-edged bitterness of those vultures of the Press who, resenting any new creative trends in the arts, fired vicious broadsides of hatred at *Façade*, seeking by distortion and calumny to inflame the passions of the public, inviting rage and insult even before the curtain rose. He described them contemptuously as 'the gossip crew, which cherished a deadly parasitic hatred and fear of all work, manual or intellectual'.[6] So charged with prejudice was the atmosphere that Osbert and Sacheverell, filled with foreboding, would not eat any luncheon, and for some hours they sat, gloomily silent, within the cloistered precincts of the Burlington Fine Arts Club. On reaching the Aeolian Hall, they found that a large audience, thirsting for blood like bull-fight *aficionados*, had assembled there. Osbert strode onto the platform and made a short speech, explaining the novel aspects of the presentation, then disappeared behind the curtain to announce the various items of the entertainment through the mouth of a mask. Soon the fanfare which introduced *Façade* sounded, the performance began and, before long, the audience, irritable and restless, manifested its rage and disgust, firstly by a salvo of goose-like hissing, and secondly by threatening poor Edith with physical violence. Badly shaken and fearing for her own safety, she stayed behind the curtain, waiting for the crowd to disperse. Recalling the event with considerable feeling some time later, she spoke of nearly being lynched by 'the inevitable old symbol of the enemy, poised, with raised umbrella, ready to smite me. . . .'[7]

The insults, volleyed anew by the popular newspapers, but excluding the *Daily Mail*, flew again next day, with, from one pseudo-critic, a vitriolic broadside captioned 'Drivel They Paid to Hear', and from another a vindictive appraisal which quoted an Aeolian Hall fireman as saying, 'never in twenty years experience of recitals at this hall have I known anything like it'—a reasonable remark not necessarily implying condemnation. The mask on the curtain was described as 'meaningless, crudely painted moonface', the poems were dismissed as 'drivel', and the music was classified as 'collected from the works of the most eccentric of the ultra-moderns'. The critic of *Vogue* was much more discerning:

> Mr Walton's music was clever. It had intuition, it understood the words. Its office seemed to be to sprinkle jewels and flowers with an apt hand on the pathway of Miss Sitwell's poetry. Only once did I observe it fail, and it failed by becoming obvious. The introduction of a few bars of hornpipe music was like underlining a phrase with the thick of one's thumb. Miss Sitwell never crosses her t's and dots her i's; and it was distressing, for the moment, to hear Mr

> Walton doing it for her. Need I say that the audience mistook Mr Walton's error of judgement for a stroke of genius? At last, in the familiar hornpipe music, it heard something it could understand. It demanded it again. The only scrap of Mr Walton's music that was not his own was precisely the scrap that pleased his hearers most. I shudder to contemplate what would have happened had Miss Sitwell quoted a line from Tennyson. The little orchestra of flute, clarinet, saxophone, trumpet, violoncello and percussion instruments played with airy delicacy and occasional pomp.[8]

It was reported that Noel Coward—presumably unable to take any more—had walked out, rather ostentatiously, before the end. As to whether or not Coward, then twenty-three years old and the much praised author of *The Young Idea*, really did make this flamboyant gesture of disapproval, is not absolutely clear. Cole Lesley, who knew him intimately, dismissed the tale as mere speculation or misunderstanding: 'Noel always told me that he did *not* walk out of *Façade*. What he actually said was "I wouldn't have missed it for anything in the world".'[9] Against this rebuttal is the fact that Coward, in collaboration with Ronald Jeans, subsequently wrote a revue entitled *London Calling*, which contained a sketch based on the first production of *Façade* and which, with Maisie Gay in the cast, opened at the Duke of York's Theatre at the beginning of September 1923. In the sketch, spiced mercilessly with satire and bearing the title 'The Swiss Family Whittlebot', the inimitable Miss Gay, plump and salubrious, with a round, pop-eyed face, appeared as the poetess Hernia Whittlebot reciting her 'poems' with her somewhat asinine brothers, Gob and Sago Whittlebot. Her prattling included the following lines:

> Life is essentially a curve
> and art is an oblong within that curve.
> My brothers and I have been brought up on Rhythm
> as other children are brought up on Glaxo.
> Drains and Sewers support the quest of eternal indulgence.
> Thank God for the Coldstream Guards,
> Guts and Dahlias and billiard balls—
> swirling along with spurious velocity,
> ending what and where and when
> in the hearts of little birds,
> but never Tom Tits.

Hernia's manic script featured Coward's own poem 'Beloved it is Dawn; I rise', taken from his collection of satires *A Withered Nosegay*; but he supplemented it with other verses which, though light-hearted enough, served his corrosive purpose adequately.

It was fortunate for the company that Edith Sitwell did not visit the theatre and see the sketch, because she was capable, under insufferable provocation, of creating a public scene. John Pearson, in his brilliant study of the Sitwells, suggests that this abnormally sensitive woman had received reports of Miss Gay's depicting her in the sketch as suffering from some unspecified, loathsome disease, with insinuations of lesbianism.[10] The gross insult and alleged obscenity of the stage parody made her bitter and unhappy, so that the illness which afflicted her a few months later—acute nervous debility, followed by jaundice—came as no surprise to her close friends.

In fairness to Coward, a fastidious craftsman and, in many senses, a traditionalist, he had an almost vehement dislike of the kind of 'modern' poetry which, rejecting metrical structure and rhythmic subtleties, glorifies meaningless, uninspired, so-called 'blank verse' which practically anyone can write. On one occasion he proved his point to a couple of friends who greatly admired Edith Sitwell by mixing extracts from her poems with some from his own *Spangled Unicorn* and, reading them aloud after dinner, according the same treatment to each selection. Then, 'which are my poems and which are hers?' he asked them, and was met with a baffled, uneasy silence.

Walton, on seeing the sketch, regarded it, in his own words,[11] as 'not unfunny', but Osbert, finding the weapons of ridicule snatched from his own hands and used against himself, his brother and his sister, grew increasingly resentful and vituperative. His dislike of Coward developed into a seething hatred, which found some relief in a pointedly sarcastic, offensive letter:

> We are delighted to have been the means of suggesting an idea to you. It is always as well to have one, even if it isn't your own; it must be a novel experience for you. All you want now is a little self-confidence—and, of course, to use your voice more.
>
> Insulting my sister is a fine beginning for you. We look forward to other triumphs. Have you tried cheating at cards?[12]

Osbert's continuing feud with Coward, unabated by the passing of time, served in the initial stages to publicize the Sitwells—and indirectly that rising young luminary William Walton—as no critical plaudits could possibly do. He had sought unsuccessfully, at the première of *Façade*, for unstinted praise from public and critics alike. Instead, the event had become famous overnight through the kind of artistic *scandale* which characterized the first performance of Stravinsky's *The Rite of Spring* in May 1913 and which has become a ritualistic feature of the Donaueschingen Festival—no patron or entrepreneur could wish for anything better. Then, to complete and reinforce the fame, if not the popularity, of

*Façade*, fate, using the mischievous pen and puckish humour of Noel Coward, had done what neither Press reviews nor theatre posters could ever accomplish. Unhappily, the vengeful, aggressive Osbert seemed unable, at the time, to recognize his good fortune and unceasingly reviled Coward for, as he termed it, 'spitting in a lady's face'. No doubt Walton, with his Lancastrian shrewdness and commonsense, was impervious to the spiteful abuse of his denigrators, and rightly so, for, to paraphrase a couplet of Goethe, 'When curs are snapping at your heels, it is a sure sign that you are on horseback.'

The next performance of *Façade*, given at the New Chenil Galleries, Chelsea, on 27 April 1926 and containing twenty-six numbers, proved to be a rattling success, and Walton, like each of his collaborators, became the toast of the town, a prodigy hailed almost with adulation. Constant Lambert, now a close, much-revered friend, composed the first eleven bars of a new item, 'Four in the Morning'; other additions were 'Country Dance', 'Scotch Rhapsody', 'Polka', 'Old Sir Faulk' and 'Tango' (colloquially referred to as 'I do like to be beside the seaside'). Walton failed to realize that the composer of the music-hall song parodied in 'Tango' was still alive (and highly indignant), but, when this rather frightening news came to his knowledge, he took prompt action to safeguard the number, which he regarded as one of the brightest facets of the entire work. Ernest Newman, reviewing the performance, used words that have been quoted many times:

> But the entertainment owed a great deal also to Mr Walton's music. All I knew of this young man's before Tuesday was a horrible quartet of his that was given at the Royal College three or four years ago. On the strength of this, I take leave to dislike intensely Mr Walton's serious music—if, indeed, that quartet *was* serious and *was* music, both of which I doubt. But as a musical joker he is a jewel of the first water. . . . Here and there Mr Walton could be seen diving into that sequestered and now stagnant pool and coming up with bits of Stravinsky sticking in his honest English hair. . . . Here is obviously a humorous musical talent of the first order; nothing so good in the mock-serious line of music has been heard for a long time as the "Valse," the "Polka," the "Jodelling Song" and "I do like to be beside the seaside"; and the deft workmanship, especially in the orchestration, made the heart of the listening musician glad. . . . At its best, "Façade" ought to incorporate the four numbers I have mentioned in "Riverside Nights." And Mr Walton ought to seek out a librettist after his own heart and give us a little musical comedy in the jazz style.[13]

It was just as well that Walton was, in Newman's words, a musical joker of the first water, and that he also had a certain toughness of fibre that enabled him to ignore or combat the irrational, aggressive element in

Osbert's nature. With their broad-brimmed black hats and capes, their aristocratic looks, dignified manner and air of lofty disdain, the Sitwells could be alarming, even frightening, to the unsophisticated and the inexperienced; but they shone brightly over the British cultural scene, giving a patina of glamour to ordinary, humdrum lives. For the young genius from Oldham they were a heaven-sent opportunity, opening up a whole new world of sensibility. Like other Sitwell protégés, who had constantly to guard against offending, and being swiftly discarded, through some hapless insult, solecism or disloyalty, Walton was never really permitted to forget his place, but, conscious that God had blessed him with a rare and priceless gift, he succeeded, nevertheless, in preserving his pride and self-respect, if not his independence.

# 3

# A Different Path . . .

If any dependable 1923 horoscope could have been compiled for Walton, it would not have shown a prodigality of milk and honey. His String Quartet, already described by Ernest Newman as 'horrible' and neither 'serious' nor 'music' (see the previous chapter) made a poor showing at Salzburg in August during the first festival of the ISCM, when the jury, which included Ansermet, also heard Berg's String Quartet, Bartók's Second Violin Sonata, Hindemith's Clarinet Quintet and Janáček's Violin Sonata. Walton travelled to Salzburg with Osbert and Sacheverell Sitwell; there he heard his own work magnificently played by the McCulloch Quartet from Liverpool. Salzburg, that beautiful, prestigious city, with its noble cathedral, presided over in the seventeenth-century by a Borgia-like archbishop of unbridled passion and profligacy, its enchanting gardens, its dignified buildings and its world-renowned music festival, mecca of some of the most illustrious and talked-about composers of the day, must have appeared to the twenty-year-old Walton as the sudden fulfilment of a fabulous, almost unrealizable dream.

During the performance of his String Quartet the restlessness of the audience probably alarmed him, but as Osbert Sitwell, writing to Frank Howes, related,[1] laughter bubbled up, breaking the tension, when the cellist accidentally pushed the spike of her instrument into a catch that operated a trap-door on which she was sitting and, still bowing furiously, she began to descend below the stage and disappear from sight. Happily, she was rescued before touching bottom and, with her bow poised for prompt action, came up, unperturbed and smiling, like a pantomime fairy godmother. The audience, not often regaled with such Hoffnung-like antics, rolled in their seats, choking with laughter.

Initially performed on 4 March 1921 at the first concert of the London Contemporary Music Centre, the quartet had since been extensively re-written and a third movement had been added, seemingly without creating any marked improvements. When the McCulloch String Quartet played the work in a LCMC concert at the Royal College of Music on 5 July 1923, one eminent critic asked Herbert Ancliffe, who sat beside him, 'Am I music-mad, or is this man?'[2] The critic, a highly intelligent and cultured person, had, says Ancliffe, a tendency to look backwards, while the composer, still immature and in the process of developing, was over-anxious to look forward, to break new ground and follow a different, more promising path. He highlighted a significant truth when he wrote: 'All the time he seemed to be trying to repress his natural instincts to be melodious. . . .' Hearing Walton's music, I have always been conscious of his painstaking, almost frantic attempts to avoid simple diatonic melody—as if, feeling ill-equipped to compete with dreary, note-spinning avant-gardists all sporting clever but facile party tricks, he suffered recurrent nightmares of being thought old-fashioned. It is interesting to recall that a year before his death Walton himself described his String Quartet as 'a horrible piece, with bits of Schoenberg, Berg and heaven knows what else'.[3]

Some of the *cognoscenti* at the Salzburg Festival certainly regarded the quartet, a work of unremitting contrapuntal severity that skated precariously on the brink of atonality, with extreme disfavour. Although the International Jury, a body of unimpeachable status and authority, had chosen it for performance, the suggestion was made that it should be withdrawn, on the grounds that it failed dismally to represent British music; but, of course, as *The Music Bulletin* pointed out,[4] the ISCM had never intended that the Festival should serve as a showcase for music 'representing' different countries. Ill-feeling flared into anger when the Italian Committee, whose members included the prestigious Casella, Malipiero, Pizzetti and Respighi, grumbled bitterly about the programmes in the Festival, then peremptorily withdrew all the works of the Italian contingent from the proceedings. Undaunted, the ISCM continued with its arrangements, and Walton's quartet, the only British contribution to the Festival, was performed by the McCulloch Quartet at the third concert on 4 August 1923, an event which drew the following comments from the music critic of *The Times*:

> It is a long work, and it was very unfortunately placed at the end of a long programme. The impressions it gave were first, that it might be considerably condensed, and second, that some passages might be re-written with a view to making the work more grateful for the strings to play. The Scherzo is the least effective part of the work. The lengthy treatment of an apparently meaningless figure of two notes lost the attention of the hall, and this was never regained. The result was that by the time the latter part of the fugue was reached the restiveness of the audience made it almost impossible to listen intelligently. A word of congratulation to the McCulloch Quartet, who bravely and

> successively overcame the many difficulties of the work—no-one grudges Mr Walton the performance of his Quartet but one may doubt the wisdom, from the composer's point of view, of forcing an immature work on the public notice.[5]

One famous and influential composer who detected some merit in Walton's quartet was Alban Berg, one of the most progressive spirits of his day. A quiet, introverted man with a certain morbidity or sadness in his manner, but also with the charm of a kindly young country priest, he took Walton and Lord Berners to see Schoenberg at a house by the side of a nearby lake which he had rented for the summer. As the party approached the house, they could hear Schoenberg playing the piano, but, despite the unwelcome interruption, he greeted his guests most cordially. Schoenberg's highly disciplined existence found little scope for frivolity, Bohemian habits or social graces; constantly occupied with productivity, he was incapable of making light of anything. His conversations with pupils and friends almost invariably revolved around music and its multifarious facets, and even the most burdensome chatter might, if it stimulated the flow of his own creative adrenalin, help to solve a spiritual or aesthetic crisis in his dark, troubled life. On this occasion, with Berners acting as interpreter, since Walton did not know much German, the four men discussed the use of the piano for composing—not the happiest of subjects for the young Oldham genius, himself an indifferent performer at the keyboard.

After the Salzburg tempest had in some measure ruffled his pride and self-confidence, the creative flame in Walton burned rather fitfully, and in 1923, back in England, he produced some mediocre works, now happily reduced to ashes by the same flame. It is a bleak, frustrating phase through which every major composer must pass. Walton conceived an opus of considerable, but variable merit, a *Toccata for Violin and Piano*, which was not performed until 1925 and which Constant Lambert described as 'a rhapsodical work showing traces of Bartók and even Sorabji'. It must be explained that Kaikhosru Shapurji Sorabji, born in Dudley, Essex, in 1892, the son of a Parsi father and a Spanish-Sicilian mother, had greatly impressed Walton and the Sitwell brothers.[6] A brilliant composer and pianist, who resided in Corfe Castle, Dorset, he wrote a number of intriguing, semi-atonal pieces, including the *Fantaisie Espagnole* of 1919.

Walton may have suffered heartache and gnawing self-doubt as he struggled to compose successfully, but he certainly enjoyed the succulent fruits of the Sitwell patronage. 'It was a gay old life,' he said, 'they knew everybody who was anybody in music and society, from Sir Thomas Beecham to the younger set.'[7] According to Peter Quennell,[8] it was not only a gay life but one with ripe, romantic overtones. Sacheverell fell deeply in love with a musical comedy actress, and he and Walton pursued her. One night, dining in a restaurant, they saw her at a nearby table with friends. Walton, who was 'very knowledgeable in such matters', volunteered to go across, make a diplomatic approach and try to persuade the actress and her party to join Sacheverell and himself. Horrified at this crude strategy, his companion forbade him to do so. Although the composer managed, rather precariously, to keep up with the glittering social cavalcade of London life in which the Sitwells moved so elegantly, he found it an exceedingly hard struggle, because he was nearly always penniless, relying on the charity of others. 'Various society friends used to bail me out with the odd donation,' he remarked, 'but I could never pay the money back.'[9] He had, by that time, mastered, or at least learned to control, his natural shyness and to associate freely with women. Once he went to a party and met a girl, Brenda Dean Paul, whom Quennell described as 'a very disreputable Chelsea character who eventually became a drug addict'.[10] When the composer first saw her, she was rather pretty and looked like a Lely portrait of Nell Gwynne. Walton danced with her, but for some reason she bit his lower lip, which swelled up so rapidly that when Quennell saw him shortly afterwards he could only mumble, 'I've been bitten by Brenda.'

One of the Walton scores which has failed to survive is the *Fantasia Concertante for two pianos, jazz band and orchestra*, written for the Savoy Havana Band, formed in 1921 by the American band-leader Bert Ralton under the title 'New York Havana Band' and directed, after his departure, by Cyril Ramon Newton. It was not Newton, however, but Debroy Somers, founder and conductor of the famous Savoy Orpheans, who, following an introduction by Richard Temple, a director of the Savoy Hotel, drew Walton away from Schoenberg and into the exciting, rhythm-pounding world of George Gershwin. He had, in 1920, been appointed as arranger and adviser to the Savoy Havana Band. Surfeited with the baffling intellect of the inventor of the twelve-note system, Walton must have found relief, and a certain challenge, in the most interesting of all the composers who have attempted to bridge the gap between jazz and concert music. Walton already had a taste for jazz and, doubtless influenced by Constant Lambert's addiction, he had introduced scintillatingly clever parodies of various jazz and popular styles into *Façade*. At a time when Lambert was living in Oakley Street, where two pianos had been installed, Walton used to come round from Carlyle Square, and together they would improvise foxtrots, blues and other tunes. Walton, after the introduction to Debroy Somers, spent more than a year studying and composing jazz, channelling much of his energy and inspiration into this massively proportioned concerto for two pianos, jazz band and orchestra. According to the *Boston Evening Transcript*,[11] on finishing the concerto he suddenly abandoned the jazz style, the pungent timbres and intriguing syncopations of ragtime, reacting with distaste against the deadly monotony of the four-square phrase, the inevitable harmonic clichés filched from Debussy and Delius, the trite nostalgia that pollutes and debilitates the whole atmosphere. This rather abrupt volte-face may have originated partly in a realization that such music, served up in the Savoy and similar hotels as a pleasant, slightly exotic background for polite chatter and romantic dalliance at the dinner table, had only restricted appeal in the more formalistic environment of the concert-hall. As evidence of this, Gershwin's *Rhapsody in Blue* had raised a storm of applause at the Savoy, but when performed at the Queen's Hall in London and on subsequent tours in the provinces, it failed to generate any real enthusiasm.

The influence of jazz on modern classical music has been considerable, yet its past development is difficult to trace. It originated among American Negroes, being distinguished from normal European music by its unusual rhythms, based on the polyrhythmic subtleties of African drum languages. Musicologists disagree about the meaning of the term 'jazz', some claiming that it derives from a Creole word meaning 'to speed up', others regarding it as a corruption of the French *jaser* (to chatter). It has also been asserted that 'jazz' is an abbreviation of 'Jasbo', the Christian name of a Negro musician who lived about 1900. Sousa, that master of brass band music known affectionately as 'The March King', believed that it was the name for the finale of a revue. Jazz is a mixture of many ingredients, the growth of which is difficult to follow precisely. One fact is certain, that many distinguished composers, who might be classed as non-practitioners in the strictest sense, have found a startlingly new improvisatory freedom in the use or influence of jazz. It enchanted Stravinsky, who, after receiving some sheets of ragtime music, made copious use of jazz rhythms in *The Soldier's Tale* and *Ragtime for Eleven Solo Instruments*. As early as 1908, Debussy utilized ragtime rhythms in *Golliwog's Cake-walk*, repeating the formula two years later in *Minstrels*; and Milhaud experimented successfully with jazz rhythms in his Negro ballet *La Création du Monde* and other works. Honegger, Krenek and Satie are among those whose music has been touched and revitalized by jazz.

During his association with Debroy Somers, while he was trying unsuccessfully to write the kind of slick, sophisticated music that the dance band needed, Walton became friendly with Vladimir Dukelsky, who had composed the ballet *Zephyr et Flore* for Diaghilev. This charming and prolific man took him to see Gershwin at his Pall Mall flat. Walton, who greatly admired Gershwin's captivating tunes as much as he did his fabulous piano-playing, found him in the middle of writing his Piano Concerto in F, a work of coruscating brilliance. Gershwin, a dominating figure with intense black eyes, framed by a face curiously reminiscent of a ram, died in 1937, at the age of thirty-eight, of a brain tumour. Modest and unassuming in manner, he had, outside the worst phase of his illness, an indomitable will-power and vitality. As for Dukelsky (his real name was Vernon Duke), much of his music, like the romantically pulsating *April in Paris*, invited popular applause rather than critical acclaim. He once published a scarifying attack headed 'The Deification of Stravinsky' in the American magazine *Listen*, referring to Stravinsky as 'I.S.' throughout his article. The infuriated Igor, no mean gymnast on the parallel-bars of public controversy and abuse, promptly sent a withering reply to the magazine, reducing Vladimir Dukelsky to the letters 'V.D.' and rending him with satire.[12]

The pre-eminence of orchestral music in the concert hall has, to some extent, persuaded outstanding British composers—including Elgar, Bliss, Rawsthorne, Fricker and Tippett—to push the highly specialized art of song-writing to one side. Walton was no exception, and although in *Façade* he matched voice and verse with uncanny insight, the result was far removed from the magical lyricism of the great nineteenth-century *lieder* composers. He did, however, excel in his own distinctive field of vocal scoring, one minor example being his conversion in 1923/4 of certain numbers from *Façade* into songs which he called *Bucolic Comedies*. They were never publicly performed as such, but in 1932 he substituted revised versions of three of them under the title *Three Songs*. The last two, '*Noche Espagnole*' and 'Foxtrot', had been incorporated into the second orchestral suite.

While the young composer, finding new forms of expression, began to strike out on his own, the apparent harmony at Carlyle Square showed signs of discord. The break-up of the Sitwell oligarchy, which had dominated the British scene so grandiloquently, a model for aspiring social aesthetes, started insidiously, as such disasters do, reaching crisis point by the spring of 1925. It was about that time that Cyril Connolly saw the formidable trio at the Washington Irving Hotel in Granada, Spain, and, with their black capes and black Andalusian hats, they looked magnificently picturesque, a dazzling monument to aristocratic superiority. How could he have known that the monument had commenced to crumble, that soon it would be glimpsed more in retrospect than reality, inviting nostalgia rather than discipleship, and amused tolerance instead of approval. The dissolution of the Carlyle Square ménage must have seemed, to those who idolized this extremely brilliant and witty trio, like the passing of a whole way of life. It was a period of hidden or suppressed crises.

Following an operation on her back at the begining of the year, Edith was in great pain and suffering so cruelly that she could hardly tackle any work. The publication of her book of poetry *Troy Park*, which she now almost disliked when comparing it with Eliot's *The Waste Land*, had triggered off some biting reviews, including an 'impertinent' one from the *Express*, a paper she detested. In her nervous agony and despair, she felt she was slipping headlong down a precipitous path.

As for Osbert, that paranoiac mandarin of letters whom Desmond McCarthy had compared with the Comte Robert de Montesquieu, the great Parisian dandy, the wolves of poverty were sniffing, if not actually howling, at the front door of his elegant house, imperilling his well-established role as *grand seigneur* of literature. Osbert was almost desperately short of money. He received £2,000 a year from the Sitwell estate, but the supplementary income from his books was pitifully meagre, as exemplified by his American earnings from *Triple Fugue*—a mere £18; so that running his large house, paying Mrs Powell, the housekeeper, and partially supporting his brother and Walton called for the stamina and fortitude of a Hercules. He grew increasingly irritable, more openly paranoiac, not only bombarding his publisher with demands for more money but castigating critics and other writers, including Michael Arlen, whom he wrongly accused of plagiarism. In his famous cloak and broad-brimmed Andalusian hat, Osbert, fulminating with rage and resembling nothing so much as a hydrophobic Count Fosco, made a frightening, almost demoniac figure.

Then there was Sacheverell, the shy, gentle poet who had had the temerity (and good fortune) to fall in love with a stunningly beautiful Canadian brunette, Georgia Doble, and who now planned, with Sir George and Lady Ida's blessing, to marry her. It was the beginning of the end. For many months Schoenbergian dissonances had been creeping into the sweet, diatonic harmony at Carlyle Square, and Sacheverell, for so long dominated by the megolomaniac stardom of his family, had gazed hungrily beyond the high-fenced paddock of brotherly affiliation to the green and succulent pastures of personal freedom. 'It had become obvious to me that my relationship with Osbert could not go on like that much longer,' he said. 'For some while I had been longing to escape, and once I met Georgia I was determined I would marry her'[13]. Although he came to accept it with a good grace, Osbert was at first greatly upset at the prospect of Sacheverell's 'defection', particularly since, having previously danced with this lovely girl, he had invited her to tea at Carlyle Square and there introduced her to his brother. He was, after all, singularly unfortunate with his charmingly highbrow society ladies, who all seemed to vanish overnight, and even William Walton, his protégé, was destined, nine years later, to provoke him beyond endurance by whisking his latest acquisition, Lady Wimborne, from under his nose. In October the 'defection' became absolute when Sacheverell journeyed with his fiancée to France and married her, without a great deal of publicity or fuss, in the Anglican Church of St George in Paris, with the Doble, but not the Sitwell, parents present. In the wedding photographs Edith looked sartorially picturesque, as well as benign, in one of her most impressive Cossack hats; but Osbert wore the sad, hurt expression of a noble patrician lord who has suffered betrayal at the hands of someone he trusted. It could have been much worse: the happy couple had, after all, decided to settle in the house next door, and Osbert was quoted in a press report as stating optimistically that the marriage would strengthen, not destroy, the Sitwell alliance.[14] He also told Rebecca West that it would ensure the survival of the Sitwell line, a prospect which filled him with joy—and his listener with astonishment, since she had never heard him profess any regard for, or interest in, the family.[15] Although his whole life had to change drastically, Osbert did manage to readjust to the loss of his beloved brother, a peerless friend, confidant and collaborator.

Walton's intimate association with the Sitwells continued as if nothing unusual had happened, and one of the celebrities he encountered, as a result of the patronage, was Lytton Strachey, a luminary of the Bloomsbury group of writers and painters. Strachey, picturesque in speech and appearance, won fame and created a vogue by his graceful denigration, in *Eminent Victorians*, of Cardinal Manning, Florence Nightingale, Thomas Arnold and General Gordon; but his Chinese melodrama *The Son of Heaven*, produced in July 1925, with music by Walton, was, in every respect, a failure. The outspoken critic of *The Curtain* described this entertainment as 'the dullest play which we have walked out of since Arnold Bennett's *The Bright Island*'[16] and the reviewer for *The Stage* called the music 'ambitious and decidedly heavy'.[17] In fairness to Strachey, it must be pointed out that he himself was not enthusiastic about the play and did not really want it to be produced.

After abandoning the jazz style, Walton, for a time, wrote nothing of consequence, then, in 1925, like a sudden burst of bright sunshine in a sky filled with grey clouds, came the overture *Portsmouth Point*, that lively and colourful picture of the teeming, ebullient life of a seaport. Constant Lambert referred to his resurgence in these words: 'It was clearly a case of "reculer pour mieux sauter" for in his next work, the brilliant overture *Portsmouth Point*, he quite suddenly and emphatically attains real self expression for the first time in his career. We can see now that his excursions into atonality and jazz were in the nature of mental exercises, studies in a foreign language that enabled him to speak his own tongue with greater knowledge and conviction.'[18]

The principal tune for *Portsmouth Point* came into Walton's head while he was travelling in London on the top of a number 22 bus, and, oblivious to the dense, fast-flowing traffic around him, he practically had to leap from the vehicle in order to write it down.[19] He composed the overture during the spring of 1925, while in Spain, accompanied by the Sitwells. It received its première at the ISCM Festival in Zurich on 22 June 1926, and when Walton heard that it was going to be played there, his elation was doubtless accompanied by 'butterflies in the stomach', since he had the formidable task of writing out sixty score parts needed for the performance. Elizabeth McCabe, herself an artist of rare gifts, once told me how her son John, the brilliant pianist and composer, had sat up two whole nights copying the intricate notation of one of his own works in preparation for a première and how he had looked 'ashen-faced and drained' when the task was completed. For Walton the undertaking involved six weeks of almost incessant copying, but the unexpected appearance of a firm of music publishers, offering a financial share in his glory, probably raised his spirits. After he had made some revisions—mostly simplifications—the full score of the overture appeared in print in June 1928. He received a royalty on every sale of *Portsmouth Point* and half the Performing Right Society's fee, the other half going to Oxford University Press, his publishers. Since the work travelled around the world on a wave of popularity, his remuneration was heartening. Walton dedicated the overture to Siegfried Sassoon, at whose instigation the publishers had provided this handsome agreement. In fact, not only did OUP, whose Music Department was headed by Hubert Foss, undertake publication, but they signed a contract to publish Walton's works over a five-year period, and in 1927 printed a piano duet version of the overture. Lord Berners had originally planned, between 1919 and 1920, to write *Portsmouth Point* as a ballet 'after Rowlandson'; he completed a piano solo version and some fifty bars of orchestral music, then abandoned the idea.

Walton's dedication of the overture to Sassoon was a tribute to a friend whose unfailing generosity over many years not only helped him to compose in a more stress-free atmosphere but saved him, again and again, from financial disaster. Indeed, the poet's magnanimity places him high in the Valhalla of those patrons of the arts who, selflessly ignoring the pressing considerations of their own highly distinguished lives, have, like Prince Esterhazy, delved deeply and repeatedly into their pockets to settle crippling debts, or provide daily sustenance, for some impoverished protégé in order that the glittering but often fragile quality we call genius might be safeguarded for posterity. A man of great sensitivity, as well as courage, Sassoon enlisted in 1915, serving in France and Palestine, and expressed in his *War Poems* (1919) the bitter disillusionment of his generation. The full extent of Sassoon's generosity to Walton will be dealt with in a subsequent chapter.

Constant Lambert, who had a beautiful speaking voice, took the role of narrator in a performance of *Façade* on 29 June 1926 which included 'Tarantella', the 'March' and 'Mazurka'. He was only twenty years of age at the time. Lambert recited again at Siena in September 1928, when Walton mounted the rostrum, and 'Popular Song', now regarded as the most appealing number, was introduced into the work. Walton, with some difficulty, wrote the tune specially for Lambert during a return visit to Oldham. 'Black Mrs Behemoth' was another addition.

For three weeks prior to the performance of *Façade* at the Siena Festival, an event of great importance, Sir George and Lady Ida Sitwell gave hospitality at Montegufoni, their castle near Florence, to a distinguished company of people, including, of course, Walton and their own children, as well as Sacheverell's wife Georgia. Among the guests was Lady Christabel Aberconway, the future dedicatee of the Viola Concerto, who, in her memoirs[20] recalled a sumptuous house-party attended by the composer, the Sitwells, Constant Lambert, Beryl de Zoete, Arthur Waley, Stephen Tennant, Siegfried Sassoon and others. She described the food as 'delicious and ample: a triumph of organisation'. The clatter of feet echoed constantly on the stone floors of the castle as a massive invasion of people—eight bus loads—swept into Montegufoni for luncheon and dinner. As a diversion from food, drink, dancing and polite conversation, the guests were driven into Siena to see the Palio, that great horse-race which, with the jockeys wearing picturesque renaissance dress bearing the colours of the different quarters of the city, fills the piazza with a blaze of visual splendour. Despite this noble, exciting event, the spirits of those intimately concerned with preparations for the *Façade* performance sank alarmingly when, a few days before the 'deadline', the painted backcloth, being created from Severini's design, failed to arrive. Walton had given the sketch to a painter named Barone whom he had met in a bar in Florence and who had promised to reproduce it and deliver the completed backcloth in good time. Unhappily, the composer had omitted to make a note of his address, and a frantic, hilarious, slapstick search for the artist began. Lady Ida, cautioning everyone 'not to panic', ordered the car and, armed with a telephone directory, drove into Florence. The names 'Baron' and 'Barone' proliferated in the directory pages—no matter, the dauntless lady knocked briskly at each door, asking in very precise Italian, 'Have you seen the backcloth of my daughter?' The only answers she received were bewildered looks, waving hands and some irate comments from people who clearly regarded her as either mad or harmlessly eccentric. Lady Aberconway, blessed with more common sense than Lady Ida, went to the bar where Walton had met the painter and elicited the help of the barman, who, to her joy, actually pointed to the elusive 'Barone', sitting only a few feet away. On being promised immediate payment of his fee, he dashed off to his lodging and, in a surprisingly short space of time, returned with the rolled-up backcloth. It was extremely heavy, but manageable, and she carried it triumphantly to a place in Florence where she had arranged to meet Sir George Sitwell at a certain hour. Her remarks about the behaviour of that perverse, highly idiosyncratic nobleman are illuminating:

> When Sir George saw the long roll, he declared, typically, because thwarting his children was a natural instinct, that it was utterly impossible to take it back in the car. I pointed out that we had to leave early the next morning; but he was adamant. I nearly burst into tears, which would have been very effective; instead, I stamped my foot at him, there in the open street, a very Victorian gesture, and announced in a loud voice that if he wouldn't take the roll and me in the car he could return alone. Shaken but obstinate, he complained that it couldn't be done; whereupon I jumped into the car, put the roll across the inside and out of the window, and appealed to the chauffeur: could he drive with this unicorn's horn sticking out sideways? Knowing the whole drama (Italian servants know everything), and much preferring the young Sitwells to Sir George, he gallantly declared that it was certainly possible. Sir George, highly displeased, sat next to him, and refused to share in the triumph of our home-coming, but instead went off to bed, there to eat a rice-pudding.[21]

Of the eighteen items performed, only six have been used for the definitive version published in 1951. They are 'Lullaby for Jumbo,' 'Hornpipe', 'Long Steel Grass', 'Sir Beelzebub', '*En Famille*' and 'Mariner Man'. Those abandoned include 'Switchback', 'Springing Jack' and 'The Octogenarian'. The definitive version of *Façade*, which had to be specially reconstructed from the numbers available because no full score had survived, was performed in London on 29 May 1942, when the audience showed warm appreciation of Edith Sitwell's verses and Walton's lively, satirical music.

It was in the early winter of 1925 that Georgia and Sacheverell, demonstrating that their union had not, in any way, changed the old pre-marital regime of literary hard work and friendship, visited Amalfi with Osbert, Walton and the handsome Adrian Stokes, whom Peter Quennell, subsequently joining the party, described as 'a striking personage, bronzed and bright-eyed, whose hawk-like profile and thatch of untidy locks—asked by the passport office to describe its colour, he had answered "old gold"—gave him the appearance somewhat of a youthful Afghan chief'.[22] Although Walton and the Sitwells loved Amalfi dearly, they had little opportunity to enjoy its visual delights: storm after storm raged across the Bay of Salerno, churning up the waves into a muddy maelstrom and drenching the narrow ledge on which the hotel stood with an almost incessant deluge of rain. The distant mountains could be glimpsed only faintly through the rain-mist, and from the streets of Amalfi, clustered around the picturesque ruin of a castle that had once belonged to John Webster's Duchess, arose 'a peculiarly damp and dispiriting smell'.[23] As mentioned in Chapter 1, the hotel had been built as a Capuchin monastery; the rooms were, in reality, cells, and one of these had been allocated to each member of the party. They remained there for the greater part of the day—Osbert writing a novel, Sacheverell creating his glowingly rich autobiography, *All Summer in a Day*, Adrian Stokes preoccupied with a piece of modern art criticism, and Walton hammering away at a rickety upright piano—issuing forth just before luncheon and dinner, to meet in Osbert's sitting-room for conversation and 'White Lady' cocktails.

Walton's next composition, a charming miniature called *Siesta*, with a prevailingly quiet, wistful mood, was first performed by Guy Warrack at one of his chamber orchestra concerts at the Aeolian Hall on 24 November 1926. He wrote it at Haus Hirth, near Munich, and dedicated it to his friend Stephen Tennant, fourth son of Lord Glenconner, whose family were also close friends of the Sitwells. The particular kind of romantic ambience that Walton evoked in the score of *Siesta*, impregnated with a carefree, impressionistic Mediterranean atmosphere, reflected his deepening absorption in, and admiration for, the Italian way of life. After attending a reception which followed the Siena performance of *Façade*, he strolled around the city with Hubert Foss, under a pitch black sky pricked with innumerable stars. In a little remote street they heard music and paused at the top of a flight of steps below which, in a small space illuminated by a single lamp, four people were playing tangos on mandolins and whistling the tunes, with the help of a flexaton, while a few couples danced. 'It was a beautiful sight, simple and peasant-like and a welcome change from the "idiotic reception," ' remarked Foss in a subsequent letter to his wife.[24]

Tennant, a shrewd and perceptive man, drew a graphic picture of the composer:

> I first met Willie, dining with Osbert, in his London house, 1925. Constant Lambert was often there, as was always Willie, at Osbert's parties. Virginia Woolf also. I was very jealous of his genius. Like all men of true genius, he was

> a remote, mysterious young man, very quiet and enigmatic. Christabel Aberconway adored Willie. But nobody understood him, really. I often went to the Russian Ballet with him. On the whole, he was not very easy to talk to and has no conversational virtuosity. He was an Enigma, a Sphinx. He was devoted to me and I to him.[25]

Tennant, a tuberculosis victim, suffered constantly from ill health, a fact which greatly worried the composer, who, with Sassoon, Rex Whistler and Beryl de Zoete, paid him many visits. According to him,[26] the 'puckish and eccentric' Sacheverell used to tease Walton about his 'Oldham background', classing it as much too 'low and vulgar' to be '*Lieu de Naissance*' for a genius. He described the Sitwell trio as 'Holy terrors, ruthless, arrogant, witty and often spiteful'.

At some time in 1928, Walton, who greatly admired and had been influenced by Stravinsky, made, at the suggestion of Angus Morrison, a concert arrangement of the 'Valse' from *Façade*. Done not as a slavish imitation but in the style and spirit of the Stravinsky arrangements from *Petrushka* and the Falla *Fire Dance*, it was published in October that year as a work in its own right and proved very popular. Walton dedicated the piece to Mrs Beverley Baxter, one of the Sitwell coterie and the extremely beautiful wife of A. Beverley Baxter, editor of the *Daily Express*.

A clever and versatile acquaintance who brought new creative experience to Walton was Lord Berners, already encountered in earlier chapters. A painter, brilliant autobiographer and writer of fantastic novels, he gained renown in the musical world for his ballets, infused with the comic and satirical pictorialism to which his gift for pastiche gave originality. One example was his ballet music for the Sadler's Wells production of *Les Sirènes*, which recaptured, hilariously, the qualities of 'high life', and its musical equivalent, in the Edwardian era. Lord Berners' most consistently delightful work in this genre is *The Triumph of Neptune*, written for Diaghilev to a scenario by Sacheverell Sitwell and produced in 1926.

In the late autumn of that year Walton prepared and orchestrated the first suite from *Façade*, to be used in the ballet as an interlude between the acts. He and Constant Lambert also helped Berners to orchestrate four large numbers in the work. Serge Diaghilev was present at the 1926 performance of *Façade*, on the look-out, as always, for another ballet to bring fresh glory to his company. Accompanied by Kochno, Lifar and other members of his princely retinue, he attended a luncheon at Carlyle Square arranged for him by the Sitwell brothers. After the meal the party went round to Angus Morrison's house in Oakley Street, because Osbert had only one upright piano, and he possessed two finer instruments. There, while Diaghilev listened attentively, Walton and Morrison played parts of Walton's projected ballet score, but, alas, he rejected it, saying that one day the composer would 'write something better'. Diaghilev did, however, agree to stage *The Triumph of Neptune*. The music Walton had written seemed much too valuable to discard, so, at Lambert's suggestion, he re-cast the score in 1927 as the *Sinfonia Concertante*, dedicating each of the three movements to one of the Sitwells. It was first performed, with great success, at a Royal Philharmonic Society concert on 5 January 1928, with Ernest Ansermet conducting and York Bowen at the piano.

The year 1927 provided Walton with a new friend, Spike Hughes, with whom, at his request, he shared a score in the gallery of the Queen's Hall during a performance of Elgar's Second Symphony, at the same time enjoying the unforgettable privilege of seeing the great composer himself at a special concert arranged in his honour. Frank Schuster, one of Elgar's most indefatigable champions, who had striven nobly, at the beginning of his career, to make his works universally known and appreciated, had determined on a final, splendid gesture,—the presentation of a seventieth-birthday Elgar concert, as an act of homage, to be given in the music-room of his house, the Long White Cloud, at Bray. Schuster, who had met the Sitwells through a mutual friend, Madame Vandervelde, invited Osbert, Sacheverell and Walton to attend the concert as his guests. Osbert has left a graphic and moving description of this historically memorable occasion:

> We motored down from London. The Long White Cloud had a garden on the river, facing Monkey Island, and as we were early, we went first, with Siegfried Sassoon—who I remember, though rather gloomy, was full of horse-play that afternoon—to look at the rooms painted with *singeries* in the hotel, and to explore the eighteenth-century pavilion in its garden. Coming out of this structure, a single large room delicately poised on pillars, I seemed to recall that we saw from the edge of the river, on a smooth green lawn opposite, above an embankment, and through an hallucinatory mist born of the rain that had now ceased, the plump wraith of Sir Edward Elgar, who with his grey moustache, grey hair, grey top hat and frock-coat looked every inch a personification of Colonel Bogey, walking with Frank Schuster. . . . The rain, as I say, had stopped, and the music-room was so crowded that, with Arnold Bennett, we sat just outside the doors in the open air. In England, only a composer, an elderly composer, could have drawn upon this solid core of enthusiasm. The programme, entitled *Homage to Elgar*, consisted of several works, for example the Violin Sonata, played by Albert Sammons and William Murdoch, and the String Quartet now given for the second time, and the Piano Quintet. . . . From where I sat I could watch Elgar, enthroned at the side, near the front. And I noticed, too, several figures well known in the world of English music, but in the main the audience was drawn from the famous composer's

passionately devout but to me anonymous partisans here gathered for the last time. . . .[27]

It was a beautiful setting, with an almost cloudless sky, with flowers nodding their heads in a gentle breeze, and with birds preening their feathers as they basked in the June sunshine: a setting whose calm English tranquillity seemed to reflect the purity and serenity of much of Elgar's music—but one strangely at variance with his own brooding, unhappy spirit, for, almost overnight, he had grown old and Death had claimed many of his dearest friends. It is probable, as Michael Kennedy has opined in his peerless and definitive *Portrait of Elgar* that, like Osbert Sitwell, some of the smartly dressed and fashionable people at the concert saw only the 'military bearing' of Britain's greatest composer, failing to notice his 'troubled and withdrawn eyes'. Perhaps, as the young genius from Oldham, gifted with a deep, introspective sensitivity, heard the wind rustling the tree-tops, he also heard, as if in some ghostly dimension, the sound of the Dark Angel beating his huge, black wings, a sound which, in the splendid cantata he was destined to write in 1931, would freeze the proud heart of Belshazzar the King.

# 4

# Belshazzar the King

Walton's indifferent skill as a pianist made the already difficult task of composition much harder. His imperfections at the keyboard drew a pungent anecdote from Basil Maine, who, at the time, was living in Chelsea. One evening he received a telephone call from Walton, who said, 'I have just completed a concerto for viola—would you like me to come round and play some of it from the manuscript?' The composer, assured of a warm welcome, arrived soon after and, according to Maine, provided 'through the indescribable idiom of his pianoforte playing . . . and occasionally a sketchy *vocalise* of the piano part', some indication of how the orchestral score would sound. Maine also related how, at one of the early performances of the Viola Concerto, given at the Three Choirs Festival, he saw Elgar pacing agitatedly up and down behind the orchestra gallery, deploring that such music should be thought fit for a stringed instrument.

It was Beecham who, towards the end of 1928, suggested to Walton that he should write a Viola Concerto for Lionel Tertis, and after some preliminary discussion the composer agreed. He was, at that time, spending the months from November 1928 to May of the following year staying with the Sitwells at Amalfi in Italy and concentrating on new compositions. Walton started work on the concerto in January, and about a month later reported progress to his friend Sassoon: 'I finished yesterday the second movement of my Viola Concerto. At the moment I think it will be my best work, better than the Sinfonia, if only the third and last movement works out well,—at present I am in the painful position of starting it, which is always full of trials and disappointments, however, I hope to be well away with it in a day or two.'[1]

Walton wrote to Angus Morrison from Amalfi, stating that the concerto was progressing well and that his style was changing. Morrison confessed that he found the remark slightly comic, but he changed his mind when, the following spring, Walton returned to London and played the concerto to him. 'In this work,' declared Morrison, 'he *had*, in fact, reached complete maturity of style and given full rein, for the first time, to his entirely personal lyrical gift.'[2]

After returning to London, the composer sent the manuscript of the concerto to Tertis, who catapulted it back in the next post with a sharp, rather ungracious refusal to perform the work. Tertis, at that time, enjoyed the highest possible renown not only as a virtuoso of the viola but as the courageous, indomitable artist who had rescued this Cinderella of the orchestra and, by his own superb attainments as a concert recitalist and soloist, had accorded it a status almost equal to that of the violin. His curt refusal must have greatly distressed Walton, who possibly regarded it as an implied denigration of the concerto in which he himself so ardently believed. Some time later Tertis wrote:

> One work of which I did *not* give the first performance was Walton's masterly concerto. With shame and contrition I admit that when the composer offered me the first performance I declined it. I was unwell at the time; but what is also true is that I had not learnt to appreciate Walton's style. The innovations in his musical language which now seem so logical and so truly in the main-stream of music then struck me as far-fetched. It took me quite a time to realise what a tower of strength in the literature of the viola is this concerto, and how deep the gratitude of we who play the viola should be towards the composer—the gratitude, too, to Beecham for having suggested to Walton the composition of a viola concerto for me. I remember that, when Walton came to me with it and I refused the honour, he was generous enough not to seem to take it too much amiss but asked me to suggest someone else to undertake the performance. I immediately thought of Paul Hindemith, a well-known and much-talked-of composer and a viola player too. So it was that Hindemith played the work for the first time at Queen's Hall. I was a member of the audience and felt great disappointment with his playing. The notes certainly were all there, but the tone was cold and unpleasing and the instrument he played did not deserve to be called a viola, it was far too small.[3]

Walton soon mastered his chagrin when Hindemith agreed to play the concerto on 3 October 1929 and when he learned that he himself would conduct the performance. He met Hindemith at the Baden-Baden Festival in Germany soon after the acceptance, and discussed the music and the arrangements. Hindemith's radio play *Lindberghflug* was being staged at the festival, and Walton found it all very interesting.

The performance of the Viola Concerto given by Hindemith and the Henry Wood Symphony Orchestra on 3 October 1929 in the Queen's Hall, London, with the composer on the rostrum, was a tremendous success and the critic of *The Times* remarked: 'Once the ear has adjusted itself to the new values, its subtlety, its rhythmic vitality, and its lyrical charm were evident enough. The mastery in the handling of the material chosen and the restraint which has been imposed upon his facility constitute a real and astonishing advance in the composer's development.'[4]

As to why Hindemith agreed to perform a Viola Concerto which the great Tertis had refused, he did so, according to his biographer,[5] for the best possible reason—because he liked it. He also admired and respected Sir Henry Wood, regarding him as a kindred spirit: a conductor who made music competently, without fuss and without thoughts of personal glory, either present or posthumous. According to the biographer, Walton considered Hindemith's playing of the concerto to be 'very brusque—his technique was marvellous, but he was rough—no nonsense about it. He just stood up and played.'[6] There was certainly nothing rough about the relationship between these two illustrious men, who had previously met only once—in Salzburg in 1923 at the ISCM festival in which Walton's First String Quartet was performed; and their collaboration over the première of the Viola Concerto marked the beginning of an extremely warm, sincere and enduring friendship. Hindemith introduced the work to a Berlin audience in January 1930, with Walton again conducting. Forty-three years later it was used as a ballet about the life of Oscar Wilde, which, alas, proved a disaster, with, as *The Times* noted, crude humour ill-suited to the nobility and lyricism of the music.

Ernest Newman, chief music critic of the *Sunday Times*, not only praised the concerto highly but, incidentally, revealed an unsuspected, almost venomous dislike of Serge Diaghilev and, by implication, Igor Stravinsky:

> . . . it confirms my previous belief in Walton as a young composer of quite exceptional gifts. He has fire, but he also has sanity, and when we remember the pathetic absurdities into which the younger men of only a few years ago allowed themselves to be decoyed by certain foreigners whose condescension towards certain manifestations of the new English music was in itself an impertinence, we cannot be sufficiently grateful that the best of our younger composers are now writing as if the malign influence of the late M. Diaghilev and others had never been. The days of quackery and mountebankery are over . . . the concerto is beautifully organised . . . the composer has a grasp of musical logic, a sense of fitness and a command of craftsmanship that are very unusual in so young a man.[7]

The year 1931 represented an even greater triumph for Walton, whose *Belshazzar's Feast*, a bold, theatrical cantata on the subject of the fall of Babylon, received its first performance at the Leeds Triennial Festival on 8 October that year, under Dr Malcolm Sargent, with Dennis Noble as the baritone soloist. He composed most of it in the stables of Weston Hall,

Towcester, Northamptonshire, the home of Sacheverell Sitwell, who, reminiscing in 1982, remarked, 'He made the most terrible din on the piano.'[8] As for the première, Walton confessed that it 'horrified' him, but seemingly no one else—'it sounded pretty bloody'.[9] As regards the creative task itself, he considered the most troublesome episode to be 'that damned Writing on the Wall'.[10] Forty years earlier Bernard Shaw had written: 'After Mozart struck the modern secular humanitarian note in *The Magic Flute* and Beethoven took it up in his setting of Schiller's *Ode to Joy*, oratorio degenerated into mere sentiment and claptrap. With the exception of a few cantatas by Mendelssohn, all the Biblical music of this century might be burnt without leaving the world any poorer.' Despite his brilliance as a playwright, Shaw seemed, when he donned the cloak and top hat of a music critic, to change from a respectable Dr Jekyll into a hydrophobic Mr Hyde who hacked and rent his victims, not with a surgical scalpel but with a razor-edged distortion of the truth. He wrote some brilliantly penetrating reviews but sometimes uttered fatuous, ill-conceived judgements in violent, intemperate language. For example: 'When people do less than their best I hate them, loathe them, detest them, long to tear them limb from limb, and strew them in gobbets about the stage or platform.' Unhappily, notwithstanding the success of two magnificent Biblical works—Honegger's *King David* (1921) and Stravinsky's *Symphony of Psalms* (1930)—Shaw's flatulent edict, delivered in the year 1889, had, in Britain, become a firm, widely held opinion forty years later.

The genesis of *Belshazzar's Feast* (it was originally to be called *Nebuchadnezzar, or the Writing on the Wall*) arose out of a BBC commission for which Edward Clark, the Director of Music, was responsible. In December 1929 the *Daily Express* reported that 'Walton is going abroad to execute the first commission ever given by the BBC to a British composer! He has chosen *Belshazzar's Feast* as a subject, but has uncertain ideas as to how his work will form itself, save that it will be built around a Sitwell narrative.'[11] Clark and Julian Herbage disclosed, however, that not only Walton but also Constant Lambert and Hely-Hutchinson had been approached for commissions, the BBC stipulating that, in view of their restricted resources, the works composed should be scored for 'small chorus, small orchestra, not exceeding fifteen and soloist'. Lambert had, as his subject, *Black Majesty* (the Emperor of Haiti), set to his own text from the book of the same name. Hely-Hutchinson's subject was *The Town*, to a text by Cecil Lewis. Fees of 50 guineas were agreed for both Lambert and Walton.[12]

A letter which Osbert Sitwell wrote to Siegfried Sassoon from Amalfi in 1930 depicted Walton as being in a state of depression, hunched up at the piano and doing little work. 'But it is a stage through which he always passes, if only he could recognise it,' said Osbert. In the letter, with just a hint of an ironical smile between the lines, he expressed his opinion that Lambert's success with *The Rio Grande* had introduced some acerbity into the friendship which Walton bore him—'. . . the other day I distinctly heard him referred to as "that little beast".'[13] Osbert wrote to Sassoon again the following week, saying of Walton, 'He has been working very slowly, like a dumb white calf, bless him.'[14]

As for the dumb white calf, Walton must, indeed, have looked dejected at the magnitude of the task he had undertaken. Edward Clark, in a memorandum to Adrian Boult, remarked: 'I saw William Walton on Wednesday, who has just returned from abroad where he has completed the composition of *Belshazzar*. It is for two soloists, small chorus and orchestra. Whilst abroad, he has shown this work to various people, whom it has evidently much impressed, and has been told by Berlin that they wish to broadcast the performance of this work, and also by Volkmar Andrae that he proposes to give it a public performance during the course of the next season at Zurich.'[15] Yet, four months later, on 4 September 1930, R. J. F. Howgill of the BBC's music staff, informed Hubert Foss of the Oxford University Press that '. . . *Belshazzar's Feast* has grown to such proportions that it cannot be considered as a work specially written for broadcasting, and the latter [Walton] therefore proposes to write something else as his commissioned work.'[16] Walton himself told Foss in 1933 that, 'In Belshazzar I got landed on the word "gold"—I was there from May to December (1930) perched unable to move either to right or left or up or down.'[17]

With resourcefulness and tenacity, Walton finally completed *Belshazzar's Feast*, which, since it had grown to full-scale concert proportions, no longer fulfilled the BBC's requirements. He never did write something else as his commission, and even his opera *Troilus and Cressida*, commissioned by the BBC in 1947 for broadcasting, was surrendered by the Corporation for stage performance.

Although by no means provocative or abrasive, the fiercely carved idioms of *Belshazzar's Feast* greatly troubled the choral singers of the day. It is probably not true, however, that during the preliminary rehearsals in Leeds the chorus, enraged by what they regarded as impossibly difficult parts, went on strike. According to one highly spiced report, Beecham sent Malcolm Sargent to charm the rebels and knock sense into them. Seemingly he discharged his task so efficiently, applying that hypnotic power which he had over choral forces, that the inflamed singers promptly fell in love with the work. The story of the 'mutiny' circulated in London for a number of years, and at one time even Walton believed it. Charles

Reid, in his fine biography of Sargent, ridiculed the alleged incident.[18] He had consulted various 'triennial' veterans who had rehearsed and sung in the first *Belshazzar*—people with clear, dependable memories of the performance and its preparation: unanimously they dismissed the revolt story as lurid fiction. Reid suggests that Beecham, the unpredictable, though gifted, eccentric, put out the story either as a practical joke or as 'cover' for having saddled Sargent with a cantata which he himself regarded as 'archaic'. One recalls the harsh derisory advice which he flung at Walton after the young composer, shaking with apprehension, showed him the as yet unscored, tremendously difficult middle section, seeking his opinion of the merits of *Belshazzar*. 'This is a work,' roared Beecham in his best seigneurial manner, 'which shall never be heard. Since it shall never be performed, I advise you to throw in all that you can. Throw in, let's say, a couple of brass bands for good and useless measure!'

Walton subsequently took Sir Thomas at his word and inserted parts for two brass bands into the score of *Belshazzar*, placing one on either side of the conductor, so that, at strategic points, they joined in with a stereophonic, or antiphonal, effect; but his action was doubtless prompted not so much by a desire to shame his tormentor, or even to vindicate himself, as by the presence of the Berlioz Requiem in the same programme as the première of his own work. Once jaded and dispirited as the sheer immensity of the challenge represented by this highly dramatic cantata chilled his blood, he found new vitality and resilience when, with the score completed, he attended rehearsals, bubbling with pride and enthusiasm:

> Mr William Walton, the composer of *Belshazzar's Feast*, was present at the rehearsal of the Leeds Festival Chorus on Saturday afternoon, when Dr Malcolm Sargent conducted for the third time in three successive weeks. After they had run through Vaughan William's *Toward the Unknown Region*, the chorus gave Mr Walton a foretaste of his own music, having made considerable headway with it after the strenuous rehearsal of the last two Saturdays. Mr Walton complimented the chorus in a modest little speech, expressing his gratitude for the trouble they had taken, and his surprise at the progress they had made.
>
> "I know it is very difficult," he said; "in fact, I have been half expecting a letter from the Secretary saying it was impossible. But, naturally, it wasn't written for a church choir."
>
> The singers, now that the toil of learning the notes is over, are beginning to feel pleased with themselves and actually to like the music.[19]

During that first performance the majestic sweep and drama, the radiant culminating optimism of *Belshazzar's Feast* persuaded the critics as well as the audience that the age of epic art was not dead. After the close of the final orchestral postlude, which Compton Mackenzie described as 'like a great explosive sunset', Sargent gestured Walton up to the platform for handshakes and backslapping, while a storm of applause swept down upon them. It was a glorious rendering, with choral climaxes that were sweet as well as earth-shaking. According to Lord Boothby, paying a birthday tribute to Sargent in a BBC 1 Television broadcast on 22 April 1965, the ironical Beecham referred to his fellow conductor in these words: 'He is the greatest choirmaster we have ever produced . . . he makes the b——s sing like blazes!' As for Sassoon, who, responding to pleading, or begging letters, had helped Walton with gifts of money and other largesse so many times, the success of *Belshazzar* fully vindicated his own faith and generosity. In a letter addressed to Sir Henry Head and his wife Ruth, the poet wrote: 'Willie's Belshazzar was a triumph . . . my heart swelled with pride when my protégé bowed (with immense ease and suavity) his acknowledgements to the audience (including Princess Mary!), the choir and the orchestra.'[20]

How deeply Sargent admired *Belshazzar's Feast* is revealed in this anecdote from Yehudi Menuhin:

> While the complete European Hephzibah [Menuhin] was bringing luxury and comfort of the old world to the Australian bush, where she and her husband had a vast and wonderful station in the Western district outside Melbourne, I went to visit them and found that they had Malcolm Sargent with them. Sargent had brought the score of Walton's *Belshazzar's Feast*, a work still new to Australia, and one of my most exciting memories is of the famous conductor expounding it to us. He sat with the score at the piano and played it sonorously through, while explaining, singing, occasionally shouting and, at times, gesticulating with insight, authority, love and knowledge. The memory of his enthusiasm and anxiety to share this work with us is something that returns to me whenever I hear Sargent discussed.

Sir Henry Wood considered *Belshazzar's Feast* to be 'truly marvellous, like the world coming to an end', and stated: 'Its dramatic power is superb, what orchestration, what vitality and rhythmic invention,—no orchestral work has ever carried me away so much!' Sir Henry's wife, Muriel, was fascinated by Walton's facial likeness to Edith Sitwell; and Harriet Cohen, the great pianist, told the composer that he must have Jewish blood in his veins—'otherwise you could not have written the chorus "By the waters of Babylon." '

One of Walton's friends, Lady Christabel Aberconway, claimed that although at the première the printed programme stated that Osbert Sitwell had selected the words of *Belshazzar's Feast*, she herself had done most of the research. This may be true, but there can be no doubt that

Osbert not only suggested the subject of the Writing on the Wall at Belshazzar's Feast in Babylon but also, in December 1929, actually worked on the libretto in Venice. During an interview, at the time of the first performance, he said:

> Ever since I have been writing, I have always wanted to make a mosaic of Biblical phrases, to give them (if possible) a definite verse form, and to have them set to music. Two years ago, when in Venice, I decided to retell the story of *Belshazzar's Feast*. I was immediately faced with one difficulty—the shortness of the original. Other difficulties followed rapidly. Mainly they centred round problems of rhythm and appropriateness. When the libretto was, as I thought, complete, I handed it over to Mr Walton. At his suggestion various passages were altered and other passages substituted. The libretto, as it stands now, is almost wholly taken from the Bible. I myself have merely added certain words in order to assist the music and poetic flow.[21]

With the strange possessiveness and personal involvement in a prized creation that often characterizes even the busiest of composers, applied right down to the most infinitesimal detail, and aware that London was to be given the first chance to hear the cantata, under Adrian Boult, towards the end of 1931, Walton not only made one or two revisions to the work but also took to copying the orchestral parts for the forthcoming performance. He decided to dedicate *Belshazzar's Feast* to Lord Berners and, for this act of grace, he received £50 from the dedicatee. There was nothing demeaning or mercenary in the transaction. Berners had acted, with much kindness, as his patron and at one time had engaged Walton and Lambert to assist him in scoring his ballet *The Triumph of Neptune*. Walton doubtless saw his own dedication as a tribute to Berners for his patronage and generosity. It is of some relevance that in Berners' novel *Count Omega*, published by Heywood Hill of Curzon Street, London, but now out of print, the hero is 'the great white hope of English music' and bears a very marked resemblance to Walton.

Shortly before commencing work on *Belshazzar's Feast*, the composer had formed a romantic association with the Baroness Imma Doernberg, and this soon ripened into love. They spent a great deal of time together and, when holidaying abroad, particularly in Switzerland, seem to have enjoyed a blissful relationship, clouded only by Imma's poor health and dwindling financial resources. Writing to Sassoon from Ascona in March 1931, where he did some work on the *Belshazzar* score, Walton spoke of being 'immensely happy', and in a postscript at the end of the letter the Baroness stated, 'We are having a nice and peaceful time together.' Ascona is a picturesque little fishing village at the top of Lake Maggiore, and it boasts at least one magnificent façade in the Casa Borrani, which, built in 1620, is beautifully decorated with plaster groups above its first-floor windows. Other letters from Walton made Sassoon fully aware of the strength and sincerity of the affection which he and Imma shared.

Not long before the association began, the Baroness had escaped by a hair's breadth from Germany, where ruthless decrees had been imposed, forbidding people to leave the country. She quickly found herself in grave financial difficulties, because her monthly income had dropped from a pitiful £15 to a precarious £7.10 as a result of her father's being involved in a bank crash. While she and Walton were in Switzerland, he brooded over her poor health (she subsequently died of leukaemia) and the uncertainty of the future. This was a period when, all over Europe, the rats of poverty gnawed voraciously at the foundations of society, and, as revealed in one of his letters, even Walton, immured in his ivory tower of music and harbouring thoughts of composing a symphony, ruminated pessimistically on the fact that by February 1932 unemployment in Britain would probably reach the horrifying total of five or six million. The position was almost as bad in Switzerland, and Imma, who had started a course of training as a stenographer, had little chance of finding remunerative work.

Whenever he was in any real financial plight, Walton, with a refreshing candour and diplomacy, would send an 'SOS' to Sassoon, and his letters, usually addressed to 'My dear Sieg' but on one occasion to 'My dear Shakespeare', demonstrated a close, almost brotherly relationship. He wrote from the Casa Angola, while staying in Ascona with Imma and, referring to the sudden and drastic reduction in her income, asked Sassoon to transfer funds to a Swiss bank, which the poet promptly did. Imma's gratitude for his generosity was conveyed in her touching letter of thanks, phrased in rather a quaint English and divulging the information that she was knitting a pullover for him.

Walton's very beautiful Baroness had an impressively blue-blooded lineage. Born the Princess Imma of Erbach-Schönberg at König on 11 March 1901, she was the daughter of Alexander, Prince of Erbach-Schönberg and his wife, who, prior to her marriage, bore the title Princess Elisabeth of Waldeck und Pyrmont and was the youngest sister of Queen Emma of the Netherlands and the Duchess of Albany, and thus was a first cousin of Princess Alice, Countess of Athlone. She married at Frankfurt on 31 May 1923 a man twenty-six years her senior: Baron Hans-Karl von Doernberg, who had had two previous wives, one of whom died in 1912, the other being divorced in 1923. His handsome son Sandro was only two months older than Princess Imma. Barely a year after this union with the Princess, the Baron died, and her subsequent movements in the twenties, before she met and fell in love with Walton, appear to be shrouded in mystery. She suffered ill health bravely, but sometimes it robbed her of sparkle and vitality, causing Walton extreme anguish. In a letter to Sassoon written on 29 May 1932, he reported that, following dental treatment, she had contracted 'a ghastly infection' which, spreading to the bones and all over her head, caused her 'fearful pain'.

Thus, life for the creative genius of *Belshazzar's Feast* was not at that time simply a blissful, untroubled period of sunshine and romance, success and fulfilment; but, although his concern for Imma's well-being must have caused him sleepless nights, his rapidly growing fame brought him the indisputable joy and consolation of kind, influential friends. One of these, Edith Olivier, held court in her sumptuous home, 'The Daye House', at Quidhampton, giving hospitality to a host of illustrious people, including Walton, Sassoon, Osbert Sitwell, Lord David Cecil and Rex Whistler. So favoured a guest and friend was Walton that she permitted him to choose the piano for her drawing-room. Immediately after the prestigious Queen's Hall performance of the cantata on 25 November 1931, she invited him and 'his Baroness' (as Sassoon called Imma) to have lunch with her. In fact, when Walton was in England, he spent many week-ends at 'The Daye House', where not only literary and artistic celebrities gathered but also, on occasion, the most brilliant and beautiful débutantes of the day.

Walton, during that phase of his creative development, had acquired a profound respect and affection for the music of Elgar, a regard which influenced many of his own compositions. He resented the pretensions and prejudices of the old British Music Society, especially those of Edward Dent, appointed a professor of music at Cambridge University in 1926 and, in some respects, a man of extreme intellectual arrogance. Dent had contributed an article on British music to Adler's *Handbuch der Musikgeschichte* (Second Edition, 1930) in which he referred to Elgar's music as '. . . too emotional and not quite free from vulgarity . . . pompous in style and of a too deliberate nobility of expression'. He devoted only a few lines to Elgar, while extolling the virtues of inferior composers at much greater length. A contribution which Dent had sent to an Italian periodical in 1925 was unearthed by a zealous campaigner; it spoke of Elgar as being 'repugnant to many English musicians by reason precisely of that chevalieresque rhetoric which badly covers up its intrinsic vulgarity'. This hissing firecracker, flung at a rapidly intensifying, flashpoint controversy, had the effect of a blazing torch dropped into a keg of gunpowder. Enraged by Dent's lip-curling insularity and abuse, Walton, John Ireland, Landon Ronald, Bernard Shaw, Peter Warlock, Sir Hamilton Harty and a dozen other signatories volleyed letters of protest to editors in Britain and Germany. Doubtless they should have ignored Dent, since widespread Press publicity can over-inflate the most inane utterance, endowing it with a dignity and importance which it ill deserves; but the outcry probably served, not only to deflate the enemy himself but to register a growing esteem for Britain's greatest composer.

As already mentioned, Walton admired Elgar tremendously—'his symphonies are much better than those of Mahler and Bruckner'[22]—and his adulation surfaced embarrassingly outside Hereford Cathedral in that most improbable of places a gentlemen's lavatory. There was a Three Choirs concert inside the cathedral, with Elgar conducting his choral setting *The Music Makers* and Walton conducting his own Viola Concerto, occupying adjacent stalls when not on the rostrum. During an interval the two men found themselves neighbours in the lavatory. Walton, normally shy and reserved, felt himself bursting with excitement and, showing uncharacteristic emotion, he stammered: 'I want to say how much I admire your work and your conducting. Your musicianship is . . . well . . . this seems hardly the place and . . .' Elgar smiled magnanimously. 'Most kind!—and do you happen to know what won the 3.30 at Worcester?' The fascination of speeding, palpitating horseflesh dominated the non-musical part of Elgar's life. Yehudi Menuhin recalled how, in 1932, he shook with delighted anticipation at being granted the privilege of recording the Elgar Violin Concerto under the composer's direction. As a preliminary to the recording he played the work at Grosvenor House, London, one morning, with Ivor Newton at the piano. Later that day the two artistes were in their places when Elgar arrived, looking like a benevolent country squire who should have had a couple of sleek hounds padding at his heels. Menuhin, glowing with pride, started to play at the soloist's entry; he had not even reached the 'English' second theme when Elgar rose to his feet. 'Very nice!–the recording will go beautifully; and now, please excuse me–I'm off to the races.'[23]

As a recognition of his rapidly growing fame, Walton, in 1931, received from the *Daily Dispatch* a commission to write a Christmas Carol which the Editor intended to publish in the paper: not an act of patronage to set the pulse racing, but a very acceptable one, since it brought what the delighted composer, in a letter to Sassoon, described—not in any sarcastic vein—as 'the magnificent sum of £10.10.![24] At that time he had not received payment. He obliged with a small, four-part carol entitled '*Make we Joy now in this Fest*', which appeared in the *Daily Dispatch* on Christmas Eve 1931, together with the following announcement:

> Mr William Walton, the famous young English composer, has specially written a carol for the *Daily Dispatch*.

The carol itself is old. English musicians will readily appreciate how aptly melody and harmony accord with the antique mode of the words.[25]

Walton's description of the *Daily Dispatch*'s payment of £10.10. for his Christmas Carol as 'a magnificent sum' gave proof of the very precarious state of his finances at that time, and, indeed, he wrote to Sassoon from Faringdon House, Berkshire, in January 1932, asking him to sign a form guaranteeing an overdraft; so his spirits must have soared immeasurably when, after the death of Mrs Elizabeth Courtauld, wife of Samuel Courtauld, the British industrialist and art collector, in February of that year, he learned that she had left him in her will a life annuity of £500, with the disposal of the capital in the event of his death. It was a munificent sum in those days and one which gave him a large measure of independence and security. 'It seems quite unbelievable; it is too marvellous for words,' said Walton in a letter to Sassoon. 'I can hardly realise what it means to my life and really to everyone else to whom I have been a willing burden.'[26] Sassoon himself wrote to Samuel Courtauld about the annuity and received the very gracious reply, 'I know that you are an old friend of Willie Walton and I am pleased if you really think that my wife's bequest will help him to produce the best that is in him.' It certainly did so.

In 1931 Walton had made an arrangement of Bach's Choral Prelude *Herzlich Thut Mich Verlangen*, not for his own private pleasure or for monetary gain but as a kind of tribute to that superb pianist Harriet Cohen. In her memoirs, *A Bundle of Times*, she referred to this and to what she described as 'an exciting new project':

Several composers, knowing of my special devotion to Bach, transcribed some of his works for organ, song or strings, so that I could play them to myself. One told the other about it until I had about ten arrangements. Oxford Press heard about these 'acts of homage' and decided to publish them,—if such a difficult project could be arranged. Elgar told me he'd try his best to do one, but in the event this did not materialise. Holst couldn't find anything he wanted to arrange, and anyway didn't feel that he could tackle the piano. I had written to Vaughan Williams to transcribe something for me, offering many more kisses although I owed him a lot from the *Hymn-Tune*. He answered: 'How can I say "no"—when such a reward will be mine if I say "yes"? I shall claim it *to the full* (and the 1580th).' His and ones from Bantock, Bax, Ireland, Bliss, Berners, Bridge, Howells, Goossens, Lambert, Walton and Whittaker finally arrived; everything was amicably decided and the title of the album would be *A Bach Book for Harriet Cohen*.[27]

During the period from December 1931 to February 1932 inclusive Walton composed his *3 Songs*, which he dedicated to Hubert and Dora Foss, who, the following October, gave the first performance in the

Wigmore Hall, London. He wrote the songs partly at Faringdon House, where Lord Berners lived, and partly at 'The Daye House', Quidhampton, the home of Edith Olivier. He had to create three versions of 'Daphne' before he was satisfied, and perhaps because of this the proposal to include the songs in the 1932 season of Promenade Concerts never materialized.[28]

# 5

# Death and Transfiguration

The genesis of Walton's First Symphony, set in motion by the dazzling success of *Belshazzar's Feast*, began with his deliberate attempt to write a piece of absolute music, with a Beethovenian simplicity and directness undiluted by the use of a choir and soloists. It was also the culminating gesture of a splendidly productive and triumphant decade in his life during which he also composed *Façade* (1923), *Portsmouth Point* (1925) and the Viola Concerto (1929). He wrote the symphony between February or March 1932, while staying at 'The Daye House', and August 1935, spreading its gestative odyssey over many places, including Weston Hall, Towcester, the home of Sacheverell Sitwell, and Ascona, Switzerland, to which, between March and May 1932, he returned once again with Imma Doernberg. In the spring, sick with anxiety, Walton reported to his publisher Hubert Foss that the symphony was 'unspeakable', but in October, only six months later, he declared more optimistically that it was 'on the move', adding, with a faint note of victory, 'I've managed to get down about 40 bars, which for me is really saying something. What hopes for it being completed for April I should hardly like to say'. The composer had promised the first performance date to Sir Hamilton Harty, then conductor of the Hallé Orchestra, whose brilliance in maintaining the high standards achieved by Richter he greatly admired. Walton had met Harty in Manchester in January 1932, when the conductor had asked him to write the symphony, and although, as he confessed in a letter to Sassoon,[1] it seemed 'a portentous undertaking', he felt that the Hallé was 'such a good orchestra and Harty such a magnificent conductor' that, with such encouragement, he might manage to 'knock Bax off the map'.

In a letter to Harty from Ascona, which bears no date but was probably sent in 1933, Walton wrote:

> I'm sorry that I've been so slow in producing my symphony, but actually I don't think it is any the worse for it; in fact, I hope and think that it promises to be

better than any work I've written hitherto, but that may be only an optimistic reaction to the months of despair I've been through when I thought I should never be able to write another note. However, the 1st movement is finished and the second ought to be in another 10 days or so. But having disappointed you once, I feel chary about fixing any date to its ultimate completion, but it ought to be ready sometime for next season.

I must say, I think it is almost hopeless for anyone to produce anything in any of the arts these days. It is practically impossible to get away from the general feeling of hopelessness and chaos which exists everywhere, however one may try—so you mustn't think I'm an exception, and one capable of compassing all difficulties and producing a masterpiece. But I'm trying my best.[2]

Writing to Foss about the same time, Walton reported that the symphony was not progressing satisfactorily and recalled how, while composing *Belshazzar's Feast*, he had found himself unable to proceed— '. . . and now I'm now in a similar distressing position, but it is not a nice chord (in fact, it is only an octave on A)'.[3]

The première of the symphony, advertised to take place at the Queen's Hall on 19 March 1934 in the London Symphony Orchestra's 1933–4 prospectus, had, of course, been cancelled because of the continuing uncertainty and delay. Walton's assurance to Harty that the work ought to be completed and ready for public performance during the 1934–5 season gave the conductor some reassurance but, with it, a nagging suspicion that perhaps he might be over-optimistic. In September 1934 he wrote to Foss: 'I shall not be sardonic, but very thankful when I say these words to Willie W.–but the poor boy is right to wait until he is quite satisfied. I do so hope (and think) it is going to be all right this time.'[4]

Alas, all was far from well, and in February 1934 the composer, after a period of illness and acute mental anxiety, made a frank and heart-searching confession to Adrian Boult, who had hoped to conduct the new work after Harty: 'There is, I am ashamed and disappointed to tell you, no hope of my finishing the symphony in time for its intended performance on March 19th; consequently, as I've promised the first performance to Harty, it will be necessary to abandon the idea of performing it at the May Festival. I am extremely sorry if this causes you much inconvenience, and I am sure that you will realise it is a rather painful situation for me to live down.'[5]

Shortly after this boyishly abject apology reached Boult, the astonishing decision was made to perform the symphony without the finale, and this Sir Hamilton Harty and the London Symphony Orchestra did on 3 December 1934. One can only assume that to release the incomplete work in this manner was not simply a compromise but a shrewd ploy initiated by Harty, with the connivance of Foss, and designed firstly to dazzle the listener with the musical 'shape of things to come' and secondly, months later, when his sense of expectation had been sharpened, to win him over completely with the whole towering masterpiece. It was like wearing a one-sleeved dinner-jacket at a party: the observer could not fail to notice—and remember—the oddity of the garment. Poor Walton, whose public utterances had not always glittered with eloquence and sagacity, made matters worse with a statement to the Press at the end of 1935 that seemed to imply that none of the finale had been written: 'All went well until I came to the last movement. I did not touch it for eight months—I had to wait for the mood—I could not think of the right thing to do. Then it came.'[6]

In any speculation as to what specific difficulties worried and temporarily defeated the composer in tackling the finale, it is interesting to note that he said to Edward Greenfield: 'It was the epilogue that was completed first. I had no problems about the actual conclusion. What worried me far more was whether I was right in using the device of a fugue in a symphony.'[7]

Walton, rightly or wrongly, exhibited a certain degree of self-pity over the precipitation of his uncompleted masterpiece into a full-scale performance. He told Murray Schafer: 'I was half-way through it at the time, but was persuaded very much against my will to let the three completed movements be performed alone. As a result, when the final movement was completed, many people considered it to be an afterthought. This is quite incorrect. Actually the coda of the last movement was the first to be written.'[8]

During the try-out of the partly finished work at the Queen's Hall on 3 December 1934, under Harty, the composer looked ashen grey and extremely ill.[9] Soon afterwards, as Samuel Courtauld revealed to Lady Christabel Aberconway, he spent a short period in hospital, undergoing certain tests and having his head X-rayed. One possible explanation for the very slow gestation of the symphony and Walton's run-down, neurasthenic condition, can probably be found in what he said during an interview in 1972:

> The reason for the hang-up appears to have been as much an emotional one as a musical one. "It is all nonsense," Walton claims, "that as they said at the time, this symphony represents the threat of war." Its message if it had one was much more personal to Walton, and the urgency, the fire, the passion, and even (remembering the marking of the scherzo) the malice, reflected his own emotional experiences at the time. After the first three movements the finale represents a world much less fraught with jagged tensions. To this day some critics find it an unsatisfactory conclusion, but plainly it should be seen in the light of what one commentator said (whether speaking literally or figuratively I

do not know): 'The trouble was that Willie changed girl friends between movements.'[10]

As regards the validity of this explanation, it is pertinent to mention that Walton's amorous relationship with Imma Doernberg seems, at some time in 1933, to have slipped its moorings and that, only a year later, finally casting himself loose from life at Carlyle Square, the home of Osbert Sitwell, he started a romance with Lady Alice Wimborne and went to live with her. Osbert, always jealous of Walton's rich society ladies, was greatly incensed at what he regarded as the shameful treachery of those he trusted; but his infatuation with the Apollo-like David Horner, who had recently been installed at Carlyle Square, doubtless brought him some consolation.

Lady Alice Katherine Sibell Wimborne, to give Walton's new 'girl friend' her full name, was one of Peter Quennell's grand society chatelaines. Her husband, Ivor Wimborne, heir to the Guest steel fortune, exercised enormous influence as one of the richest, most powerful industrialists in Britain. Born on 26 September 1880, with the surname Grosvenor, she was the younger daughter of the second Lord Ebury and a cousin of the Duke of Westminster. She married Ivor Guest, the elder son of the first Lord Wimborne, in 1902 and bore him a son and two daughters. Her husband, a Liberal MP for a large Cardiff constituency, was made a Privy Councillor in 1910; he was raised to the peerage, as Lord Ashby St Ledgers, during his father's lifetime and, in 1914, succeeded him as the second Lord Wimborne. Serving as Lord Lieutenant of Ireland from 1915 to 1918, he was shortly afterwards honoured by the King and became a Viscount. With her pale, aristocratic beauty, her charming manner and her great influence, Lady Wimborne reigned, as a much-loved patron of the arts, at her large, opulent house in Arlington Street, off Piccadilly, inviting to her almost legendary parties writers, artists, musicians and distinguished people of all shades of political opinion. She may, at one time, have been in love with Osbert Sitwell, whose *Triple Fugue* she admired tremendously; but, with her free-ranging, highly romantic spirit and appetite for life, she was inclined to show affection, in the most proper way, to any man of talent, including Walton, who soon recovered from what seems to have been a stress or domestic-problem crisis and began composing again in 1935. As regards the success of his First Symphony, which demonstrated his marvellous ability to write soaring tunes, this work, instantly recognized as one of the outstanding achievements of its kind, became a popular classic within a few years, although when Eugene Ormandy conducted it in Philadelphia on 16 October 1936, over two hundred outraged listeners walked out of the audience.

John Ireland, a warm-hearted composer who, in his own music, often allowed his unaffected emotions to become partly hidden by complicated harmonies derived from the impressionism of Debussy and Ravel, wrote to Walton from 'The Studio', 14a Gunter Grove, Chelsea, praising the merits of the symphony, a gramophone recording of which he had played again and again: 'My dear Friend, there is no doubt that this is the work of a true Master—unlike any other English symphony, this is the real line of symphonic tradition. It is simply colossal, grand, original, and moving to the emotions in the extreme degree . . . it has established you as the most vital and original genius in Europe. No one but a bloody fool could possibly fail to see this.'[11]

Walton undoubtedly realized that he had created a major work of striking power and originality, but instead of instantly dreaming up some other huge, heroic concept, he sensibly resumed composing in a more relaxed, unpressurized atmosphere. Drawn to the world of film music through the sagacity of Dallas Bower, a studio executive, he found a welcome, contributory source of independence, one which helped him to purchase his own house in Eaton Place, London. Bower, who was personal assistant to Paul Czinner during the making of *Escape Me Never*, recommended Walton as the most suitable composer for the important ballet in the film. Herbert Wilcox, managing director of the British and Dominion Film Corporation, tried to persuade Czinner to use Vivian Ellis, who had written music for many successful West End shows, but the growing prestige of Walton, coupled with the robust advocacy of Bower, gained him the commission, though he subsequently admitted that writing the score nearly drove him insane until, through greater familiarity with his task, he found with some surprise that he could compose about ten minutes of music a day without too much difficulty. The ballet sequences, filmed at Drury Lane in December 1934, under the control of Frederick Ashton and Ninette de Valois, were notable for the glimpses they gave, in long-shot, of the young Fonteyn, although occasionally they showed Beatrice Appleyard, her understudy. Efforts made shortly after to create another ballet, this time based on Walton's *Belshazzar's Feast* and reputedly intended for performance in the late autumn of 1934, proved fruitless, the cost of staging a large choral work and providing scenery and costumes being regarded as prohibitive.

It is pertinent to mention that the relationship between Walton and Osbert Sitwell, irreparably damaged by the composer's 'elopement' with Lady Wimborne, had, at that time, come very close to freezing-point. Osbert, who expected a blind loyalty and obedience, a compliant, subservient attitude, from those he patronized, still seethed with a righteous anger. In a letter to David Horner his rancour exploded: 'Saw

Willie and Alice Wimborne walking down King's Road yesterday,' he reported. 'She looked old and footsore and slummy.'[12] If Walton had heard of this bitter, frustrated and cruel remark, he would probably have tossed it philosophically into his mental waste-paper basket. With his ripening interest in film scores, he had more important matters to brood upon.

Vaughan Williams once said: 'Film contains potentialities for the combination of the arts such as Wagner never dreamed of.'[13] Until the full realization of his vision comes, the best film composers—people like John McCabe, Carl Davis and Wilfred Josephs—wage a kind of guerrilla warfare in the underbrush of contemporary music, sweeping aside the disdain of the critics and the pigheaded ignorance or stupidity of some directors to practise and, as far as possible, perfect, with genuinely inspired scores, the mysterious, often beautiful art of illustrating pictorial events with musical tones in such a way as to create atmosphere, shade emotions, imply, suggest, define character, refine personality and, with many subtle touches, play upon the imagination of the audience. As for the past attitude of some directors—even great ones—Tony Thomas related an amusing anecdote concerning the late Alfred Hitchcock. During the making of *Lifeboat* at Twentieth-Century-Fox in 1944, composer David Raksin was stopped in the studio annexe and told, rather too bluntly, by a friend that Hitchcock had decided against using any music in the score of the film. Raksin, aware of the denigration and cheap cynicism heaped upon film music, deliberated for a moment, then asked why and how that strange decision had been reached. Said the friend, 'Well, Hitchcock feels that since the entire action of the film takes place in a lifeboat on the open ocean, where would the music come from?' Replied Raskin: 'Ask Mr Hitchcock to explain where the cameras come from, and I'll tell him where the music comes from.'[14]

Despite the many chilling and infuriating examples of musical ignorance that must have come his way, Walton found a certain creative fulfilment, as well as reward, in writing film-scores; but other equally tempting offers reached him from the world of theatre. Charles B. Cochran, the impresario, had, since March 1930, been trying to persuade him to write music for one of his revues. The composer wrote to Sassoon on 2 March 1930 that Cochran wanted his help 'both as a ballet and a jazz merchant' and that he had cordially agreed to provide it.[15]

Cochran subsequently met Walton and invited him to write a score for the musical comedy book *Cat and the Fiddle*, by the famous American librettist Otto Kern. Although the composer was interested and spoke of Cochran as 'the only man in England today acutely responsive to new ideas',[16] the impresario finally commissioned Jerome Kern to write the music, some of the ballet being designed by Frederick Ashton. It was not until 1935 that Walton collaborated with Cochran by composing another ballet, *The First Shoot*, as part of the spectacular revue *Follow the Sun*, with a scenario by Osbert Sitwell, designs by Cecil Beaton and choreography again by Ashton. This ten-minute ballet, which formed Scene 19 of the revue, first shown at Manchester's Opera House on 23 December 1935, starred the American actress and dancer Claire Luce and related how the wife of an Edwardian peer, an ex-chorus girl, was accidentally killed at a country house shooting-party. Walton subsequently remarked, with characteristic irony, that there was more money to be made from music of this kind than from writing symphonies. Unfortunately, the music is no longer in existence, although in 1942 the composer used the waltz as radio music for *Went the Day Well?* and, at a later date, for the dream sequence of *3 Sisters*. The ballet, though brief and partly tragic in theme, was a delightful miniature, and Ashton thought so highly of its possibilities that he harboured the notion of reviving it in an extended form, with additional music, but nothing came of this.

The death of King George V, that wise but unobtrusive counsellor, had caused the Manchester première of *Follow the Sun* to be postponed. Despite the national mourning, Ashton, full of admiration for the British composer, staged on 24 January 1936 another short dance irradiated by his music. This was *Siesta*, first performed as an orchestral piece by Guy Warrack at one of his chamber music concerts at the Aeolian Hall, London, in the autumn of 1926. Walton had also written music for Cochran's other production, *The Boy David*, but the première, scheduled for 15 February 1936 in Edinburgh, was put back because of Bergner's illness and received its first performance on 21 November, with the pre-recorded music being relayed from the roof of the theatre. Nothing of the score now remains.

Walton wrote a considerable amount of music for Paul Czinner's production of *As You Like It*, but it is probable that Hyam Greenbaum helped him to orchestrate it, since, on its completion, the composer gave him the manuscript of his First String Quartet as a token of thanks. Indeed, the versatile Spike Hughes, in his book of reminiscences *Opening Bars*[17], confessed that he himself instinctively turned to 'Bumps' (Greenbaum's nickname) when he needed technical advice, 'as did William Walton and Constant Lambert and Alan Rawsthorne'. He also remarked that, 'A great deal of Willie Walton's film music was scored at great speed and with typical expertness by Bumps Greenbaum when the composer was pressed for time.' Walton was certainly under pressure when he tackled the music for *As You Like it* and resourcefully seized upon some music he had written for the second act of a stage production of *The*

*Merchant of Venice*, popping it, with the new title 'Tell me where is fancy bred', into the finale of the Paul Czinner production. He also composed a song, 'Under the Greenwood Tree', doubtless inspired by his reading of *As You Like It*; but this attractive piece was not used in the film. Walton, recognizing its merit, persuaded Hubert Foss of the Oxford University Press to publish it separately.

The ceremony of investing a king—on this occasion, George VI—with the emblems of royalty in the hallowed precincts of Westminster Abbey is one to stir the imagination and passionate loyalty of any true Briton and Walton, in 1937, the Coronation Year, was no exception. Even in November of the previous year he longed, as a memorandum in the BBC archives testifies, to pay his own special homage:

> Walton . . . would love to be commissioned by the Corporation to write a really fine symphonic Coronation March. No one will doubt that his immense technical ability should produce a March of exceptional repertoire of equal value to the existing Elgar Marches. He is the one person of the younger generation of composers most able to do this, and I should like the Corporation to give its approval in principle to the matter being gone into from a financial point of view. . . .[18]

By the following March the Corporation commissioned Walton to write 'a symphonic march for Coronation Week', and the composer agreed to accept a fee of 40 guineas. Full of enthusiasm for what he undoubtedly regarded as a highly important assignment, he finished the march within fourteen days. At the Coronation Service in Westminster Abbey on 12 May 1937, the resplendent music of *Crown Imperial*, with its majestic *cantabile* melody broadening into a truly magnificent climax, was played for the entry of Queen Mary, just before the ceremony began.

Another festive commission came to Walton when the organizers of the 1937 Leeds Festival invited him to compose a choral work to celebrate the event. He decided on a cantata, using for its text a poem by the Scottish poet William Dunbar, bearing the title *In Honour of the City of London*, most of the score being written in the summer of 1937, while he was living in Ravello, Italy. Although difficult to sing, with a good deal of harmonic asperity or ferocity—characteristics of the Walton style—it aroused no resentment among the singers, as *Belshazzar's Feast* had done, and, with Malcolm Sargent in charge of the rehearsals and subsequent performance in Leeds Town Hall, the new cantata won immediate acclaim. One reviewer commented that, 'With the first performance of William Walton's choral ode *In Honour of the City of London* the chorus without a doubt added a new line to Festival history. One felt convinced, by the time the rehearsals denoted that the singers had mastered the "strenuity" of this setting that they would give a remarkable demonstration of its "vigour". Next to the word "lusty", which occurs five times in Dunbar's six verses, "vigour" and "strenuity" are the keywords of Walton's setting.'[19]

After the première, Richard Capell, a former *Daily Telegraph* music critic, wrote: 'Encouraged by Dunbar, Mr Walton depicts old London as a scene of riotous splendour and jollity—and it may be that he had almost swamped the poet's stateliness in his concentration on the tumultousness suggested by the terms of the Scottish bard's praise. However, the stanza about the Thames, "Above all rivers thy river hath renown," is the occasion for a contrasted flowing movement still rich in cross-rhythms, and the final stanza, "Strong be thy walls," crowns it all with massiveness'.[20]

This was a bountiful year for Walton, because it brought not only the Coronation assignment—nobly discharged—but also two significant tributes: his election to a Fellowship by the Council of the Royal College of Music, and the conferment on him by Durham University of his first honorary degree. He must have gained immeasurable self-confidence from these recognitions of his musical gifts, and perhaps his determination to vindicate himself, to rise to even greater heights, prompted him to refuse a financially tempting offer from Gabriel Pascal to compose the music for his film of George Bernard Shaw's play *Pygmalion*, an offer which the great Arthur Honegger, untroubled by such considerations, subsequently accepted. Walton was also invited to write a suitable choral work for the City of New York for inclusion in a music festival which Olin Downes was planning as part of the New York World Fair, held during the period 30 April to 31 October 1939; but, with other requests for compositions coming in and pressure building up, he had to refuse. He did, however, while staying in Rugby, write a score for Paul Czinner's *Stolen Life* at the end of 1938, and this followed the composition of 'Set me as a seal upon thine heart' for the wedding of Alice Wimborne's son on 22 November that year in St Mary Abbot's Church, Kensington. Walton and Lady Wimborne had become very close companions, and until her death in 1948 he visited her home regularly.

# 6

# A Young Man Named Walton . . .

In 1936 Walton had been introduced by his friend Spike Hughes to Jascha Heifetz at the Berkeley Hotel, London, and some time later—the exact date is uncertain—he received from that illustrious virtuoso of the instrument a commission to write a Violin Concerto, to be reserved for his own personal use over a period of two years. Hughes described the genesis of the concerto in these words:

> While William Walton makes his place in the history of English music more certain with every new work, I feel I can claim a tiny share of his success in one instance.
>
> Some years ago Jascha Heifetz asked me if I knew a young man by the name of Walton with whom he wanted to discuss a violin concerto. I said I did. Why? Well, could I bring him to lunch. I could and I did, and out of that lunch at the Berkeley (smoked salmon and tournedos) came Jascha's commission for the Walton violin concerto. As a reward for my part in the affair, I have a nicely inscribed score presented "To Spike from William", with the letters written alternatively in red and blue pencil.[1]

Heifetz, who was idolized for his phenomenal technique and beautifully expressive tone, had become something of a legend in music, and rightly so. Leopold Auer chanced to hear him play when he was only nine and arranged for him to enter the St Petersburg Conservatoire, where, as the youngest member of Auer's own violin class, he rapidly outshone the other students. Six years later the boy appeared with the Berlin Philharmonic Orchestra, under Artur Nikisch. He had the ability to start playing confidently and spontaneously without any preliminary practice, striving for a control so complete that every performance would be identical.

Heifetz, a naturalized American citizen, invited Walton in the spring of 1939 to visit him in that country, to incorporate into the solo part of the new concerto a number of suggestions he had prepared for making the violin technique more effective. This was characteristic of a great artist who, in music, planned everything minutely, indicating marks of expression with unusual detail, even to the placing of tiny *crescendi* and *diminuendi* on single notes. To many people Heifetz, aloof and slightly disdainful, seemed a cold, forbidding figure. They saw in him a Buddha-like blandness, because of his moon-faced impassivity, the fixed stare of his heavy-lidded eyes and his, at times, almost frozen detachment. He had a page-turner for many years named Sam Epstein: throughout the whole of this period all they said to each other was 'Hello' and 'Goodbye'. One day Epstein told the violinist Benno Rabinoff, a close friend of Heifetz, how magnificently the great man had recorded Saint-Saëns's *Introduction and Rondo*. Rabinoff encouraged Epstein to tell Heifetz how he felt; he did. Startled that his 'silent' partner had spoken at last, Heifetz, stared into the page-turner's adoring eyes and replied, 'you mean I finally played something you liked?' This anecdote seems to confirm the popular impression of Heifetz as having a rather caustic temperament, but, as Yehudi Menuhin has indicated[2] his visible personality was probably the result not of a crabbed, unfriendly nature but of an underlying degree of discipline and method which no other violinist of his time possessed.

As the concerto took shape, Walton encountered many grave problems, which resulted in a measure of self-doubt and pessimism. It was Antonio Brosa, another famous violinist, who, with practical help and advice, restored some of his confidence. At a time when Walton had completed two movements, Brosa was playing in the film *Dreaming Lips*, in which the male lead (taken by Raymond Massey) was a violinist. The never-to-be-forgotten actress in the film was Elisabeth Bergner, directed by her husband, Dr Czinner, who, since Walton had composed a rumba 'Rose of Mexico', a tango 'Highlights of Havana' and other brief music for the production, appointed him sole musical director, with Boyd Neel in charge of the London Symphony Orchestra. According to Brosa, the high-spirited Czinner wanted to perpetrate a harmless little joke on the musicians and, as pre-arranged, when the violinist had successfully played the Beethoven Violin Concerto, with cadenza, the orchestra called for an encore. He responded with a Tchaikovsky waltz which, in Brosa's own words, begins 'da de-da da de-da da de-da', making everyone present think he was giving them the Beethoven concerto again.

Walton, greatly amused, was also there, and Brosa, seeing him in a gay, affable mood, asked him if he had written anything for the violin. 'Well,' replied Walton, 'I am writing a concerto for Heifetz.' 'How interesting,' said Brosa. 'May I see the concerto, please—will you show it to me?' Walton remarked that he would be delighted to do so, but added: 'As a matter of fact, I am very fed up because I do not know very well how to write for the violin.' After his companion had reassured him with the cheerful comment, 'Well, nowadays you can write anything at all, anything you like, for the violin,' the composer had a copy made of the partly finished manuscript and lent it to Brosa, who practised the two movements. Walton visited Brosa at his home and the two men played through the score. The violinist made a few suggestions for improving it, and Walton wrote to Heifetz, informing him of this and enclosing the two movements as samples. Back came a letter from the great man saying that he was not at all sure that he liked the movements as Walton desired them, and he invited the composer to spend some time in America and work the problems out with him. Walton was angry and upset. 'For tuppence I would give it to you,' he said to Brosa. 'I am not like Heifetz,' said the other. 'He can play it anywhere he likes. He can make records—I cannot.'[3]

Mrs Dora Foss wrote to her husband, then in America, in January 1939, informing him that Walton, clearly in a very troubled frame of mind, had telephoned her from Rugby to say, 'I am having great difficulty in making the last movement elaborate enough for Heifetz to play it.' She also reported that, during an hour-long conversation, he had expressed the fear that Heifetz would not, after all, play the new work when it was completed and felt that perhaps he ought to ask Kreisler to play. Asked what he proposed to do next, Walton replied that he was going to study composition and start with a duet, a trio and a quartet, progressing to more advanced pieces. Attempting to cheer him up, Mrs Foss said of the concerto, 'anyhow, I'm sure it's better than anyone else could write' (or something similar), to which, with a characteristic, breezy self-esteem, he answered, 'Oh, I've no doubt about that!' He subsequently telephoned again with the news that Heifetz had cabled the cryptic, but heartening message 'accept enthusiastically'.[4]

Walton went to America in the spring of 1939 to consult Heifetz about the concerto. According to Brosa, there was an international fair in New York, and not only did the British section send Solomon to play the Bliss Piano Concerto but Walton, who was making his first visit to the United States, had been chosen to represent them in some capacity and was thus able to see Heifetz, with whom he worked on the third movement of the Violin Concerto. Heifetz did little more than edit the score, adding accents and dynamic markings in the explosive section of the *scherzo*, which is full of rushing, scampering phrases, and in only one place—the descending passage in the central cadenza of the first movement, which the violinist regarded as 'far too easy'[5]—did he actually change some of the notes. Interviewed by the Press during his stay in America, Walton expressed the gloomy opinion, shared by so many people who treasure music as a rarefied, elitist art, that a vast increase in knowledge of it through radio and gramophone had reduced its 'life expectancy' and remarked: 'Today's white hope is tomorrow's black sheep. These days it is very sad for a composer to grow old—unless, that is, he grows old enough to witness a revival of his work. I seriously advise all sensitive composers to die at the age of 37. I know: I've gone through the first halcyon periods, and am just about ripe for my critical damnation.'[6]

In New York on 2 June 1939 he put the finishing touches to the score. Walton had intended to visit the USA again, to be present at the première, but, of course, the outbreak of World War II prevented this, as he indicated to Heifetz:

> Alas, I don't think, owing to this something war, there is the slightest likelihood of my being able to get over for it, what with the difficulties of travel and the difficulty, not only of expense, but of obtaining any dollars; also I'm of military age and am liable to be called up, but when, the powers that be (there are far too many of them!) will decide. Meanwhile, I have become an ambulance driver for the local A.R.P. though I must admit that it doesn't entail much, as everything, as you will have read in the papers, has been very quiet as regards air raids. In fact, this is a peculiar war and not working out as predicted and it looks as if the side that can bore the other most will win.[7]

In this letter Walton asked if the concerto was to be broadcast and, if so, whether Heifetz would have a recording made as it came 'over the air' and send it to him—the only way in which he might hear his own composition, 'at least for a very long time'. He conveyed his approval of an alteration in the score which Heifetz had made and, at the same time, enclosed some alternative passages on a separate sheet of paper, expressing the hope that these would not be obliterated by a 'well-meaning, if unmusical censor who regarded the symbols as a code'.

As regards Heifetz's opinion of the Violin Concerto, Artur Rodzinski reported him as being 'very crazy about it'.[8] It was Rodzinski who, at Cleveland, Ohio, on 7 December 1939, conducted the Cleveland Orchestra in the first performance, with, of course, Heifetz in the solo part. The concerto was first heard in New York on 5 February 1941, when the same orchestra, conductor and soloist played it at Carnegie Hall. One assessment of its merits appeared next morning in a review by Virgil Thompson, who wrote: 'Its material is inoffensive, but extremely vague. Its violin writing is glittery, its texture is continuous. The whole surface of it is dainty and luxurious. There is very little substance beneath. If Elgar's music could be described, as it once was, as "holy water in a German beer barrel", Walton's might well be summed up as Strauss and soda. There is more than that in it; there is a lump or two of Sibelius and a slight zest of

Stravinsky; but mostly it is Straussian "effect" music watered down and sparkled up with French Perrier.'[9]

From this highly spiced but astute phraseology, which smacks a little of *The Good Food Guide*, Thompson might well be a *Cordon Bleu* judge assessing the merits of a richly iced and decorative cake. A student of Nadia Boulanger, he was, in fact, a brilliant composer who, like Debussy, wrote progressive music in a tonal framework, his greatest success being the opera *Four Saints in Three Acts*, which has a stringently simplified score and libretto. His ability to find opportunities for wit and malice was remarkable and prompted John Tasker Howard to say of him: 'He is our musical satirist, our Erik Satie.' Thompson had a sharp ear for the inflections of words, a gift which makes his songs—often simple to the point of audacity—particularly interesting.

The first British performance of the Violin Concerto should have been given at the Sheldonian Theatre, Oxford, early in February 1941, when Walton received an Honorary Doctorate, but, as the parts had not arrived from America, this did not take place, and Henry Holst, the soloist, played the Brahms concerto instead. Walton himself conducted the première at the Royal Albert Hall on 1 November 1941, when Holst, appearing with the London Philharmonic Orchestra, was again the soloist. Composers are not immune to the misfortunes of war, which, on this occasion, almost resulted in the cancellation of the concert. Heifetz's personal proofs of the concerto, bearing his meticulous bowing and fingering directions for the solo part, were lost in the Atlantic during a convoy sinking while in transit to Britain. Happily, a photographic copy had been made in New York as a precautionary measure, and this, despatched by air to the Oxford University Press in London, averted disaster. A gramophone recording of the concerto, performed by Heifetz, also went down with his proofs. Since neither Walton nor Holst had previously heard the work played, they had no interpretative signposts to guide them. Moreover, according to Malcolm Arnold, who played trumpet in the London Philharmonic Orchestra, the first printed score contained so many incredible errors that he felt sure it was 'junked' and regarded his own copy of the score as 'a curiosity to be prized'.[10]

The precarious tonality of much of the concerto, the ambiguity of key, the sharp, tricky rhythms, the hairpin dynamics, causing the soloist to snatch repeatedly with single strokes of the bow at differing numbers of notes, have made the task of presenting a lucid, shapely performance extremely difficult, even for a virtuoso artiste. Sir Adrian Boult, who conducted the concerto many times, undoubtedly found it so. Peter Beavan, formerly principal cellist of the LPO, related how Boult rehearsing the work, said to the players: 'Gentlemen, it gets a little complicated here. I'll keep a steady two; you'll have to fish about for yourselves.'[11]

Walton managed, while composing the Violin Concerto, to write the music for Paul Czinner's film *Stolen Life*, shown for the first time on 18 January 1939 at the Plaza Theatre in London. He was living in Rugby at the time and was under great mental strain because of the grave problems involved in making the concerto worthy of the illustrious and exacting Heifetz; but he succeeded, nevertheless, in creating some highly imaginative, atmospheric music for the film. The music, recorded by the BBC Television Orchestra and conducted by Hyam Greenbaum, was warmly praised, and the film itself, starring Elisabeth Bergner and Michael Redgrave, proved to be first-class entertainment, with superb photography involving beautiful mountain and sea scenes—the former filmed on location in the French Alps, the latter in Brittany.[12]

If Walton had not, in 1936, been commissioned by Heifetz to write the Violin Concerto, he might, instead, have accepted the invitation sent to him by Benny Goodman and Joseph Szigeti to compose a work for clarinet and violin. Faced with the much more important and exciting challenge of the concerto, he declined the offer, which was subsequently passed on to Bartók and, in 1938, fructified in his *Contrasts*, a charming and popular piece which shows his mastery in exploiting instrumental tone-colours.

The re-scoring of Bach is the favourite pastime of many composers, and in this respect Johann Sebastian has posthumously endured more compositional surgery than ever Mussorgsky did at the well-meaning hands of Rimsky-Korsakov. Schoenberg, Respighi, Busoni, Stravinsky and others, including the poachers of the 'Pop' world, have all played ducks and drakes with his most eloquent scores, often with fascinating results. Even in provincial Leipzig he was considered an old-fashioned, conservative type of musician, and perhaps the modern transcribers so regard him, although for many people—trained musicologists as well as ordinary concert-goers—he is the composer of all composers. Certainly Bach is of such magnificent fibre that his place in posterity is unaffected. It was at Frederick Ashton's request that Walton, in 1940, agreed to orchestrate some Bach selections which Constant Lambert, director of the Sadler's Wells Ballet, had made for a Frederick Ashton-Rex Whistler ballet, *The Wise Virgins*, given its première on 24 April 1940, with Margot Fonteyn and Michael Somes dancing the principal roles. Fonteyn and other members of the company were greatly amused when they saw the ballet advertised on a bill-board as 'THE WISE VIRGINS (subject to alteration)'.[13]

The genesis of the ballet began some years before, when Ashton and Lambert spent an evening with Boris Ord, a mutual friend. After a long discussion about Bach's music, Lambert and Ord, seating themselves at the piano, played an impromptu recital exemplifying his work. Among the pieces performed was the beautiful aria 'Sheep may safely graze', which moved Ashton greatly with its contentment and serenity. 'I would very much like to arrange a ballet to such music,' he declared. A subsequent reading of the Gospels convinced him that the parable of the wise and foolish virgins would provide a splendid subject for a ballet to music by Bach, but with the simple theme elaborated into a morality play, rather than left in its original form. Michael Somes recalled that, when the Sadler's Wells Ballet visited Cambridge early in 1940, he visited Dr Paddy Hadley's rooms in King's College, where Constant Lambert and Hadley played several Bach pieces for Ashton, who, after consulting his guests, chose what he needed for the varying moods and sequences of the ballet. Walton orchestrated these brilliantly, while Rex Whistler designed scenery and costumes reported to be some of his most inspired creations. Curiously enough, the artist, writing to Edith Olivier on 18 April 1940, remarked: 'I fear the scenery and dresses are going to be intolerably hideous, but we must all *face the music*, I suppose (or Constant Lambert will be offended—not to mention Willie).'[14]

According to David Vaughan, the work was, in a sense, a product of the war, which kindled flames of spirituality in every phase of life. Ashton, a devout Christian, though not a Roman Catholic, could sometimes be found on his knees in the Brompton Oratory, the Catholic church near the Victoria and Albert Museum in London, praying for guidance before starting work on a new ballet. Both he and Vaughan undertook to occupy their spare time, while touring with the ballet company, by reading the whole of the Bible. This lovely ballet gradually became popular with audiences and, in Vaughan's own words: '. . . it was exquisite as a spectacle, one of the most beautiful the Vic-Wells Ballet has ever presented. Above all, the ballet reflected Ashton's faith in Fonteyn as an interpreter. . . . Ultimately it was dropped from the repertory, a solo for the Bride only being revived and danced by Fonteyn, in a new production by the Royal Ballet, as a tribute to Sir Frederick Ashton, at the Royal Opera House on 24th July 1970.'[15]

A suite of six numbers from *The Wise Virgins*, published in December 1942, was used in May 1970 for another ballet, *Cantus Firmus*, created by Jeanne Brabants for the Ballet Vlaanderen in Amsterdam.

In 1940 the Chicago Symphony Orchestra commissioned Walton to compose music for the celebration of the fiftieth anniversary of its foundation. This act of faith was also a manifestation, in a sense, of the high esteem in which he was held by American music-lovers. The once popular belief, prevalent at the time, that only Britten had achieved great fame abroad was, of course, a fallacy, and even before 1940 the works of Walton were eagerly sought after in the concert-halls of Europe and America. His Violin Concerto, which received its first performance in Ohio, showed him to be a superb melodist with a rare sense of beauty who, like Elgar, could write the kind of score which illustrious virtuosi felt happy and privileged to include in their repertoires. They and other connoisseurs, aware of the stimulating freshness and vitality of his music, and of its capacity to hold the listener spellbound with a fascinating fusion of the old and the new, recognized him as a major composer in the romantic mainstream.

Walton commenced work on the Chicago project, a comedy overture to be called *Scapino*, in July 1940, and it proved to be the only 'serious' concert-hall piece he produced during the war. His work as a war-time ambulance-driver employed by the Ministry of Labour took up part of his time, but he managed, despite this, to compose regularly throughout the summer and autumn, completing the overture at his London home on 28 December 1940. The score bears on its cover the portrait of its roguish hero, and its title page declares it to be 'after an etching from Jacques Callot's *Les Trois Pantalons*, 1619'. It is dedicated to the Chicago Symphony Orchestra and its conductor, Dr F. A. Stock, who, in Chicago on 3 April 1941, gave the overture its première, according the composer the unusual tribute of a repeat performance a fortnight later. Some years after this, Boyd Neel, the conductor, heard a BBC broadcast rendering of *Scapino* and wrote to Walton, who was also a friend, suggesting that he had quoted *Scheherazade* in the music. Walton, in a characteristically brief and breezy postcard, replied, 'Ass, don't you know *Tancredi* when you hear it?!!' Neel was not convinced and held steadfastly to his own opinion.

It was also in 1941 that Walton toiled unremittingly on a film score for Gabriel Pascal's production of George Bernard Shaw's play *Major Barbara*, a gruelling, uphill task. Shaw had commenced work on the script in 1939 and, fortified by his prodigious knowledge of, and insight into, music—sharpened by many years of experience as the critic Cornetto di Basso—he gave expert, painstaking attention to the score, declaring that 'music is just as important as dialogue'. He and Pascal, the director, had hoped to commission Arturo Toscanini, the hallowed, almost legendary maestro of La Scala, Milan, to provide the musical score, and the Irish playwright had worked on the crowning scene of *Major Barbara* with him in mind; but the great conductor, always remote by temperament and sympathy from this kind of commercial project, gave such a tardy, grudging 'Yes' that the explosive Shaw ran out of patience. 'No use waiting for Tosca,' he barked, decisively. 'I cut no ice with him. . . .' So the commission fell into Walton's lap, accompanied by a suggestion from

Shaw that he should 'try the effect of a single trombone sounding G flat quite quietly after the others have stopped. Undershaft pretending to play it. It ought to have the effect of a question mark.'[16]

As a result, Shaw had to write another version of the Announcer's speech, which occurs just before the choral ode, a copy of which is held in the British Library[17] as part of the typewritten cutting-room script; inscribed in ink on twelve-stave music paper by someone other than Walton, it commences with the bass solo 'In this our hour'. The composer, in a letter to Stewart Craggs,[18] recalled that Pascal took him to lunch with Mr and Mrs Shaw 'somewhere in Whitehall Mansions', and remarked humorously, 'My eyes were glued on him, for every time he opened his mouth his dental plate came down and then went up—very off putting.' Concerning the ode, Shaw made various suggestions, of which the following is an example:

> In bar 37 the major third does not suit the word 'lamenting.' Make it minor: flatten the B.
>
> If I were a musician I should not presume to suggest an alteration; but an amateur's comments should always be listened to. Even when they are technically asinine they often draw attention to some hitch or other. Mozart did not disdain the idiocies of Schickaneder. Otherwise extremely OK.[19]

The filming of *Major Barbara* took place partly at Denham Studios and partly at Dartington Hall, Devonshire, between April and Christmas 1940. It was the black period of the Blitz on war-time Britain and, as Denham Studios were close to a war factory, the frequently wailing air-raid sirens sent the actors and the film crew racing into underground shelters, wasting valuable time and money. Finally, the whole staff and professional entourage, 'stiffening their sinews', decided to ignore the German bombers, and filming progressed more rapidly. After being released, *Major Barbara* opened triumphantly in Nassau on 21 March 1941 under the patronage of the Duke and Duchess of Windsor.

Many composers have, with varying degrees of success, written music for children. Debussy, in Part 1 of his *Children's Corner*, sub-titled 'Doctor Gradus ad Parnassum' (the name is copied from Clementi's studies), describes a child practising the piano and pokes gentle fun at his frustrated attempts to come to terms with Clementi's complicated harmonies. Stravinsky's son Soulima, himself a brilliant keyboard performer, wrote his *Piano Music for Children*, which, in a simple way, introduced pupils to classical forms and textures, making juvenile understanding much easier. Both men knew how extremely difficult is the task of composing either music that fledgling pianists can play with eagerness or, alternatively, music to which they can listen with pleasure or delight.

So, too, did Walton when in 1940 he composed his *Duets for Children*, dedicating them to 'Elizabeth and Michael', his niece and nephew; but he did not wholly succeed, as Debussy or Stravinsky *fils* might have done, in suiting them ideally to child performers. In fact, they originally began as *Tunes for My Niece* in solo piano form, but Dora Foss considered them to be much too difficult and told Walton so. Although classed as 'not really too hard for young pianists to play', some of the duet pieces require more sensitivity in the blending and balancing of tone than might be expected from four amateur hands. Paradoxically, it is hard to play easy pieces exactly—that is, faithfully observing every single marking, while adjusting details, even subconsciously, during an interpretation. At the end of 1940 Walton orchestrated the *Duets* under the new title *Music for Children*, and the first performance was given in the following February at the Queen's Hall, London.

On the manuscript of the *Duets* is the intriguing dedication 'For Alfred Chenhalls (Cheneg) in celebration (surtax!) from William'. Chenhalls had worked as an executive of Pascal Productions on *Major Barbara* when Walton was composing music for the film. He was killed with the actor Leslie Howard in June 1943 when the plane carrying the two men was shot down. Howard had been giving a lecture tour in Spain and Portugal, and it has been suggested that the Germans imagined Churchill was on board.

In December 1941 Walton shared a concert at Cambridge with Arthur Bliss and conducted the second half of the programme. Immediately after the performance he sat in Paddy Hadley's room in Caius College, laughing and arguing about life and music with Constant Lambert, Alan Rawsthorne, Hadley and Bliss. It was well into the morning when the men, whom Bliss described as 'having a real grand set to',[20] broke up their happy discussion.

# 7

# Music for Films

As previously mentioned, Walton, around the end of 1940, was called up for service in the armed forces, but Jack Beddington, Director of the Films Division of the Ministry of Information, subsequently pleaded passionately for his exemption and succeeded in having him officially attached to the MOI as a composer. He had done his best for the war effort by driving an ambulance in London, but could never master double-declutching, and after he had propelled the vehicle into a ditch several times, he was told, 'Perhaps you had better not drive an ambulance after all.' So, as he had written music for films before, he was allowed to concentrate on doing precisely that.

One can only regard Walton's work as a film propagandist, inspiring and encouraging the people of Britain with music that was often patriotic and stirring, as a vital, constructive part of his career that increased his own versatility and helped others to endure suffering and privation. Hubert Foss, however, regarded the MOI secondment with some bitterness, and in 1945, as reported in *The Listener*, he complained that '. . . for nearly six years we have had no major work from William Walton, whom a beneficent but bureaucratic government "directed" into writing music only for films. Thus comes about a curious situation, that Walton's latest compositions—he has written some five-and-a-half hours of music during the war—have reached the ears of a vast public who would not dream of going to a concert of his important works, while the musicians and music-lovers have been starved of his music, past and present.'[1] If, however, the War Office had chosen to 'direct' Walton into the Infantry, instead, and he had got himself killed, music-lovers would have been permanently deprived of what would have been his post-war music, including the gloriously rich and tuneful opera *Troilus and Cressida*.

In December 1940 the War Office discussed with Producer Michael Balcon and Director Thorold Dickinson, who had offered their services to the nation, the making of a two-reel, twenty-minute instructional film about counter-espionage and security, submitting a list of points which should be included. Such was the length and wide scope of the list that the running-time of the film, which used a script by the technical consultant Sir Basil Bartlett and bore the title *Next of Kin*, eventually stretched itself to a hundred minutes. Dickinson, with War Office authority, invited Walton to write the score, tactfully indicating that, since the music had to reach an extremely wide 'common man' audience, the style should perhaps be more 'music hall' than 'opera house'. He was delighted when Walton accepted the advice as well as the commission, and was even more pleased when the composer delivered a score which, in its dignified, unpretentious idioms and utter propriety to the sentiments and facts conveyed in the script, was a model of its kind, although, according to Dickinson,[2] the fox-trot he wrote was neither characteristic Walton nor good dance music. He scored the thirty-two minutes of music between 2 and 22 December 1941, as is made clear in a postcript to a letter which he sent to Dallas Bower in January 1972.[3] The film, its production, and all matters directly concerning it were made subject to the Official Secrets Act; all involved personnel had to swear a strict oath of secrecy, and all scripts of the film, once the relevant parts had been completed, were ceremonially burned. Only people working on the picture were allowed on the set.

After finishing the score, Walton was co-opted onto the Films Division for the duration of hostilities. As for *Next of Kin*, it ran, in the old Curzon Cinema, specially requisitioned by the War Office, from January 1942, being shown to members of the armed forces and civilians with security passes. The first version shocked its audiences, and even Winston Churchill, who banned it during the St Nazaire raid of 28 March 1942, demanded that the violence be cut down. This was done and the film re-released. Michael Balcon and Jack Beddington won the right to show it publicly, after the War Office transferred the civilian rights to the MOI for release through United Artists.

In the summer of 1941, doubtless relieved to have some respite from the exacting, chronological finesse of film scores, Walton began corresponding with Cecil Gray about the libretto for a proposed opera concerning Carlo Gesualdo and Maria d'Avalos. A neurotically hypersenstive member of an old aristocratic family—one of his uncles having been canonized—Carlo Gesualdo di Venosa, madrigalist and murderer, virtuoso lutenist and Neapolitan prince, showed sado-masochistic tendencies, experiencing a delirious pleasure in being flogged, for which purpose he kept a trained servant. He wrote superb music with one hand and assassinated his enemies—including his wife, Donna Maria, and her seducer—with the other; all, so it is said, out of love or an overwhelming sense of duty.

Gray wrote to Walton in considerable detail from Harrogate, outlining a suggested synopsis for the opera.[4] Act I contained a boudoir, ballroom and garden scene; Act II revealed Carlo's private apartment and Donna Maria's chamber; Act III presented a final chapel scene. He had obviously made useful progress on the text early in 1942, because at the beginning of the year Walton told him in a letter that the sketch for the opening of Act I, Scene 1 seemed to be 'just what is needed and will give just enough to establish Laura Scala as a semi-important character'.[5] He expressed the hope that Gray would be left in peace to continue the good work and added, 'I shan't be rid of my film entanglements until the end of March.' Walton wrote to Gray again in December, thanking him for what he had accomplished and praising the last scene:

> It ought to be very effective if I can do my stuff. I'm all for the ghost scene from reading the extracts and I think it would be dramatically right.
>
> I'm slightly worried about the many scene changes in Act 1. There will be a break of about 5 mins after the Prologue. Which is as it should be, but I feel there should be more in the music, and that it should carry on between the scene changes which shouldn't take more than 1½ mins at the most. If the changes are going to take more than that perhaps it might be an idea to interpolate two extremely short scenes between 1 & 2, 2 & 3, before a drop curtain, and have some courtiers or someone (Ping, Pong and Pang) discussing the situation. In fact, anything to stop the lights being put even half up and continuity being broken by the chattering of the audience.[6]

Gray considered that there were the makings of a great opera in the story of Carlo Gesualdo and Maria d'Avalos and, being himself a composer of some brilliance, he had on several occasions thought of creating such a libretto for his own purpose. Some years before, he and Philip Heseltine ('Peter Warlock') had produced a book about Gesualdo; so, having undertaken tremendous research as his share of the task, he had a treasury of expert knowledge. Nevertheless, with refreshing honesty, Gray realized that he could not himself do full justice to such an opera, but he felt that the project was ideally suited to Walton. He was greatly disappointed that, after he had prepared what seemed to be a splendid libretto for his collaborator, month followed month and it remained unset. He referred to the matter in these words:

> Whether the composer felt that it was a failure or merely unsuited to him, or alternatively that he did not feel equal to the task, I do not know—a bit of each, perhaps. I shall think often of attempting to set it to music myself and probably in the end I shall do so, if Walton does not; and he does not seem likely to do so at present, if at all. My difficulty consists in the fact, already mentioned, that I did not feel that the subject was entirely suited to me; and this aspect of it became intensified as I wrote the libretto, which was intended, not for myself

> but for the very different Walton, affording opportunities for musical developments of which he is supremely capable, but I, up to the time of writing, do not feel myself to be.[7]

Gray died in 1952, at the age of fifty-six, his dream of a Gesualdo opera still unrealized. A brilliant critic as well as composer, he had an inbuilt resistance towards the new and important phenomenon of his day, atonality, or serial music, and in his book *A Study of Contemporary Music* he crystallized the prevailing climate of music in the early twenties. His rather unperceptive and ill-humoured attitude to pioneering trends on the Continent caused him to describe Hindemith in 1924 as 'a sandbank in the wide ocean of notes in musical Germany', a comment which nowadays may draw a smile of understanding.

John Gielgud, in 1941, was planning a production of Shakespeare's *Macbeth*, and in May or June he invited Walton, through H. M. Tennant Ltd, to write the incidental music, which he did, starting on Christmas Day that year and finishing on New Year's Day. The recording sessions (by HMV) took place at Ealing Studios in London, where, as Gielgud recalled[8], he had to make out large cheques for the musicians, to cover their unexpectedly long periods of overtime.

Walton attended a few rehearsals. Gielgud, bearing in mind the particular rhythms of the verses, tried in the scenes of the Witches to achieve apposite rhythms from the actresses involved, and Walton, with an uncanny faculty for finding precisely the right phrase and inflections, made careful notes, while, at the same time, beginning to compose music for those scenes in accordance with the rhythms. Gielgud gave him the timings for the interludes and scene-changes and was astonished to observe how meticulously the composer followed them, without having to consult him again. He didn't hear the music—superbly played by the London Philharmonic Orchestra under Ernest Irving—until about six months later, when it was ready to be used, and he was delighted at the richness, pathos and drama of the score. According to Gielgud, the recording was used again some years later in the London production of Thornton Wilder's *Skin of our Teeth*, with Vivien Leigh in the cast and directed by Laurence Olivier at the Piccadilly Theatre.

The new production of *Macbeth* opened in cold, rain-swept Manchester in January 1942, with an impressive Arthurian-looking set, inspired partly by Tchelitchew, with a hint of the Burne-Jones manner, and designed by Michael Ayrton in collaboration with the gifted and fashionable young painter John Minton. The inimitable Gwen Ffrangcon-Davies, cutting short a tour of South Africa, returned post-haste to England to play Lady Macbeth, with Leon Quartermaine as

A childhood photograph of William and Noel Walton. William is on the right
*(Original photograph restored by Kaye Photography and reproduced by kind permission of Mrs C. E. Walton)*

William Walton as a schoolboy

William and Noel Walton standing in the front garden of their home at 93 Werneth Hall Road, Oldham. The smaller of the two figures (on the right) is William (*Original photograph restored by Kaye Photography and reproduced by kind permission of Mrs C. E. Walton*)

Walton shortly after his adoption by the Sitwells

Walton in the 1920s—probably about 1923 when *Façade* was first performed

Walton in 1925 with six of his friends at Stephen Tennant's house in Wiltshire. Left to right: Rex Whistler, Cecil Beaton, Georgia Sitwell, William Walton, Stephen Tennant, and Zita and Tessa Jungman

Cecil Beaton's profile portrait of Walton in 1926 when, according to Osbert Sitwell, he resembled 'a handsome and elegant snipe'

Edith Sitwell in 1927 and Osbert Sitwell in 1929

Sir William with Dame Edith, Sir Osbert and Sir Sacheverell Sitwell and their nephew Francis, October 1962

Christopher Hassall, Sir William Walton and Sir Malcolm Sargent examining the score of *Troilus and Cressida*

A scene from *Troilus and Cressida*

Sir William with Magda Laszlo, the Hungarian soprano who sang the part of Cressida in the première of the opera in 1954

Peter Pears (right) as Pandarus in *Troilus and Cressida*

The picture by Thomas Rowlandson (1756–1827) which inspired the overture *Portsmouth Point*

Walton the conductor: conducting *Scapino*, 1941

Scapino. From an etching by Jacques Callot (1592–1635)

Banquo and Milton Rosmer as Macduff. For the rest, it was a rather makeshift company, since war-time conscription had gathered up many bright young actors who might have shone in the supporting parts. One exception was Alan Badel, at that time not widely known but already, as one of Macbeth's servants, striding the stage with great distinction.

In the second half of 1941 the Films Division of the Ministry of Information gave Walton his first official assignment, namely the creation of a score for *The Foreman Went to France*, a propaganda film based on a story by J. B. Priestley describing an actual incident following the surrender of France. In the story some extremely valuable special-purpose machines have just been delivered to France, and a foreman in the factory concerned, showing great courage and pugnacity, persuades his manager to let him cross the Channel to retrieve them. The producer, Michael Balcon, asked Priestley to write the script. He readily agreed but stipulated that he must be allowed to invent what happened to the foreman after he arrived in France. The film, made between 1 August and 9 November 1941, was not publicly screened until next April. The composer told Dallas Bower that it was 'a boring one—only just taken on as a "fill-in" . . .'.[9]

The score contained some beautiful French-flavoured music with some glorious diatonic tunes, and Ernest Irving, moved by the refugee sequence, described it in these words: 'William wrote a piece of music for the French refugees scene in *The Foreman Went to France* which was completely different from the idea given to him by the producer, who, by the luckiest of mistakes, failed to make himself understood. The music thus composed under a misapprehension really makes your feet sore and your knees sag and excites the exact emotional reaction required.'[10]

Walton's music for *The First of the Few*, his next most immediate assignment for the Ministry of Information, has a peculiar excellence of style, a graphic unity of concept with the film, which raises it to an extremely high level in the genre. Leslie Howard, the film actor, conceived the idea for the film after hearing for the first time the inspiring story of R. J. Mitchell, who, though suffering from an incurable disease and in continuing pain, with only a year to live, devoted himself unsparingly to the design and production of his brain-child, the Spitfire aircraft. Walton regarded the film as a first-rate one and, although in bed recovering from influenza at the time he received the commission, was impatient to begin. David Niven, serving then in the 60th Rifles and released for a short time to undertake this special assignment, starred with Leslie Howard in the film, which spanned twenty years of aeronautical development and included scenes of the Battle of Britain, shot at an RAF station with real service pilots, not actors, portraying their immortal part in the salvation of the United Kingdom.

Both the film and Walton's music for it were highly praised when the finished product was first shown to the public in August 1942:

> *The First of the Few* has been made into something of an English occasion; and memorable it is as a film, and patriotic in the true sense.
>
> This is a sincere, exciting, well-constructed and well-acted English film. Walton's music deserves special recommendation. His fugal movement for the assembly of parts of the Spitfire adds immensely to the most moving sequence in the film.[11]

By the end of the year, heartened and encouraged by the unstinting praise heaped upon his music, Walton had rescored the opening section, a rousing, Elgarian call to arms, irradiated by noble fanfares, and also the fugue, which conveys the noise, bustle and intense activity of the aircraft factory. He combined the two for use in the concert hall, under the title *Prelude and Fugue (The Spitfire)*. The first performance was given in the Philharmonic Hall, Liverpool by the Liverpool Philharmonic Orchestra, conducted by the composer, on 2 January 1943. The orchestra—which was granted the prefix 'Royal' in 1957, the year when John Pritchard, then chief conductor, inaugurated his famous *Musica Viva* concerts—has distinguished itself in many ways, not least by a progressive policy, spread over four or more decades, of introducing new, often exciting works in its programmes.

Switching his concentration and efforts once again from film music, Walton agreed, at the request of Arthur Bliss, the BBC's Director of Music, to write a short brass band suite for the Corporation, although he was anxious to tackle a much bigger and more gripping project: the incidental music for Louis MacNeice's radio play *Christopher Columbus*. He was ill in bed at the time, but writing to Bliss in March 1942 he promised to do the brass band suite as a 'thanksgiving offering', with a request that he be sent 'the requisite amount of tunes necessary and the instructions of what is exactly needed'.[12] The notes, together with lists of tunes for his sketches, were posted to him the following month while he was staying at Ashby St Ledgers. Alas, the composer, writing a few months later to Kenneth Wright, Overseas Music Director of the BBC, confessed that he knew precisely nothing about brass bands; could he therefore have a list of instruments, with relevant compass and characteristics, and also the loan of some or all of the volumes from which he was to take the tunes? 'Never having gone in for folk songs, etc., I must again confess almost complete ignorance of those in the list,' said Walton, 'so what I turn out may be a complete disaster.'[13]

After this baring of his musical soul, nothing more was heard of the suite.

It was on 12 October 1492 that Christopher Columbus, sailing from Palos in Portugal with three small ships, landed in the Bahamas (probably at Watling Island), and the BBC chose this date for a planned commemoration of the 450th anniversary of the discovery of America. The Corporation asked Louis MacNeice, the Anglo-Irish poet, and Dallas Bower to suggest a subject suitable for the occasion. They decided upon one of MacNeice's finest and best-known works, *Christopher Columbus*, choosing it in preference to Darius Milhaud's huge and monumental opera on the same theme. Bower was appointed to produce the radio play, because the project bristled with difficulties and MacNeice, at that time, had not gained sufficient experience and sagacity to handle so complex an undertaking, not the least problem of which was the music specially composed by Walton, involving the use of the BBC Chorus, the BBC Symphony Orchestra and three soloists with guitarist.

Exactly how Walton came to write his massive and picturesque score for *Christopher Columbus* is revealed in the original letter sent to him by Bower:

> Dear William,
>
> This is at once an official and unofficial letter of exploration.
>
> The Corporation intends broadcasting a large-scale programme on Christopher Columbus. Louis MacNeice is writing it and I shall produce. It is, in a sense, a development of the 'Alexander Nevsky' programme, ie, the full resources of the Music Department will be available, including, of course, the Chorus and Orchestra A. Would you be interested in undertaking the incidental music? At one time I considered the possibility of using the Milhaud opera, but no full score exists except in Vienna.
>
> The programme has to be ready for performance in mid-March.
>
> The second matter concerns a private effort of my own to raise money for the Greek Red Cross. I am proposing to produce Yeats' translation of the 'Oedipus Rex' in the Albert Hall. I have asked Donat to play Oedipus and he is willing, but please keep this strictly under your hat at present. My intention is that the choruses shall be reset (for unaccompanied voices only) and I want to put a specific proposal to Malcolm Sargent as the obvious plan would be to use the Royal Choral Society. The entire venture is, of course, to be on a voluntary basis where everyone is concerned. Would you cooperate in this?[14]

*Oedipus Rex* for the Greek Red Cross remained a pipe-dream, and Walton did not compose any music for it; but as regards *Christopher Columbus* he replied to Bower's letter with a touch of acerbity:

> This is most irritating—there is nothing I should like better than to accept both propositions (I can do the second, though no appropriate date is mentioned).

> Unless you can get the Corp to postpone the date to mid-May instead of mid-March, I don't see how I can do it. . . . If Christopher Columbus could be shifted to even early May or late April I could manage it. In fact I don't see how else you can do it, as there are precious few composers about nowadays. I don't suppose it would be possible to get Alan Rawsthorne out of the army again, as he was given 8 weeks leave in Dec & Jan to do the Golden Cockerel. He would be best, but as I've said I doubt the Corp being able to get him so soon after, in fact they wouldn't have got him at all if it hadn't been for yours truly. But anyhow it would be worth trying & he is most frightfully good & would suit excellently. Benjamin Britten is by way of returning—he may be already back, but I gather he joins the RAF music dept on landing. Who else is there except the old gang of V. W., J. Ireland, A. Bax, if you want any of them.[15]

Bower replied immediately to Walton's letter, enclosing an approximate scheme for the *Christopher Columbus* programme which MacNeice had prepared and which he hoped would convey to the composer the proposed size and scope of the work. Anxious not to alarm Walton, the producer pointed out that although the total running-time of the whole feature would be from 1¾ to 2 hours, it should not be assumed that 'an enormous quantity of music' would be necessary, since not all the dialogue or action would have a musical accompaniment. Bower offered the cheering news that, in consultation with the Controller of Programmes, he had postponed the date of presentation until late April. He also gave various reasons why Britten, Rawsthorne and Vaughan Williams could not be approached to undertake the commission, and reaffirmed his own heartfelt wish that nobody but Walton should compose the *Christopher Columbus* music. 'I am really delighted to think that we shall be working together once again,' he concluded, enticingly.[16]

After reading MacNeice's detailed synopsis of the scenario, Walton, writing again to Bower, confessed that he was a little scared of accepting the commission, because he doubted if he would be free of 'the Howard film' in sufficient time to give *Christopher Columbus* the full attention, trouble and care that such a fine project needed. The music would have to be first-class and not rely on the usual quick film extemporisation technique. He pleaded for a further delay and to be provided with 'a rough idea of the extent of the music'.[17]

Doubtless realizing that *Christopher Columbus* was going to be a programme of gigantic stature—the kind of programme that could be matched by the comparable stature of his own music, Walton did accept the commission and in due course submitted what Bower called 'a number of excellent ideas'.[18] The inevitable delays that plague such artistic enterprises like malevolent poltergeists caused first one postponement then another; but finally Bower, in a memo[19] to Adrian Boult, stated that *Christopher Columbus* would definitely go out on a transatlantic broadcast on Monday 12 October 1942, that date being the 450th anniversary of the great explorer's first voyage to America. He reported that Walton was 'busy with the music' (about fifty minutes of it, including songs) and that he hoped to make the score available by 1 September.

The composer, now full of enthusiasm, continued working on the *Christopher Columbus* score throughout July and August. In the following month, to meet the requirements of the truly resplendent music he had created, arrangements were made to augment the BBC Chorus with thirty singers, and by October preliminary rehearsals were under way in London and Bedford.

Unease about his future with the Ministry of Information, and the full extent or depth of his involvement in the war effort, surfaced in a letter which Walton sent to Bower. In it, besides raising various points relating to *Christopher Columbus*, he reported:

> Saw the War Office yesterday: 13 films on the stocks and three for middle of August. What with Ealing these 3 & C.C. I don't quite know what will happen. There is no room for me in the unit as an officer but I think I'm to be made civilian music adviser to the Army Film Unit.
>
> My first experience of a government department, it stank of red tape but found everyone very nice.[20]

Bower informed Dr Stewart Craggs that Walton did not compose any music for the Army Film Unit's productions but simply gave unofficial advice.

In a memo to Boult,[21] the producer expressed his deep regret that Walton would be in Wales during the performance but said that the composer was being violently overworked. He reported that Hedli Anderson would play the Marchesa and sing her song, that since Margaret Rawlings, the Beatriz, was not a singer, a good mezzo-soprano must be found to double for her, and that the other solos could be taken by members of the Chorus as and when they occurred. Writing to Walton, he expressed his bitter disappointment that the composer could not be present at the performance and remarked that Adrian Boult was 'a little fussed at the complicated nature of the whole undertaking'.[22]

The broadcast was a magnificent triumph, referred to by Leonard Cottrell of the BBC's Features and Drama Department as 'one of the most moving examples of radio drama which I have heard in ten years of listening'. He added: 'It shows what can be done when a first-class composer, writer and producer are given their heads with a subject worthy of their talents.'[23] Bower told Walton: 'There has been nothing but praise for the music (from the public, one or two critics and personal friends).'

He also lauded Boult, who had 'worked like a navvy', compassing the whole musical tissue of the production with only the cue sheets which he and the Stage Manager provided. Bower explained that he had cut out the 'court' music entirely because he did not like it; the scene was redundant anyway, and the production running three minutes over schedule in the first Act. Two stanzas of Hedli's song had been sacrificed for dramatic reasons, but she had sung the remaining two superbly. Bower considered that Laurence Olivier, Stephen Murray and Marius Goring had served him admirably, but wrote in a niggling manner of Margaret Rawlings, who had been miscast as a result of the producer's being told that Vivien Leigh was not available. He revealed with some rancour that Vivien had, in fact, been free for the broadcast, as there were no performances on Monday nights of *The Doctor's Dilemma*, in which she was playing. When he learned of this, it was too late for anything to be done about it. Bower found it 'pretty sick-making to have an actress of that calibre "on the premises" merely sitting with me in the Control Room and not playing in the entertainment'. Because of poor reception on his North Wales hotel radio set, Walton did not hear the whole broadcast.

Probably the warmest, most illuminating review of the *Christopher Columbus* broadcast was the one published by *The Listener*:

> Could anything more be wanted to make the two and a half hour celebration of the 450th anniversary of America's discovery a supremely worthy effort? Yes,—great verse and great music. And lo, and hark, here was William Walton providing lashings of the latter. Here were saintly choruses and semi-choruses. Here were sultry serenades—tawny, smoky, authentically Spanish. Here were rich orchestral bursts interrupting Columbus's disputes with the Cardinals and the nobles and his reasonings with Queen Isabella. Here was sea-music-open air, stinging, full of weather—with the sound of the straining of the sails as its persistent ground-bass. Mr Walton has, in a word, been inspired by his great subject.[24]

Christopher Palmer's more detailed review in the *Musical Times*[25] referred to Beatriz's song 'When will he return?' as one of the most affecting that Walton had written and expressed the hope that Oxford University Press would issue it as a separate publication. This was done in July 1974, when OUP published an arrangement of the song with guitar accompaniment.

*Christopher Columbus* was Walton's first and last incursion into radio music, and soon a new propaganda film from the Ministry of Information's Film Division occupied much of his time. In this film, *Went the Day Well?*, based on a story by Graham Greene, the inhabitants of an English village, Bramley Green, watch unsuspectingly, on a certain day in

1942, as lorry loads of Royal Engineers suddenly appear and the soldiers commandeer every building and vehicle within sight. Before long, small details, noticed by observant villagers, result in the discovery that the visitors are, in fact, German invasion troops, and the enemy promptly seal off the village from outside. A frantic SOS to the Home Guard and the Army is despatched, and a fierce battle ensues. The Germans are killed and buried in Bramley Green churchyard.

Walton wrote the music for *Went the Day Well?* in September and October 1942 and, being a self-confessed slow worker, he enlisted the help of Roy Douglas, who orchestrated a few small sections, so that the score would be completed in time for the recording sessions. Douglas had rendered similar assistance with the scores of *Major Barbara, Next of Kin, The First of the Few, The Foreman Went to France* and *Christopher Columbus*. In the music for *Went the Day Well?* a simple diatonic tune formed part of the opening and closing titles—'Went the day, went the day, went the day WELL?'—and Douglas, in a letter to Dr Stewart Craggs, recalled how Walton mockingly scored the last bars of this tune in order to inspire him. 'Those who wrote music for propaganda films and broadcasts during the war,' said Douglas, 'usually found that the goods had to be delivered in a hell of a hurry and the music sometimes rebelled against forced labour, so we often used to encourage "inspiration" by repeating the words of the title of the production until the rhythm suggested a tune. Hence bar one of this sketch.'[26]

'In a hell of a hurry . . .' is a fair summary of the highly skilled, steam-pressurized agony—and joy!—of writing music for films. I remember discussing the subject with Elizabeth Lutyens, during one of her rare visits to Liverpool. This delightfully idiosyncratic but gifted composer wore an habitually cynical and disgruntled look on her sharp-eyed, intellectual face (probably caused by her dislike of music critics), and an almost permanent cigarette, with an inch or so of ash dangling precariously at the end, seemed to intensify the humour of the droll remarks that fell from her lips. I asked Elizabeth how she liked writing for films. She focused a bleary, penetrating eye on me. 'It's bloody awful,' she replied. 'One minute you're slogging away at a palpitating love scene, straining your guts and your imagination to create an atmosphere of sweetness and romance; then, hey presto!, along comes the director—"Drop that," he orders, "I want you to write some rousing Western music for a cowboy film we're doing. You know the kind of thing . . . galloping hooves, noisy, stampeding cattle, cracking whips and all the rest of it." ' She coughed asthmatically on her cigarette and added, with a philosophical shrug of her shoulders, 'One learns to cope, to be flexible and cooperative.'

And that precisely is what Walton did. *Went the Day Well?* was released in 1942 and received a favourable, if brief review from the *New Statesman*:

> Good story (Graham Greene), good direction (Cavalcanti), everything water-tight from Walton's score and the English countryside to the acting of a large cast and the anonymous quotation: 'Went the day well? We died and never knew. But well or ill, Freedom we died for you.'
>
> It is the sort of film that, after three years of war, with little show and no great expenditure of money, we can make better than anyone.[27]

Walton went to Huddersfield in December 1942 to conduct a performance of *Belshazzar's Feast* for a recording which, commissioned by the British Council, was to be sent abroad as cultural propaganda. He joined the Council's music committee the following May. During his brief stay in that city an enterprising reporter interviewed him and obtained some clarifying comments about his then unfashionable attitudes to Elgar: unfashionable because they extolled and honoured a man of whom many of the avant-garde *cognoscenti*, themselves incapable of producing a really inspired and memorable tune, invariably spoke of with a lip-curling contempt. Walton had always admired the power and eloquence of Elgar's best work and in his own *Crown Imperial* coronation march he paid unforgettable tribute to the *Pomp and Circumstance* genius.

It was in January 1943 that the Government gave certain instructions to the Campaigns Division of the Ministry of Information concerning the organization of a massive celebration in the Royal Albert Hall on 21 February of the 25th anniversary of the founding of the Red Army. The producer, Basil Dean, who organized the event, stated that the MOI 'had not the faintest idea of how to set about it'.[28] They sought his help, having so far collected nothing for the project except a promise from Louis MacNeice, one of the BBC's most valued collaborators, to provide a story line. As director of ENSA, which had considerable financial and other resources, he was able to meet the challenge.

After a friendly consultation, Dean and MacNeice planned a story line that involved all branches, civil and military, of the British war effort. Music, the responsibility on this occasion of the ENSA Musical Council, was to be a dominant part of the celebrations, and special fanfares were written by Walton and Sir Arnold Bax (then Master of the King's Musick), while Alan Rawsthorne composed music to highlight and illustrate MacNeice's rhythmic repetitions.

Two thousand people, drawn from areas as far apart as Scotland, Wales, Northern Ireland and Cornwall, were to participate in the great apotheosis of the performance, spreading themselves over three acting areas. The first of these was the orchestral platform, backed by a huge panoramic perspective, designed by Denis Wreford, of the city of Stalingrad. This magnificent set, 120 feet wide and 60 feet high, gave noble and lofty dimensions to the whole production. The second area consisted of the existing arena, with all seating removed. The third comprised a space at the opposite end of the auditorium created by the further removal of seats: an area which would accommodate the London Philharmonic Orchestra, augmented by the BBC Symphony Orchestra and the Royal Choral Society, with Malcolm Sargent elevated on a high rostrum to conduct the various musical events. In the large circle of boxes and the tiered seats beneath them would sit an illustrious invited audience—Ambassadors, Heads of Government Departments, Lord Mayors, Mayors and Councillors from every part of the United Kingdom.

Several distinguished actors, including Laurence Olivier, John Gielgud and Marius Goring, gave dramatic and emotive shape and expression to MacNeice's ode 'Salute to the Red Army'. Positioned in steel towers, placed on either side of the orchestral platform, Ralph Richardson (the Spokesman) and Sybil Thorndike (the Spokeswoman) delivered their narrations with a moving eloquence. Walton, the vice-chairman of the ENSA Advisory Music Council, who had composed some fanfares, took an active part in all the musical planning.

Before the celebrations ended, Anthony Eden, the Foreign Secretary, made a speech. As reported in *The Times*: 'He called the audience to stand in silent tribute to the memory of the glorious dead of the Red Army. The audience stood in silence while a solemn fanfare composed by Sir Arnold Bax, Master of the King's Musick, and the Last Post were sounded. This was followed by a triumphant fanfare to the Red Army written by William Walton.'[29] This fanfare, which the composer used in March 1945 as the basis of his *Memorial Fanfare for Henry Wood*, is no longer in existence.

Shortly after his involvement in the Red Army celebrations, Walton rejected an invitation to compose music for another propaganda film, *The Bells Go Down* (Roy Douglas subsequently provided this), and instead, at the request of Frederick Ashton, agreed to provide a score for a new ballet, *The Quest*, a patriotic spectacle to be staged by the Sadler's Wells company which, under its musical director, toured indefatigably throughout war-plagued Britain. Granted special leave from the RAF, in which he served as an intelligence officer responsible for the interpretation of aerial photographs, Ashton found in *The Quest*—a somewhat crude allegorical study of the conflict between good and evil, with St George as the hero—not only a formidable challenge but an almost impossible task. Drawn from Spenser's *The Faerie Queene*, the subject, dense in texture and needing more drastic condensation, seemed unsuitable for characterization and difficult to choreograph. John Piper's designs, the first he created for a theatrical production, were attractive enough, but, as Frank Howes, who saw the ballet, testified,[30] the costumes were most unappealing, and St George's white tunic and golden wig made Robert Helpmann look slightly ridiculous. According to another observer, Miss Mary Clarke,[31] this great character actor—*danseur noble*, usually ebullient, even satirically amusing, when faced with stilted heroics, walked about with an air of patient resignation, obviously depressed by his costume. Other principals in the ballet were Margot Fonteyn, Beryl Grey, Moira Shearer and Leslie Edwards (recently invalided out of the forces). Despite the problems arising out of Doris Langley Moore's libretto, Ashton, managing to simplify the scenario, choreographed the work superbly, with exciting pyrrhic dances and excellent groupings.

Ashton had originally thought of using Delius's music but on reflection felt that a new ballet required a newly commissioned score, as much as new wine needs new bottles, and he chose William Walton as the composer.

As already mentioned, the creation of *The Quest* was a formidable task, even though the ballet lasted only forty-five minutes, and the work was rehearsed on tour, while Walton, composing with painful slowness, fed the music to Ashton a page or two at a time. Occasionally, almost frantic with worry, Ashton had to telephone Walton at Rugby to beg for more, only to be told by the composer that 'inspiration' had dried up and he could progress no further. The music never arrived fast enough, even though, at times, Walton entrusted pages of manuscript to the guard of a train, who handed them over to the choreographer when the train drew into the station where he stood waiting impatiently. On reaching the finale, Ashton was still short of vital music, and in desperation he persuaded Hilda Gaunt to improvise at the appropriate duration and tempo, then adjusted the music to fit when the missing pages of the manuscript arrived. Michael Somes recalled 'that bits of the score of Sir William's for "The Quest" arrived on backs of envelopes, piece by piece, and Sir Frederick would then choreograph the latest bit!'[32] And Beryl Grey remembered that,

> The last Act of the ballet was finished during the last week of rehearsal time. He had to choreograph before the music arrived! This was at the Coventry Theatre. I rehearsed mainly out on Tour in the Provinces.
>
> It was the first role that was created for me. I was just 15 then. It seemed very odd for a 15 year old to be taking the part of a seductress! I was very thrilled at being chosen by Ashton and having the choreography worked out on me, some of which was with Robert Helpmann.
>
> The music was most exciting and inspiring, as were the John Piper costumes and sets.[33]

The ballet, first presented at the New Theatre in London on 6 April 1943, in aid of Lady Cripps's Aid to China Fund, won glowing tributes for its choreographer, Frederick Ashton, its designer, John Piper, and its composer William Walton, whose music was warmly praised by *The Times*: 'Mr Walton . . . has written music which drives the dancers along with the crackling rhythm to be expected of him. The question, which has been much canvassed, whether he could write dramatic music for the stage as well as the film has been answered affirmatively in a score which avoids too thick a texture and is clear in its characterisation.'[34]

Walton, writing about *The Quest* to John Warrack, said that,

> The music was composed under adverse circumstances . . . some of the ideas were not too bad and some better not mentioned, but as it had to be done quickly, as Freddy had only a limited "leave," it had to be done that way—45 mins music in less than 5 weeks. . . . I remember having to "bribe" guards on trains to take a minute or so's music to wherever Freddy happened to be with the ballet—to Wolverhampton, Preston or somewhere and some of the dances were done before the music arrived! . . . at the moment I can't recall a note of the music. . . .[35]

Since the ballet had such a distinguished cast and a favourable first performance, it might seem strange that it had dropped from the repertory and that the score itself vanished for eighteen years; but there was not a great deal to commend it—not only was *The Quest* hastily constructed, but its patriotic theme, dominated by the superman figure of England's dragon-slaying saint, which stirred the blood in 1943, provoked no comparable response in a post-War Britain seeking to forget the horrors of war and the jingoist sentiments of its protagonists. There were some persistent efforts to revive the ballet, but Walton and Ashton firmly opposed them.

Aware that the score had vanished, John Warrack, between August 1957 and July 1958, made attempts to locate it.[36] Having failed to elicit any useful information from either the Oxford University Press or Walton, he set off to make enquiries at Sadler's Wells. From there he was directed to a warehouse somewhere in North London, where various papers, documents and other oddments were stored. And among these, to his joy, he found a brown paper parcel with the manuscript inside it. The music having been recovered, a suite in four movements was arranged from it by Vilem Tausky after Alan Frank of the Oxford University Press had telephoned him to report that he had parts of the ballet score.[37] The first performance of the suite in 1961 persuaded the critic of *The Times* that these excerpts 'would have been better left in obscurity . . . even the concluding passacaglia, which climbs higher than the rest, now sounds cold and contrived'.[38] Walton, however, conducted a performance of the suite at the opening night, 21 July, of the Promenade Concerts of 1962, which drew a more flattering response from the same newspaper: 'The suite, if not Walton at his most inspired, suggests in its vivid and attractive character, a viable stage work that our Royal Ballet might find it rewarding to revive.'[39]

Two unusual commissions reached Walton in 1943: one for an anthem to celebrate the overthrow of Hitler, the other for a work to be premièred during the fiftieth anniversary of the Henry Wood Promenade Concerts in 1944. A list of the composers invited to submit works for the first performance in the 1944 'Prom' series included Bliss, Britten, Alan Bush, Lambert, Ian Whyte and, of course, Walton, from Britain; Milhaud, Roy Harris and Stravinsky from America; Prokofiev and Shostakovich from the USSR, and Honegger from Switzerland.

As regards the 'victory anthem' to commemorate the downfall of the arch-monster Hitler, both Walton and Vaughan Williams (who had also received an invitation) declined a commission because 'they felt unable to comply with the official ruling that the work should be "symbolic" of all the fighting freedom nations and not take longer then 5 minutes to play.'[40]

It was Sir Henry Wood who asked Walton to write a piece of music for the fiftieth anniversary of the 'Proms', and Walton, in a letter of acceptance from Rugby, told the great conductor that he felt honoured to be asked, although, because of a busy film schedule, he was 'pushed for time'.[41] He wrote again the following month[42] to report that he was 'safely launched on the "Te Deum" for chorus and orchestra' and to express the hope that Sir Henry would regard this as an appropriate choice. Having sent such an assurance, Walton, surprisingly, in a letter addressed to Julian Herbage at the BBC only two months later, made what must have seemed a very depressing announcement:

> Before it is too late, wisdom dictates that I should take some evasive attitude about this projected 'Te Deum.' The situation is this—Henry V should have been finished six weeks ago—and, I need hardly add, through no fault of my own, there is no prospect of it being finished before the end of March. Which would give me about 6 to 8 weeks in which to write the 'Te Deum' and with another 4 weeks for copying the chorus parts it would mean that whatever chorus is going to sing it wouldn't have it before the beginning of July!
>
> Therefore rather than be late again especially for such an auspicious occasion, I think it would be wiser to withdraw it altogether, or what I would prefer, to not have it announced at all.[43]

This letter highlights the enormous pressure which had fallen on the composer since he began writing film scores for the Ministry of

Information and the BBC. He had, for some time, been working on a score—destined to be one of the finest of its kind—for the film *Henry V*, and, as this was a major project, it required all his time and concentration. After receiving the letter, Herbage discussed with Sir Henry Wood the possibility of the 'Te Deum' not being ready in time for the Jubilee Promenade Concerts and subsequently reported to Walton that, unless the work was sufficiently far advanced to be included in the programme, it would hardly achieve the necessary effect if announced at the last moment.[44] The subject of the 'Te Deum' was therefore mutually discarded.

Dallas Bower, originally a sound engineer and now a much-esteemed film-maker, conceived the idea of creating a film version of Shakespeare's *Henry V*, and in 1938 he prepared a script for BBC Television, the pundits of which, regarding it as too ambitious for the new medium, promptly rejected it. During the war, Bower, conscripted into the Army, found time to work on the rejected script and transform it into a film scenario. On being reassigned to the Film Division of the Ministry of Information, he suggested the making of a film based on his scenario; but, without hesitation, his superiors shook their heads, since they were interested only in short propaganda and information pictures. It was not until 1943, after Bower had left the Ministry to join the BBC, that his dream of a splendid film version of *Henry V* materialized, almost magically, through a fortuitous collaboration between himself, Laurence Olivier and producer, Filippo del Giudice, who, regarding Walton as 'England's most promising composer', commissioned him to write the music.

Work on the film commenced on 6 January 1943 and ended on 3 January 1944, although the music and sound effects were recorded in March and April of that year. Walton described the process of composing and synchronizing the music as 'an unusually complex and close collaboration of sound and screen from one bar, or visual movement, to the next'.[45] After the music, dialogue and sound effects with footage had been successfully combined and final processing in the laboratories carried out, the film opened at the Carlton Theatre in London on 22 November 1944, earning some very favourable reviews and the rare distinction of being featured in a *Times* leading article.[46]

Composing the music must have placed tremendous pressure on Walton, although, as he himself admitted,[47] he discussed and planned everything in advance with Olivier, who was not only a great help but 'marvellous and stimulating'. Olivier, in a graphic appraisal of the music, returned the compliment: 'The music had more guts, more spunk, more attack and more venom than one would have thought was hidden in Walton's personality.'[48]

The two men concocted what Olivier described as 'a very artistic way of going about things'. It seems that Walton wrote the music first, especially that for the battle scene, and that shooting of the scene was engineered in such a way as to fit it. The actor reaffirmed his admiration for Walton's score: 'I have always said that if it was not for the music, *Henry V* would not have been the success it was.'[49]

James Blades, that jolly, invariably kind and charmingly anecdotal percussionist, related an incident which occurred during the recording:

> Sir William was also keen to experiment with percussion sounds, though perhaps he had forgotten the occasion at Denham Studios when he became my assistant and played (remarkably well) on my set of tubular bells. I was doing my best to imitate the clash of a great number of church bells, an effect required by Sir Laurence Olivier (now Lord Olivier) for the film *Henry V*. To produce what Larry wanted from my array of tubular bells needed several pairs of hands, so I enlisted his help as well as that of the composer.[50]

A suite containing four numbers from the *Henry V* score appeared in 1945 and gained the important distinction of selling well commercially—something which had not previously happened in the realm of film music; then, in 1964, as part of the Shakespeare birthday celebrations, yet another suite was produced, arranged by Muir Mathieson, a conductor of whose brilliance Sir Arthur Bliss, reminiscing, wrote in these words:

> One of the enjoyments of going down to the sets in Denham was watching the skill of the camera men, the recording engineers, the cutters, and especially the musical direction. This was in the hands of a young Scotsman, Muir Mathieson, who was to gain a great reputation as a conductor for musical film scores, and in his determined way to influence directors to commission special music from our own composers, Vaughan Williams, Walton, Alwyn, Arnold and many others. It is a fatiguing and anxious job fitting music to a film and I used greatly to admire Muir at work, baton in one hand, stop-watch in the other, one eye on the film and the other on his players. He was so type-cast for this particularly exacting work that his great abilities as a conductor of public concerts have been overlooked, and that is the musical world's loss.[51]

Sir Henry Wood, the much-revered 'Father of the "Proms" ' who had a unique place in British music, died a few days after he conducted the last concert of the Jubilee series in Bedford. Knighted in 1911 and made a Companion of Honour in 1944, the year of his death, he was the first conductor in Britain to perform works by Debussy, Fauré, Franck, Ravel, Rimsky-Korsakov, Tchaikovsky, Stravinsky, Mahler and Sibelius; in fact, by establishing the 'Prom' tradition of introducing new and rarely heard compositions into programmes of popular pieces, he aroused the interest of a multitude of people, young and old, in classical and good modern music. In addition to his arduous work as a conductor, he found time to write oratorios, theatre music and songs, as well as arranging the *Fantasia on British Sea-songs* which became the regular closing item on the last night of the Promenade season. A perfectionist in every detail, he used to stand, often still wearing his overcoat, in the 'wings' of the Queen's Hall, London, just before the start of any concert he was to conduct there, holding up his famous tuning-box for all to see. Whenever a violinist went past him onto the platform, he would strike an A with his great tuning-fork, and the musician would then have to play the note back to him as he went on. Not surprisingly, Sir Henry raised the standard of orchestral playing in Britain quite remarkably.

The passing of such a titanic figure called for a special tribute, and early in 1945 it was decided that a memorial concert should be held in the Albert Hall on Sunday 4 March. W. W. Thompson wrote to Walton concerning this and confirmed a previous telephone message to the effect that the concert—to be known as the Henry Wood Memorial Concert—was being organized by Lord Camrose, a member of the *Daily Telegraph* committee, who had asked if he, Walton, would kindly consider writing a fanfare for the occasion.[52] Thompson also reported that Boult, Barbirolli and Cameron were giving their services, that three orchestras—the London Philharmonic, the London Symphony and the BBC Symphony—would take part and that the total instruments on the platform would be 38 First Violins, 34 Second, 28 Violas, 26 Cellos, 20 Basses, 9 of each Woodwind, 12 Horns, 10 Trumpets, 12 Trombones, 3 Tubas, 2 Timpani, 4 Percussion, 3 Harps and Organ. He informed Walton that his fanfare would conclude the concert, following the Bach-Klenovsky Toccata and Fugue. The name Klenovsky, coupled with that of Bach, will puzzle no one who is familiar with Sir Henry's career—it was under the pen-name of Paul Klenovsky that he published an orchestral arrangement of Bach's Toccata and Fugue in D minor.

Walton was not in the best of health when he received Thompson's invitation, but in a very short period of time the score of his *Memorial Fanfare for Henry Wood* was safely in the hands of Thompson, who wrote to acknowledge it, saying, 'all concerned are most grateful for the gesture you have so very kindly made', and promising that his best copyist (de Mauny) would supervise the copying of the parts and the duplicate score.[53] The speed at which the brief but gripping composition was written can probably be explained by the fact that it was not a newly minted piece but an extended version of Walton's *Red Army Fanfare*. After the performance *The Times* reported that, '. . . the *Memorial Fanfare*, specially composed by William Walton, militated against the sonority of this dignified and elegiac short piece making its proper effect, though it was sufficiently impressive to restrain applause.'[54]

The Fanfare was heard again at the beginning of the first concert of the following series of Promenade Concerts on 21 July 1945 but has not, as far as I know, been performed since.

In September 1945 Charles B. Cochran received the 'book' of a light opera by Sir Alan Herbert and, with a view to producing the finished work in Manchester the following spring, invited Walton to write the music. The composer, however, declined, feeling that he was not 'right' for the commission. He recommended that gifted musician and writer Spike Hughes, who likewise considered that it was not his genre. Cochran then approached Vivian Ellis, who had provided lyrics and music for many successful London shows, and he readily agreed to create a score for the operetta, which took the title *Big Ben*. Walton had a long-standing association with the impresario, and at Manchester in 1935 a new Cochran revue, complete with his famous 'Young Ladies', had included a short ballet, *The First Shoot*, a product of the combined talents of Osbert Sitwell, Frederick Ashton and Cecil Beaton. Walton wrote the music, and the distinguished author and music critic Michael Kennedy confessed years later that it had not only set his feet tapping but made him an immediate Walton convert.

Various rumours, seemingly ill-founded, concerning music which Walton was reported to be composing or about to compose, drifted suddenly into public awareness from time to time and, like puffballs, vanished just as abruptly. One rumour, heard in 1945 and never substantiated, alleged that he was collaborating with Frederick Ashton on a choral ballet, *Agamemnon*, for Sadler's Wells. And during a visit to Scandinavia between October and December 1945, at a time when he had just arrived in Stockholm, the Svenska Dagbladet made an announcement which, once again, failed to fructify: 'Englishman will set music to Strindberg. *Dreamplay* tempts William Walton. To set music to Strindberg's dramas is an idea which occupies William Walton.'[55]

If Strindberg's dramas did tempt Walton, they did so briefly, since he was currently involved in another tribute to the late Sir Henry Wood. It had been decided in January 1945 that a stained glass window, specially installed in his memory, would be unveiled in St Sepulchre's Church, Holborn Viaduct, London, where, as a boy, he learned to play the organ so thoroughly that, at the age of fourteen, he was persuaded to give public recitals on the instrument at various trade exhibitions. His ashes were laid beneath the window. Walton had been invited to set to music some verses by John Masefield, the Poet Laureate, and, in accepting, had written to Masefield, describing his ideas:

> Lady Wood has forwarded me a copy of your letter about the poem you have so kindly undertaken to write for me to set to music. My idea is for a piece not lasting longer than ten or fifteen minutes and not on any considerable scale—at the most say 6 verses of poetry to be set for small chorus and orchestra with perhaps the 3rd and 4th verses with a solo voice. I go to Sweden shortly for about six weeks and should be very pleased if you could have the poem ready on my return in early December. I hope that this idea will meet with your approval and I may add that I feel deeply honoured to be in association with you in this project.[56]

Masefield obviously sent a reply, because there is a letter from the composer thanking him for his own, enclosing six pages of printed poetry and stating: 'I think that verses like XXIV with perhaps a longer one in the middle to avoid too much regularity would be just right for what is intended.'[57]

Following this brief correspondence, Walton, although he had already set two verses of it, decided not to use Masefield's poem, which for some reason seemed to be unsuitable for what he intended, and concentrated instead on writing a non-choral work as a tribute to Sir Henry Wood. Explaining his decision, he offered a short string piece to Lady Wood, who expressed the hope that he would conduct it himself.[58] Deeply troubled by the turn of events, Walton told her in a letter that he could not make a worthy work out of the poem but that the last thing he wanted to do was offend the Poet Laureate or hurt his feelings. 'I am loth to make this decision,' he remarked, 'as I have so much respect for Mr Masefield. . . . Nor do I think it wise to ask him to write another—the same thing might happen.'[59]

Action had already been taken to obviate any possibility of his offending the Poet Laureate. At a meeting held in January to discuss the music for the unveiling ceremony—scheduled for 26 April—it was agreed unanimously that the Masefield verses should be read. Lady Wood suggested to Walton that this might assist him out of a difficulty, in that he could inform the Poet Laureate that he had decided to write a piece for orchestra only, providing whatever reason he wished. She added that if he was not in sympathy with the suggestion, perhaps he would allow her to write to Masefield, explaining that, having been abroad, working hard on film and other scores, he, Walton, had found himself unable to proceed with the choral work.[60]

Any unease that still flitted through the composer's mind as a result of the difficulties he had recently faced must have gone completely between the January meeting and March 1946, because, during that period, Masefield apparently wrote a short poem, 'Sir Henry Wood', which Walton, taking his title from the first line, set to music as *Where does the uttered music go?* The new work, performed at the unveiling service on 26 April by the BBC Chorus, under Leslie Woodgate, received warm praise from the critic of *The Times*: 'A noble piece of music worthy of the occasion, and sure to survive its occasion.'[61]

Walton, writing to Lady Wood, expressed his gratification, tinged with an irony and bitterness concerning those he so often regarded as enemies—the critics:

> I am so pleased you like the Masefield setting. It turned out to be much better than I expected and was most beautifully sung.
>
> It would, I think, be a good idea if it was performed sometime during the Proms. The more often the better as I have assigned all monies accruing from it to the Memorial Fund.
>
> I received a batch of press-cuttings this morning, & one must admit that it hardly received an overwhelming reception. But I have given up all hopes of critics a long time ago.[62]

Masefield, too, had written to Lady Wood with a modesty that was characteristic of this gentle, unassuming man who had penned some of the finest lines in English poetry: 'It was so little that I could do, but I am told that Dr Walton hid my deficiencies with wonderful music.'[63]

According to Henry Nevinson, the Poet Laureate was 'a shy man, with a smallish flat head and dreamy, light-brown eyes set in a delicate face that were full of sadness, as if brooding upon the misfortunes of humanity'.[64] Tall and athletic, with a slender frame, he spoke faultless English and had a courtly, old-world manner that other people found both delightful and strange. Masefield died in 1967, mourned and esteemed by a host of admirers from every walk of life.

# 8

# A Girl in Argentina

In 1945, when World War II ended, Walton was released from the Ministry of Information and promptly resumed work on his second string quartet, which he had started composing in the summer of 1945, although Kenneth Wright of the BBC had invited him in August 1939 to write this work for Harry Blech and his quartet.[1] It proved to be a full-blooded piece, distinguished by his own peculiar mixture of nostalgia and pugnacity, very different from the first quartet which, Stravinskian in technique, reveals Walton in his lightest and most sarcastic vein. The new work, dedicated to Ernest Irving, who had conducted much of his film music throughout the war years, received its first performance at Broadcasting House on Sunday 4 May 1947, when the BBC broadcast it in the Third Programme, although the London Contemporary Music Centre had previously advertised the première to take place in the Wigmore Hall on 4 February 1947—the reason for the change of plan seems not to have been explained. On the day following the broadcast, the Blech String Quartet gave the first public performance in the Concert Hall of Broadcasting House. The distinguished critic Desmond Shawe-Taylor made the following comment: 'In spite of the lapse of time since his last major work (the Violin Concerto of 1939), it is also in all essentials the familiar blend of harmonic astringency, rhythmic and contrapuntal ingenuity, and nostalgia meditation.'[2]

At this time, Walton, casting his eyes on more verdant and variegated pasture-land, was contemplating the composition of an opera and, according to rumour, was looking around for a suitable libretto; but the BBC, aware of his growing fame and importance, sought more and more to utilize his undoubtedly rare and distinctive gifts. In February 1947 the Corporation's representative John Lowe invited Walton—unsuccessfully as it turned out—to write a new work for a choral and orchestral concert to celebrate, on 29 September of that year, the first anniversary of the inauguration of the Third Programme.[3] With a view to planning the first studio performance, mention was also made of the new opera which Walton hoped to write during the next eighteen months.

Imma Doernberg, the enchantingly beautiful Baroness who, at one time, had meant so much to the composer, died on 14 March 1947 in London of the dreadful scourge leukaemia. There seems to be no recorded account of how she lived since those halcyon days in Ascona, Switzerland, but it is known that in 1938 she occupied a 'grace and favour' address at Kensington Palace and that on 1 July 1940, acquiring British nationality, she married the fifty-five-year-old Captain Neil Boyd Watson McEacharn, MBE. He died in Italy on 18 April 1964. In her memoirs,[4] Princess Alice, Countess of Athlone described Imma as 'the most alive and buoyant person imaginable', and Sassoon wrote of her as 'very pretty and a most sweet creature, very lively and courageous, with a clear, ringing voice and a tall, graceful figure'.[5]

Another unfulfilled request from the BBC for a new work came in August 1947 in a letter from Gerald Abraham, whom Walton had met in Czechoslovakia during the Prague International Music Festival earlier in the year:

> I wonder whether you would care to take part in what promises to be a rather interesting experiment? We have commissioned six poets of some standing, each to write for the Third Programme a poem specially for musical setting; the poems should be in our hands by the middle or end of September. The idea is then to send all six poems, the authors of which will remain temporarily anonymous, to you and to five or six other leading British composers and invite you to set any one of them that appeals to you, either for voice and piano or in any other way you prefer. At the same time we should ask you to make notes on the poems, stating the reasons for your choice and so on; if none of the poems appealed to you, it would be equally interesting if you would say why they did not. The results would be collated, edited and generally shaped into one or two radio programmes which would, I think, make not only very attractive listening for their own sake, but might throw considerable light on such points as the suitability of words for music, the nature of musicians' varied approaches to poetry, even possibly on the nature of musical inspiration. If you are interested in the idea and willing to collaborate, as I very much hope, I will arrange for you to receive a formal commission and a set of questions which you may answer or ignore as you please, but which will guide you as to the kind of notes we should like.[6]

If Walton bluntly declined this invitation—as appears likely—one can hardly be surprised. For a busy composer of considerable status to be asked to participate in 'a rather interesting experiment', to make detailed analytical, critical or explanatory notes on six poems, advancing equally detailed reasons if he didn't like any of them, seems a gross imposition and the kind of cerebral exercise hardly calculated to set the pulse racing.

At the beginning of 1947, Olivier brought to fruition the dream he had nurtured four years earlier (while making *Henry V*) of creating a really stunning production of Shakespeare's *Hamlet* and, cheered by Walton's ready agreement to write the music, spent much time in Italy, preparing the script, the shooting sequences, the camera work and the lighting. The actual shooting of the film began in May 1947 at Denham Studios, which Olivier, banning all visitors from the set, had isolated with Pentagon-like security measures. By mid-December, while Walton slowly and fastidiously composed the score, the completed film was passing through the cutting and editing stage, prior to its final release on 6 May 1948.

In a published record[7] of how this gripping film was produced, Walton warmly praised Olivier, who had given him 'every consideration', spreading the recording dates over a whole month, so that he had ample time to ponder the results of each recording and to discuss relevant points before proceeding to the next music section. Walton had, throughout the filming, maintained the closest possible collaboration with Olivier, basing some of his musical ideas on suggestions made by the great actor-producer.

Altogether *Hamlet* contained about fifty minutes of music, and this, performed by the Philharmonia Orchestra of London, assembled in the Music Theatre of Denham Studios on certain days, was, like the individual picture 'shots', recorded in short sections and transposed onto the sound-track. Ted Drake, the music mixer (also responsible for the microphones and orchestral 'balance'), made the recording, with Olivier, the composer and the film-editor present in the studio. Muir Mathieson, the musical director, wrote of Walton's music for *Hamlet* with outstanding eloquence:

> I have recorded many of Walton's film scores and believe him to have excelled himself in the case of *Hamlet*. He has a tremendous dramatic sense, and his music for the two Olivier Shakespearean productions must surely augur well for his first opera. A single instance from the score of *Hamlet* will perhaps be sufficient to illustrate the extraordinary ingenuity Walton brings into his screen writing, making his one of the famous names in film music all over the world.
>
> The arrival of the Court is heralded by trumpet calls and a superb march theme which appears to keep step with the retinue as they take their places around the King's dais. Then the players make their entry, accompanied by a small group of musicians. For this, Walton hints at the idiom of the period and uses an orchestra of two violas, cello, oboe, cor anglais, bassoon and harpsichord. He opens with a sarabande, music in slow three-in-a-measure dance time often encountered in 17th and 18th century music, and follows this with a slower, sinister passage for the entry of the poisoner.

As the camera moves round to show the reactions of the audience, and particularly of the King, the stage music dissolves into the Players' theme, which is taken up by the full symphony orchestra, as the dramatic undercurrent of the scene, and the tension of the Court, rises.

The camera, from its circular tracking orbit, returns to the Players, and the music reverts to the quiet accompaniment of the play. The actor-king has been poisoned; the King can no longer stand the strain ('The play's the thing, Wherein to catch the conscience of the King'). The full power of the orchestra rises up, swamping the soft sounds of the cello, oboe and harpsichord, and ends in a tremendous chord, as the King roars out 'Give me some light.'

William Walton's score was a constant delight to record, being so perfect in detail and sure in its dramatic conception. It will certainly prove the perfect complement to a great subject.[8]

James Blades, that master-percussionist and raconteur, was also involved in making the film and in his autobiography *Drum Roll* gives a characteristic anecdote:

Another sound which called for a great deal of experiment was the background 'heart beat' effect for the film *Hamlet* (to intensify the drama of the ghost scene). Laurence Olivier (the producer and director) let me hear a recording of a heart beat taken through a stethoscope. This sounded like someone consuming thick soup with a rhythmic intake, and was absolutely useless for our purposes. What was required was a steady, gentle 'poom-poom-poom-poom.' I made experiments with various kinds of drumsticks on muffled kettledrums, bass drums and tenor drums. The only sound which seemed in any way suitable to Sir Laurence was when I placed a blanket on the skin of my largest bass drum and prodded the rhythm with my fingertips. As it happened Vivien Leigh was an interested spectator, and I wondered if her fur coat would be better as a muffle. This was tried and Olivier got the quiet 'shush' and the deep though light-sounding 'poom-poom' he wanted. A similar effect was required some time later for the prison scene (ie, the death of Clarence) in *Richard III*, but it was extremely difficult to repeat it.[9]

Part of Walton's magnificent score survives because the *Funeral March*, abstracted by Muir Mathieson for concert use, has been published separately. Mathieson also took other passages and arranged them as a poem for orchestra, *Hamlet and Ophelia*. And Malcolm Sargent collated a number of isolated fanfares into a single piece entitled *Fanfare for a Great Occasion*.

When the brilliant and high-minded Alice Wimborne died on 17 April 1948—an event which must have saddened Walton greatly—her affection and concern for him found expression in a very handsome legacy. She left him the sum of £10,000, the leasehold residence Lowndes Cottage, Lyall Mews, Westminster (including the fixtures), her Sunbeam Talbot car and, among other effects, a carpet, a statuette and some fine pieces of furniture. All his life fortune smiled upon Walton like a warm Mediterranean sun: firstly in the patronage of the Sitwells, giving him financial as well as artistic encouragement; secondly in the funds provided so generously by Sassoon; thirdly in his life annuity of £500 from Mrs Elizabeth Courtauld; and finally in Lady Wimborne's magnificent bequests.

The composer went to Buenos Aires in 1948 at the invitation of the British Council, who had organized a tour, presumably in order to impress the Argentinians with British musical talent. Mr Boosey of Boosey & Hawkes, the music publishers, piloted him to a reception where a large crowd had gathered to do homage. Although an uninvited guest, he stood in front of Walton and took over the proceedings, then, having introduced him, glided swiftly over his achievements like a skater warming up for the acrobatic *pièce de résistance*, which consisted of the embarrassing comment, 'of course, Walton isn't our most important composer—Britten is!' During a perfunctory ripple of applause, the discomfited Walton caught sight of a lovely Argentinian girl, Susana Gil, the daughter of a Buenos Aires business man, and promptly forgot Mr Boosey's rudeness so completely that the two men subsequently became good friends. Years later, in an interview with John Warrack, the composer described what happened:

> The first item was a conference to meet Mr Perón (President of Argentina). He got up and made a speech of which no one understood a word, then all his backers got up and screamed 'Perón, Perón, Perón.' Then Mr Boosey got up and made a speech in reply, and when he finished I said 'Boosey, Boosey, Boosey.' And that became the cry of the opposition in Buenos Aires for some time, I was told. After that there was a press conference which I had to give, and I saw a rather attractive girl in the corner. Of course one of the journalists asked what I thought about Argentinian girls, so I nearly said, do you see that girl over there, I'm going to marry her, but I controlled myself just in time. Anyhow we met, went off to lunch and I proposed to her the next day. As far as I can remember she said "Don't be ridiculous, Dr Walton." But we got engaged three weeks after that. They played my Coronation March at the wedding, terrible it was. It was the most appalling sort of wedding-at nine o'clock at night in devastating heat.[10]

Lady Walton, reminiscing in 1982 about this memorable first meeting with her future husband, confessed that, at the time, she thought she was about to be saddled with yet another drunken, post-war Englishman. He proposed to her every day for three weeks and always she refused; then he failed to do so, and she became extremely worried. When he asked her again, she promptly said 'Yes'. This delightful girl worked as a secretary for the British Council in Buenos Aires. 'What a courageous chap he was,' she remarked, looking back. 'Argentine women were very secluded. Education was very old-fashioned. We weren't allowed to go out without chaperones. When I got my first job the whole family fell backwards in disgust. Poor William—when he proposed he didn't know he was going to have to battle with a virgin. Anyway, he went into the first bookshop he saw and bought a little book with very neat designs, so that I could get on with it! Mama had very definite ideas. The moment we got married, she had my tonsils taken out, because that would keep me out of trouble, she said.'[11]

It is clear from other, more detailed sources of information that Lady Walton's remarks about education being 'very old-fashioned' in her own milieu were not exaggerated. Although by no means a facsimile of the egocentric tyrant of Wimpole Street immortalized by Rudolf Besier, her father had rigid Pan-American principles. Up to the age of sixteen, Susana was taught only English, so that in order to communicate with her and her brothers, her aunts had to master that perverse, inconsistent, yet gloriously poetic tongue. Burdened with a German governess, the children, as they grew older, made only a perfunctory acquaintance with English, and in later years Susana described her own knowledge of it as 'deficient'.[12] Her parents sent her to a State school, an act which, considering their wealthy, upper-middle-class status, must have shocked many people who knew them intimately. Susana and her brothers were transported to and from school in a private car. There is just a hint of cloistered respectability, of the chaste insularity of a closed religious house in her remark 'I never talked or played with anyone of my own age until much later.'[13]

At the age of ten, when the buds of independence first began to flower, she created a domestic rumpus, as a result of which Señor Gil allowed her to go to a convent school, instead; but, characteristically aglow with 'progressive' ideas, she insisted on taking a commercial, rather than an academic, sixth-form course. After all, no other girl of her own immediate social background had done this, and she saw herself as a trail-blazing pioneer. A demure, seventeen-year-old who wore a hat with a veil to hide her pretty face, Susana taught English for a couple of years at the British Institute in Buenos Aires, an occupation which subsequently facilitated her acceptance of the post of social secretary at the British Council, only, it must be mentioned, after bitter opposition, then capitulation, by her father, when she threatened dire sanctions. 'I shall take my toothbrush and never enter this house again,' said the girl, with an endearing blend of Victorian drama, injured adolescence and unconscious humour.[14]

Her marriage with William Walton took place at the Church of San

Martín de Tours on 13 December 1948, in the presence of the British Ambassador and Lady Balfour and four other ambassadors, and with two thousand guests at the reception.

Walton and his bride discovered a happiness they had never known existed. It was, by all relevant standards, a union of improbable compatibility, since she was twenty-six years younger than her partner and totally unmusical; but the strange, pulsating and irresistible force we call love created an immediate rapport. Walton and Susana spent their first few months of married life in London, sustained during the bleak aftermath of war-time rationing partly by a sack of sugar and two hams which they had received as wedding gifts, and partly by a consignment of five kilos of meat which the Argentine Meat Company delivered weekly by taxi. The couple stayed for a time at Lowndes Cottage and also made a flying visit to Oldham, where the composer introduced his wife to his mother and his brother Noel, at the same time promising to conduct the Hallé Orchestra in a concert in Oldham in October 1949. (He did so, on the 2nd of that month, steering the orchestra through a programme of his own music, which included the *Sinfonia Concertante*, with Phyllis Sellick as the soloist, the *Façade* Suites 1 and 2, and the *Coronation March* of 1937). Noel described his sister-in-law as 'lively' and 'the independent type'. Asked whether his brother was engaged on a new composition, he replied: 'Willie doesn't like being asked questions, so one doesn't ask, but I suspect he is working on an opera.'

Walton and Susana were very fond of Italy, having spent happy days touring that country in an old Bentley, and the composer, increasingly aware that London did not suit them as a place in which to settle permanently, longed for a home on the island of Ischia. During his visit to Oldham he had bumped into a man who told him that his aunt had a villa on Ischia which she wanted to let. This at least was a beginning, and Walton promptly paid the rent. Before the end of 1949 he and his wife, illegally stuffing into two hot-water bottles enough money to see them through the winter, hastened to Ischia and took possession.

The villa, a big, dilapidated old place, looked more like a convent, which, indeed, it had once been, and over the years at least two armies had been billeted in its shambling rooms. There were no chairs, and the beds had poltergeistic springs which coiled sideways instead of upwards: during the night these devilish contraptions would suddenly unwind with what, years later, Susana desribed as an 'orchestral twang'.[15] Not only the bed-springs but also the huge primitive stove had Satanic characteristics: only half of it could be used and through the other half rats the size of well-fed cats would unexpectedly push up the lid and jump out. At least Susana Walton's cooking helped to make this diabolic ménage more endurable, for the culinary art was a revered tradition in the Gil family, and Susana's grandmother, the author of a fine recipe book, had taught all her twelve sons how to prepare first-class meals. In continuing discomfort, plagued but undefeated by the twanging springs and the pantomimic rats, the indomitable Susana, perched on a seat taken from the back of a 1923 Lancia car found in the garage, sat doing needlework by the dim light of an oil lamp.

After what, many years later, she described to me as 'two dreadful winters' in this most unconventional of convents, she and her husband moved into an abandoned cellar owned by the caretaker: a man whom they nicknamed with affectionate humour 'Don Pasquale', and the composer settled down to continue work on his romantic opera *Troilus and Cressida*. They remained in the cellar for eight years, during which Susana Walton searched the island for a suitable residence to serve as their future home, and in 1956 she discovered what, after they had purchased it, was to become a Garden of Eden: a plot of volcanic earth unexpectedly rich in humus, but uncultivated, which slithered down a craggy hillside into a valley. Here, over a period of time, they built, first of all, what Lady Walton described as 'a reef of tiny villas', flanking the bottom of the garden and providing not only a protective barrier against anticipated foreign tourists but also a source of income in summer lets (rents). They camped in the villas while they painstakingly designed the house, planning every detail, from the installation of an eighteenth-century wooden fireplace to the exotic kitchen tiles. When the house was finished, they had it painted and stoned in a charming natural grey that blended miraculously with its backdrop, so that, clamped to the side of the cliff, it clung there as unobtrusively as a martin's nest.

The Italians love to adorn the roofs and walls of their villas with bright, often garish colours, and the self-effacing anonymity of this new dwelling must have seemed like a gesture of defiant insularity, proud though they were of the English milord and his lady. Indeed, as time went on, not every Italian family in the vicinity looked approvingly at the Waltons, whose efforts to transform a barren hillside into a place of beauty and order provoked, through a misunderstanding, not only a flare-up of hostility but the possibility of court litigation. Petty lawsuits are almost a popular sport in Italy, and many property-owners practise it with the healthy ebullience of a British football team heading for a cup final. The discordant bleating of goats tethered in an adjacent pasture, the asthmatic death-rattle of a vintage car disturbing the peace, a slight reduction in the daily ration of sunlight caused by an overhanging tree in the next garden—with small grievances like these, the scales of justice are filled to overflowing.

Accordingly, when Susana Walton converted that bleak, neglected patch of land into what Colin Graham (Artistic Director of the London Coliseum and a close friend of the composer right up to his death) has described as 'an earthly paradise', carefully raking, enriching, cultivating and irrigating the soil, she aroused some degree of envy, or resentment, in the breasts of the peasant farmers who lived on adjacent property. It was clear to them that the Waltons, with a disregard of human rights, were cutting off, or drastically reducing, their neighbours' water supply by a system of diversion. The indignant farmers thereupon swore a complaint to the Ischia *polizia*, and such was the response of the official dealing with it that the possibility of one or both of the Waltons being arrested could not be discounted. Happily, the complaint was carefully investigated, and to the chagrin of the informants it transpired, firstly, that the hut on the Walton estate regarded as the basis of the grievance contained nothing more sinister than two mechanical water-softeners and, secondly, that what passed through them was merely water already coursing down the hillside, without in any way being diverted from its natural channel. The case collapsed like a squeezed puffball. Annoyed and frustrated, the informants went to a highway flanking the Walton land and retaliated by turning off the official mains water supply. Fortunately, the boiling lava of suspicion and resentment rapidly cooled down. Not only Susana but also the composer was accepted as a good neighbour, with outstanding qualities of sincerity and friendliness, just as Walton's music, once regarded as prickly and idiosyncratic, has charmed his critics into a warm, if slightly grudging admiration.

Despite the inevitable worries and setbacks accruing from the process of settling into a new home, Walton applied himself diligently to the composition of his opera *Troilus and Cressida*, a project which will be fully discussed in the next chapter. Prior to his marriage he had been working on a Sonata for Violin and Piano, a composition which owed its birth to the fact that, while travelling in a train in Switzerland, he met Yehudi Menuhin's wife Diana and persuaded her to commission the sonata for 2,000 Swiss francs.[16] He was under great financial and emotional strain at the time and, with Alice Wimborne in a nursing home at Lausanne, suffering from cancer, he desperately needed the money. After her death and his own marriage, he returned to London and completed the sonata, which was first performed at a Zurich concert on 30 September 1949 by Yehudi Menuhin, the dedicatee, and Louis Kentner. The first British performance, at the Theatre Royal, Drury Lane, on 5 February 1950, drew appreciative comments from the critics.

Still concentrating on small-scale works, Walton, soon afterwards, wrote his *Two Pieces for Violin and Piano*, which he dedicated to Larry and Vivien Olivier; but no record can be found of where the première was given, or by whom. He then composed, probably at the request of Boris Kochno, a *Galop Finale* for a ballet devised by John Taras called *Devoirs de Vacances*, which, with designs by Cecil Beaton, was staged at the Théâtre des Champs-Elysées in Paris on 8 November 1949. Richard Buckle, the well-known critic, described the costumes of the ballet—a mild and gentle *divertissement* to Walton's own *Music for Children*—as 'bright and pretty', with 'gentle music', but thought that the production would have been much better 'if William Walton's specially written finale (ie, the *Galop Finale*) had not arrived, unorchestrated, at the last moment, too late to be used'.[17]

1951 was not only Festival of Britain Year but a particularly happy one for Walton, since it opened on 1 January with an announcement in the Prime Minister's List of New Year Honours that William Turner Walton, composer, had been made a Knight Bachelor.[18] Shortly after receiving the accolade, Sir William wrote to his father-in-law. 'I should never have accepted the knighthood,' he said, 'only I wanted to make Sue a lady.' Señor Gil was not amused. He replied at once, angrily pointing out that his daughter was a lady long before William Walton met her![19] As regards the Festival, a number of leading composers, including Walton, were asked to compose suitable new works to celebrate the event, but as his opera was making 'tolerable progress', he declined to become involved. Walton did, however, assist in preparing the definitive version of his *Façade Entertainment* for publication on 26 July 1951 by the Oxford University Press. He was made a member of the Swedish Academy of Music early in 1952, but, instead of travelling to Stockholm to receive the honour, he continued to work assiduously at his opera.

In February 1952 the whole of Britain and her dependencies mourned the death of that man of high ideals and indomitable courage King George VI, and preparations were made for the crowning as Queen Regnant of his daughter Elizabeth, the second of that name to ascend, and bring a special lustre to, the English throne. John Denison, then Music Director of the Arts Council of Great Britain, was responsible for inviting certain composers to write music either for the actual Coronation in Westminster Abbey or for the celebrations that would accompany this great event. He wrote to Walton, in Italy, on 29 October 1952,[20] asking him to participate in a project involving several composers. He explained that the idea for the project sprang from the Oriana collection of madrigals and called for a number of *a capella* pieces to be set to appropriate texts from living poets. Each composer would be required to write one piece. Denison enclosed some notes for guidance and stated that the 'collection', to be edited by Dr Edmund Rubbra, might be entitled *A Garland for the Queen* or *An Oriana Garland*. He remarked that the Arts Council were willing to pay Sir William a fee of £50 and hoped that the completed work would be heard at a special concert in the Royal Festival Hall on the eve of the Coronation, 1 June 1953. Would he, Walton, accept a commission of this kind?

Seemingly he would not! One senses a note of acerbity in the postcard reply that Walton sent: 'You can hardly expect me to say "Yes" when all my best sides are verboten—besides I don't want to be accused of making a corner in the Coronation music.'[21]

Unscathed by the broadside, but much wiser as to what great composers may and may not be asked to undertake, the Arts Council, in a letter from Mr W. E. Williams on 31 October 1952[22] put a new proposal to Alan Frank at the Oxford University Press. He promised to discuss the contents with Sir William. The suggestion was that the Arts Council should commission Walton, for a fee of £50, to write a new march on the occasion of the Coronation of Her Majesty Queen Elizabeth II. The work must be ready in time for performance at the Coronation Ceremony on 2 June in Westminster Abbey if required for that purpose by the authorities concerned. The first public performance would be given on 7 June 1953 in the Royal Festival Hall by the London Symphony Orchestra under Sir John Barbirolli, at the first concert of the Royal Philharmonic Society's special Coronation series. No release of any recording, and no broadcast, could be permitted before this performance.

Walton, who had written the splendid *Crown Imperial* march for the Coronation of King George VI and Queen Elizabeth, found the new proposal much more to his liking, and by 28 November he had agreed to compose a Coronation March to be entitled *Orb and Sceptre*. It was completed in mid-January 1953, and after Oxford University Press had sent the full score to the Arts Council for perusal, Alan Frank wrote to John Denison to say that Walton ardently wished to dedicate his Coronation March to the Queen—could appropriate action be taken to implement this desire? In his reply,[23] Denison quoted some helpful but inconclusive comments by her Assistant Private Secretary, who first of all pointed out that the Sovereign accepted such dedications only very rarely, permission being granted during the fifteen years of the previous reign in only four instances, one of these being the *Musica Britannica*. He agreed, however, that the Queen should be formally asked, and promised to get the Chairman of the Arts Council to submit the necessary request. It says much for Walton's lofty status and integrity that Her Majesty did authorize the dedication in April, and the presentation copy bearing his signature on the page recording this act of homage was duly prepared. The march, which formed part of the programme music preceding the actual ceremony, was performed for the first time in Westminster Abbey on Coronation Day, 2 June. On the 7th of the month, in the Royal Festival Hall, the London Symphony Orchestra, under Sir John Barbirolli, gave *Orb and Sceptre* its first public hearing, after which *The Times* reported: 'It makes a joyful noise in the March proper, and it is in the trio that Majesty comes to the fore with a sweeping diatonic tune in C Major, reminiscent of Parry as well as Elgar.'[24]

Sir William McKie, the Abbey Organist and Director of Music for the Coronation Service, who worked in consultation with the Master of the Queen's Musick and an advisory panel of distinguished musicians, met Walton on 16 September 1952 and managed to persuade him to compose a new *Te Deum* for use in the Abbey should it be required. The phrase 'should it be required' was not in any way demeaning but simply meant that any scheme of Coronation Music proposed by Sir William McKie had to be submitted for approval, firstly to the Archbishop of Canterbury and secondly, by him, to the Queen. In the words of the Director of Music: 'Sir William received the proposal very kindly and was most co-operative. I was most impressed by the thoroughness of the briefing which he asked for. He came down to the Abbey, asked for most precise information about the size and composition of the choir and the orchestra and how they were to be placed. He also wanted to know what would be happening in the ceremonial just before the *Te Deum* was to be sung, and what music would precede the *Te Deum*.'[25]

Walton was, indeed, thorough, as various letters which he sent to Sir William McKie confirm. He discussed the ideal length for the piece and suggested a duration of six to eight minutes. Commenting on a 'shortened version' of the text, he asked if it would not be better to finish with 'And we worship thy name: ever world without end', perhaps adding an 'Amen'. Walton enquired as to the numerical strength of the Queen's Trumpeters, as he might want to use them for an added effect; but what did the Director of Music think about that? 'It might be overstaffing too much!'[26]

In one letter[27] Sir William asked the Director of Music to intercede with the Archbishop to allow him to set the whole of the *Te Deum*, since in his opinion a suggested cut would result in 'a most frustrated and truncated ending', as well as making the short setting, about 5½ minutes in duration, slightly undignified. Unusually for him—almost invariably taciturn and non-committal about his own work—he expressed the view that his *Coronation Te Deum* was 'going to be rather splendid'. Walton wrote five days later, acknowledging the news that the Archbishop had no objection to his 'having done the "Te Deum" complete', and making a characteristic plea for 'a harmonisation of the National Anthem without the flattened seventh'.

Sir William McKie received the completed work with joy: 'I put the *Te*

*Deum* into rehearsal at once. Its first actual performance took place in the Abbey Song School, with Sir William conducting the Abbey Choir and myself at the piano. Sir William was most helpful (and most successful) in showing us exactly what he wanted. He also came later to one or two of the final rehearsals in the Abbey (ie, 26th May 1953) and again was most helpful in his comments and suggestions. Both singers and orchestra were delighted with the work.'[28]

At McKie's suggestion, the Earl Marshal of England (the Duke of Norfolk), acting on behalf of the Queen, invited Walton and his wife to attend the Coronation Service, and they gladly consented. After the first performance the critic of *The Times* wrote; 'This is a splendid piece of ceremonial music which made use of all the Abbey's resources, the trumpeters, the organ, the orchestra and the choir in a grand antiphony.'[29] While he and his wife were in England for the Coronation and its attendant celebrations, Walton, on 20 May, was presented with an honorary Doctor of Music degree by Manchester University.

A month after his music had helped to glorify the crowning of Queen Elizabeth II, the first performance of Britten's new opera *Gloriana*, commissioned by the Arts Council, was given on 8 June in a gala concert at the Royal Opera House, Covent Garden. At the beginning and end of the concert the National Anthem was played in a special arrangement by Walton. It has been said that he disliked and subsequently disowned his arrangement, but this is not true, although he must have found the first performance, before the curtain rose on *Gloriana*, a disturbing experience. I am indebted to Lady Walton for a factual account of what happened. Both the Queen and the Queen Mother had come to the Opera House for this notable event, and a restless, obviously excited audience sat in the auditorium, ready to stand as the illustrious visitors entered the Royal Box. Then the familiar drum-roll sounded as the conductor John Pritchard led the orchestra with a flourish of his baton into the noble strains of the National Anthem and the audience rose with one accord in respectful homage. Alas, the Queen and the Queen Mother were at that moment standing in a corridor some distance away, chatting to a distinguished person, and the box remained embarrassingly empty. The conductor, apprised of his mistake and probably feeling like a shipyard worker who has accidentally launched a new battleship before the appointed day, abruptly halted the orchestra and, after a rather bewildered pause, the loyal, upstanding citizens sat down; whereupon, with disconcerting suddenness, the two royal ladies came into view, the orchestra hastily set off again, and the audience, now settled comfortably in their seats and taken unawares, had to shoot up again with mingled speed and disarray. John Pritchard must have been considerably rattled by this contretemps, which resulted in a letter of apology being sent to the Palace. He seems to have had a special and enduring love-relationship with the National Anthem and while principal conductor of the Royal Liverpool Philharmonic Orchestra took pleasure in serving up a succession of different arrangements, like a proud chef producing one culinary delight after another. What happened at the Royal Opera House was the kind of poltergeistic mishap which can afflict the most reliable and fastidious of conductors—a description which certainly fits Sir John, as we are now privileged to call him.

It was during Coronation Year that Walton collaborated with other composers in creating a piece for string orchestra, *Variations on Sellinger's Round*, which was performed on 20 June 1953 at a concert organised as part of the 6th Aldeburgh Festival. He and his wife toured America in August that year, and the pressures upon him, partly resulting from his work on the opera *Troilus and Cressida*, which began in 1947, must have been considerable. The idea for the composition of the *Variations* arose at a programme-planning conference for the 1953 Aldeburgh Festival attended by Benjamin Britten, Peter Pears and Imogen Holst, and, with Britten himself committed to making a contribution, invitations were sent to Arthur Oldham, Michael Tippett, Lennox Berkeley, Humphrey Searle and Sir William Walton.[30] It proved to be a brilliant, compelling work, and at the concert in Aldeburgh Parish Church members of the audience, who had the names of the composers involved on printed programmes, were, at Walton's suggestion, challenged to record their opinions as to who had written the variations in the sequence of performance. Those who guessed correctly would be given free seats at the Festival of 1954. Imogen Holst thinks that no one succeeded in doing so.[31] The names of the composers ran in the following order: Arthur Oldham, Michael Tippett, Lennox Berkeley, Benjamin Britten, Humphrey Searle and Sir William Walton.

# 9

# Operatic Rapture from the Convent

The slow and painful genesis of Walton's only full-length opera, *Troilus and Cressida*, which, after a lengthy hiatus, progressed a little further when he settled on Ischia after his marriage to Susana, spread itself over a total period of 8½ years. I have deemed it sensible, therefore, to deal chronologically with the composition of this important work as a complete creative process, rather than as a piecemeal entity broken up by the production of smaller, more inconsequential works. The real impetus for the opera seems to have been activated in his temporary abode, the converted Convent of San Francesco, during those early, blissful days on Ischia, and perhaps some of the romantic bloom and refulgence of the music is a reflection of the happiness he experienced at that time.

Walton had for many years wanted to write a work of this kind, and the initial stimulus or provocation came in 1945 with the production at Sadler's Wells of Benjamin Britten's *Peter Grimes*, whose clouds of glory seemed overnight to illuminate the whole dismal landscape of British opera. The seeds of his ambition fructified when, in a letter from Victor Hely-Hutchinson, the BBC commissioned him to compose an opera for broadcasting, subsequently transferring it to the Royal Opera House. According to Gillian Widdicombe[1] it was Walton's dear friend Alice Wimborne who persuaded Christopher Hassall to write the libretto, helping the poet in his painstaking search for a subject that would suit the composer's music. Seemingly his choice of *Troilus and Cressida* delighted her. She had a burning admiration for Hassall, a man of many rare gifts. A poet, the author of two successful biographies, an actor, a competent musician, he had an inquiring mind and a generous spirit, as well as a beautiful speaking voice which many concert-goers may recall with pleasure from his performance as the orator in Bliss's *Morning Heroes*.

There is some evidence that Lady Wimborne, shortly before her death, did, in fact, bring Walton and Hassall together, one positive indication being a letter[2] which she wrote to the poet on 7 June 1947, inviting him to meet her for luncheon in Claridge's and saying, 'We are going to have a grand review of all the librettos this week-end.' Against this is the fact that, soon after receiving the BBC's request, Walton himself wrote to Cecil Gray in these words: 'I've forgotten whether I told you that the BBC had commissioned me to write an opera (*not* specifically for "broadcasting") *and recommended Christopher Hassall* whom you may know of to go into the question of the libretto. And I believe that we have at last hit on one in "Troilus and Cressida"—not founded on Shakespeare, but on Chaucer, Henryson and Boccaccio.' [3] (The italics are mine.)

The truth of the matter is probably of no great importance, and certainly Lady Wimborne prodded both Walton and Hassall into undertaking such a formidable task. After the luncheon at Claridge's she wrote to Hassall, saying, 'I believe that you should not be perplexed or worried by the unbouncing ball; and equally that he, Walton, should think you quite unmoved by procrastination! So that he doesn't fear being, as it were, pushed into anything because a decision is expected of him. . . . The difficulty is to find the perfect subject. Many that would suit his music have other drawbacks — as a case in point, Byron.'[4] It was after receiving this letter that Hassall suggested *Troilus and Cressida*, and Chaucer's long poem, which was taken from Boccaccio's *Il Filistrato* and has no basis in classical antiquity, seemed to him — and Lady Wimborne — to be the best subject for the libretto.

Collaboration between Walton, in Ischia, and Hassall, in Highgate Village, London, was not easy and had to be charted through a continuous spate of letters. 'I kept a pile of envelopes ready stamped and addressed for prompt reply,' remarked the poet, 'and our rather extraordinary correspondence over a long period would fill, I should imagine, several volumes.'[5] He discussed with Walton such matters as precise motives or moods at particular points in the libretto and, since the stanzas ranged from measured rhyme to free verse, the appropriate shape or style of the utterance.

> For Cressida's free-verse monologues in Acts 1 and 3 [said Hassall], I made a careful study of the technique in Matthew Arnold's *The Strayed Reveller*. The result was very different, but Arnold's conception of the classical world, as also shown in his *Myceninus*, has always been congenial to me and must have been helpful in my effort to lift Chaucer's story out of medieval England into a convention that at least suggested the pre-classical world of Troy. A librettist is his composer's literary limb: and it is not to disclaim any detail of the libretto, but rather to acknowledge the great benefit of a close collaboration, when I say that in the last analysis a composer of opera is his own dramatist.[6]

An early draft of Hassall's libretto was sent to Ernest Newman, the distinguished music critic, who found many of his lines much too poetical. 'There are far too many long words for music,' he remarked.[7] Knowing that human sensibilities are sharpened and intensified under the influence of music, he pointed out that, in consequence, any infusion of the commonplace may introduce an element of grotesque humour. 'I fancy there would be a touch of the comic, for the ordinary spectator, in the episode the morning after, with Troilus lying, half-dressed on top of the bed-clothes, while Cressida leans out of the window and sings.'

Walton, aware that Hassall had written lyrics for Ivor Novello and had not previously created an operatic libretto, seems to have viewed their collaboration with growing unease. 'I'm quite unable to cope with "Child of the grey sea wave",' he wrote. 'It evokes the worst type of music from me — real neo-Novelloisms, which I fear cannot be tolerated on the operatic stage.'[8] The poet, deeply hurt by this remark, felt even worse when, coincidentally, Ivor Novello died a month later. During an interview when the opera was revived in 1976, the composer stated bluntly: 'If Hassall had been alive, I would not have been allowed to re-write *Troilus*. Every time I took out a word or note there was a row. I think his style had been ruined by Ivor Novello. He didn't take it at all well when I suggested that Ivor's influence should be subdued. I remember I put "I.N." all over his libretto. That didn't please him at all.'[9]

Difficulties between composer and librettist are not unusual, as is made clear by published accounts of the troubled relationship between Puccini and Giocoso during the creation of *Tosca*, to mention only one famous collaboration. Ernest Newman, who had considered many of Hassall's words not suitable for a musical setting, with a slightly bookish and therefore comic aspect, seems finally to have capitulated, since he rather ludicrously described the finished libretto as 'the best poetic opera text since Hofmannsthal'.[10] The composer, however, remained a little disenchanted and, reiterating his chief grievance, told Alec Robertson shortly before the première that he thought some of the music would be called 'Ivor Novello-ish!'

As with other major works of Walton, including the First Symphony, the gestation of *Troilus and Cressida* was beset by minor difficulties, major problems and frustrating delays. Some of the problems related to Act III, a particularly tantalizing one being the big sextet 'Troy false of heart'; but W. H. Auden, at that time a neighbour of Walton's on Ischia, gave very helpful advice. Indeed, the draft of a new version of the words of the sextet has been found among the poet's posthumous papers. It had originally been hoped that the composition of the opera would be completed within two years. John Lowe of the BBC wrote to Walton in March 1947 referring to 'the new opera which you hope to write during the coming eighteen months' and expressing the hope that plans could be made for 'the first studio performance for the Third Programme',[11] but not until January 1948, almost a year later, did the Press announce that, 'The BBC has commissioned Dr William Walton to write an opera.'[12] Walton himself informed Stanford Robinson (Head of BBC Opera) in March 1949 that 'the opera position is a little brighter. At last Christopher and I, with the help of the producer, Otto Erhart, have really got the libretto into shape, so it only now needs the music. The idea at the moment is to get it ready for the 1951 Exhibition.'[13] Incidentally, it was not only Erhart who assisted him but also Franz Reizenstein.

After taking up permanent residence on Ischia at the end of 1949, the composer started work not on the political, war-infested themes of Act I but on the radiantly passionate music of Act II, with its heart-throbbing love passages. Progress was painfully slow, however, as a letter which he sent in March 1950 to Steuart Wilson, Head of Music at the BBC, clearly indicates: 'On the whole I'm not keen about a concert performance of Troilus during 1951. For one thing I don't think it would stand the cold hard light of a concert performance, and it may, with luck, just get away with it on the stage. . . . I've been fairly stuck for the last fortnight and I shall be pleased if I get it finished in sketch by this time next year. I aim for a Cov. Gar. performance about June 52.'[14]

In August 1951 *The Times* announced that, 'The opera will be performed at the Royal Opera House, Covent Garden next year. It will be produced by Sir Laurence Olivier, with scenery painted by Mr Henry Moore.'[15] In fact, the great artist and sculptor, whose remarkable drawings of London air-raid-shelter scenes in World War II highlighted his flair for the graphic yet symbolic portrayal of life, had been invited to design the scenery and costumes for a Covent Garden production of *The Ring*, but after pondering for a lengthy period on the advisability of carrying out theatre work of this kind, he felt that he must decline,[16] a difficult decision, since he was a close friend of Walton. The composer, in January 1953, told Angus Morrison that, 'The opera, after some progress, came to an enforced standstill while I wrote a Te Deum for the Coronation, rather splendid, and a Coronation March, neither better nor worse than the last and I hope a bread-winner.'[17] Whatever the delays, problems or setbacks that followed the over-optimistic reports of a firm, or anticipated, date for the première, the manuscript score of *Troilus and Cressida* is dated 13 September 1954 and bears the simple dedication 'To my wife.'

Walton had not only wanted Elisabeth Schwarzkopf to take the part of Cressida but had actually composed it specially for her, in the confident expectation that she would sing it on the first night. As to why she declined to do so, I am obliged to her husband, Walter Legge, for clarification.[18] One reason was that she always disliked singing in English because of the impure vowels which she, a scrupulous perfectionist in the matter of diction, had to contend with. Schwarzkopf also feared that her slight German accent might invoke hostile criticism from diehard purists. Additionally, having carefully read the libretto, she found little to admire in either the story-line or the characters, and, as if all this was not sufficient to justify rejection of the part, she could not accustom herself to Walton's melodic line, however hard she tried. One must respect this magnificent and much-loved singer for her honesty and integrity, as Walton undoubtedly did.

In the event it was Magda Lazlo, a Hungarian soprano, who, at the première, sang the part of Chaucer's ill-fated heroine. Hugh Casson, with David Gentleman, Sheila Miller, Jocelyn Herbert and Clement Glock as collaborators, designed the sets for Walton's opera. Gentleman created a noble painting of a goddess for the Temple Wall in Act I, and Glock, the Chief Scene Painter at Covent Garden (who died shortly afterwards) reproduced it full-scale, cleverly 'fading' the colours to convey a realistic semblance of antiquity. Miss Miller, an ex-RCA student, was responsible for the very tasteful curtain used in the 'penthouse' of Act II, and Malcolm Pride for designing and executing the splendid costumes. According to Casson, the composer was always merry and polite but preserved a poker-faced attitude towards the designs.[19]

The first performance of *Troilus and Cressida* took place at the Royal Opera House, Covent Garden, on 3 December 1954, and, this being Walton's first opera, patrons undoubtedly looked forward to a gala occasion, to the opulence, the picturesque beauty of sound and imagery, and the romantic panache that, since the war, had seldom appeared in English opera. Rehearsals began in November, with Walton present at all the orchestral sessions, helping Sargent whenever he could; but as the première drew near, the public heard rumours of difficulties, bitter words and hard feelings at rehearsal.[20] Some of the rumours contained more than a grain of truth. Sir Malcolm Sargent, chosen to conduct *Troilus and Cressida*, rattled many of the singers by declining to beat some of their unaccompanied passages. 'Without the beat it's terribly difficult,' they would complain, whereupon Sargent, with his special kind of impenetrable blandness, would reply that a beat was unnecessary. He would remind them that these bars were silent for the orchestra—why should the singers worry! When the dissidents pointed out that, silent or not, the players had to follow the ongoing rhythm, which sometimes had a change of metre on the way, he switched to a barely concealed irritation and embarrassment.

Sargent, doubtless activated by his own burning zeal for perfection, also sought, in a courteous but persistent way, to alter Walton's scoring, with a view to making it 'safer'. He suggested, for example, that, acoustically, some intrumental or other combination might be precarious in the theatre, that gaps between the rhythmic stresses of chorus and orchestra produced seeming discrepancies which for some listeners might imply that the singers were coming in off beat. Sargent also pounced on a passage in the score (deleted on revision) where a bass-flute was doubled by a clarinet, denouncing it as dangerous. 'The clarinet won't come in on the beat—let's have it out,' he argued. Walton, obviously not placated by Sargent's rostrum solicitude, insisted on retaining the clarinet.

Although the increasingly myopic conductor had a Bertie Wooster eye-glass in a tortoise-shell frame, he seldom used it and also refused to wear spectacles. Singers and orchestra, watching him at rehearsal peering short-sightedly at the notes in a hardly legible, not yet engraved conducting score, felt uneasy and discouraged. Despite this and other difficulties, including the acrimonious atmosphere at rehearsals, the company familiarized itself with, and finally mastered, the new opera.

The first night proved to be a dazzling event, with more fashionable and important people in the opera house than regular patrons could recall. Many stayed behind after the performance for what was reputed to be the biggest first-night party ever held there. According to *The Times* next morning, Sir Malcolm 'was vigilant, served the singers with tact and elicited from the orchestra that stringency which is one of the marks of Walton's orchestral writing'.[21] Those on the stage the previous evening might not have wholly agreed, since, during the performance, they could see the myopic, though indomitable maestro counting the bars to himself, mouthing, 'one, two three, four', etc—a sight as disturbing to a cast as the spectacle of a doctor, about to undertake surgery and studying a first-aid handbook, might be to a patient on the point of being anaesthetized. Geraint Evans, then a singer preparing to soar into the starry operatic firmament, had the small part of Antenor, Captain of the Trojan Spears. In the first act, during a heated encounter with the High Priest, who wants to parley with the Greeks, he had to sing an impetuous 'Never! Never!' For this entry Sargent imperiously flung out his left arm, like a traffic policeman urging a dawdling motorist to hurry along. Unfortunately he volleyed his cue a bar too soon, and poor Geraint Evans, riveted to the stage in a kind of shocked disbelief, faced his first real crisis—should he respond or resist what he knew to be a palpable error? He made the right decision and came in a bar later, as the composer intended him to do. The première could hardly be classed as a musical triumph: the Waltonians damned it as 'inaccurate' and over the succeeding years, in various revivals, referred to *Troilus and Cressida* as 'this unfortunate opera'.

At least the *Manchester Guardian* greeted the new opera with unstinted praise: 'This fine opera, a grand opera in the true sense, is a work of splendid craftsmanship; it is large, with long, soaring vocal lines. The music is effective, dramatically: it's seriously beautiful and it's rigorous in a way characteristic of a composer who always has something to say.'[22] At the Italian première, at La Scala, Milan, on 12 January 1956, a fusillade of boos and hisses was fired at the opera, but since the performance was reputedly mediocre, this might well have been the reason.

It must have delighted the countless admirers of the great, almost legendary Schwarzkopf that, after being coached by Herbert von Karajan, she sang the role of Cressida in an EMI recording of excerpts from the opera made in 1955 by the Philharmonia Orchestra, with Walton conducting and Richard Lewis as Troilus. Her decision not to play Cressida on the stage, disappointing though it must have been to the composer, never once clouded the warm friendship which she and her husband had shared with him for so long. It began in 1937, at the time when Walton's cantata *In Honour of the City of London* received its first performance in the Leeds Trienniel Festival, and it remained steadfast over the ensuing years.

Walter Legge, an Englishman by birth and a European by choice, was a supremely gifted musician, a conductor with particular insight into twentieth-century music, and possibly the greatest classical producer of gramophone records the world has ever known. Gerald Moore once described him as 'a Diaghilev where music is concerned'.[23] He founded the Philharmonia Orchestra and, with the subsequent help of Herbert von Karajan, raised it to prestigious heights of excellence. Legge had a marvellous flair for spotting new talent and although, in ruthlessly spurning all but the first-rate, he trod heavily on many toes, he also showed immense kindness and vision in promoting the careers of countless young musicians. This remarkable man, who supervised more than 3,500 recordings of separate works, large and small, not only championed Walton's music, extolling its virtues to famous and important people, but in many discussions and arguments he also shared with the composer his own rich storehouse of knowledge and experience. His death on 22 March 1979 inspired an almost unprecedented, often deeply moving, series of tributes.

Dr Schwarzkopf told me that she always 'stood in awe of Sir William', adding with an amused chuckle, 'I was just a little scared of him, despite our friendship.' When I remarked that I found it intriguing that she, one of the world's greatest singers, should have felt like that, she replied, with obvious astonishment, 'But my dear, he was a major composer—a wonderful man!—and he wrote *beautifully* for the voice; it was nearly always so marvellously singable!'

Walton found a challenging as well as rewarding creative outlet in film music and managed, despite the notorious frustrations and tensions of this highly specialized art, to keep a sense of humour, as exemplified by his famous, light-hearted 'ham, lamb and strawberry jam' instruction on the score of *Richard III: con prosciuto, agnello e confitura di fragole.* He wrote this music for the film which Sir Laurence Olivier, at the invitation of Sir Alexander Korda, produced and directed at Shepperton Studios in 1955, and which had its first public viewing at the Leicester Square Theatre, London, on 13 December that year. The music was played by the Royal Philharmonic Orchestra, under Muir Mathieson, who, with Walton's approval, subsequently prepared from it a suite prefaced by the Prelude depicting the Coronation of Edward IV with which the film opened. It was early in 1954, when Olivier visited him on Ischia, that Walton first had any real knowledge of what the commission entailed; but he was firmly instructed not to write any of the score until February and March 1955, when the recording would be made at Shepperton Studios—and, in consequence, the composer was placed under very considerable pressure. Nine years later he remarked in a *Sunday Times* interview:

> I did learn some facility with film music, but hated writing it until I came to work with Larry Olivier. The thing about film music is that it needn't necessarily be good or bad, only it must fit. They all say the great characteristic is that it shouldn't be heard. . . . There was one patch in *Richard III* that I just couldn't face—only some two minutes. Well, I filled it in somehow. Larry Olivier was furious. 'You really have played it down this time,' he said. But the engineers said that it was just what was wanted.[24]

Also in 1955, doubtless swept along by the fondness for ceremonial music already manifest in the score for *Richard III*, the composer made full orchestral arrangements of 'The Star-Spangled Banner' and 'God Save the Queen', intended for Herbert von Karajan and the Philharmonia Orchestra to use on their United States tour in October that year. In June the degree of Doctor of Music was conferred on him by Cambridge University, and in November he received a similar honour from the University of London.

November also saw the following report appear in *The Times*: 'It is understood that Sir William Walton is at work on a cello concerto, and that he has been invited to compose a 2nd symphony for Liverpool,'[25] but at that time Walton had, in fact, received a more urgent commission from Johannesburg, the largest city of South Africa and centre of the world's gold-mining industry. The city wished, through its Festival Committee, to celebrate its seventieth anniversary, and he responded with a *Johannesburg Festival Overture*, which had its première in the City Hall there on 25 September 1956, when Sir Malcolm Sargent conducted the South African Broadcasting Corporation Symphony Orchestra. The approaches to the City Hall were packed with motor cars for this prestigious event, and the huge demand for seats necessitated some people being relegated to the organ steps at the back of the platform. Audiences at the City Hall have nearly always consisted of happy, demonstrative people who have communicated their sense of enjoyment to others. It seems that, a few years before Sargent's concert, some visiting players, with a fustian, starched-collar outlook, described Johannesburg as 'a place where classical music, on the rare occasion when it was performed, had to compete with the crackle of chocolate wrappings, the crunch of ice-cream wafers and monkey nuts, the striking of matches by chain smokers and assorted coughs and groans and snores'. Sargent, moved and inspired by his own contacts with City Hall patrons, swept this harsh stricture into oblivion when, speaking on the radio, he told Johannesburgers: 'You probably do not realise that you are a charming people. A stranger feels he is welcome and and appreciated here and forgiven his differences of behaviour and speech . . . that is not always so, even in our Commonwealth of Nations.'[26]

As regards the music, one Johannesburg journal, *Forward*, damned it obliquely by asking, 'Why do we persist in rushing for "imports" when we should be giving home talent a chance?' and added pungently, 'A local composer would have written something more indigenous . . . at half Walton's fee.'[27] According to the *Rand Daily Mail*, however, 'Good tunes made the strings sing, vivid scoring gave scope to the orchestra to use its forces in deployment and in close formation; vigorous rhythms (based on a 2-4 beat) made the air gay.' The critic did claim that 'there was little substance' but declared that his paramount inpression on a first hearing was of 'an attractive, animated piece of festive intent'.[28]

The same critic also referred to a hint of African themes in the music: 'With intent listening one might detect certain allusions, and the use of percussive wood strengthened the sense of recognition.' David Rycroft, writing in the *British Institute of Recorded Sound Bulletin*, made some interesting comments about these African melodies: 'On listening recently to the first broadcast performance in England of Sir William Walton's 'Johannesburg Festival Overture,' it was interesting to detect frequent snatches of indigenous African thematic material and some effective polyrhythm . . . Congo guitarist Mwenda Jean Bosco is clearly responsible for one of the subsidiary themes. It appears that, upon agreeing to compose this overture, the composer was supplied with a representative selection of recordings of African music issued by the African Music Society.'[29]

Frederick Ashton, at one time, had fond hopes of choreographing *Macbeth* as a full-scale ballet with music by Walton, and accordingly he prepared a detailed scenario with 'minutage' for the composer. Dame Ninette de Valois felt so confident about the project that at the end of the 1954–5 Sadler's Wells season she appeared in front of the curtain to announce the production of an unnamed three-act ballet by Ashton and Walton the following year. Alas, after first abridging the concept to a lengthy single act, then considering *The Tempest* as an alternative subject, he discarded both possibilities in favour of *Ondine*, which Margot Fonteyn, an important factor in the process of selection, much preferred. Walton was too busy to compose a score for *Ondine*,[30] which seems regrettable: the simplicity and directness of his own genius would have perfectly complemented that of Ashton who, after listening to a few bars of music while choreographing, 'would fling himself into some swoops and twists and dives, his movements just flowing out of the music, apparently spontaneously, then stop and say to the watching dancers "What did I do? Now you do it!" '[31] Walton suggested that the German composer Hans Werner Henze should write the *Ondine* music, instead.

Although disclaiming all ability to play a musical instrument with any real efficiency, Walton spent much of his creative life writing concertos. It was in 1956 that Gregor Piatigorsky commissioned him, through Ivor Newton, to compose a Cello Concerto. When the famous pianist asked him if he would accept the invitation, Sir William replied, 'I'm a professional composer. I'll write anything for anybody if he pays me.' A moment later came an afterthought in which his impishness, one of the qualities that audiences have learned to recognize in his music, came to the surface. 'I write much better when they pay me in dollars,' he said.[32]

Piatigorsky, born in 1903 at Ekateroslav in the Ukraine, Russia, grew up in a bleak hinterland of adversity. At the age of nine he was helping to support his family by playing the cello at the cinema in his home town, and at fourteen he was engaged by the Imperial Opera in Moscow. When the Revolution swept like a raging fire across Russia, he made several attempts to flee the country. It was not until 1921, when a band of smugglers escorted him to Poland, that he succeeded; but as they also stripped him of his clothes and money, he found himself destitute. Begging lifts from charitable car-drivers and stopping here and there to make a little money from casual work, Piatigorsky went to Berlin, where he earned a living playing at cafés and cinemas. He was lucky: the great pianist Artur Schnabel heard the young man coaxing magical sounds from his instrument and persuaded him to take part in the performance of a work by Schoenberg. This proved to be the turning-point in Piatigorsky's career. After winning a competition for the position of principal cellist in the Berlin Philharmonic Orchestra, he gained rapid fame, touring first the USA, then other countries, as a concert soloist or recitalist.

When Piatigorsky met Walton, after inviting him to write the Cello Concerto, he was deeply impressed.

> I have never [he told Ivor Newton] encountered such a rare combination of greatness and simplicity. A great composer like Walton needs no suggestions from me. The concerto should not be too long—twenty or thirty minutes. The orchestral *tuttis* can be grandiose enough, but while the cello is playing the orchestral accompaniment must be light. No orchestra really observes *pianissimo* markings; it is important for a composer to write so that the orchestra cannot help playing softly. The greatest problem in writing for the cello is to make it heard. And yet, there must be symphonic *tuttis*. The ending should be brilliant and the coda fairly long; all the existing concertos end abruptly, even the Dvorák. I can't tell you how much I am looking forward to a really good concerto by Walton. He must not hestitate to ask me anything.[33]

Sir William took the last sentence at its face value, and throughout the composition of the work there was a constant interchange of letters between himself and Piatigorsky. He wrote the concerto at his villa on the island of Ischia between February and October 1956. It was not a propitious time for such an enterprise, because the stalwarts of musical tradition were about to be challenged by the young avant-garde protagonists of a revolution whose banners flaunted the names of such composers as Webern, Schoenberg and Stravinsky. Seeking to change the stereotyped concert repertoire, they had little respect for the music of old favourites like Sibelius, Strauss, Vaughan Williams, Bax and, of course, Walton.

A graphic description of the resourceful process of composition came from Alan Frank:

> For months, using the small boat that plies between Ischia and Naples, wads of closely-covered manuscript paper had been passing between Walton and Piatigorsky, sometimes to the 'cellist's home in California, sometimes further afield to Japan where Piatigorsky was playing last autumn.
>
> Italian and Japanese postal authorities collaborated with efficiency, and customs officials with a commendable lack of inquisitiveness.
>
> All went well with this world-wide exchange of ideas until one day when Piatigorsky was changing planes in Chicago during the course of a journey. The entire manuscript, the only one in existence, mysteriously disappeared. A few days later, equally mysteriously, it turned up again. Apart from this minor crisis, the work of composition and checking went forward smoothly.[34]

Piatigorsky, to whom the Cello Concerto is dedicated, gave the first performance with the Boston Symphony Orchestra, under the direction of Charles Munch, on 25 January 1957.

Two projects involving Walton which failed to materialize concerned a work to be written specially for the Birmingham Symphony Orchestra and the music for a film of Shakespeare's great tragedy *Macbeth*. It was in 1957 that comments in the music Press indicated that Sir William's future commitments included an orchestral composition for the BSO and that the Feeney Trust might commission him to do it; but the proposal never progressed beyond the preliminary discussions. Sir Alexander Korda, in 1955, announced that he intended at some future date to make a film of *Macbeth*. He died a few months later. In 1958 his plans nearly fructified through the efforts of Sir Laurence Olivier, who invited Walton to provide the music towards the end of the year, when the production team hoped to have completed shooting the film. Unfortunately, Sir Laurence could not raise sufficient money for the enterprise, although he tried diligently for nine months, and reluctantly it had to be abandoned.

On 15 January 1957, while motoring along a road near Rome *en route* for London, the Waltons were involved in a serious accident when their car, driven by Lady Walton, crashed into a long, lorry-towed trailer. Both were rushed to hospital—Sir William with a cracked pelvis and extensive contusions, his wife with cuts to the head, a broken left wrist, a fractured right foot and rib injuries. Happily they made good recovery and, while ensconced in his hospital bed, Sir William heard the first London performance of his Cello Concerto, given by the BBC Symphony Orchestra, under Sir Malcolm Sargent, specially relayed by the Italian Broadcasting Corporation. A visitor heard his remark, 'Piatigorsky was magnificent!'

Although the Birmingham Orchestra project of 1957 came to nothing, Walton had received from the Cleveland Symphony Orchestra a commission for a composition to be performed by the orchestra under George Szell during its fortieth anniversary season of 1957–8. One of ten pieces commissioned to celebrate this event (the other composers were Alvin Etler, Paul Creston, Howard Hanson, Peter Mennis and Robert Moevs of America, Gottfried von Einem of Austria, Bohuslav Martinu of Czechoslovakia, Henri Dutilleux of France and Boris Blacher of Germany), it could not be of any great length, and accordingly Walton, starting work on the assignment at his home on Ischia, chose to create a fifteen-minute *Partita* in three movements. After its first performance on 30 January 1958, the *Cleveland Plain Dealer* described it as 'one of the best works by Sir William Walton heard here', adding, 'It is masterfully orchestrated and precise . . . filled with boisterous blasts of colour and sturdy, uninhibited tunes that suggest sly, good-humoured satire.'[35]

This appealing work was heard in Manchester at the end of April the same year, when the composer conducted a performance by the Hallé Orchestra in the Free Trade Hall. One of the viola players, Malcolm Tillis, has described the preparations for the première, and the event iself, in a published account of his life as an orchestral musician:

> And so, after weeks of painstaking preparation made more arduous by carelessly printed parts, a new work was ready to receive its first performance. Time and care had been lavished on it; the orchestra knew it backwards. The public was eager to hear it, as is usual with any new work from one of the world's leading composers.
>
> There was a good house in the evening. When Walton appeared he received a warm reception. He looked confident and conducted competently enough; but although no great heights were reached—he didn't pay much attention to his dynamic marks—everything went smoothly and the performance did ample justice to the composition. This contrasted violently with Beethoven conducting the first performance of his C minor Symphony exactly a hundred and fifty years before in Venice; there was a breakdown in one of the simplest passages and the composer was forced to stop the orchestra and start again.
>
> So yet another first performance had been given; another new work had been launched. It was well received by the audience and Walton was given a thrilling ovation at the end. But whether or not it will take its place in the standard repertoire remains to be seen.[36]

Walton was doubtless happy and relieved to have finished with the *Partita* and to have read the *Cleveland Plain Dealer*'s opinion of it as one of the best of his works heard in that city—he could now focus his attention on his Second Symphony, which the Royal Liverpool Philharmonic Society had commissioned in November 1955. Or could he? In fact, as often happens with a much-esteemed composer, more commissions came his way. The first of these was a *Fanfare for the Queen's Entrance at the opening of the Nato Parliamentary Conference*, held in Westminster Hall, London, on 5 June 1959.

There was also a mysterious *March* which he composed in 1958 for a series of one-hour films based on Sir Winston Churchill's *The History of the English Speaking Peoples*: mysterious because, although intended to be heard against the opening and closing titles, this very brief piece of music, commissioned by ABC Television and Harry Alan Towers Production Ltd, was recorded but apparently never used.

Another commission, which came this time from Peter Pears and Julian Bream in 1959, kept Walton busy; it consisted of a set of six songs entitled *Anon in Love*, the poems in the cycle having been chosen by Christopher Hassall from anonymous sixteenth-and seventeenth-century lyrics, with a guitar part edited by Bream, who, with Pears, gave the first performance in the thirteenth Aldeburgh Festival on 21 June 1960. Of this event *The Times* remarked: 'They must surely be universally welcomed. Fired by the artistry and virtuosity of these two musicians, Walton has distilled the fruits of his experience into a potent and concentrated musical utterance, sometimes direct and sometimes curiously subtle. *Anon in Love* had a brilliant première, and will be heard everywhere with delight.'[37] The cycle was arranged for tenor and orchestra in 1971, and the first performance of the new version—part of a festival of music-making—took place on 21 June of that year at the Mansion House, London.

In 1959 Walton flung his energies and his inspiration wholeheartedly into the composition of his Second Symphony, working on the ideas which he had sketched during 1957 and 1958. The symphony had been commissioned by the Royal Liverpool Philharmonic Society to commemorate the 750th anniversary of the granting of the charter of incorporation to the borough, and the Society, which reserved to itself the right of its first performance in Liverpool, magnanimously volunteered to give that performance at the Edinburgh Festival, as requital of the honour of being asked to appear in that illustrious event. It was, perhaps, Walton's misfortune to have produced much of what many critics regard as his finest work before he was thirty, and, finding himself not only isolated by a vast desert of avant-garde experimentation but seemingly ineligible to qualify immediately for a 'reflective and relaxed final period', he must have regarded the new symphony—separated from its predecessor by a quarter of a century—as a daunting task. The world première had been scheduled for 30 December 1958 in Liverpool, but in fact much of the composing was done in the first half of 1960, although an earlier version of the first movement had been written in 1959 and was subsequently revised. After John Pritchard conducted the Royal Liverpool Philharmonic Orchestra in the première of the symphony at the Usher Hall, Edinburgh, on 2 September 1960, the critics generally classified the work as 'the same old mixture'. There has been a favourable reappraisal since, and certainly Frank Howes, reviewing the symphony and the Edinburgh performance in *The Times*, highlighted the splendid, even imposing structure and the manifold beauties of the scoring:

> The compact new symphony bears Walton's unmistakable fingerprints, the electrical discharge of energy in short and rapid fingers, the urgent melodies depending largely on the interval of the seventh, the tight but withal clear contrapuntal web, and the mastery of orchestral effect. Its emotional roots seem to be apprehension (in both senses) of the turbulence of our lives, meditation upon it, and resolute action which, after the conflict presented by a clash of tonalities, succeeds in containing that disquieting turbulence.
>
> The last movement is the longest and most elaborately organised: the

> exercise of the will is conducted in a powerful passacaglia and its decisive stroke in a fugato. The first movement is thus a brutal exposition in a kind of scherzo recalling the con malizia marking of his first symphony. The slow movement weaves melody in and out of melody poignantly and urgently. Nothing showed Mr Pritchard's skill in reading the composer aright than the beauty he extracted from this central movement by sheer elucidation of the texture, though the excitement of the piled-up tension in the complex finale was realised so surely as to bring immediate acclamation from the audience. Here at last was something by which to remember this festival.[38]

Walton, always a painstaking perfectionist, carried out some revisions to his *Sinfonia Concertante* and Violin Concerto in the direction of greater clarity. He also re-examined his Viola Concerto in 1960 and 1961: a work already beautifully scored but improved by the extensive changes he made, which included reducing the density of the brass and woodwind colour and introducing an important, as well as ravishing, harp part. In 1962 he made certain minor revisions to *Siesta*, a sweet, unhurried little piece composed in 1926.

Oldham, the much-loved place of his birth, honoured Sir William, who had travelled from Ischia for the occasion, when, in a twenty-minute ceremony at the Town Hall on 22 April 1961, the Mayor (Alderman G. F. Holden) presented him with the freedom of the borough, handing over the traditional illuminated resolution and a sterling silver salver. Two immensely proud spectators were Walton's only sister, Mrs Nora Donnolly, who had come post-haste from New Zealand, and his brother Noel. On the front of the illuminated resolution conferring the freedom of the borough was a drawing of the opening part of the anthem 'O Lord our Governor'—the test piece which Sir William had sung fifty years previously to gain admission to Christ Church, Oxford. In a speech of much eloquence, the Mayor spoke with pride of the many distinctive tributes—including the Royal Philharmonic Society's Gold Medal—already paid to the composer: six universities had conferred on him the honorary degree of Doctor of Music; the Royal College of Music, the Royal Academy of Music and the Royal Swedish Academy of Music had granted him honorary membership; he had also been awarded the coveted Gold Medal of the Worshipful Company of Musicians. 'You have attained the front rank as an orchestral composer and writer of choral music,' said the Mayor. 'As a writer for the ceremonial occasion your work has proved to be of striking and enduring value and, indeed, your film music, by its very excellence and original quality, unlike the great majority of film music, continues to be appreciated. Finally, you have abundantly proved yourself as a composer in the difficult field of opera.'

'You, sir,' continued the Mayor, with an inspired flow of rhetoric, 'are one of the rare beings who can ascend into the realms of creative imagination and beauty; who can perceive musical sounds hitherto undiscovered; whose wave-length is more receptive than ours. . . . In making this presentation, I assure you, sir, of our enduring regard for your qualities as a man and our profound respect for your endowments of mind and spirit.'

Sir William's wave-length was certainly perceptive of the great honour conferred on him by his home town, as well as of the lustre which his own genius and international renown had shed upon Oldham. A picture in the *Oldham Chronicle*, which reported the event[39] shows him sitting beside Lady Walton, studying the illuminated resolution with a look of happy contentment on his face. 'You have brought this on yourselves,' remarked Walton drily in his speech of thanks to the Mayor, 'so you can't hold it against me if I stand before you this afternoon as the local boy who makes good, as the saying goes!' And he promised at an early date to dedicate a piece of music to the town of his birth, a promise which was never fulfilled.

His next major choral work, after the Coronation 'Te Deum', was the *Gloria*, which he composed for a double celebration by the Huddersfield Choral Society in 1961: the 125th anniversary of the Society itself and the thirtieth year of Sir Malcolm Sargent as its conductor. Walton completed the orchestration by September 1961, and on 24 November that year the first performance, given in Huddersfield Town Hall, drew the following appraisal from *The Times*: 'The new work lasts some 20 minutes but crowds a good deal of musical action into them; it leaves the impression of a more spacious and eventful piece than its duration suggests. The spirit of the music, its impetus and its specific gravity, is altogether fresh, as it has not always been in Walton's recent music. There is no sensation of old ground retilled, but of new ground made fruitful by an old, still vigorous hand.'[40]

In February 1961 the Waltons visited America for the première in that country of the Second Symphony, played by the Cleveland Orchestra in Carnegie Hall. They travelled to Ulster in April, when Sir William conducted a performance of the same work. His highly original carol 'What Cheer?' appeared in a set of *Carols for Choirs—I*, published by Oxford University Press in the same year.

Photographs of the composer which appeared in various publications at that time showed that not only his tall, slight figure, with its deceptively delicate frame, had acquired immense dignity as well as maturity, but also his face, whose prominent well-cut nose had once made him seem to Osbert Sitwell like 'an elegant snipe'. In the *Radio Times* of 24 January 1930, a critic, after seeing Walton conduct a performance of *Façade*, had described him as 'a pale young man in shirtsleeves with a narrow head and rat-trap mouth', and that was, more or less, how he looked when suffering extreme annoyance or tension. On the occasion mentioned, it was undoubtedly stress, because the contriver of the BBC programme featuring the performance wanted to conclude it dramatically with the midnight stroke of Big Ben. Alas, the programme was running late and, as twelve o'clock approached, Walton, feverishly inciting his players, started a race to be in time for the chimes, while, according to the critic, Constant Lambert 'chanted about "parrot-coloured sunlight" till his face shone'.

Although, in 1961, Sir William still experienced tension and was capable of peevishly irascible outbursts, his whole personality seemed to have mellowed, with a hint of sweetness as well as sadness and mischief in that pale, brooding face. When he conducted, it was as a modest, unattitudinizing musician with no other desire than to obtain the best performance possible. Walton's prowess as a conductor improved greatly as time went on, and I shall have more to say about it in a subsequent chapter.

# 10

# A Song in Praise of the City

A highly unusual honour with a rather florescent title came to Walton on 4 February 1962, when he was appointed an 'Accademico Onorario di Santa Cecilia (Roma)'. It was his sixtieth birthday year and, to celebrate it, Oxford University Press gave a reception in the drawing-room of the Arts Council's headquarters in St James's Square, London. There were also concerts featuring his music. Making his first visit to Canada in the same year, Walton took part in a programme for the Canadian Broadcasting Corporation, sharing it with the American composer Aaron Copland and Louis Applebaum from Canada. He then visited Los Angeles for the American première of his *Gloria*, given on 10 June 1962 in Royce Hall, after which he returned to Ischia.

It was in 1962 that the Worshipful Company of Goldsmiths, ruefully aware that, unlike many great cities, London had no festival that it could call its own, decided on remedial action. By donating £500 from the Goldsmiths' Charitable Donation Fund to the City Arts Trust, they were instrumental in commissioning Walton to compose a celebratory song-cycle, the spirit and purpose of which he subsequently conveyed in the dedicatory title *A Song for the Lord Mayor's Table*—this came from the title of the opening song, a setting of a rumbustious poem by Thomas Jordan calling upon the Nine Muses 'to pen us a ditty in praise of the City'. That ever-resourceful word-spinner Christopher Hassall arranged the texts of the songs, taking them from poems by Jordan, William Blake, Charles Morris, William Wordsworth and two anonymous eighteenth-century poets, and by the end of June Walton had completed the music. In choosing him to compose this commemorative piece, given its first performance as a part of the City of London Music Festival in their own noble hall in London on 18 July 1962 by Elisabeth Schwarzkopf with Gerald Moore at the piano, the Worshipful Company of Goldsmiths paid the Lancashire-born Walton an implied tribute, since he had spent little of his creative life in the capital and could not in any sense be regarded as a Londoner by adoption.

Years later Moore made the following comments about the music and the event:

> As you know, the songs were written *for us* and my copy sent by William has this inscription in his own hand 'For Gerald, il bravissimo, from William, 23.3.63', but the performance took place in July '62 before the songs were published.
>
> You may be certain I practised them for weeks before E.S. and I rehearsed and we had manuscript copies. The quick songs with so many words would present difficulties to a foreigner, especially 'Wapping Old Stairs', but E.S. is a fine linguist and sang them as if she were an English woman. The final song 'Rhyme' has problems of balance: the chiming of the bells can easily cover the voice altogether. They are superb songs and had a triumphant success at the Goldsmiths' Hall: if anything, our favourite of all the splendid set is 'Glide Gently' (Wordsworth).[1]

Apart from a subsequent broadcast with Heather Harper, who sang the songs with complete mastery, this recital with Schwarzkopf was the only performance of the cycle in which Moore took part. He deplored the fact that the songs are so seldom heard and told me that, although they are tricky to 'put across', the enunciation of John Coates, the Yorkshire tenor who gave such poetic and sparkling interpretations of the *Façade* songs in the 1920s, would have made the texts crystal-clear to the listener. Mr Moore expressed the view that, with the right kind of singer, this work could become more popular with concert-programme organisers.

A special 'Service of Dedication' for the Festival took place at St Paul's Cathedral on 9 July 1962 when, headed by the Lord Mayor, the resplendently robed Masters and Prime Wardens of Livery Companies moved in solemn procession down the nave, doubtless pleased, as well as overawed, at the chance to wear their fur-trimmed ceremonial dress in public. During the proceedings the Cathedral choir sang the première of the 'Te Deum' by Edmund Rubbra commissioned for the event. Afterwards, at the Tower of London, a spectacular performance of *The Yeomen of the Guard*, conducted by Lawrence Leonard, delighted a huge audience. Anthony Besch's clever production made strong visual impact from the moment when spotlighted Yeomen appeared on top of the grim walls as part of the brass in the overture.

Walton subsequently prepared an orchestral version of *A Song for the Lord Mayor's Table*, and during another Festival of the City of London the first performance of this was given in the Mansion House on 7 July 1970 by Janet Baker, mezzo-soprano, and the English Chamber Orchestra, conducted by George Malcolm, who in 1976 wrote of the event in these words: 'The only single detail which sticks in my mind is a very trivial one concerning the clarinet parts. Sir William writes these in actual pitch. In this particular work he specifies clarinets in A, although the low C is used (as far as I remember) only once—somewhere in the cycle. The copyist had taken him literally, with the result that in the first song the clarinet parts were in seven flats. This was so asinine, and so inconsiderate, that it *angered* me, and I have remembered it ever since.'[2]

Granada Television commissioned Walton in June 1961 to compose a 'Prelude', 'TV Call Signs' and 'End Music' for use in their broadcasts. He delivered the score in August 1962, when the late Gilbert Vintner re-orchestrated the 'Prelude' (in the form of a march) for Symphonic Wind Band. The March was recorded—but not the other pieces—and transmission began in 1965 and ended in September 1973.

Walton's first orchestral composition since the Second Symphony of 1960 was the *Variations on a Theme by Hindemith*, which he wrote in honour of the Royal Philharmonic Society of London, who intended the work to be performed at a special 150th Anniversary Concert at the Royal Festival Hall. During a visit to Salzburg in 1923 to hear his early String Quartet played at the Festival of the International Society for Contemporary Music, an exciting and profitable experience, Walton had met Hindemith, a bold, round, jolly little man, and had fallen under the spell of his vibrant personality. Six years later Hindemith had played the solo part in the first performance of Walton's Viola Concerto in London, and the two men remained close friends throughout the ensuing years. The première of the *Variations*, given by the Royal Philharmonic Orchestra, with the composer on the rostrum, took place at the Royal Festival Hall, in the presence of HM Queen Elizabeth the Queen Mother, on 8 March 1963; exactly 150 years since the Society's first concert at the Argyll Rooms in Regent Street. *The Times* appraised the work in these words: 'Walton's Variations renew and revive many of his familiar and well-loved fingerprints. There are some strikingly new, but obviously characteristic effects too. Most intriguing of all, though, is the interplay between Walton and Hindemith—for the composer of the theme continues to exert his personality throughout the variations.'[3]

Walton thought highly of Hindemith and dedicated his own *Variations* to him and his wife. It was not only a tribute to a distinguished friend but a token of thanks to him for having resolved the first major crisis of Walton's career by undertaking the performance of his Viola Concerto after Tertis had rejected it. There can be no doubt that Hindemith warmly appreciated the gesture, as this letter to Walton confirms:

Vevey, poste restante,
July 29th, 1963

Egregio Amico:

Finally our criss-cross journeys came to an end and we could sit down in front of the exhaust of our gramophone and play your piece, score before us. Well, we had a half-hour of sheer enjoyment. You wrote a beautiful score and we are extremely honoured to find the red carpet rolled out even on the steps to the back door of fame. I am particularly fond of the honest solidity of workmanship in this score—something that seems almost completely lost nowadays. Let us thank you for your kindness and for the wonderfully touching and artistically convincing manifestation of this kindness (even old Mathis is permitted to peep through the fence, which for a spectre like him seems to be some kind of resurrection after artificial respiration!). I am glad that George Szell had a great (and well deserved) success with the piece in the States. I also shall put it in my programs as soon as possible. I wrote to the Oxford Press people that this could only be the case during the next season, i.e., starting autumn 1964, since I received the score at a time when all programs for 63/64 were settled and could not be changed. I hope this will be all right with you, and I shall do my best to be a worthy interpreter of W.W. Again my and Gertrude's heartfelt thanks!—We shall be in Naples around the middle of October and we hope to see you.

Love to you both as ever, yours
Hindemiths.[4]

Christopher Hassall, the librettist for *Troilus and Cressida*, died in 1963. When, in 1952, he had just written a play for the Edinburgh Festival, he told Walton that he had found a young actor to play the lead. 'Oh yes', said the composer, 'what's he called?' 'Britt*o*n,' replied Hassall. 'Britt*e*n, oh, no!' Walton said, aghast. 'Don't tell me he can *act*, too!' Joking aside, Sir William greatly admired Benjamin Britten (although Colin Graham told me that they enjoyed a kind of love-hate relationship), and in 1953 he had joined Britten, Oldham, Tippett, Berkeley and Searle each composing a variation on *Sellinger's Round*, which proved to be a musical quiz (see page 128).

During a visit to Britain in 1963 he attended the first performance of the revival of *Troilus and Cressida*, given on 23 April 1963 in a production which contained minor cuts—less than ten minutes in all-but few changes, although a number of small additions had been made to the original scenery designed by Hugh Casson. One reviewer seemed completely disenchanted with this musical face-lift: 'To have revived successfully the old 1954 production of Walton's *Troilus and Cressida* would have required rather more artificial respiration than there was at Covent Garden last week. In the original production everything was at least under control, whereas on this occasion many of the exits and entrances were simply a means of getting on and off the stage. The lighting and the operation of various stage machineries were often haphazard and some of the singing sounded perilously like sight-reading.'[5]

Always a zealous ambassador for his own music, though often disinclined to talk about it, Sir William spent a busy year travelling abroad, his first visit being to Israel, where he conducted three concerts and where, during the month of July, the first performance of *Belshazzar's Feast* in Hebrew was given by the Tel Aviv Choir and the Israeli Philharmonic Orchestra in Tel Aviv, Haifa and Jerusalem. Walton then flew to Ravinia, Illinois, summer base of the Chicago Symphony Orchestra, where three concerts, each featuring one of his string concertos, drew large, appreciative audiences.

In February 1964 the composer was in New Zealand, where he conducted concerts of his own music in Auckland, Wellington, Dunedin and Christchurch. Unfortunately, Lady Walton broke a leg shortly before the departure date and could not accompany him. He was, she subsequently told me, 'very lonely and unhappy' without her. For nearly three months Sir William toured Australia and again occupied the rostrum for concerts of his own works, one of these forming part of the Adelaide Festival of the Arts. Whilst he was in Australia, his remark that our National Anthem 'should be played only at the beginning and at the end of the concert season'[6] attracted wide, slightly controversial Press publicity. On arriving in Sydney he received a collection of poems sent to him by the Australian poet Douglas Stewart and, concurrently, the Press reported that he might write a composition with an Australian theme; but Walton returned to Ischia at the beginning of June and promptly started work on two new commissions.

One of these, which he subsequently called *The Twelve*, was for an extended anthem for Christ's Church, Oxford. Dr Cuthbert Simpson, the Dean, had little regard or affection for most of the anthems in the church repertoire popularized by frequent use and since, in particular, he could find few suitable ones for singing at the feasts of the Apostles, he asked both W. H. Auden, one of his closest friends, and Walton to remedy the deficiency, in part at least, by creating a new anthem. The commissioning and all relevant details were communicated verbally, and seemingly there were no letters on the subject, as Auden confirmed: 'I sent Sir William my text and later saw him on Ischia, so there was no correspondence.'[7] Walton subsequently orchestrated the organ part of *The Twelve*, and the new version, complete with introductory recitative, short solo passages and a big fugal chorus, was performed under his baton on 2 January 1966 in Westminster Abbey at one of the concerts celebrating its 900th anniversary.

The other commission tackled by Walton after his return to Ischia from abroad was for a *Missa Brevis* and came to him from the Friends of Coventry Cathedral, acting as patrons for the choir. It was David Lepine, the organist, who sent the invitation to him, requesting a work on a time scale similar to that of Britten's *Missa Brevis*, since the Cathedral congregations were not accustomed to long-winded settings of the liturgy. Lepine had expected Sir William to decline and was delighted when he accepted with a great show of interest, making helpful remarks, including the suggestion that only the Gloria should use an organ accompaniment. For some reason the first performance, scheduled for Easter Day 1966 in Coventry Cathedral, failed to take place.

Walton, doubtless pleased with the success of *Troilus and Cressida* and the magnitude of conception which he had been able to achieve in the work, had, for some time, been sniffing around for a libretto for another opera—a daunting task since, with the death of Christopher Hassall in 1963, he had lost a most valuable, if not always consistent, collaborator. His need of a libretto was pressing, however, because on 6 October 1958 the Serge Koussevitzky Foundation in the Library of Congress had offered him a commission which, if fulfilled, would satisfy his burning ambition to write another opera. Happily, that fastidious, gentlemanly, almost unique singer Peter Pears suggested to Walton that he should read Chekhov's three vaudevilles or jests: this the composer did, choosing *The Bear* for his new project but deciding to call it a one-act extravaganza, and not an opera. He began to create his own libretto but, probably realizing what others can hardly have failed to notice—that he had no great fluency or precision in the literary craft, he asked Paul Dehn, a professional writer of immense versatility, to discharge the task. Dehn, successively film critic over a period of eighteen years of the *Sunday Chronicle*, the *News Chronicle* and the *Daily Herald*, published several volumes of brilliant light verse, as well as libretti, including one for Lennox Berkeley, and a number of songs. He started work on the new libretto in the spring of 1965, progressing by means of correspondence between himself and Walton, on Ischia, until on 28 October that year he flew to Italy and, settling down on that enchanting island, worked closely with the composer until mid-November, when he produced a first draft and departed for home, leaving Sir William to his own musical devices.

Alas, in January and February 1965 work on *The Bear* was interrupted when Walton's health seemed gravely imperilled by one of the dread scourges of our time. During an interview the following year he remarked with the characteristic brevity of a courageous man, 'I went to the doctor for quite another reason, and he just happened to discover there was a shadow on my lung—it was cancer at the rather young stage. I had it nipped out in the London Clinic. The operation was 100 per cent successful.'[8] He omitted to mention that he had to undergo what Lady Walton subsequently described to me as 'eleven weeks of gruelling ray treatment'. At the beginning of February the composer was able to write to Dr Stewart Craggs, saying 'I am making marvellously good progress and hope to be out of here soon.' After a period of extra specialized treatment on a Sussex health farm, Walton made a complete recovery and, on being discharged by the hospital, he and his wife returned to Ischia, where he resumed work on *The Bear*, now earmarked for the English Opera Group, who expected to perform it in London the following September.

It had been decided, however, that the première should take place at Aldeburgh in June, and consequently there must have been considerable pressure on Sir William to finish the score; in fact, the first music rehearsals started before he had completed it, although, with sections arriving by instalments as soon as he had written them, the performers had ample time to learn and practise their parts. Walton attended many of the rehearsals for both the London and Aldeburgh productions and offered valuable advice on interpretation. The opera, as it is now regarded, was recorded in August 1967, after the composer had made various revisions. Andrew Porter described the new work as 'one of the strongest and most brilliant things Walton has written',[9] and other critics praised it.

November 1967 saw Sir William honoured once again when he and Professor P. M. S. Blackett, the physicist, received the Order of Merit. Academic tribute came to Walton in April 1968 with the conferment by the University of Sussex of the degree of Doctor of Letters; he was attending the Brighton Festival at the time, his first public appearance since his hospital operation of two years before. Difficulty in making any real progress on his latest commission—an overture for the New York Philharmonic Orchestra, supposed to be ready by June 1968—prompted him to say, 'I've done it about four times and thrown it away four times. But it's getting better although it hasn't got a title.'[10]

It did have a title inflicted on it—by the sponsors, not the composer: the exceedingly dull, pedagogic title *Philharmonic Overture NY '68*; but Walton subsequently re-named it *Capriccio Burlesco*. He took from May until September 1968 to write the overture, and in consequence the anticipated performance in the season of Promenade Concerts for that year did not take place; but the world première was given in New York on 7 December 1968, inspiring one American critic to write that the music 'consists of about five minutes of sly musical gesticulation; weaving of saucy ideas; scampering in and around corners and in syncopations; winking dismissal at any ponderous touch'.[11]

The first British performance of *Capriccio Burlesco* took place at the Royal Festival Hall in February 1969. Walton, accompanied by his wife, was in America the previous month, appearing as guest conductor of the

Houston Symphony Orchestra. During an interview he spoke of various commissions in the pipeline:

> Though six projects 'near to his heart' are urgently pending, composer William Walton sticks with his conviction that number of performances is more important than number of premières. 'I'm not one of those fellows who can turn out something in a week,' explained Walton. 'I do take longer, to make it last longer. I'm made that way. But it has generally paid off.'
>
> He ticked off 'all the music I shall be writing'—major pieces for the New York Philharmonic and the San Francisco Symphony, a double concerto for his friends Heifetz and Piatigorsky, 'something' for George Szell.
>
> 'And that double bass player, Gary Kerr, he's on my track,' he said.[12]

There was another musical assignment of considerable importance that slipped from Sir William's mind during the interview: a commission to compose the music for a new multi-million dollar film called *The Battle of Britain*, to be made by United Artists Ltd under the direction of Guy Hamilton, with a notable cast headed by Michael Caine, Laurence Olivier, Michael Redgrave and Susannah York. Harry Saltzman, the producer, had sent a script of the film to his home on Ischia the previous summer. After seeing a rough-cut of *The Battle of Britain*, the composer agreed enthusiastically to write the score. He was able to write the complete film version on 17 February 1969 and had from then until mid-April to create a suitable theme and suite. A writer in the *Guardian*, describing the recording session held in Denham Studios on 10 April 1969, reported that the commission had been forced on Walton at the last minute and that he had only ten days in which to write the dog-fight sequence, a gruelling task for a composer known to be rather slow and inhibited. He described the recording of the 'grand super-dambusting' march:

> No troubles of synchronisation this time (the march comes at the end over the credits) and after the jagged syncopations of the dog-fight, the plain 4/4 time is restful for everyone. There are the usual Waltonian clearings-of-throat, and then with an outrageous whooping on the horns comes a grand patriotic tune to out-type and out-glory any that Sir William has yet written, whether for films or coronations.
>
> The first three notes may be blatant crib from the opening of Elgar's Second Symphony, but they turn at once into the purplest Walton.[13]

Malcolm Arnold, that versatile composer who gave us the ingeniously scored *Beckus the Dandipratt*, conducted some of the numbers during the recording sessions and also orchestrated the accompaniment to the Blitz sequences. Although, generally speaking, the processing of Walton's music went as smoothly as could be expected and the tapes were flown to

New York without delay, the *Sunday Telegraph* reported him as saying, 'I have been treated in the most extraordinary way and will never write another bar of film music.' The reasons given made Sir William's anger understandable:

> Walton and Arnold were delighted with the recording, but when the recording was delivered Walton was told that it was unsatisfactory. The reason, Mr Arnold explains, is that United Artists, who are distributing the film, intend to produce an L.P. record of the music, and Sir William's compositions are not long enough to fill it.
>
> So Spitfire Productions have commissioned a whole new score from Ron Goodwin, They first approached John Barry, but he declined. Mr Arnold is astounded at the cavalier way in which Walton has been treated. "The music is Walton at his very best," he says, "it would be lunacy to reject it."
>
> Sir William expressed his feelings in more homely language: 'It's bloody cheek, all these Americans want is money and I had never even heard of Ron Goodwin.'
>
> Mr Goodwin is to finish the substitute score next month. Spitfire Productions will then do Sir William the courtesy of revealing whose music they will use.[14]

Goodwin subsequently informed Dr Stewart Craggs that not only had the incident greatly embarrassed him, but 'the unfortunate and mistimed publicity surrounding it' had aroused his anger.[15]

Laurence Olivier, outraged by the callous and insulting behaviour of the film moguls, informed United Artists that he would have his name removed from the credits unless they retained some part of Walton's music. He had the important, crucial role of Air Marshal Dowding in the film, and the deletion of his name might have caused a public scandal. The producers compromised by agreeing to use a small segment of the score. It was a five-minute, superbly photographed sequence near the end, where planes, with their roaring engines unheard, swoop dramatically in a surrealistic cat's-cradle of dog-fights. Olivier, with characteristic good taste and diplomacy, made his protest privately, so as not to embarrass Walton.

After the première of *The Battle of Britain* in September 1969, *The Times* commented: 'Handsomely shot, soberly put together, it is weighed down somewhat by a platitudinous score from Ron Goodwin (the only sequence of the rejected Walton score ie, Battle in the Air—turned down allegedly because it was not long enough to fill an LP—is not perhaps vintage Walton, but at least lifts the film with moments of sharp excitement.'[16]

As a result of this unsavoury episode, Walton had threatened not to write any more film music, but the passionate dedication and interest he had shown in this highly specialized genre indicate that the decision was made in anger and not in earnest. At all events, in 1969 he composed a score for Laurence Olivier's film version of the National Theatre production of Chekhov's play *The Three Sisters*, subsequently screened for the first time at the Venice Film Festival in August 1970. The score was recorded at Shepperton Studios on 29 December 1969 under Marc Wilkinson, who had received the manuscript of the music ten days previously while Sir William was on Ischia, but the composer arrived in London in time to attend the recording sessions, which took place in the morning and afternoon.[17]

The music of Benjamin Britten, like that of Walton, has nearly always given rise to controversy, and when he returned from the United States in 1941, bringing with him the score of the *Sinfonia da Requiem*, his work continued to arouse excitement, hostility and anger, as well as fervent admiration. He and Walton had a relationship based largely on a sincere, warm-hearted respect, rather than upon any real bond of affection, and when Sir William, in 1969, found in Britten's Piano Concerto a theme that seemed ideal for transforming into a set of variations, he did not hestitate to write, asking if he could borrow it. 'Of course you may vary that tune from the third movement of the Piano Concerto,' came the reply, 'with the greatest of pleasure. Perhaps it will be my way of going down into the future!—anyway, I feel very honoured.' Walton was delighted, and during the summer of 1969 he sketched most of his musical ideas for the new work, *Improvisations on an Impromptu of Benjamin Britten*, a score commissioned for the San Francisco Symphony Orchestra by the scientist and benefactor Dr Ralph Dorfman—further evidence, if any were needed, of Walton's lofty reputation in the United States. The work received its première in the War Memorial Opera House, San Francisco, on 14 January 1970, with Josef Krips on the rostrum. The first European performance was given at the Aldeburgh Festival on 27 June 1970 by the Royal Liverpool Philharmonic Orchestra, under Sir Charles Groves. Dr Dorfman told Stewart Craggs[18] that, after offering to provide financial sponsorship for a new work in memory of his first wife, Adeline Smith Dorfman—to be dedicated to the San Francisco Symphony Orchestra—he left the choice of a composer to the conductor Krips, making the sole request that it should be a joyful, not a mournful, piece. The stipulation is understandable, because Adeline, a highly trained amateur pianist, had been passionately devoted to music, with a sparkling vivacity and zest for life. The maestro's choice of Walton pleased Dorfman greatly, and the resultant *Improvisations* fulfilled all his hopes and expectations. An earlier title, *Elegiac Variations on a Theme of Benjamin Britten*, had been used but was discarded on 13 November 1969.

After the American première the *San Francisco Examiner* described the piece as 'an elegant, well balanced set of variations on a thoughtful stately theme evoking some deserted place' and added, 'Sir William Walton is one of the last sensible composers on this earth.'[19]

At the Annual Luncheon of the General Council of the Performing Rights Society, held on 1 July 1970, the Master of the Queen's Musick, Sir Arthur Bliss, on behalf on the Council, presented to Prince Charles, the guest of honour, a superb red leather volume, tooled in gold and bearing the gold-blocked inscription *Music for a Prince*. This magnificent volume was the result of the Council's decision to mark a very auspicious occasion in some appropriate way, and since the Prince played both the cello and the trumpet, it seemed fitting that a bound collection of short pieces for these instruments, written by selected composers, should be presented to him. Walton was one of those invited by Laurence Swinyard, Chairman of the PRS, to contribute a score and, accordingly, he wrote his *Theme (for variations) for Cello Solo*, which was included in the volume. In view of the fact that the recipient was the Prince of Wales, the Guild for the Promotion of Welsh Music was requested to nominate two Welsh composers to participate in the project.

In 1970 Oxford University Press published another collection of carols, which bore the title *Carols for Choirs II* and included Walton's 'All This Time'. scored for full choir and written in response to a verbal invitation from the publishers. The text had been taken from a collection of sixteenth-century English carols.

Neville Marriner, one of the most revered British musicians of today, met Walton in the Ritz Hotel, London, in 1970 and invited him to write a composition for the Academy of St Martin-in-the-Fields; when Sir William refused, he then persuaded him to orchestrate his Second String Quartet. The orchestration for the new work, *Sonata for String Orchestra*, was carried out in Ischia in September and October 1971, but not by Walton alone. His friend and collaborator Malcolm Arnold had offered to arrange the piece, under his supervision. Arnold referred to his own part in a characteristically modest way:

> When I arrived, he had already completed the first two movements and was half-way through the slow movement. This did not surprise me, and the reason for my offer was to give him encouragement to do it himself. However, I stayed with him until I had completed the last movement under his supervision, and we more or less had a race, meeting for luncheon and dinner to report progress. I am sorry to say he beat me by almost two days, but after all mine was a quick movement with so many semiquavers.[20]

Marriner and the Academy gave the première of the new work in

March 1972, as part of the Festival of Perth, and also performed the *Sonata* for the first time in the UK later that year in Bath.

Early in 1971 Sir William, accompanying André Previn and the London Symphony Orchestra, paid his first visit to Russia, where his First Symphony, performed before a Moscow audience, had what the *Financial Times* called 'a phenomenal success'.[21] Later that year he spent a week at a slimming farm in Suffolk, subsisting on hot water and lemon, with only the television to provide entertainment. He saw a film about Harrison Birtwistle, whose chunky, brittle music he greatly admired, and found himself deeply affected by this narrative profile of a fellow-Lancastrian who, like himself, had risen above the unromantic 'waste land' of the cotton towns to achieve world-wide fame. Watching the scene showing Birtwistle returning to his native country from an overseas tour, Walton grew strangely emotional, perhaps experiencing a sudden nostalgia for the past. He had, incidentally, always shown reluctance to express opinions about the younger generation of composers, or, indeed, about the avant-garde practitioners as a whole, confining himself to a few pithy and sporadic remarks. Of Stockhausen he said: 'I know very little about him. What I have heard I dislike intensely. Berio I'm inclined to like. . . .'[22] He had a great respect for the music, though not the Marxist philosophy, of the German composer Henze, another migrant to the halcyon refuge of Ischia, and visited Britain for the première of *We come to the River*, music richly inventive and steeped in colour. 'I think he's the only proper composer going today. I hate to say it, but it's no good mentioning Britten or Tippett or myself in the same breath as Hans. The only thing I've got against him is that he takes on so much.'[23] Walton, a self-critical, fastidious craftsmen who ruthlessly cut and revised his own works, usually after hearing them performed, makes a curious contrast with, and idolator of, the volatile, precocious Henze, who, seldom retracing his own steps and moving confidently from one shining rebirth to another, poured out an almost incessant flood of music. On one occasion Sir William spoke to Henze about an operatic act that lasted about an hour and a half: 'I told him, "My dear chap, you've just got to start cutting." '[24]

Julian Bream, who, with Peter Pears, had commissioned Walton in 1960 to compose the song-cycle *Anon in Love*, approached him with another assignment, this time for pieces solely for guitar. Malcolm Arnold related[25] how, in January 1971, Sir William, after five weeks of work on the *Bagatelles* he was writing for Bream, had only the first six notes, all to be played on the open strings. 'Not all that good,' mused Walton. 'I've been worrying. I'm wondering if when he begins they'll think he's tuning the bloody thing up.'

Despite this droll self-depreciation, the *Five Bagatelles for Guitar* delighted a large audience at the 1972 Bath Festival, and not only the audience but also the critic of the *Bath and Wiltshire Evening Chronicle*: 'The first showed Walton's professionalism in writing for solo guitar while yet retaining his own personality; the second was a simple valse, the third had some fine choral textures and a tune which seemed vaguely familiar, and the last gave Bream a chance to show off his own complete mastery of his own instrument and virtuosity.'[26]

Walton subsequently transcibed the *Five Bagatelles* into a charming suite bearing the title *Varii Capricci*, and in the Royal Festival Hall, London, on 4 May 1976 this was performed, as a 75th birthday tribute, by the London Symphony Orchestra, under André Previn. During the gestation of the *Five Bagatelles*, Sir William met Lina Lalandi, the Artistic Director of the English Bach Festival, in the Ritz Hotel—'a very happy meeting,' according to her,[27] because he promised to write a short composition for her 'as a present'. The gift proved to be an extremely beautiful setting of the 'Jubilate', which, given its first performance in Christ Church Cathedral, Oxford, on 22 April 1972, moved Miss Lalandi to tears. 'It is a very beautiful piece and I am honoured and happy that he wrote it for me,' she said.[28]

At the beginning of the year, in recognition of his 'work for Anglo-American understanding', the Benjamin Franklin Medal of the Royal Society of Arts was conferred upon Walton. According to the citation, the regular performance in the United States of his works, impregnated with the British idiom, had contributed greatly to American culture. In the middle of March the Manchester Royal College of Music paid tribute to Sir William by making him an honorary member.

In March 1972, after a forty-year separation, revivified and doubtless nostalgic following the celebration throughout Britain of his seventieth birthday, he met his two brothers, Noel and Alec, at the Midland Hotel, Manchester. Alec, the younger of the two, a director of the Bank of Canada and a resident of that country, had come over specially for the occasion. Noel, a skilled pianist and a citizen of Oldham, held the appointment of music master of Hulme Grammar School in the town until his retirement. Interviewed by Joan Lane, he stated that as a child he had been a choirboy and might, like William, have gone to the Oxford voice trials in 1912, but that, alas, his voice had broken a few days previously. Noel, slightly whimsical in manner, sported a dry humour. He referred to himself as a BOFM—'brother of a famous man'—and recalled visiting 'Willie' while stationed in London during the First World War. 'He used to sit at the piano, composing, and usually smoking a cigarette in one of those long black holders,' said Noel. 'He never could play the piano, though—used to just bang away at it!'

Congratulations to Sir William on reaching his seventieth birthday came also from the *Oldham Chronicle*, whose editor, one of his most ardent admirers, proudly drew attention to the fact that Oldham's greatest son had been offered the Freedom of the Borough only after his paper had suggested that this honour be conferred. He complained bitterly that no one had installed commemorative plaques either outside the house where Walton was born or inside the church where he had sung as a boy. His indignation warming up to flashpoint, the editor reported, with a faint note of irony, that consideration was being given to calling a new Oldham traffic by-pass 'Walton Way'—not, however, as a tribute to the composer of *Belshazzar's Feast*, but to honour Mr Harry Walton, the town surveyor, for his services![29]

Walton's seventieth birthday was celebrated in Britain not only by special performances and profile tributes from Press, radio and television but also by the publication of a beautifully bound and printed edition of *Façade*, which contained *Herodiade's Flea*, a previously rejected twenty-seven-bar piece based on rhythmic *ostinati* with woodwind accompaniments which had not been heard since the first public performance of *Façade* in the Aeolian Hall on 12 June 1923.

Edward Heath, then Prime Minister, gave a concert at No 10 Downing Street to celebrate Walton's seventieth birthday on 29 May 1972 and, as an ardent admirer, took a special delight in sponsoring this because he felt that the composer had not always received the recognition he deserved from both the public and the critics. The concert represented an act of homage in which many of Walton's contemporaries could share. Herbert Howells contributed a grace, whose words had been written for the occasion in Heath's private office. After its performance at dinner, the grace was sung before every subsequent dinner at No 10, with its words adapted to common use. Sir Arthur Bliss wrote an amusing piece to an equally droll poem by Paul Dehn, a former collaborator with Walton; bearing the title 'An Ode for William Walton' and making witty comment on a number of his compositions, it was sung, together with Sir William's 'Set me as a Seal upon Thine Heart', by the Martin Neary Singers. The final verse in the 'Ode' must have moved Walton deeply, and perhaps saddened him as he contemplated his growing infirmity:

Tonight we hope devoutly one and all
For further writing on your fancy's wall.
Go from strength to strength! At least
This is not *Belshazzar's Feast*.
And the air on Ischia
Seems to make you friskier
May there flower from your pen

A symphony called 'Number Ten'!
Fa-la-la, fa-la-la, fa-la-la, fa-la-la
Coupled with a seventy-fold 'AMEN'!

While the guests clustered around a small horseshoe table, David Atherton conducted the London Sinfonietta, with Alvar Liddell as narrator, in a performance of ten movements from *Façade*.

As the evening wore on, the distinguished company moved into the pillared drawing-room. Seated on the sofa were the Queen Mother and the Waltons; those around them included the Blisses, Herbert Howells, Benjamin Britten, Malcolm Arnold, Richard Rodney Bennett, Lionel Tertis and his wife, the Soltis, Sir Frederick Ashton, Sir Laurence Olivier, Bryan Forbes, Nanette Newman, Lord Clark, Lord Goodman, Jenny Lee and the Droghedas. As midnight approached, Mr Heath told his guests how he had heard an interviewer ask Walton, on his sixtieth birthday, whether there was any piece of music he would like to have composed himself and how the prompt reply had come, 'Yes, Schubert's B flat Trio'. To the delight of everyone present at No 10, especially of Sir William himself, John Georgiadis and Douglas Cummings, leader of the London Symphony Orchestra, and the first cellist, together with the pianist John Lill, played the Trio with a mastery that reminded Heath of the days when Thibaud, Casals and Cortot performed the same work—a remarkable achievement in itself, since the recitalists at No 10 had not previously tackled this music in public, although they had rehearsed it together during the previous week-end.

Heath greatly admired the wonderfully atmospheric scores which Sir William had written for those popular films *Spitfire* and *First of the Few* in 1942, scores which had placed his name high in the annals of music, and knowing something of the unhappy events which had followed the completion of the music for *The Battle of Britain* and the distress which the shabby treatment meted out by a United Artists official had caused the composer, the Prime Minister, with typical kindness, persuaded the film company shortly before the Downing Street birthday celebrations to return the manuscript to Walton. It was a poignant moment at the party when he presented Sir William with a copy of the agreement. Alas, the one part of the music which had been used in the film was missing from the score, since United Artists had somehow managed to lose it! As I sit at my desk in March 1983, completing this book, the music of *The Battle of Britain* has not, as far as I know, been publicly performed, although in May 1971 that highly gifted and resourceful musicologist Dr Stewart Craggs was able, with Walton's assistance, to purchase a recording and copies of the score from United Artists. Indeed, in April 1982 the *Daily Telegraph* reported that, 'Walton fans have been urging United Artists, who commissioned Sir William to write the score, to release it for performance' but that the film company had imposed stringent conditions which prevented this being done, because they were 'quite unacceptable' to the composer.[30] The conditions were said to concern the title of the score.

At the seventieth birthday concert held in 1972 the conductor André Previn announced that Walton had promised a third symphony for the London Symphony Orchestra, but the work did not materialize, although in May 1973 the composer told Robert Ponsonby, the BBC's Controller of Music, that it was 'on the move',[31] and Previn, interviewed by Robert Keenen at the beginning of 1978, claimed that, 'There's a third symphony on the way. . . . I've had the first page, with a very kind inscription and dedication, so I've duly framed it; but I'm still waiting for further pages. . . .'[32]

Indeed, after 1972 Sir William, wrote no major choral or orchestral pieces, restricting himself to undemanding works of not more than a few minutes' duration. One of these, a fifty-five second 'Fanfare', he composed in 1973 for EMI's seventy-fifth anniversary on 22 November of that year. Peter Andry, General Manager of the International Classical Division, told Walton that he wanted something that would 'start the evening off with a bang' and added, 'you may even, if you like, include "Happy Birthday" . . .'[33] Sir William did include it, or at least the first six notes, after Keith Prowse had granted permission, and the 'Fanfare', completed by September 1973, was played by the Kneller Hall Trumpeters on 29 November the same year, under the direction of Lt.-Col. R. B. Bashford, in a concert conducted by André Previn at the Royal Festival Hall, London. On the manuscript score, held by Oxford University Press, the composer stipulates that in performance it is 'to be *immediately* followed by the Coronation March *Orb and Sceptre* (1953)', He had, in fact, with great cunning so devised the closing bars that the music could blend almost imperceptibly into the brazen opening of that piece of royal ceremonial grandeur.

Walton, invited by Professor Aloys Fleischmann, representing the responsible committee, to write music for the coming-of-age in 1974 of the Cork International Festival, composed his *Cantico del Sole*, dedicating it to Lady Dorothy Mayer, who had approached him unsuccessfully in 1972 regarding this commission, and to Sir Robert, her husband. The invitation, which had been sent also to Boris Blacher, Roman Vlad and Brian Boydell, the Irish composer, was for an *a capella* part-song between three and ten minutes in duration and to be sung, if possible, by an amateur choir to be mentioned by the composer. An added inducement was the fact that the Senate of the National University of Ireland had expressed its willingness to grant honorary doctorates in music to the four composers who had been commissioned to write music for the Festival. At first, Walton, faced with formidable difficulties, seemed reluctant to accept the invitation.[34] He knew very little about British choirs, especially those of amateur status, although he promised to make enquiries on the subject during his next visit to London. In his reply to the composer,[35] Fleischmann asked him to reconsider his decision, as planning for the Festival had reached a point of no return, and, by way of encouragement, he suggested that Walton submit a brief work—possibly an early, unpublished part-song which he had not used—and that he accept the honorary degree *in absentia*. Sir William did accept the commission, and on 25 April 1974, at University College, Cork, the BBC Northern Singers, under Stephen Wilkinson, gave the first performance of his *Cantico del Sole*, which has since proved to be an extremely popular piece—'. . . there is a new, almost Latin sensuousness about the harmony, particularly at the work's radiant climax . . .' reported the *Daily Telegraph*.[36]

Shortly after completing this composition, Walton, in response to a commission from Rt. Rev. Walter Hussey, the Dean, started work on his 'Magnificat' and 'Nunc Dimittis' for the 900th anniversary celebrations in June 1975 of Chichester Cathedral. Dean Hussey had peviously asked him to write something for the Jubilee Festival of his church, St Matthew's in Northampton, and although unable or unwilling to do so, the composer did, in fact, attend the Jubilee celebrations, highlights of which were the unveiling of a sculpture by Henry Moore and the première on 21 September 1943 of Britten's 'Rejoice in the Lamb', which he dedicated to the Dean and his choir. The fee paid to Sir William in 1974 for his celebratory setting of the canticles for Chichester Cathedral came from money given by the Bishop Bell Memorial Fund to the Cathedral for commissioning works of art. The first performance of the 'Magnificat' and 'Nunc Dimittis', together with the première of Sir Lennox Berkeley's new setting of 'The Lord is my Shepherd', was given at Evensong on 14 June 1975, and Walton, zealous as ever in the search for perfection, noted the sound and feeling of his own work and, prior to publication some time later, made a few alterations to the voice and organ parts, mostly in the 'Nunc Dimittis'.

Happily isolated in the Shangri-la paradise of Ischia, he found his visits to Britain a physical and mental strain, since they permitted few opportunities for relaxation; but he did allow himself to be interviewed by BBC 2 in October 1975 as a corollary of the performance of *Belshazzar's Feast*, under Owain Arwel Hughes, broadcast from the Free Trade Hall, Manchester. On the previous evening the *Aquarius* series of London

Weekend TV screened a beautifully reflective profile film called 'Sir William and our Gracie', which, made in 1974, was focused separately on Walton at home on Ischia, and Gracie Fields, the much-loved comedienne and singer, on the Isle of Capri across the Bay of Naples, also relating how they first met in a restaurant on Capri. The meeting of these two Lancashire musical 'exiles' must have been a happy, as well as nostalgic, occasion, because their childhood social upbringing and environments had been much the same. It was raining heavily when Sir William arrived on Capri with his wife, doubtless reminding him of the often damp East Lancashire climate. He expressed his regret that Gracie had never become an opera singer. 'A lot of people told me that,' she replied, 'but I've had a better time my way! You've had the training, haven't you? Mine just fell out of me mouth!'

Probably as a result of the *Aquarius* interviews, London Weekend TV commissioned Walton to compose a *Fanfare for the National*, to be used in a programme celebrating the completion and opening of the National Theatre, which the producer, Derek Bailey, having spent five years planning the film and collating material, expected to be an artistic triumph. Administrative difficulties arose, however, and not until late October 1976 did the official opening take place, although the programme itself was televised nationally on 21 August that year, several versions of the *Fanfare* being played in different styles throughout.

Early in 1975 the composer revised the last two pages of his Cello Concerto for Gregor Piatigorsky to play in the Royal Festival Hall on 24 June 1975, but the great man became ill and the concert had to be cancelled. Piatigorsky died in August the following year, and the manuscript of the rescored passages is now held by Paul Tortelier, that other supreme virtuoso of the instrument. Writing of Tortelier's gifts as a concert artist, during a tour of the United States, the critic Samuel Chotzinoff said: '. . . in his hands the cello loses its limitations; his playing is as light and brilliant as if he were playing the violin'.[37]

John Sanders, organist of Gloucester Cathedral, approached Walton in September 1975 on behalf of the committee organizing the 250th Three Choirs Festival to be held in Gloucester in 1977, and offered him a commission for a choral work, but the composer refused. Sanders would have settled for an overture, if Sir William had wished to supply one.[38]

In the summer of 1975 the Greater London Council commissioned Walton and other composers to write commemorative pieces for the twenty-fifth anniversary, in May 1976, of the building of the Royal Festival Hall on the South Bank in 1951; but the project foundered for Sir William at least when Herbert von Karajan, invited to conduct the *Adagio ed Allegro Festivo* which he intended as his contribution, declined. The composer, in March 1976, began orchestrating his *Five Bagatelles for Guitar*, details of which, including the première of the new score, have already been given in this chapter.

Walton, with his profound love of ceremonial pomp and splendour, showed great flair and affection for the fanfare, and in 1975 his friend Lord Zuckerman, the Secretary of the Zoological Society of London, visited him on Ischia and invited him to write a piece of music to celebrate the Society's 150th Anniversary in the following year. He received the completed work, *Roaring Fanfare*, in May 1976, and on 3 June that year the Kneller Hall Trumpeters played it for the first time in public as the Queen arrived to open the new Lion Terraces at London Zoo.

The fact that Walton's promise of a third symphony was not fulfilled, as already mentioned, may perhaps have been due not to any ineptitude or irresolution but to ill health, which surfaced alarmingly in November 1976 when, after attending all the performances of *Troilus and Cressida* in a new production at Covent Garden and returning to Ischia, the composer, showing signs of a stroke, became a very sick man and was unable to work. It must be mentioned in passing that, for this production, originally scheduled for his seventieth birthday, Walton, choosing Janet Baker as his ideal tragic heroine, had made small changes in *tessitura* to bring the top notes within her contralto range. He transposed some of Cressida's music down a tone, one large alteration being in the aria 'At the haunted end of the day', whose sombre poignancy was intensified when he lowered it a third. Walton also reduced the length of each act by five to ten minutes. He had not been in good health while revising the opera and, after being taken ill in London, he remained inactive on Ischia, making only a partial recovery; but with characteristic gallantry he visited Britain at the end of March 1977 for his seventy-fifth birthday celebrations and, although confined to a wheelchair and looking extremely fragile, he managed his usual kind, if somewhat non-committal, smile.

Sir William attended the London concerts given in his honour, and by a unanimous vote the Incorporated Society of Musicians nominated him as 'Musician of the Year'. This award was presented to him by Miss Ida Carroll, the Society's President, at a gala concert in Fishmongers' Hall, London, on 22 March, and she paid glowing tribute to the 'tremendously varied' compositions he had produced over the years.[39] Oxford University Press, his publishers, celebrated 1977 as a birthday year by releasing several Walton scores, including *The Bear*, and they were doubtless gratified to realize that, by a fortuitous coincidence, their first publication of a Walton piece—the arrangement for piano duet of *Portsmouth Point*—had been issued exactly fifty years previously.

It must have gladdened the hearts of many Walton admirers when, by

June of that year, following a very effective course of acupuncture, he was reported as being much improved and working again. In November he and Lady Walton returned to Britain and took part in a thanksgiving service held at the Chapel Royal, St James's Palace, to commemorate the 75th Anniversary of the Order of Merit; after which they joined other members of the Order at a special luncheon given by the Queen and Prince Philip at Buckingham Palace.

As a semi-invalid in a wheelchair, with a restricted range of movement and energy, Walton continued to compose in a small way, but major works became too daunting to contemplate. His indomitable spirit was one of his most endearing facets, and the flag of courage fluttered bravely over 'La Mortella', his home on Ischia.

It was early in January 1976 that Peter Hurford, organist at Westminster Abbey, started to examine the possibility of incorporating into the Ninth International Organ Festival, scheduled for St Albans in July the following year, a concert involving three or four choirs. Acting on his behalf, Christopher Morris of the Oxford University Press invited Walton to contribute something suitable, and Sir William stated that he was 'taken with the idea and would be delighted to undertake it'.[40] Alas, because of the precarious state of his health, the extended choral piece on which he was engaged had to be abandoned. Max Aitken had also offered Walton a commission to write an orchestral piece, bearing the title *Prospect* (after Aitken's house), for the London Sinfonietta's Silver Jubilee Concert to be given on 3 June 1977, but the composer had to drop this also. He did, however, rally sufficiently to produce a new score: the choral work *Antiphon*, with words by George Herbert, for the choir of St Paul's Church, Rochester, New York, which he had been asked for in the summer of 1975. His commission was for a festive anthem with organ accompaniment, to be sung by a choir of forty-five mixed voices, and for this Walton chose the text 'Let all the World in Every Corner Sing'. The duration of the piece had to be seven to eight minutes, with music appropriate for the 150th anniversary of the church. The first performance of *Antiphon* took place on 20 November 1977. In the summer of that year Sir William also completed a small carol, 'King Herod and the Cock', for *Carols for Choirs 111*, to be published by Oxford University Press in 1978, and the first performance was given in King's College Chapel, Cambridge, on Christmas Eve during the Festival of Nine Lessons and Carols. Ever zealous in restructuring or polishing the facets of earlier compositions, he sent to OUP in early November a revised finale for *Varii Capricci*, for publication as the official one to the set of orchestral pieces.

In January 1982 Walton completed his *Prologo e Fantasia*, which was commissioned by the great Russian cellist Mstislav Rostropovich for his

National Symphony Orchestra of Washington, who gave the world première in the Royal Festival Hall, London, on 20 February, shortly before the composer's eightieth birthday. The privilege of presenting the first British performance went to the Royal Liverpool Philharmonic Orchestra, under Norman Del Mar, who included in his Philharmonic Hall birthday celebration concert of 20 March not only this brief work but also *Belshazzar's Feast* and Vaughan Williams's *Five Tudor Portraits*. The Royal Liverpool Philharmonic Society, founded in 1840, is the fifth oldest concert-giving organization in Europe. Its conductors have included such prestigious masters as Julius Benedict, Max Bruch, Sir Charles Hallé, Sir Henry Wood and Sir Thomas Beecham. The orchestra gave the first British performance of Walton's Second Symphony in 1960, under John Pritchard, and his *Improvisations on an Impromptu of Benjamin Britten* at the 1970 Aldeburgh Festival, under Sir Charles Groves.

Rostropovich also persuaded Sir William to write a *Passacaglia for Solo Cello*, and on 16 March 1982, at the Royal Festival Hall, he himself gave the world première in the presence of the obviously delighted composer. Walton, a man of strong, independent views and immense courage, greatly admired Rostropovich, who, while in Russia, had so bravely incurred the wrath of the Kremlin oppressors. Walton must have found the task of writing the *Passacaglia*, intended for Rostropovich's own use, very much to his taste, and of course it demonstrated, during the composer's eightieth birthday celebrations, that he could still create a pleasantly entertaining, if all too brief, 'conversation piece'.

# 11

# Every Man is an Island . . .

Death came to Sir William Walton not fearsomely and with an awe-inspiring grandeur, as it did to Belshazzar the King, but quietly, like a sudden breeze blowing across a calm, unruffled lake; for on the previous Sunday, filling his head with music—music as blithe as the figures in a Benozzo Gozzoli fresco—he had completed the score of a ballet version of his *Varii Capricci*. He died of a lung haemorrhage on 8 March 1983, following what Dr Amalfitano called 'a cardiac crisis', at his villa, 'La Mortella', on the island of Ischia, cradled in the arms of his wife, Susana, the lovely Argentinian of whom, at a first heart-plucking glance in Buenos Aires in 1949, he had whispered, 'That's the girl I'm going to marry.'

The measure of the love and esteem which the people of Ischia bore him may be judged by the fact that within four hours of his death nearly a thousand men, women and children flocked to the villa to pay homage to the man they called '*Il Maestro*'. Big, black-bordered posters, containing a splendid tribute from the local mayor and mourning the loss of 'our most illustrious and sincere friend', were put up on walls all over the island.

For three days condolences from friends and admirers, including Lord Olivier, for whose films *Henry V* and *Hamlet* the composer had written glorious music, reached Lady Walton, and then on 11 March at Florence came the funeral. When that other twentieth-century musical genius Igor Stravinsky died, his body lay in state in the thirteenth-century church of SS Giovanni and Paolo in Venice, under whose marble floor twenty-one Doges—the city's medieval rulers—lay buried. While three thousand people packed the church for the service, an Italian choir and orchestra, conducted by Robert Craft, intoned Stravinsky's *Canticum sacrum*. Afterwards the body, in a rose-covered coffin, was ferried in a black gondola to the island of San Michele in the Venice Lagoon. For the humble, Lancastrian-born Sir William Walton, the obsequies were strikingly different, consisting of a cremation attended by a few friends. The manner of his passing, devoid of panoply and ostentation, seemed entirely fitting for a man who, self-deprecatory and modest, vehemently detested all fuss or flattery. In the ravine garden of 'La Mortella', filled with massive Australian tree ferns of ancient growth and other exotica, a recess in a huge boulder projecting from the wild hillside provided a resting-place for his ashes, as he himself wished.

Hearing of his death, I imagined him as he appeared on television during his eightieth birthday celebrations, seated on the terrace of his home, wearing a floppy, broad-brimmed straw hat tilted at a rakish angle, fondling his favourite walking-stick and, with his faintly challenging, ironic smile, looking like one of Somerset Maugham's more ruminative tea-planters. It was a picture as poignant as the photograph I once saw of the blind Delius, hunched, fragile and unreal, in a reclining-chair outside his house at Grez-sur-Loing, with Eric Fenby, his amanuensis, friend and *alter ego*, standing beside him. Both composers, I sensed, were gazing with the blurred, nostalgic eyes of memory at a world of subtle kaleidoscopic beauty slowly vanishing into the mists of time and forgetfulness. It was a picture so unutterably moving that one could cry merely to think of it.

One of Walton's favourite expressions was 'I have no regrets', and perhaps, reborn in God's perpetual summer, cleansed and purified by death, he has already spoken those words, looking back with that endearingly wry, laconic smile at the triumphs and the failures, the heartache and the bliss. Not the least of his triumphs was in the realm of conducting. He never aspired to stardom in this difficult and highly specialized genre, competing against the whizz-jet-baton breed, with their managers, accountants, private planes, luxury hotel suites and the like, but quietly, doggedly and with great resourcefulness, he built up a fine, enduring reputation as an interpreter of his own works. If he never conducted the music of other composers, it was probably because, having gained such mastery over his own scores, often ruthlessly cutting and revising them to achieve more finesse or cohesion, he knew that he had a special flair for elucidating their rhythmic difficulties, which, in the early days of his career, even Ansermet found perplexing. Walton realized that many professional conductors were not projecting his music properly, and that he himself must demonstrate how it should be done.

He learned to conduct not by intensive studying at some prestigious college of music but by his own imitative genius, with a good deal of help from others. Although he conducted *Façade* as far back as 1929, 'holding his baton with something of the air of an elegant and handsome snipe', as Osbert Sitwell put it, Walton's real début on the rostrum was with *Portsmouth Point*, an ordeal for which he prepared, firstly, by making a fresh appraisal of every detail of the score and, secondly, by prolonged practice in front of a mirror. His grasp of the technique of conducting grew much more confident in the late twenties, when an orchestral player in Berlin advised him to keep his left hand in his pocket; but, always self-critical, Walton, poised on the rostrum at rehearsal, would turn to the leader and say 'Is this all right?' He conducted economically, with a neat, precise beat, using his baton as little as possible, communicating his wishes to the players efficiently and charging them with the intense electrical energy that flowed from his deceptively shy, self-effacing personality. Elisabeth Schwarzkopf told me that he never quite overcame his nervousness while on the rostrum but that when he mentioned this to Sir Thomas Beecham he received the reply, 'always have a stiff drink before you go on, my boy—it helps enormously!' Walton toured abroad with great success—notably in Scandinavia (1945), Australia and New Zealand (1964) and the USSR (1971)—gaining the respect and admiration of world-famous orchestras.

Coupled with his authoritarian status as an interpreter of his own works in concert-halls were his equally remarkable achievements in the recording studio, which resulted in the promotion of his music for a much wider public. He made his first recording in 1929 for the newly established Decca company, when he conducted the chamber ensemble needed for the *Façade* entertainment, with Edith Sitwell and Constant Lambert as reciters. Only eleven of the poems were used, and Walton was prudently advised to take cash for his services 'in case the company went bust'. It was the small Decca company that put two of his major works on disc in the 1930s—the First Symphony, with Sir Hamilton Harty conducting the London Symphony Orchestra, and later the Violin Concerto, with Frederick Riddle as the soloist and Walton himself conducting. RCA in America then recorded the Violin Concerto in the early days of World War II, with Eugene Goossens conducting the Cincinnati Symphony Orchestra and with the dedicatee, Jascha Heifetz, as the soloist. This recording, which marked a change of allegiance, came out in Britain on the HMV label, and thereafter, in the days of 78-rpm records, it was EMI rather than Decca that recorded Walton's music, usually with the composer conducting.

When the long-playing record arrived, he had for more than a decade been warmly accepted by the British Establishment, and in the 1950s he made some major recordings for Columbia, with Walter Legge and his Philharmonia Orchestra, which had never been surpassed. Like his illustrious predecessor Sir Edward Elgar, he had a marvellous instinct for bringing out the full essence of the music—bright, clear, unpretentious, but vibrant with life—and his musical style was immediately recognizable in every bar. In the matter of recordings, Walton conducted by Walton is an unforgettable experience, because nobody seemed to be able to master the spring of his rhythms as he did.

Sir William was an extremely shrewd, practical man. Noting how the First Symphony neatly spanned twelve 78-rpm sides, Edward Greenfield asked him if he had planned this division when composing the work, just as Puccini, according to common belief, wrote his arias to fit records. 'Of course I did!' replied Walton emphatically, albeit with an enigmatic smile.[1]

He enjoyed great happiness on the island of Ischia, which provided the tranquillity and seclusion which he needed for his work. In that almost unblemished paradise few people penetrated his genial, fatherly but slightly blunt, uncompromising exterior. His delightful and vivacious wife, Susana, was both his companion and his protector. For some famous men the act of composition has come as naturally as breathing, but for Walton it was agonizingly difficult, so that commissions were dragged out of him in self-doubt, chaos and misery. He rarely spoke about this, although he once remarked whimsically to Caroline Moorehead, 'I have never found composing easy. You would be saddened for me if you saw the scraps of paper littered around my room at the end of each day!'

After having the diseased lung removed in 1965, and for a long time afterwards, he had to ration his creative and physical energy. A tall, frail figure with a tantalizing air of mingled gentleness and inner amusement, he seemed as if immured in a windowed tower, watching the pageantry of life outside through shrewd, half-regretful eyes. His opprobrium scarified both Schoenberg and the abrasive 'pop' groups on whose gramophone recordings he refused to waste his money. He loathed aleatoric and electronic music—'Who gets the royalties?' he asked cynically. Adhering, as Stravinsky did, to a strict regimen of 'office hours', he worked with painstaking slowness in a white, sound-proofed studio backing into the cliff behind his home, aware of the continuing pitfalls of success, with its reliance on self-repetition, and a little frightened, perhaps, of the noise and aggression of bright young men purveying strange musical idioms with more ugliness than beauty. He used to start work early, carry on through the morning and then, after a break for relaxation and other activities, continue in the evening from about four until eight o'clock. In the twilight of his life he rose late, pottered around during the day and worked only in the evening. 'I have nothing else to do,' he remarked sadly.[2]

The philosopher Nietzsche deliberately wrote in a veiled allegorical style, hiding plain speech and truth behind a tangled hedgerow of parable and figurative allusion, so that, to use his own words, 'Swine and herdsmen may not break into my gardens'. Walton, in his bantering, ironic and elusive responses to interrogations about his own life and music, his philosophical opinions or his relationships with others, adopted much the same cautious, defensive and slightly aggressive attitude. For example, how much did he really know about Osbert Sitwell and his remarkable, often idiosyncratic family? In those halcyon days of patronage and broadening horizons, did he ever hear the skeletons rattling in the cupboards of Renishaw Hall and Carlisle Square, feeling, with his blunt, uncompromising Lancastrian sense of propriety, just a little bewildered and uneasy about the future? Did he, in later life, realize for the first time that Osbert had maintained a permanent homosexual affair for forty years while periodically staying with, and amusing, members of the royal family? Or had he been aware of the association much earlier? Whatever he knew or felt about the Sitwells, Walton never publicly maligned or repudiated them, and even in the closing phase of his life, when he sat reminiscing in a wheelchair on Ischia, sick and crippled in body, he spoke of them with a fond, if rather punctilious, gratitude.

Although Sir William, who loathed pretentiousness and self-aggrandisement, usually avoided making any comment about himself and his music, he and his wife would chatter proudly and excitedly about their garden, with its beds of camellias that filled the summer air with brilliance and sweetness. The unspectacular name of their home, 'La Mortella', meaning 'The Myrtles', and suggesting a slightly prim Victorian residence hiding demurely in a copse of trees, conveyed nothing of the modernity of the house, or its fortress-like amenities. At the back of the villa a small funicular railway, clamped into a channel scooped out of the hillside, carried guests—two at a time, standing—up the cliff to a blue swimming-pool, set in an olive grove, high above the sea, for coffee. The front gate of the house was a massive, electrically controlled wooden door, looking rather like a portcullis, which rolled backwards and forwards whenever switches were pressed either in the house or in the Waltons' cars. Another switch in one of the rooms sent plumes of water shooting from fountains in the gardens. There was always a great sense of fun in the household, seemingly modelled, as far as its range of electronics was concerned, on the comic film *Mon Oncle*, and Alan Jefferson recalled how Lady Walton picked up a telephone receiver, listened for a moment, then, with twinkling eyes, remarked briskly, 'No, this is *not* T. Walton, Fruiterer: our business is music!'

One of her favourite hobbies has always been needlework, and she used to spend many hours working devotedly at a tapestry: a copy of a sixteenth-century canvas, four metres long and two metres high, showing the long-since-vanished mansion of Stoke Edith. She brought knowledge and care to her supervision of the garden which Russell Page designed, with its chain of lily ponds, fountains, Mexican tropical plants, rare ferns and rockeries tended by two men. An excellent cook, she prepared connoisseur dishes for the many regular visitors to her home: such celebrities as Colin Graham, Hans Werner Henze, the Oliviers, Sir Lennox Berkeley and Lord Goodman. A vital, sharp-eyed compendium of diverse gifts, whom Edward Greenfield described, not inappropriately as 'Maria Callas with the mouth turned upwards instead of down',[3] she frequently wore gay sailor-suits and radiated immense charm, co-ordinating travel arrangments with a brisk, encyclopaedic efficiency and, although she knew very little about music, applying a gentle and mature understanding to Sir William's busy, complex life.

Complex it may have been, but the man himself had a refreshing honesty of purpose, a fundamental sincerity that found no room for conversational sham or artifice. The mischievous delight he took in deflating egos did not spare even his friends, however lofty their professional status and accomplishments. André Previn recalled how, after conducting a very successful concert of Walton's music, he asked the composer to write something in his copy of one of the scores performed that night. Sir William took out his pen and opened the score, carefully wrote for a whole minute, then placed the score on Previn's dressing-table. The room was filled with people, including critics and reporters who had been covering the great man's eightieth birthday celebrations. Before the conductor could peruse Walton's inscription for himself, one of the reporters grabbed the score and, in a loud voice, read out the most flattering enconium that Previn had ever received. While the conductor squirmed with mingled delight and embarrassment, the journalist turned to the composer. 'Sir William, do you really mean all the nice things you wrote in Mr Previn's score?' he asked. Walton put on a gentle, teasing but inscrutable smile. 'Of course not,' he replied, and said no more.[4]

'No man is an island . . .' wrote the poet and theologian John Donne, and in the sense in which he meant this profundity he was undoubtedly right; but a composer like Sir William Walton, increasingly marooned and isolated by changing cultural standards and tastes, by the inexplicable and the ugly, can often seem like an island. Not some barren, unproductive lump of dead volcanic rock, but a place where sunlight, filtering through still, silent trees, conjures up a kind of unreal, florescent make-believe. It is difficult to recall this great man without feeling that he belonged to another, more leisurely, more fruitful and reflective era.

In April 1981, accompanied by his wife and balanced precariously on a seat in a small Soho cinema, he was given a preview of Tony Palmer's film biography of his life. Broadcast by the BBC on Easter Sunday the same year, it showed Sir William, pale and fragile, leaning on his piano and, with extreme difficulty, composing. His eyes were large and sad. 'I have reached the part now where it will go very quickly and be over before I know it,' he said. Expressing relentlessly gloomy views about old age, Walton spoke of the fits of black depression that engulfed him so frequently. This was not surprising, for most of his friends and coevals—Hindemith, Christopher Hassall, Lord Britten, Lady Wimborne, Stravinsky, Imma Doernberg, Sassoon, Lambert and others—had vanished, like ghostly figures, into the pages of history. Only Sir Sacheverell Sitwell, now reclusive with his wife Georgia at Weston Hall, Towcester, Northamptonshire, survived from the formidable Sitwell trio. As a result of their friendship and patronage, Walton had acquired a polish and sophistication that served him well in the higher echelons of society; but, as André Previn observed, no matter how many honours were heaped upon him, no matter how imposing his personality became, the plainspun image of the Lancastrian-born Willie Walton lurked tantalizingly behind that of the much revered Sir William Walton. The writer and critic Clifford Burwyn Rees contributed this portrait of the composer:

> The longish pallid face could belong to a young successful Ambassador. No secrets are being blurted; or he could be, very nearly, Sherlock Holmes. He is not the kind of personality that blows the candles out. Slim, cool—the word persists in recurring—poised, alert, disciplined, he always has an air of distinction. He observes the human scene without apparent excitement. I should guess that he often finds it amusing. . . .
>
> His generosity is known only to his friends, and only to them. He will do you good behind your own back. Try to get him to talk about his work and he will ask you for a match, seek a receptacle a little way off in which to deposit it, and you have lost him. I know few persons who 'keep out of the way' who are so unmistakably there when they choose. His brilliant career is public property. But he has no eye for the limelight and follows no fashion.[5]

In extolling Walton's generosity, the many acts of kindness he did by stealth, Rees did not exaggerate. One such act came to my notice a few days after Sir William died. It concerned my friend Dr Stewart Craggs, the Sunderland author of a unique, superbly documented and wholly indispensable catalogue of Walton's compositions. For his Master of Arts degree, Stewart wrote a splendid thesis on Walton's life and music. In the course of doing so he exchanged many letters with the composer. Some of the replies he received were extremely helpful, but inevitably, when permission was sought to use some biographical facts, Walton, with a characteristic flare-up of aggressiveness, would volley a blunt, almost rude refusal, reminding one of what he said to Gilliam Widdicombe concerning manuscripts of letters he had destroyed: 'If I'd known that somebody like you was going to be on my track, I'd have torn up a hell of a lot more!'[6] Remarks like these were often part of his breezy bonhomie, his good-natured way of 'putting up the shutters' when the wind of inquisitiveness blew too strongly, and perhaps even Stewart, with his sharp percipience, failed to realize fully the affection with which Sir William came to regard him. He did so in November 1982 when, out of the blue, a letter from Walton reached him, enclosing the score of a Duettino for Oboe and Violin which he had composed for Stewart's two adorable children, Barnaby and Cordelia. Earlier that year Sir William had collapsed only six days after celebrating his eightieth birthday and was rushed to hospital, where he had spent a week in the intensive care unit, festooned with needles and tubes. Despite the pain and suffering, the weariness and the sadness, which he must have experienced during the few precious months of his life that remained, he had the love and generosity to make so noble a gift to the children. Perhaps, in a sense, nothing that Walton did in the whole of his life—not even the First Symphony, rugged and awe-inspiring in its Sibelian grandeur—was finer than this.

A glowing testament to the huge and kindly spirit that illumined the character of Sir William Walton was paid by a fellow-composer, Elizabeth Lutyens, who died on 14 April 1983. In her absorbing book *A Goldfish Bowl*[7] she described him as a tremendously beneficial influence on both music and his contemporaries, a man who would selflessly 'stick his neck out' to support a good cause, who would unhesitatingly extend a helping hand to a deserving colleague. Walton, she affirmed, was the very best of company, 'devoid of that "safety first" cautious respectability of the middle classes . . . whose very virtues rob musical bread of yeast'.

Walton, for some considerable time, had known her father, Sir Edward, the great architect who designed the Whitehall Cenotaph, and other members of his family, so, meeting the composer by chance, she asked if he would give her an introduction to Muir Mathieson, musical director to most of the large British film companies, as she wanted to obtain work. Sir William immediately replied, 'Of course I will; but I'll do more than that. Write any work you like and dedicate it to me, and I'll give you £100.' This magnanimous and spontaneous act imparted fresh courage and hope to Elizabeth Lutyens in what she described as 'one of my darkest hours', and, as the immensely shrewd Walton had undoubtedly realized, his £100—proof that she could actually earn money by composing—restored her self-confidence in full measure. The work she wrote for her benefactor was *The Pit*, a dramatic scena for tenor, baritone and women's chorus.

Spike Hughes, in his autobiography *Opening Bars*, appraised Walton in these words:

> If I were to analyse exactly what it is about the music of William Walton which attracts me, I think I would say its virility. It is English music, but written by an Englishman who has something to say for himself in his own language, not in the olde-worlde droolery, folk-chantery of Somerset yokels. It is music by an Englishman who is aware of his nationality but is also aware that the world is a much smaller place than it used to be; William Walton is a Lancashire lad who had lived in Italy, lain in its sunshine, breathed its clean air and absorbed its music. The Italian influence on Willie's music is strong; it gives his music clarity, wit and colour and acts as a natural antidote to the English composer's national obsession with temperate half-tones and melancholy reflection on the mysteries of autumn and the holiday camp atmosphere of old Stonehenge. Willie can be gay; thank God he is never 'merry'. He can be serious; he can be aggressive. But he is serious and aggressive with all the guts of a man of strong convictions; his seriousness and aggressiveness are never the self-pity and cantankerousness of the misunderstood Chelsea drunk. One of William Walton's most endearing qualities is his ability to regard his own music with alarming irreverence; but it is the irreverence of a parodist who has a genuine affection for the thing he parodies.[8]

This irreverence probably stemmed not so much from modesty as from the nostalgic regret which retrospective self-examination so often conjures up, for hidden behind Sir William's impish and whimsical humour one detected a sad, frustrated, rather disillusioned man who, even after being acclaimed by many of his contemporaries as one of the major figures in British music, seemed to behave as though it had all happened in the land of make-believe and might suddenly vanish in a puff of smoke. His powerful urge to debunk and denigrate his own music, as well as that of other composers, could be embarrassing to his friends and admirers. He once described *Belshazzar's Feast*, which remains his most popular big work, as 'a beastly noise'[9], and, while reminiscing on the occasion of his eightieth birthday, he remarked, 'I'm a disappointed man. I could have done much better. Rather sad, really!' He often brooded over the validity of what he was doing when it appeared to conflict with the pseudo-progressive trends of the day and, in some of his large-scale 'abstract' compositions like the Second Symphony (a commissioned work for which he kept the Royal Liverpool Philharmonic Society waiting a year beyond the 'deadline' date), one hears, faintly beneath the glitter of the notes, the troubled voice of Walton asking 'Where am I going? What is it all worth?' He was frequently at the home of Sir Lennox Berkeley, whose son Michael, himself a composer, said that after chatting to Walton he had the impression of an 'insecure' man who did not quite believe that people loved him and his music as much as they were supposed to do. 'He didn't realize in what respect he was held.' Tony Palmer, the well-known musicologist and writer, spoke of Walton as having a sense of inadequacy which was reflected in the anguish of some of his music. This is how really great men react to their own mighty achievements, and the climber who stands, weary but exhilarated on the summit of Everest, knows that he has only come closer to heaven, not reached it.

Walton had an insatiable thirst for knowledge, with an absorbing interest in music of every kind, ranging from Ravel, Wagner and Villa-Lobos to Henze and Stockhausen by way of Schoenberg and Bartók, and, notwithstanding his marvellous professionalism, he was largely self-taught, which doubtless had some bearing on the sense of failure or inadequacy which haunted him throughout his life. The first Manchester performance of his First Symphony was given by Malcolm Sargent and the Hallé Orchestra on 24 February 1938, and the *Oldham Chronicle* reported that, on the previous day, 'A tall, fair young man crept into the Free Trade Hall while the orchestra was rehearsing an intricate movement' and that 'at the first break in the playing he hurried up to the platform and tugged at Dr Malcolm Sargent's sleeve to make a modest suggestion.'[10] It was, of course, William Walton, and after Sargent had invited him onto the platform, he sat beside the conductor, not only explaining his own ideas about interpretation but also carefully noting the various 'tricks of timing' and harmonic subtleties used in the rehearsal. This is but one example of how, profiting from the friendly advice and collaboration of others, he greatly enlarged his range of understanding, expertise and self-confidence. Walton had gleaned much valuable knowledge during his early, productive years at Oxford, helped and encouraged by such fine teachers as Dr Hugh Allen, Dr Henry Ley, Dr Ernest Walker and Dr Thomas Strong, but the musical giant he became resulted from his own divine gifts as a composer, and from a certain imitative genius and resourcefulness, a capacity to find out for himself 'how things worked'.

As part of the eightieth birthday celebrations, the BBC, on 25 March 1982, broadcast a television account of an interview which Russell Harty had with Sir William at his home on Ischia. Speaking to Harty in a slow, gentle voice, wearing his familiar broad-brimmed straw hat and surrounded by clumps of camellias and jasmine, Walton acknowledged his 'enormous debt to the Sitwells', who had 'behaved ideally', never imposing any pressures or restrictions upon him. Harty's references to 'certain myths and stories' that Sir William was actually, by blood relationship, an offspring of the Sitwells drew a merry chuckle from the composer, who countered it with the information that, according to Constant Lambert, his mother had been Dame Ethel Smythe! Remarking that many people had come to believe that he would not compose any more music, Harty asked him why, unexpectedly, he had written his *Prologo e Fantasia* for Rostropovich, who commissioned it. 'We met him in Russia when the London Symphony Orchestra invited us to accompany them on a tour,' interrupted Lady Walton, 'and William, who had always been sad that Rostropovich had never played his Cello Concerto, wanted to know when he would do so. And the old boy sat down and said "You do *me* a favour . . . I do *you* a favour. You write new work and I play new work and old work." Well, he was delighted with the new work, and the other day he sent us a telegram confirming that he will play the Cello Concerto.' During his wife's animated explanation, Sir William remarked, in a dry, conspiratorial aside, 'We did a bit of a deal.'

At the end of the programme, Lady Walton, questioned about her husband's application to the sheer mechanics of composing, recalled that a very cross Sir Malcolm Sargent had told her, 'You must lock William up in his music room, so that he will work longer hours,' but she added whimsically, 'It isn't true. Wives do lock composers up, but they escape through the window, as Puccini did, because his wife couldn't tell who was playing the piano inside the room—of course it was the pupil and meanwhile Puccini had jumped through the window and gone shooting.' Asked about the future of the Walton estate when she and her husband were no longer there to look after it, Lady Walton reported that they had founded a Walton Trust which will keep the garden open in perpetuity.

'A hole will be scooped out of a pyramid of rock in one part of the garden,' she said, rather sadly.

'And what's that for?' asked Russell Harty.

"For my ashes,' remarked Sir William, 'like playing cricket, you know!'

Walton, with his curious way of smoking a pipe, dangling it in his mouth without those puckerings of the lips and contorting grimaces in which other men indulge, had a striking but impenetrable air of distinction. He stimulated conversation, not usually by provocative or profound remarks but by saying very little, observing the human scene with shrewd, penetrating eyes that, in themselves, induced others to speak their minds in the hope of stimulating his. Although orchestral players referred to him affectionately as 'Willie', he was never the easiest of men to understand or even tolerate.

When his vituperation, rising steadily inside him like the boiling, molten rock in the belly of a volcano, finally erupted, it burned and blistered those it touched. Walter Legge, husband of the great singer Elisabeth Schwarzkopf, sat with Walton in a box at Covent Garden on the first night of *Troilus and Cressida* and subsequently related[11] how his companion kept up a running commentary on the performance which consisted largely of four-letter words, and one six-letter word repeated incessantly with uncontrolled rage and bitterness. Doubtless the composer's wrath focused chiefly upon the myopic Sir Malcolm Sargent, whose conducting rapport with stage and orchestra seemed precarious. In the earlier days when prowling critics sank their teeth into Walton's music, he reacted violently. Once, at the Aeolian Hall, he raised his crutch and vigorously assaulted a reviewer who had shown him calculated rudeness. 'I have never quite known what the role of a critic was,' he remarked sardonically during a 1976 interview. 'Do they develop a cult of a certain composer or do they sometimes quite deliberately set out to destroy him? Critics can do you a lot of damage, but most of them don't do you much good. They could do if they tried, if they weren't so vitriolic. . . .'[12]

Now, when Sir William is no longer with us, a vibrant, compelling, larger-than-life personality seen only in retrospect, his music is classically acceptable and widely appreciated; the hostility and the acid dissonance are gone. In the twilight of his years, looking around the British musical scene with a wry sense of humour, he must, despite his bitter regret at not having written mightier, more enduring works, his tragic sense of lost opportunity, have felt some pride over his achievements. Honours, including a knighthood and an Order of Merit, had been heaped upon him. 'I was very lucky,' said Walton, reminiscing to an interviewer. 'I was so damned stupid, all I could do was to write music.' For stupidity such as this, diverting a natural genius from the barren hills of commerce into green pastures of melody and counterpoint, rhythm and nuance, suffused with the glory of his matchless creative imagination, posterity is grateful. Sir William's modesty, his innate simplicity of character, his almost childlike sincerity and dedication, find a fitting eloquence in these lines by Arthur William Edgar O'Shaughnessy:

We are the music-makers,
We are the dreamers of dreams.

# *The Music*

# Introduction

Sir William Walton's personality and genius have proved attractive to a wide range of twentieth-century musicians, notwithstanding the fact that he came at a particularly fractured time in the history of composition when many new and experimental trends jostled for recognition. He must have been keenly aware, even at the age of twenty, of the musical climate around him, and, with his innate conservatism, his love of pure diatonic melody—a love which he sometimes self-consciously concealed behind harmless asperities—it must, at times, have filled him with unease and foreboding. In order to assess fully the courage and dedication of the man, as well as the significance and value of what he achieved, let us examine briefly some of the major developments in music since those exciting days when Wagner, with his daring chromaticisms, flagrantly breached the frontiers of traditionalism and, as it then appeared, brought the edifice of simple diatonic melody crashing to the ground.

Prominent among the innovators were Schoenberg, Berg and Webern, the progenitors of the 'Second Viennese School' who pioneered the state of total harmonic permissiveness known as atonality, or serialism, which fired the imaginations of Krenek, Hartmann, Steinecke, Nono, Ligeti, Kagel, Maderman and other avant-gardists. Stravinsky, in his *Petrushka*, popularized 'bitonality', the simultaneous use of two keys, and this was succeeded by 'polytonality', the deployment of several keys at once, much favoured by Darius Milhaud, the French tradition-breaker. Another startling innovation, that of 'microtones', or intervals smaller than a semitone, has appeared, although it has not so far settled on the periphery of music. John Cage championed 'aleatoric' music, in which chance plays a decisive role, with the performer making a random choice from various 'solutions' as to which passage or phrase he will play; and, dominated by the father-figure of Karlheinz Stockhausen, the complexities of electronic music, or *musique concrète*, have staked their claims to recognition.

Walton reacted to all this neither by servile conformity to the up-and-coming order nor by a sweeping rejection of radical trends but by evolving a highly individualistic musical language that best served his creative purposes. A composer who looked to the past for guidance and precept—rather like Johann Sebastian Bach in relation to his many precursors—he presented his discoveries to the world not by anachronistic repetition but by inventing a tone and a rhythm which were unmistakably his own. Even the most frivolous of the *Façade* pieces revealed a greater solidity and substance than anything produced by the school of Cocteau and 'Les Six'; and while the pagan *Belshazzar's Feast* revived the tradition of oratorio, its barbaric exhortation of cruel idolatry, involving harsh dissonances and flamboyant effects, blew the same tradition sky high. When his rebel days were over, Walton continued to compose with a fertile imagination, using no 'modern' formula but often surprising and delighting the listener with a certain air of defiant, innovatory brightness. After the performance of his Second Symphony, some critics denigrated him, not because the work was old-fashioned but because, in its psychological or mental growth, it displayed no protean evolutions. This did not deter Walton from progressing along the path he had chosen, creating music of no decreasing vitality, strength, beauty and personality: music on which I have commented in the following chapters. If he had lived in a more stable, unsophisticated age, he might have explored greater depths of consciousness, touched more exhilarating heights; but neither speculation nor regret can dim the glory of his achievements.

# 12

# The Symphonies

## Symphony No 1 in B Flat Minor

This work, towering to Sibelian peaks in its rugged, hostile grandeur, was born into a world in which the seven mighty symphonies of the Finnish composer were frequently performed in Britain, but a world in which doubts about the relevance of a form so popular and over-exploited were only slowly and with great difficulty being dispelled. The major composers of the previous generation had largely avoided it, but Walton, taking the plunge, restored its credibility, and what he produced, after much heart-searching and despair, was an indisputable masterpiece and probably the finest British symphony since Elgar. With its massive structure held together by pedal points and *ostinati* under very free dissonant harmony, it has many characteristic asperities, including jagged cross-rhythms and jazzy syncopations. The symphony, which stands firmly in the conflict-and-triumph tradition of Beethoven's Fifth, is fundamentally Romantic, notwithstanding its high-voltage electricity, and although the music has a shattering range of power, the scoring is fairly conventional: double woodwind, brass and strings, with only two players involved in the percussion. Few listeners will fail to recognize the influence of Sibelius in this many-voiced composition, but they should also note how Walton mixes his instrumental tone-colours in a manner somewhat similar to Elgar.

The first movement, *Allegro assai*, begins *pianissimo* but soon generates enormous strength and vitality, creating a massive structure from a few basic ideas. As in Beethoven's Ninth Symphony, there is a rhythmic insistence on the interval of the fifth, although the ghost of Sibelius flits uneasily through the movement, manifesting itself firstly in a poignant oboe solo focused upon D flat, then through a more aggressive and forceful personality. This oboe melody has been copied, perhaps unconsciously, by other composers, including the late Herbert Howells, who used it, commencing at bar 47, in his *Saraband for the Morning of Easter*, and Francis Chagrin, who deployed it in the first movement of his symphony. Against firm pedal points, sometimes on the home-base B flat, sometimes on C, Walton, with an obsessive intensity, repeats the oboe melody and three other preliminary ideas—a calm, ascending figure on the horns, a flurrying passage on the violins, and a gruff, descending figure on cellos and basses—until, like a rumbling volcano suddenly blowing off its top, the music explodes into another key. After the first explosion, the woodwind elaborate the original oboe melody *fortissimo*, while the strings voice a savage theme until, once again, the tumult subsides to usher in a long, impassioned melody on the violins. A new conflict of awe-inspiring ferocity is unleashed for the development, and, with the opening rhythm and the oboe melody triumphant, the impetus of the music sweeps forward into a shortened, but immensely gripping, recapitulation.

Walton's much-publicized malice (*malizia*) sends a riveting electrical current through the *scherzo*, in whose inimical themes and bitingly perverse rhythms a hovering, often spiteful animosity flickers like a snake's tongue; but there are broader, more stable episodes, including a passage for all the strings playing together, *martellato*, which serves as an introduction to the melancholy (*malincolia*) slow movement, one of singular beauty with a nostalgic, other-worldly atmosphere and a rousing climax. A feature of this marvellously compact and organized movement, which makes use of pedal points, is the Waltonian *ictus*, or rhythmical stress of two semiquavers before a sustained note.

The finale (*maestoso—brioso ed ardamente*) is heralded and concluded by a noble introduction and epilogue. Bernard Shore, that much esteemed viola-player, compared the exultant glow and ceremonial splendour of this movement with the shattering force of the trumpets that flattened the walls of Jericho; and certainly the great dramatic peak of the closing bars, rocked by violent, unpredictable explosions, is a gripping piece of rhetoric. Nevertheless, hearing the finale after the tremendous first movement, the savage *scherzo* and the sad, brooding *andante*, I am all too conscious that, as mentioned previously in this book, Walton, after a long delay, completed it with extreme difficulty when the rest of the symphony had already been premièred. Until the coda is reached, the music, whose mood suggests a rhetorical affirmation rather than a proud cry of '*Consummatum est*', is not so intense in feeling. The movement is shaped like a triptych, the first panel presenting a *maestoso* prologue, launched with a battering fanfare and rooted in B flat; the second, a stretch of pungent, jabbing *Belshazzar*-like rhythms leading to a fiery fugue in 3/4 time commenced by second violins and violas; the third, an imposing climax, in which the two main themes are luminously transformed on the high strings, heavy brass and timpani (six in all, manipulated by two players), then sweeping on *fortissimo* in the full orchestra, to end with a typical Waltonian flourish of defiance. The symphony is an irresistibly compelling work, romantic in style and of lofty dimensions. Perhaps, as the years pass and the music can be assessed in closer, more balanced perspective, the manner in which Sir William wrote the finale, contrasting it rather oddly with the rest of the symphony, may be seen as yet another example of his intuitive and capricious mastery.

### Symphony No 2 in G

The loud scoring, truculence and sustained bitterness of feeling in Walton's First Symphony reflected a temperament which seemed to hover between the extremes of romantic melancholy and expressive high spirits. He was never a prolific composer, and twenty-five years passed before he wrote another symphony, in response to a commission from the Royal Liverpool Philharmonic Society to celebrate the 750th anniversary of the granting of the charter of incorporation to the borough. Some critics have regarded the Second Symphony as 'a less uncompromising work' with (a term which Sir William heartily disliked) 'romantic qualities'. It is perhaps more of a massive *divertimento* than a symphony, although it uses a larger orchestra than its predecessor (triple woodwind, brass and strings, timpani, piano, celesta, two harps, vibraphone), and the music, intensely personal, is unmistakably Walton throughout. Certainly no one could justly upbraid him for being unadventurous, since he uses a twelve-note structure in the finale.

The first movement, *Allegro molto*, derives principally from the leap of a major seventh, and the opening theme, announced over a background of strings and celesta in G minor, carries the harmonic flavour of much of the Violin Concerto and some of the *Troilus and Cressida* music. A certain ambiguity of tonality, reminiscent of the *Scapino* overture, attaches to the rather feebly characterized second subject, which lingers briefly in a *grazioso* mood before being displaced by the zestful brilliance of the opening, whose bite is now sharpened by syncopations—a typically Waltonian device of 6/8 within a 3/4 frame which occurs also in the music of Brahms. Then follows an interlude in which the two moods—one pungent and incisive, the other much gentler—are foiled against each other, with the first of these predominating. The music ends softly in G minor.

In the elegiac second movement, *Lento assai*, we find what appears in perspective to be an almost continuous, unbroken web of sumptuous *cantilena* writing, rather than of isolated separate themes, but which does, in fact, contain some passages of nervous agitation. Opening with a few bars of rising fourths in the woodwind, the music flows into a section where mellow woodwind solos are set against muted strings. After the strings have delivered, unmuted, a few more elaborate bars, the pace gathers momentum in a largely direct, unadorned section full of sharp rhythmic ejaculations which introduces a soft, chordal woodwind motive with a slightly dark, ominous feeling. Horns take up this motive, strings are added, then a stretch of lyrical scoring is ruffled by the sharp ejaculations already noted and, with brass and percussion used more assertively, the music gravitates for the first time in the movement towards a climax. Suddenly the drama subsides into a beautifully expressive section, with figurations on strings, woodwind, celesta and two harps constantly rising and falling, like a scintillating fountain, around a slow horn solo. At a point where the ascending fourths of the opening bars are heard descending, the music, whose dynamic energy has gradually been intensifying, sweeps forward into the stunning, if slightly unconventional, full climax, which ends in some ravishing bars where, typical of Walton's caprice, the tonality hovers intriguingly between B major and B minor.

The finale is a *passacaglia*, comprising a twelve-tone theme which, framed in a clear tonal context of G minor, is not in the least Schoenbergian. There are ten variations, many of them short with considerable contrasts in mood, a *fugata*, based on the *passacaglia* theme, and a *scherzando* which, serving as a coda, leads to a G major chord, reiterated many times by the full orchestra.

# 13

# Concertos, etc

## Viola Concerto

Despite the powerful influence of Paul Hindemith and the magnificent advocacy of such players as Lionel Tertis and William Primrose, the viola, that Cinderella of stringed instruments, has never been really popular with the average music-lover as a concert-hall soloist, although Tertis's wonderful virtuosity inspired a large number of chamber works, as well as a fine concerto in the modern idiom by Elisabeth Machonchy, in which the viola sings with great eloquence. A fifth lower than the violin and altogether heavier, it is a difficult instrument which looks almost big enough to warrant being played between the legs like a cello and, unlike the violin, is best used not as a purveyor of dazzling pyrotechnics and aerobatic brilliance but as a highly distinctive voice bringing gravity and beauty, strength and drama, within the inner harmony of an orchestra or string quartet. To hear the viola, with its unmistakable contralto tone, played soloistically and with surpassing mastery for the first time is to become aware of a richer, more picturesque and resonant form of communication.

Walton's Viola Concerto evolves by gentle means, not by flashy ostentation or heart-throbbing rhetoric, reserving its most profound feelings for the more intimate dialogues between one instrument and another. It has the usual three movements, but, introducing a characteristic touch of novelty, the composer puts the slow movement first, a precedent which he was to follow in the Violin Concerto. In 1962, thirty-three years after Walton conducted the *première*, with Hindemith in the solo part, he rescored the work for a smaller orchestra, using double instead of triple woodwind, omitting one trumpet and tuba and adding a harp.

In the first movement, *Andante comodo*, muted strings, with a single clarinet in its chalumeau register, establish the tonality of A minor, seeming, by the restlessness of the phrases, to be searching for an elusive idea. Scarcely three bars pass before the solo viola enters with an extended theme whose haunting beauty is to illuminate the finale with unforgettable eloquence. It starts with a rising interval, a lift onto the higher note that is one of the appealing facets of the music. Soon, against a fine web of counterpoint, the solo viola introduces the second subject, whose cantilena allows the instrument to sing like a prima donna. This arresting theme, flavoured with drama as well as poetry, provides an abundance of lyrical music which enriches the whole movement. The development draws upon both main themes, its frequent time-changes, with syncopated rhythmic versions on muted brass, producing much of the soloist's fast passage-work. Soaring to its highest register, the viola, now passionate and impetuous, delivers in sixths yet another version of the main second subject, which the orchestra foils with a vigorous account of the first main subject. As the tension subsides, the viola reiterates the opening argument, poignantly highlighting its contemplative nature, and the movement ends, as it began, quietly.

The second movement, *Vivo, con molto preciso*, has great vivacity and a definite *scherzoso* character. Again the solo instrument is heard in the opening bars, throwing out a rhythmic tune which is volleyed backwards and forwards with much brilliance between soloist and orchestra until the fun stops abruptly when *pianissimo* muted brass introduce a syncopated second subject of contrasting design. The soloist develops this in his own right, showing it to be perfectly relevant to the vocabulary of stringed instruments; but first he announces another important theme, which the orchestra seizes upon, demonstrating in a breezy *Portsmouth Point Overture* manner that it can express the idea more fully than a solo viola. Finally, when the three main themes of the movement have been exploited in a sparkling display, with rapidly shifting rhythmic patterns, the music burns itself out.

In the closing movement, *Allegro moderato*, the longest and most highly organized of the three, a bassoon plays a somewhat arid solo melody, but when it finishes its course, the viola takes it up, enlarges and enriches it, brings it to a high climax, then hands it over to the orchestra. The next large theme is announced by the solo viola and answered by the clarinet. As the music swells orchestrally, a noble broadening of the bassoon tune is heard, treated canonically over a static bass, and then comes the crowning glory of the work, an affectingly sincere and exalted passage. In an atmosphere of contemplative sadness the solo instrument, accompanied by *tremolando* strings, plays a transfigured version of the concerto's opening themes, while the principal theme of the finale hovers in the bass. The effect is spellbinding.

Violin Concerto

Of the three concertos that Walton wrote the one for violin and orchestra, deeply felt with haunting flights of fancy and a heart-plucking sweetness of tone, is the most romantic. The expansive and rhapsodic cantilena of the Violin Concerto, as exemplified by the inspired second subject of its finale, makes the beautiful melodies of the Viola Concerto sound rather demure in comparison. Walton's rising sevenths, often heard in passages of great emotional intensity, are as overwhelming to the listener as Elgar's falling sevenths. The solo part, painstakingly edited by Jascha Heifetz, is of almost phenomenal difficulty. In order to highlight the player's artistry, the composer re-states themes in different shapes, with a good deal of filigree counterpoint.

The first movement, set in the key of B minor and marked *Andante tranquillo*, is, like that of the Viola Concerto, the slowest of the three, and the opening bars give no hint that this is to be a brilliant display piece. Not until after the orchestra has announced the second subject on the first violins does the soloist begin his flamboyant flights of rhetoric, with dazzling arpeggios, scales, wide leaps, and broken octave passages that lead to a brief cadenza ending on a held note. The speed quickens and the orchestra, playing in compound time, builds up an impressive climax and the free recapitulation follows, after which the movement closes with the same calm atmosphere as prevailed in the opening. One is constantly aware, in the slower passages, of the very subtle harmonisations, coloured by a typically Waltonian bitter-sweet melancholy.

In the second movement, *Presto capriccioso alla napolitana*, a bar of orchestral helter-skelter sets the mercurial mood, then the solo violin commences what proves to be a virtuoso showpiece. This movement, played at demonic speed and introducing almost every trick of violin technique, can be seen as a conventional *scherzo*, with a trio central section marked *Canzonetta*, which, beginning with a songlike melody on the solo horn, comes as soon as the *scherzo* themes have fulfilled their roles with dash and sparkle. A captivating passage of 'Mediterranean' music in languorous waltz rhythm justifies the *napolitana* part of the title. The return of the *scherzo*, punctuated by explosive recollections of the opening bars, is not in any sense a formal reprise and merely recaptures the spirit of the first section, with an intriguing hint of remembered experience.

The finale, *Vivace*, shows the influence of Shostakovich in some of the spiky melodic lines, and of Elgar in the extensive accompanied cadenza towards the end of the work. It commences at a lively 3/4 tempo, but soon the soloist is heard in one of Walton's most eloquent and serene inventions. First delivered on the lower strings and bassoons, the main theme becomes a springboard for several subsidiary ideas, which are superimposed on the solo 'voice' to provide contrapuntal interest. After much interweaving of the various thematic elements, Walton astonishes and delights us by bringing in a brilliant synthesis of the opening theme of the first movement, now played in sixths, with its long slow tune beautifully embellished in thirds by the soloist. This music serves to unify the whole concerto: it flavours the finely constructed cadenza and reappears in the ensuing *alla marcia* immediately preceding the splendid flourish which ends the work. Walton revised the concerto in 1943, changing various expression marks and altering certain tempo directions. The revisions were embodied in the score which OUP published in 1945.

Cello Concerto

The cello more nearly approaches the human voice than any other instrument, and just as the operatic bass infuses regality, profundity, sadness and a monolithic nobility into rôles like those of Mussorgsky's *Boris Godunov* or Szymanowski's *King Roger*, so this magnificent, richly timbred instrument brings a throbbing beauty and poignancy, an uplifting spirituality or surging passion, to whatever is being performed on the stage or concert platform. As the player coaxes those long, swan-like melodies from his cello, he must seem to many listeners like an incurable romantic, dreaming of fair ladies and castles with gleaming white towers. A comparatively small number of illustrious composers have written notable concertos for this *bel canto* string vocalist—Bach, Haydn, Boccherini, Schumann, Dvorák, Saint-Saëns, Elgar, Delius, Shostakovich, Martinu and, of course, Walton, but the repertoire is meagre. That Walton should have written a Cello Concerto at all is remarkable, since he always disclaimed any real ability to play an instrument—courage, however, was one of his dominant characteristics and, with it, adaptability.

In his concerto he has made the most of the cello's rich *cantabile* voice by giving us what are in effect two slow, rhapsodical movements, instead of the usual one, and has created the necessary balance and contrast by putting a fast, substantial *scherzo* between them. His orchestra is fairly modest in size, so that the soloist can be clearly heard at all times; but Walton produces a dazzling range of colour, with strings divided into glowing chords, and the percussion instruments, which include a vibraphone and celesta, achieving a delicate as well as full-blooded variety of expression. As a means of intensifying the colour range, all the second woodwind players are required to double up on the first part.

In the opening *Moderato* movement the orchestra, mostly light and transparent, highlights the songful solo part, which falls into seven roughly equal portions or paragraphs, the first of which is heard three times. The movement starts with a 'splash' from the vibraphone and harp, enhanced by gentle viola trills, and after two bars the soloist enters with the principal melody, a meditative, though widely ranging, tune that ends with a prolonged diatonic cadence, its final bars dropping through five octaves. There are constant shifts of colour in the short but gripping development, with the solo voices of the winds brought forward to complement that of the cello. The movement has no cadenza.

Constructed in the ABBA (coda) design which the Germans call *Bogen*, the middle movement, an *allegro appassionato* in triple time, is based on a rapid rhythmic figure used to introduce the soloist's first theme (A). A quieter, more contemplative melody is heard before the material is elaborated; then a march-like theme, initiated by the soloist, but soon appropriated by the orchestra, ushers in the second section (B), culminating in a triple-stopped phrase that subsequently reappears twice. This fresh group of themes leads into a highly expressive flight of *cantabile*, after which the group is restated, with a partly accompanied cadenza inserted into the section. The movement, crowned by a very precise coda, ends with a quotation from the opening bars.

There can be few parallels to Walton's *tema con improvvisazioni* finale, which exploits the original concerto concept of antithesis by allotting two variations to the orchestra *tutti* and two (second and fourth) to the soloist, unaccompanied. As regards the theme itself, this is long and highly organized. The orchestra repeats it quietly in the first variation, while the soloist provides a filigree of triplet counterpoint. The second variation, played by the soloist, is marked *risoluto* and *brioso*: not being simply *bravura*, it faintly resembles a cadenza but can hardly be described as one. An orchestral toccata in compound time forms the very full-blooded third variation, which brings in a plethora of percussion, *glissandi* and bright, chirpy woodwind. The fourth variation, marked *rapsodicamente*, allows the soloist and the listener plenty of excitement, ending in a flurry of trills that leads to the 'epilogue', an *adagio* based on quotations from the previous movements. This device clearly establishes the unity of the whole work.

*Sinfonia Concertante*

A clever and entertaining piece free from the grimmer features of Walton's mature style, the *Sinfonia Concertante*, given its first performance in 1928, represents a phase of his career (including *Façade* and the *Portsmouth Point* overture) when his attitude to music, definitely anti-romantic and flavoured by a satirical gaiety, resembled that of Stravinsky. It was not until he wrote the Viola Concerto that the poet in Walton, thirsting for self-expression, displayed another, vastly more appealing side of his personality. Infused with a greater sobriety than he had shown previously, the *Sinfonia Concertante* needs a first-class pianist; but since it has little to play that is really memorable or rewarding, few distinguished artists are willing to perform it. In the revised version of 1943, described as 'with piano obbligato', Walton, doubtless inspired by his new phase of neo-classical dalliance, removed much of the counterpoint in the first and last movements. Dealing with the slow movement, he transferred the introduction from the solo piano to the orchestra, simplified the keyboard writing, and lengthened the piece by one bar at the end, where the final chord is held for an extra bar and a half. After a slow *Maestoso* introduction of massive scale in which the opening piano chords are duplicated by the strings, with 'added' notes making the texture richer and denser, the *Allegro spiritoso* movement arrives and, after being announced in canon by the piano in double octaves and by the horn, it deploys several ideas consecutively and with much ingenuity. In the second movement, marked *Andante comodo*, brass is used very sparingly, and the music, revealing strange cross-rhythms, is often sensuous or devotional in feeling, striking a deeper emotional note than anything in the composer's earlier works. Walton concludes the *Sinfonia Concertante* with a high-spirited finale, *Allegro vivo sempre scherzando*, full of twisting, leaping phrases, off-beat accents and bright skirmishes into the realm of jazz-like syncopation.

In 1928 Walton made an arrangement for two pianos of music from the *Sinfonia Concertante*, and this, edited by Roy Douglas, was published in 1947.

*Fantasia Concertante*

Some time before *Portsmouth Point* he wrote a piece called *Fantasia Concertante*, scored for two pianos, jazz band and orchestra. The work has been lost, but Constant Lambert described it as using jazz rhythms in a Gershwin style, although with a profusion of clichés, some dull melody and harmony.

Sir William Walton recording *Belshazzar's Feast*

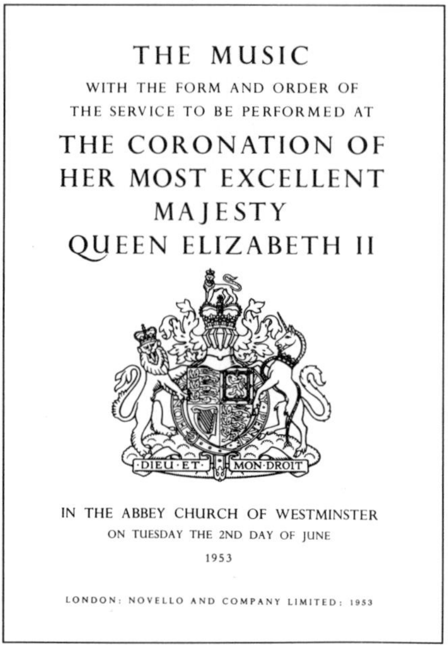
THE MUSIC

WITH THE FORM AND ORDER OF
THE SERVICE TO BE PERFORMED AT

THE CORONATION OF
HER MOST EXCELLENT
MAJESTY
QUEEN ELIZABETH II

DIEU ET MON DROIT

IN THE ABBEY CHURCH OF WESTMINSTER
ON TUESDAY THE 2ND DAY OF JUNE
1953

LONDON: NOVELLO AND COMPANY LIMITED: 1953

Title page of the Coronation Service Book used for the Coronation of Her Majesty Queen Elizabeth II in Westminster Abbey, 2 June 1953, and (right) first page of Walton's *Coronation Te Deum*

Sir William with Elisabeth Schwarzkopf and her husband Walter Legge

Discussing the score of his Second Symphony with Sir John Pritchard, who conducted the first performance in Edinburgh with the Royal Liverpool Philharmonic Orchestra on 2 September 1960

Alan Frank with Sir William and Lady Walton at the first performance of the Second Symphony in Edinburgh, 2 September 1960

Walton discusses his Second Symphony with George Szell

'La Mortella', the enchanting home of Sir William and Lady Walton on the island of Ischia

Sir William and Lady Walton in a happy and relaxed mood outside their home

Sir William received the honorary degree of Doctor of Letters from the University of Sussex in April 1968, and is here congratulated by Professor Asa Briggs, the Vice-Chancellor

Following a performance of his First Symphony at the Leningrad Philharmonic Hall, Sir William received an ovation from audience and conductor alike. He visited the Soviet Union early in 1971 with André Previn and the London Symphony Orchestra

Walton and the famous violinist Kyung Wha Chung discuss the score of his Violin Concerto

Dame Janet Baker, Sir William and Christopher Morris of the Oxford University Press admiring a new EMI recording of *Troilus and Cressida*. In 1972–1976 Walton made some revisions to his opera, changing the role of Cressida to that of mezzo so that Dame Janet could sing it

Sir William with his brothers Noel (left) and Alec (standing). A rare meeting at a Manchester hotel during his seventieth birthday celebrations

Sir William and Lady Walton photographed in London shortly before the celebration of the composer's seventieth birthday

The 'Grand Old Man of Music' smoking his favourite pipe

Sir William Walton at the Royal Festival Hall, 20 February 1982, during a rehearsal of the first performance of his *Prologo e Fantasia*, 1982

# 14

# Other Orchestral Music

*Façade*

Ever since Schoenberg composed *Pierrot Lunaire*, a set of twenty-one 'melodramas' on poems by Albert Giraud, the principle of having verse declaimed to music became increasingly popular with the Modern Movement, one example being Cocteau's *Parade*, which, presented with Picasso's décor and Satie's music, aroused hostility and censure but also a measure of warm admiration when performed in Paris in 1917. There was, of course, a huge stylistic and temperamental difference between the grandiose, many-sided, sombre and sad picture of Giraud's moonlight Harlequins, as portrayed in Schoenberg's music, and the satire, mock-sentimentality and parodistic humour so brilliantly highlighted by Walton's timeless and witty *Façade* score; but the device of the spoken melody that conforms to a notated pitch, while recognizing the difference between a sung note and a spoken note, was fundamentally the same. And the curious, dreamlike quality of Schoenberg's text found a mirrored reflection in the unreal frivolity and sophistication of Edith Sitwell's poems, which, thanks to the music, have much of the ghostly, other-world quality of those late-Victorian sepia photographs of family life that are now highly prized and priced in the antiquarian world. In both works instrumental colouring is one of the strongest means of contrast, exploring a simple but widely varied sound-palette.

According to what Edith Sitwell told Elizabeth Salter, her secretary, the genesis of *Façade* began when the nineteen-year-old Walton gave her certain rhythms and said, 'There you are, Edith, see what you can do with those',[1] whereupon she went away and wrote some poetry 'for fun'; but Sir William's recollection was that she had already penned the verses, which to him cried out for a musical setting. How the work began is not as important as the manner in which the project, involving a marvellously close Sitwell-Walton collaboration, rapidly fructified into a full-scale artistic achievement. Music meant a great deal to both of them, and, indeed, for some time, fascinated by the melody, the stresses and the inflections of language, Edith had been trying to create special musical effects by experimenting with assonances, dissonances, rhythms and repetitions, using words in much the same way as a composer uses notes and phrases. Walton, at first nonplussed as to a suitable title for the new work, finally decided to call it *Façade* on the strength of a grumbling remark made at Edith's rented, fifth-floor flat in Pembridge Mansions, Moscow Road, London, by her charlady: 'All this carry-on is just one big façade.' Marking and accenting the verses to indicate where the precise stress and emphasis fell, he began creating a magical Stravinsky-inspired fusion of poetry and music—a score full of nostalgic imagery, colouristic nuances and sly, pungent humour.

Mention has already been made of Schoenberg's *Pierrot Lunaire*, which, like *Façade*, adumbrates the principle of having verses declaimed to music. The two works, though different in other respects, have much the same aphoristic, spectral and fleeting unreality, evoking fantasy through a highly specialized blend of music and poetry—poetry which, as described by the Belgian writer Emil Cammaerts, is 'poetry run mad, poetry on the verge of becoming music'. Edith Sitwell's verses for *Façade* are made of subtle, vibratory overtones that run together as softly as the broken, fragmentary chiming of tiny silver bells, not as each line is expressively spoken, but at the precise moment when the listener hears the next one uttered and the sound-memory of the first lingers on. One example of this can be found in the first two lines of the verse used in *Valse*:

> Daisy and Lily,
> Lazy and silly. . . .

Set in the score to pitchless notes of no definite time-value which, like the megaphone, serve to depersonalize the voice and increase the hallucination of a romantic fantasy, the verses should be spoken in strict time and level tones. The music, written with a deft and natural touch, though often with a parodistic, rocket-like ebullience, completely adapts itself to the curious, other-world quality of the text. As a creative effort in a single, consistent style, as an artistic phenomenon, *Façade*, like *Pierrot Lunaire*, towers high among the musical peaks of the twentieth century.

The work is not a stage or concert entertainment with a story line but a succession of cameos in which Sir William pokes fun at European manners and habits, and this music-hall type of gentle, light-hearted satire is the only real connecting tissue. In its original form, the music, involving a chamber ensemble of seven instruments, provided an illustrative commentary on eighteen of Edith Sitwell's dadaistic poems, preceded by a 'general salute and prologue'.

A private performance of *Façade* took place in Osbert Sitwell's house in Chelsea on 24 January 1922, followed by the public première on 12 June 1923 in the Aeolian Hall, London, when the work, comprising twenty-four 'facets' prefaced by the same 'General salute and prologue' unleashed a storm of critical rage and hysteria. After this, Walton revised the score, so that it consisted of twenty-six numbers and included a fanfare. This adaptation, heard at the New Chenil Galleries on 27 April 1926, proved extremely successful, enslaving those who heard it with what Ernest Newman called 'an unholy fascination'. *Façade* was also performed twice in the same programme at the Festival of the International Society for Contemporary Music at Siena on 14 September 1928, when the composer, with Lambert reciting, conducted twenty-two of the items.

The music, suitably adapted, was used for a frivolous, but highly sophisticated ballet which, with seven of the numbers choreographed by Frederick Ashton, was staged by the Camargo Society at the Cambridge Theatre, London, on 26 April 1931. A new production at the Sadler's Wells Theatre on 23 July 1940 included ten of the numbers, and, although arranged in a different order, they correspond to the two orchestral Suites which have been played many times in concert-hall programmes. The tangled skein of continuity and development created by the various revisions and adaptations of *Façade* must confuse may otherwise knowledgeable music-lovers, and even Walton, presented by Gillian Widdicombe with her solution to the 'Chinese puzzle', resulting from a careful examination of the relevant manuscripts, could only remark, somewhat perplexedly, 'Looks all right to me.'[2] The two Suites can either be performed separately or mixed and played as a separate entity, spread over twenty-five minutes, but the recommended order or sequence is as given in the following commentary:

1 *Fanfare*: The music, in the key of C and reminiscent of Stravinsky, was inspired by a travelling showman with a devil in a bottle at Palermo, Italy, and is very brief, opening with a trumpet summons which, soon reinforced, first by horns and more trumpets in canon, then by alto saxophone and/or cor anglais, leads straight into

2 *Scotch Rhapsody*: A kind of Scottish reel which is used in the ballet as a *pas de trois* for two girls and a boy in Highland dress. One detects a strong flavour of mimicry in the music. A lively dotted-note rhythm is thrown out by the woodwind, to be joined by *pizzicato* strings and, at irregular intervals, the rattle of a side-drum. The principal tune is shuttled from one instrument to another, like a ball in a children's game. The music makes a brilliant and copious use of percussion.

3 *Valse*: This delicious parody of various waltz-styles flits

imaginatively through the late nineteenth-century salons of Vienna, Russia and France, flirting mischievously with the sensuous languor of Johann Strauss, the romantic swirl and sentimentality of Tchaikovsky, Ravel and others. Opening in C major with a spurious bit of *Casse-Noisette*, the number has a middle section whose Viennese tune cavorts with the jolly inebriation of the gaoler Frosch in *Die Fledermaus*, bringing in the characteristic broken figures, cross-rhythms and disjunct accents of a jazz accompaniment. After the key changes to F, a capricious passage in the Johann Strauss manner is followed by a recapitulation of the C major opening.

4 *Tango-Pasadoble*: It came as no surprise to learn that in the ballet this number is danced by a slick, over-dressed gigolo who partners a demure, rather unresponsive girl. The music opens with the old music-hall tune 'I do like to be beside the seaside', played on the saxophone or cor anglais against a somewhat drowsy bassoon syncopation. A flurry of string trills and rising thirds coincides with a key change from E flat to G, ushering in another popular street ditty, which is tossed about like a scrap of paper in a gust of wind. The original key returns in a kind of South American tango, with a slinky trumpet recalling the seaside tune and oozing gigolo caddishness at every smeared semiquaver.

5 *Swiss Yodelling Song*: Two unaccompanied bassoons (*con trisezza e sentimento*) negotiate the up-and-down contours of Swiss yodelling, soon acquiring a decorative fringe of flute trills, a fragment of the *Ranz des Vaches* (*à la William Tell*) played on the oboes, horn calls in the brass section and ruminative sighs from the woodwind. Even if the Swiss scene pictured in the music is a little Germanic and the keys get very mixed up at the end, this open-air vignette, with its hints of cowbells on glockenspiel and xylophone, has a charmingly fresh, invigorating sound.

6 *Country Dance*: The scoring of this number, used in the ballet to accompany a dramatic sketch involving a Maiden, a Yokel and the Squire, is remarkably simple, being restricted to woodwind and strings without double bass. Instead of starting the piece with the tapping of a drum, to set the rhythm, Walton uses a cello *pizzicato*, increasing the volume and that of the rest of the strings as flute and clarinet pipe a tune in canon, reinforcing a kind of coy milkmaid, nobody-asked-you-sir-she-said rustic atmosphere. There are no sophisticated saxophones in the number, and the element of parody is not conspicuous.

7 *Polka*: This gay, exhilarating number deploys the full woodwind. A

rhythmically emphatic opening is followed by shrill outbursts from that hard-driven section, with rapid scale passages and flurries of notes from different solo instruments in a satirical development spiced by a tantalizing, 'vamp'-flavoured accompaniment. Despite the wild *fortissimo* flourishes, the listener will catch the faint semblance of a tune through all the spluttering gaiety, and at length the trumpet brazenly announces this—the familiar music-hall song 'See me dance the polka, See me clear the ground. . . .'

8 *Noche Espagnole*: This is a typically exotic, bitingly satirical piece of 'Spanishry', featuring a swarthy, flashily dressed dago and consisting largely of cadenza-like solos for trumpet, woodwind and those picturesque instruments—castanets, tambourine and triangle—that evoke the sultry Andalusian landscape, the swirl of gaily coloured skirts and the rhythmic stamping of feet. Certain military allusions in the poem—'The white soldiers pass . . .'—are conjured up by a trumpet call, set against the clatter of castanets that represent the heroine, a 'tall Spanish jade', and following this a gliding phrase on the clarinet introduces a free-wheeling rhapsody for the saxophone over a buoyant tango on the strings. The music, inflated by a grand *tutti*, acquires once again the sensuous allure of southern Spain in a passage of great rhythmic elaboration.

9 *Popular Song*: A skit on a music-hall tap dance executed by two extremely bored young men who heartily detest what has become a stale, repetitive routine. Walton deliberately and fittingly wrote banal, cliché-ridden music with more than a whiff of breezy vulgarity. The simplicity of the tune masks the cunning with which, imposing a Sousa-like side drum and cymbal effect, a flavour of jazz, and the frequent reiteration of the same melodic figure, he tickles our ears with a parodistic mastery. The tune, dominated by flute and saxophone, flits from one instrument to another and back again.

10 *Old Sir Faulk*: This is a fox-trot for two couples, and a mocking, but not malicious, skit on the typical dance-hall music of the 1920s which suggests, but never directly imitates, what it satirizes. The score does, however, include a saxophone, the usual percussion of the period, with 'traps', bass drum, side drum, cymbal and Chinese blocks. At one point in the score wa-wa mutes are used alternately with ordinary mutes by trombone and trumpet. The saxophonist is instructed to 'slap' his tongue and the horn-players to flutter theirs—all indications of the astonishing command of instrumentation which the nineteen-year-old Walton had acquired.

11 *Tarantella Sevillana*: An exhilarating Italian dance in 6/8 time

which, casting affectionate glances at Rossini, spins blithely along until, after a series of heavy detached chords from the full orchestra, the strings, with a flourish of 'Spanishry', break into a 3/4 pulse against the 6/8 in the wind, whose playing is enhanced by *acciaccatura* prefixing each note. With the primary rhythm broadening to 9/8 time, the *Tarantella* sweeps along to a colourful, animated finish.

Concerning the definitive version of the full *Façade* score, published in 1951, this derived from a performance at the Aeolian Hall on 29 May 1942, when, with Lambert again reciting, the twenty-two pieces, including a Fanfare, which now comprise the Entertainment, were presented, although not in the order in which they are known today. Walton re-examined the existing score in 1947–8, made various amendments and probably authorised or established the present order. The revised score of 1951 was dedicated to Lambert, who suggested that the poem should be arranged into seven groups of three as a parody of Schoenberg's 'three times seven' in *Pierrot Lunaire*, which also uses 'speech-song':

Fanfare.
Group I: I. Hornpipe. II. En famille. III. Mariner Man.
Group II: IV. Long Steel Grass. V. Through Gilded Trellises. VI. Tango-Pasodoble.
Group III: VII. Lullaby for Jumbo. VIII. Black Mrs Behemoth. IX. Tarantella.
Group IV: X. A Man from a Far Countree. XI. By the Lake. XII. Country Dance.
Group V: XIII. Polka. XIV. Four in the Morning. XV. Something Lies Beyond the Scene.
Group VI: XVI. Valse. XVII. Jodelling Song. XVIII. Scotch Rhapsody.
Group VII: XIX. Popular Song. XX. Fox-Trot 'Old Sir Faulk. XXI. Sir Beelzebub.

Several arrangements of music from the *Façade* entertainment were made over a period of forty-two years, and these are listed below:

*Façade: Piano Duet Arrangements*

Suite No 1 (arranged by Constant Lambert): Polka, Valse, Swiss Jodelling Song, Tango pasodoble, Tarantella Sevillana. Published by OUP in 1927.

Suite No 2 (arranged by Constant Lambert): Fanfare, Scotch Rhapsody, Country Dance, Noche Espagnole, Popular Song, Old Sir Faulk. Published by OUP in 1938.

*Façade: Arrangement for Concert Band*

1. Fanfare and Scotch Rhapsody. 2. Jodelling Song. 3. Polka. 4. Popular Song. 5. Old Sir Faulk. Arranged by Robert O'Brien and published by OUP (New York) in 1969.

*Four Dances from Façade*

Polka; Tango; Tarantella; Popular Song (Tap-dance). Arranged for small orchestra by Walter Goehr and published by OUP in 1939.

*A Façade Suite for Harmonica and Orchestra*

Polka; Tango, Swiss Jodelling Song, Popular Song. Arranged by Roy Douglas. Manuscript held by OUP.

*Three Pieces from Façade*

1. Tango pasodoble. 2. Swiss Jodelling Song. 3. Popular Song. Arranged for harmonica and piano by Roy Douglas. Published by OUP in 1959.

*Façade: Piano Solo Arrangements*

From Suite No 1: Polka, Valse, Swiss Jodelling Song. From Suite No 2: Scotch Rhapsody, Popular Song, Old Sir Faulk. Arranged by Roy Douglas. OUP published Popular Song and Valse in 1942 and the rest of the pieces in 1943.

Walton himself made a piano arrangement of the Valse, dedicating it to Mrs Beverley Baxter, and this was published in 1928.

*Façade: Two-Piano Arrangements*

Arranged by H. Murrill: Valse (Suite No 1) (1934); Swiss Jodelling Song (Suite No 1) (1949); Polka (Suite No 1) (1949); Old Sir Faulk (Suite No 2) (1949); Tarantella Sevillana (Suite No 1) (1950).

Arranged by M. Seiber: Popular Song (Suite No 2) (1939).

*Variations on a Theme of Hindemith*

In this work Walton took a beautiful singing *arioso* in 9/8 time from the middle movement of Hindemith's Cello Concerto and fashioned nine contrasted variants and a fugal finale in an idiom strongly and unmistakably his own. It consists of an extended passage of thirty-six bars which, in the concerto, is given chiefly to the soloist, with one short, though brilliant orchestral interlude, and whose ending contains a reference—perhaps unintentional on Hindemith's part—to a prominent theme in *Mathis der Maler* which occurs in both the opera and the symphony of that title. Walton scored his own *Variations* for woodwind, strings (including harp), horns and timpani. The taut, nervous phrases, spiky rhythms, graciously shaped melodies, a natural, flowing polyphony and powerful, well-judged climaxes are all present in the music, and so too are constant echoes of Hindemith.

Walton makes bold use of the *Mathis der Maler* element in the Hindemith theme—easily recognizable because its notes are formed out of successive major triads—and in Variation 7 firmly establishes the reference by quoting four bars in the original harmonization. The first twelve notes of the theme provide the basis of a sequence of key changes in the variations; they are: E, G-sharp (A), F-sharp, B, C-sharp, D, A, C, B-flat, F and E, with the third note, A (bracketed), reserved as a key-change when it reappears five notes later. Thus the first variation progresses from E to G-sharp (or A-flat), the second from G-sharp to F-sharp and so on. The last one acts as an introduction to the Finale. Here are the nine variations:

*Theme* — *Andante con moto.*

Variation 1: *Vivace.* A characteristic Walton *scherzo*, mostly light in texture.

Variation 2: *Allegramente.* A slightly faster passage with sharp, syncopated rhythms activated by those of the horn's opening sharp phrases.

Variation 3: *Larghetto.* This opens in a Sicilian 6/8 with a dialogue between cor anglais and bassoon and with muted *pizzicato* strings.

Variation 4: *Moto Perpetuo* (*con slancio*—with abandon). Brief, of coruscating brilliance and heading for the new key of C-sharp.

Variation 5: *Andante con moto.* Here, with ornamentation and trills, Walton makes use of both the retrograde version of the theme and its inversion, with the clarinet voicing the *Mathis* reference as the variation ends.

Variation 6: *Scherzando.* Strings and wind, playing in 5/4 time and executing some remarkable *glissando* effects, shuttle fragments of the theme to and fro. After a fierce climax the excitement slowly ebbs.

Variation 7: *Lento molto.* The slowest and most profound variation, with a tranquil opening for lower woodwind and then for horns. Later in the variation we hear the beautiful four-bar quotation from *Mathis der Maler*, marked *espansivo*, after which the music plunges without a break into

Variation 8: *Vivacissimo.* The shortest variation in the work, which flutters past with a faint reference to the theme and a brief pause before the end.

Variation 9: *Maestoso.* An imposing preparation for the Finale, with massive preludial brass and explosive outbursts that create a tingling expectation.

Finale: *Allegro molto.* An intensely dramatic and gripping *fugato* which builds up to a great climax and then slowly subsides into the serenity of a coda in which the composer quietly restates and contemplates the opening theme in a new orchestral passage which, with angelic effect, comes to rest on a long-drawn chord of E major.

*Porstmouth Point: An Overture*

Walton was never a prolific composer, but rather one who considered every work slowly and with great care before and during the act of composition, with a fastidious attitude of mind which imprinted the hallmark of quality on almost everything he created. In consequence he wrote only a few major opuses that will ensure his place in British musical history, but happily he also produced a good deal of light, cheerful music which, though not of Olympian scale, reaches an appreciative audience with absolute directness.

One of these pieces is the overture *Portsmouth Point*, the inspiration of which was a picture by Thomas Rowlandson (1756–1827), an English painter and caricaturist. The scene, with its cluster of tall-masted ships in the harbour, its groups of sailors engaged in horseplay or cosseting bosomy females, flanked on one side by a tavern and on the other by the moneylending establishment of one Moses Levy, bustles with activity. Walton depicts all this admirably with music which, scorning academic devices, revels in prickly rhythms, capricious cross-accents and bars of 5/8 and 2/8 time bumping against each other like dodgem-cars in a fairground, with clattering tambourines and huge tonal outbursts from the orchestra. In the first section of the overture strings, brass and woodwind meet, converse, then skirmish to and fro in a hornpipe-flavoured tune that conjures up the figures in Rowlandson's picture. The following section, switching from C to E flat, makes a half-hearted attempt to form a second subject, but the music, harsh and discordant, 'runs amok' in a manner indicative of squabbles and fights. There is a solo for a boatswain's pipe—seemingly the rowdy sailors are being summoned aboard ship—and, with a flourish of the hornpipe, the music comes to an ebullient ending. Constant Lambert made an arrangement of the overture for small orchestra, and Walton, in 1927, prepared one for piano duet.

*Scapino: An Overture*

The overture *Scapino* was also inspired by a print, in this instance an etching by the French draughtsman Jacques Callot (1592—1635), and the music splutters with high spirits. Scapino, the knavish servant of the Commedia dell'Arte and a prototype for so many comedies (Molière's *Les Fourberies de Scapin*, for example) assisted his master in certain amorous adventures—indeed, the name Scapino survives in the word 'escapade'—and excelled as a rogue in his own right.

The work is scored for a very large orchestra with triple woodwind, trumpets, cornets and a whole battery of percussion. Scapino is characterized at the very beginning by a syncopated trumpet tune which conveys the brazenly impertinent side of his nature, while the cellos play a honeyed theme redolent with his more plausible roguery. A change of key-signature introduces a new subject on the violas, and we hear this highly suggestive theme later in an augmented version which hints at some Casanovarish intrigue (*come una serenata*), with the violins, *pizzicati*, serenading like a guitar, but, here and there, with mocking comments by the woodwind. The *scherzando* mood returns, and the opening themes are freely reiterated.

*Johannesburg Festival Overture*

Walton's third composition in the 'curtain-raising' genre was the *Johannesburg Festival Overture*. In response to an invitation from Ernest Fleischmann, musical director of the Johannesburg Festival, he composed it for the seventieth anniversary celebrations of the city of Johannesburg, describing it to his publisher as 'a non-stop galop . . . slightly crazy, hilarious and vulgar'. Most of this is perhaps a fair assessment, but vulgar the music is not—indeed, the score blends exuberance with a sleek elegance, an air of nonchalant whimsicality.

The work is scored for a large orchestra of triple woodwind, with harp and a nine-instrument percussion battery requiring three players. Asked by Fleischmann to include 'some African themes', Walton compromised by supplementing the battery with maracas and rumba sticks, but the statement made in so many concert programme-notes that the score contains no actual African themes is incorrect. The original music on which the overture is based, a theme used in the middle of the work, is *Masacanga*, by Jean Bosco. A recording of Bosco's composition was issued in 1954,[1] and Walton wrote the overture in 1955–6. More of a symphonic composition in its own right, the *Johannesburg Festival Overture*, marked *Presto capriccioso* and devoid of any metrical complexities, takes the form of an elaborate *rondo* in D major whose sixteen-bar tune recurs five times as the glittering, frolicsome music whizzes along at a furious pace.

*Crown Imperial: Coronation March*

No composer had a better sense of a royal occasion than Sir William Walton, whose *Orb and Sceptre* and *Crown Imperial* perfectly conjure up the grandeur and dignity of the Coronation ceremonial. Commissioned by the BBC to write a march for the Coronation of King George VI in 1937, he created a piece of music which, opulent and grandiloquent like Elgar's *Pomp and Circumstance* nationalism, proved worthy of a glorious occasion. A firmly diatonic masterpiece of uncomplicated rhythms and broad melody, scored for a large orchestra with organ (optional) at the end, it bore the title *Crown Imperial: Coronation March* and a quotation from William Dunbar (1465–1520): '*In beawtie beryng the crone imperiall*'.

The opening section, brisk and rhythmically pointed, makes an effective contrast with the slow trio section, which has a long, unforgettable *cantabile* melody in A flat, sung first by clarinet, cor anglais and violas, with the rest of the strings providing a rich accompaniment. The radiant brass chords preceding the trio are the basis for a splendid coda which, as all the material is recapitulated more expansively, sweeps into a conclusion of breathtaking magnificence.

W. J. Duthoit made an arrangement of *Crown Imperial* for military band, published in 1937, and there is also an arrangement of the 1963 version of the Coronation March made by David Stone for amateur orchestra. Other arrangements include one for solo piano by Walton (1937), one for organ (1937) and one for piano duet (1949) by H. Murrill, as well as Doris Arnold's vocal adaptation, 'That we may never fail' (1948), commissioned by the BBC for a Gala Variety Concert in honour of the Royal Silver Wedding.

*Orb and Sceptre: Coronation March*

Sixteen years after the Coronation of King George VI and Queen Elizabeth, the Arts Council of Great Britain commissioned Walton to compose another Coronation March, this time for the crowning as Queen Regnant of their daughter, another Elizabeth, who succeeded to the throne while touring Kenya with her husband. Given the fittingly emblematic title of *Orb and Sceptre* and scored for full orchestra, it comprises a main section and a slower trio section in the middle.

The march, which was performed in Westminster Abbey by the same orchestra and conductor as on the previous occasion, is more complex than its predecessor. It opens ceremonially in E major with a two-bar trumpet fanfare; then, ornamented and chromatically harmonized, the music swings into a broad and spacious passage. After eight bars a beautifully expressive phrase is delivered, with characteristic Waltonian syncopation, by the second violins; this is followed by music of coruscating brilliance, which soon fades into the songful trio section. A glorious C major tune—one of those memorable airs that Walton always did so well—is heard on gentle strings with harp chords, and this is restated *maestoso* in a very elaborate coda. The speed increases and the march, making further reference to the trio tune and with organ added, swells into a majestic conclusion crowned by a final fanfare of brass.

Arrangements of music from *Orb and Sceptre* include one for military band (1953), one for organ (1953) by William McKie, and one for piano (1953) by Roy Douglas, who in the same year also prepared a reduced version for small orchestra.

*Partita for Orchestra*

Walton's *Partita*, commissioned by the Cleveland Orchestra for its fortieth anniversary, is a virtuoso piece written solely for enjoyment, and in, Sir William's own words, 'It poses no problems, has no ulterior motive or meaning behind it and makes no attempt to ponder the imponderables.' It consists of three short movements, the titles of which (I, *Toccata*. II, *Pastorale Siciliana*. III, *Giga Burlesco*) indicate the character of the music. The first and third, deploying the full orchestra, fairly crackle with energy, high spirits and scintillating rhythms. Ebullient surges of colour and bold, uninhibited tunes are spiced with characteristic touches of satire. In contrast, the central *Pastorale* is gently romantic, with a slightly whimsical flavour, opening with an unaccompanied duet between solo viola and solo oboe. 'The eighteenth-century forms are invoked, but only as a frame of reference,' said Howard Taubman. 'Sir William's procedures have the tang of our century—the early part of it, one would say.'

*Improvisations on an Impromptu of Benjamin Britten*

Mention has been made in a previous chapter of how, in 1969, Walton, commissioned by the scientist and benefactor Dr Ralph Dorfman to compose a piece of music for the San Francisco Symphony Orchestra, asked Benjamin Britten if he could borrow a theme from his Piano Concerto and received a flattering letter of consent. The work he produced, *Improvisations on an Impromptu of Benjamin Britten*, showed spare melodic scoring that made no attempt to ape the mannerisms of the avant-garde. It has five distinct sections. Walton used an orchestra of normal size without extras. A theme on the solo clarinet is followed by a slow, contemplative section. After this come two related paragraphs, a sprightly triple-time variation and a passage marked slightly less fast. In the fourth improvisation, which is preceded by a brief pause, the Britten theme is transformed into an appealingly fresh and lyrical subject by the widening of some of its intervals. The work has a stylishly urbane and courtly ending.

*The Quest*

Metaphorically speaking, Walton was never a *danseur noble* in the make-believe land of ballet music. Although in *The Wise Virgins* he arranged music by Bach, and also saw his own orchestral version of *Façade* adapted to stage choreography, he created only one original ballet score, *The Quest*, and this, produced by the Sadler's Wells Company in 1943, has remained comparatively unknown. The suite which Vilem Tausky, assisted by Walton, arranged from the original score has also, to a large extent, been neglected. Based on the first book of Spenser's great allegory *The Faerie*

*Queene*, the plot of the ballet concerns the chivalric adventures of St George of the Red Cross, the symbol of Holiness, who, in a raging storm, is separated from his lady, Una, representing Truth; they fall under the spell of the magician Archimago, who stands for Hypocrisy, but are joyfully reunited after St George has defeated three Saracen Knights and triumphed over the Seven Deadly Sins.

A brief introduction to the first movement of the Suite graphically depicts the storm, then Archimago, popping maliciously out of a ten-bar whirlwind of atmospheric wizardry, propelled by splintering rhythms, catches us unawares. A central cross-section, which briefly ushers in Una's theme, depicts the Transformation to the Palace of Pride. The second movement presents this theme in the form of a Siciliana—a charming flute solo set against a bright counterpoint of oboe and cor anglais, with harp, strings and horn (six notes only) enriching the tonal background. In the very martial third movement, full of prancing, cut-and-thrust metres, dotted notes and off-beat accents, the Saracen Knights challenge St George; the music, progressing out of a kind of fanfare, undergoes extensive variation and development. The finale, a *passacaglia* on a sequence of falling fourths in the bass, uses quasi-religious harmonies to symbolize the victory of Holiness in the person of St George, who is reunited with Una; also important in this respect is the smooth flowing flute melody which rises ecstatically with the bass up to the final climax. Although not one of Walton's most compelling scores, *The Quest* has many appealing features.

### *Siesta*

Written and performed in 1926, shortly after the *Portsmouth Point* overture, *Siesta* is a reflective and serene work scored for an orchestra without brass, save for two horns, and with one each of the woodwind section, provision being made for a second clarinet and for a piccolo alternative to a flute. Throughout this leisurely piece, Walton placed the emphasis on solo instruments, with the first tune, *Andante tranquillo*, delivered by the oboe, accompanied by a gently undulating figure in the lower strings and the woodwind. In the more richly scored centre of the work, where the cellos redouble the tune played by the horns, this kind of repetitive device is a constant feature of the music; dotted-note figures are kept buoyantly in motion, while solo instruments present fragments of these as a commentary on the main flow of ideas. With the full lilt of the opening theme returning on the oboe, *Siesta*, harnessing a tonic chord with an added second and added fourth, ends *pizzicato* in a slightly discordant voice, made more congenial, as it ceases, with a sustained A from the violas and oboes.

In 1928 Walton made an arrangement of the music for piano duet.

*Music for Children*

It takes a master to compose tiny pieces that mean something, and Walton undoubtedly succeeded in *Music for Children*. The whole suite of ten items requires only about fourteen minutes to perform, and one lasts a mere forty seconds; yet the music, scored with a Schumann-like artistry, conveys feeling, mood and atmosphere in a few notes. First written in 1940 as piano duets entitled *Duets for Children* and dedicated to 'Elizabeth and Michael' (the composer's niece and nephew), the pieces acquired a richer, fuller life when they appeared in orchestral garb. Following the publication in 1949 of an arrangement for piano solo by Roy Douglas, the pieces were given separate titles, but, at the same time, their sequence in the orchestral version was changed, and conductors not wishing to present them all were permitted to make arbitrary selection. No one could rightly pretend that the music has a substantial concert-hall appeal, but it can be profitably used in TV or radio feature-programmes.

No 1, 'The Music Lesson', is a beautifully neat and artful miniature which, based on a five-finger exercise in the scale of C, but omitting E in some bars and rising to A, has the crystal-clear simplicity of the old clavecin music.

It is followed by

No 2, 'The Three-Legged Race', a dainty titbit in which the bass-end pianist (or trombone and cymbal) play on the off-beats of the bar against a nursery-rhyme tune until (in the orchestral version) the side-drum and harp crisply conclude the piece on a chord of F, with 'added notes'.

No 3, 'The Silent Lake' (*adagio*), is a charming example of *genre* painting which steers a brief but eventful course in A minor with a double pedal of tonic and dominant most of the way. How curious are the pungent interpolations of a C sharp with an F a ninth below which occur half-way through this progression, and the repetition with tiny structural variations of the two-bar tune.

No 4, 'Pony Trap', is a jolly and vivacious jog-trot. In the orchestral version harp, glockenspiel and tambourine conjure up a picture of glinting, chiming bells on smooth, well-polished harness.

No 5, 'Ghosts', creates a slightly chilling atmosphere with its shadowy spectres flitting capriciously up and down the G minor scale inflected with semitonal astringencies, B flat or B natural, F sharp and F natural, to send youthful imagination scurrying through the cobwebbed imagery. 'Swing Boats' bears the number 5 in the orchestral suite, and 'Ghosts' appears there as No 9.

No 6, 'Hop-Scotch' (*leggiero*), played with a loose, flexible wrist, bounds along at a fair speed in 5/8 time, with the characteristic 'hop' of childish play induced by a gap in the scale-passage five-finger exercise.

No 7, 'Swing Boats' (*giocoso deliberamente*), which begins Book 2 of the *Duets*, is listed as No 5 in the orchestral suite, where the tune, gliding 5/8 in the key of D and yet another variation on the five-finger exercise, is played by the tuba. On its last appearance strings complement the tune with a bright, neatly constructed counterpoint.

No 8, 'Song at Dusk', is a simple, but highly effective item in which the two-bar tune is moved up from B flat minor into its relative major, uses a change of pitch, with little prefatory variations, to usher in the second section and is a capital 'teaching piece', whatever that may mean.

No 9, 'Puppets' Dance', is also instructional, since it roams waywardly in and out of the key, with irregular bass chords and tricky finger-work stretching the skill and resourcefulness of the young performers. In the suite, where this item is listed as No 6, the figures are shuttled to and fro by different woodwind instruments, while bassoon and horn highlight the choreographic problems of the puppets.

No 10, 'Trumpet Tune', provides a splendid, though microcosmic finale in both the *Duets* and the suite. Set in the key of C major, with bright, unexpected skirmishes into E, the music has just the merest hint of an Elgarian type of march. The tune in the Trio section, which moves to A flat, is allotted to the oboe.

Bram Wiggins arranged parts of *Music for Children* into a work entitled *Miniatures for Wind Band*, which contains two sets. The first comprises Nos 1–4, and the second Nos 9, 8, 6, 5 and 10 of the original score. An arrangement of *Music for Children* for piano solo, published in two books (1950), was made by Roy Douglas.

### *Prologo e Fantasia*

*Walton's Prologo e Fantasia*, commissioned by the great Russian cellist Mstislav Rostropovich for his National Symphony Orchestra of Washington, is a brilliantly sculpted piece of ceremonial music. Barely seven minutes long, it opens with serene, recitative-like passages for all the string groups in turn, and these, reinforced by the woodwind, with brass interjections, complete the *Prologo*, which ends with an explosive outburst. A trombone call, answered quietly by the cellos, introduces a typical Waltonian *scherzando*, with repeated notes and bustling rhythms. Then follows a mock-fugue, described by the composer as make-believe and ending rather precipitately (at a point where the listener might have anticipated a first episode) with a frustrating coda. As a tribute to Rostropovich, that most generous, high-minded and dedicated musician, this brief work, which carries the intriguing flavour of a baroque overture, showed the Grand Old Man of Music composing in a strangely new but appealing manner.

Sonata for String Orchestra

It was Neville Marriner who suggested to Walton that the String Quartet of 1947 could be successfully re-scored for a full orchestra, and the composer, impressed by his eloquence, re-arranged the piece accordingly.

The opening is deceptive, because for a page and a half Walton gives us the original solo version, but just at the stage where the immediate repeat of the ravishing first theme might be expected to produce no surprises, the whole ensemble enters, flooding the texture of the music with opulent sound. Throughout the work he entrusts the more intimately expressive passages to solo instruments and, in doing so, introduces many vivid contrasts.

Uncharacteristically the strings are not muted in the slow movement, the reason being that the *scherzo*, after a rather tough and sinewy exposition, suddenly changes its clothing, like a magpie transformed into a nightingale, and for the rest of the movement has a lovely, hushed nocturnal quality. As to why the composer indulges in these party tricks, the listener soon discovers when, as a result of what has gone before, the long crescendos in the finale acquire tremendous striking power and impact. What, in quartet form, might have been a lightweight ending, becomes a dynamically gripping conclusion. The sonata is a finely scored piece worthy to rub shoulders with Elgar's great *Introduction and Allegro* in the concert-hall string repertory.

Other Orchestral Music

Among the smaller, more unsubstantial works that Walton wrote are the four-minute-twenty-second *March: A History of the English Speaking Peoples* (probably in 1959), the score of which has not, to my knowledge, been published; and the 2½-minute *Memorial Fanfare for Henry Wood*, the manuscript of which, dated 5 February 1945, is held by a Mr O. W. Neighbour. He also, in 1953, created a finale for *Variations on an Elizabethan Theme (Sellinger's Round) for String Orchestra*, to which five other composers (Arthur Oldham, Michael Tippett, Lennox Berkeley, Benjamin Britten and Humphrey Searle) contributed music.

The ebullient *Capriccio Burlesco*, commissioned by the New York Philharmonic Orchestra for its 125th anniversary year (1968), lasts only seven minutes but has a tantalizing *Till Eulenspiegel* elusiveness which, to use Michael Kennedy's apt description, appears to be 'spinning like a gaily coloured top from start to finish'. The scoring is for a fairly conventional orchestra, but with the percussion reinforced by such 'exotica' as castanets, whip, block and bongo.

Walton's transcription of his five guitar *Bagatelles* under the title *Varii Capricci*—a suite written with a masterly finesse and requiring equally delicate handling if they are to make an impact on the listener—comprises a series of variations, almost skittish at times, on a number of musical conventions, and features some beautifully harmonized string solos.

Among several of Walton's early pieces which have disappeared is *Dr Syntax*, a pedagogic overture inspired by a Rowlandson etching and, according to Angus Morrison who saw the score, a highly elaborate work.

# 15

# Film Music

*Henry V*

All too frequently, in the film soundtracks of today, the romantic highlight, the poignant ending or the tragic and bitter anti-climax, is pinpointed not by music of epic strength, dark, brooding menace, soft atmospheric subtlety or consuming passion, but by a nostalgic adolescent male voice, poor in diction, crude in tone and wayward in pitch, pouring out some treacly, infantile song against a twanging guitar or electronic synthesizer.

Let us then be grateful for the glorious film music of Sir William Walton.

Not the least of his magnanimous deeds was to give us the music for the film *Henry V*: it has a stylistic splendour and beauty that raise it above most of his other music in the genre. Lord Olivier remarked in a BBC radio broadcast: 'I have always said that if it was not for the music, *Henry V* would not have been the success it was.'[1] In composing the score, Walton had to adapt his music to three sharply contrasted periods in such a way that he could vividly capture the atmosphere of the reigns of Queen Elizabeth I and Henry V with a contemporary idiom that summoned up, but never directly reverted to, the styles and mannerisms of the past. In certain sequences he used organum and plainsong—both measured and unmeasured music—sensitively conveying the dramatic aura, rather than painting it in the usual bright Hollywood or Wardour Street colours.

In the opening playhouse scenes he cleverly imitated the style and instrumentation of Elizabethan theatre music. His flair for creating exactly the right mood for a scene or episode resulted in two magnificent string passages: the beautiful *passacaglia* 'The Death of Falstaff' and 'Touch her soft lips and part', which makes Pistol's farewell to Mistress Quickly unbearably moving. Also hauntingly poignant is the music associated with the French scenes, which intensifies the drama of Burgundy's speech made against the background of a horribly devastated countryside.

Walton based it on a folk song, 'Balëiro', originating in the remote and mountainous district of central France called the Auvergne. In this speech the Duke of Burgundy makes a passionate plea for peace, deploring the tragic and destructive impact of war on the hearts and minds of the French people. Almost any other experienced composer of film music, well versed in the clichés and impedimenta of elegiac screen epics, would have solemnized this most eloquent of speeches with muffled drum beats, muted ceremonial brass and strings, throbbing softly in deep registers, as Purcell did for Queen Mary II with his famous *Funeral Music.* Not so the unpredictable Walton; instead, recognizing in Burgundy's opening lines the finer vision of attainable peace and prosperity, he sustained it in music of gently lapping, pastoral delicacy, whose woodwind shimmers and rustling strings are touched by a Delian magic. The crescendo of the French cavalry charge which commences the Battle of Agincourt is utterly spellbinding. In the film a long 'crossfade' highlights the music, spicing it atmospherically with harness and armour—clinking sound effects; but, as the charge gains impact, the crescendo pounds along at full gallop, creating, as the banners and surcoats of the knights blaze with bright primary colours, a climax of overwhelming panoply and excitement—one of the supreme moments in cinema entertainment. Also memorable are the splendid fanfares that herald a new scene or the arrival of some noted personage. A fitting preface to this noble film is Walton's 'title music', where the delicate roulades of a solo flute swirl around a fragment of paper which, tossed about by the wind, finally resolves into a playbill of the Globe Theatre; and the overture on the Globe itself, quaintly evocative, but never imitative, of Elizabethan tunes—a marvellously apt and simple piece of scoring. The entire score is brimming over with character, and to summarize its many virtues one can do no better than to quote Lord Olivier once again: 'The music had more guts, more spunk, more attack and more venom than one would have thought was hidden in Walton's personality.'[2]

In 1964 Muir Mathieson, the British conductor and, for many years, musical director to Korda's London Film Productions, adapted the following items into a *Suite for Henry V* for concert-hall use: 1. Overture, The Globe Playhouse. 2. *Passacaglia*: The Death of Falstaff. 3. Charge and Battle. 4. Touch her soft lips and part. 5. Agincourt Song. Malcolm Sargent, in 1945, arranged another Suite bearing the same title and comprising: 1. London 1600 and Overture: The Globe Playhouse. 2. *Passacaglia*: The Death of Falstaff. 3. Touch her soft lips and part. 4. Agincourt Song. Other derived publications are:

*Two Pieces for Strings*

1. *Passacaglia*: Death of Falstaff.

2. Touch her soft lips and part. OUP (1947)
*Passacaglia: 'The Death of Falstaff'*
Arranged for organ by Henry G. Ley
OUP (1949)
*Two Pieces from Henry V*
Arranged for piano duet.
OUP (1972)

*Hamlet*

Muir Mathieson thought highly of Walton's fifty-minute score for the film *Hamlet*, which the Philharmonia Orchestra recorded under his guidance. He described it as 'perfect in detail and sure in its dramatic conception . . . the perfect complement to a great subject'. One glowing example of Walton's insight and ingenuity is the players' scene, in which regal trumpet calls herald the arrival of the Court, then a stately march theme accompanies and paces the picturesque retinue as they take up positions around the King's throne. The players follow with a small group of musicians, and for this Walton provides a typical seventeenth-or eighteenth-century slow, three-in-a-measure sarabande, switching to a slow, blood-chilling passage for the entry of the poisoner. He uses an orchestra of two violas, cello, oboe, cor anglais, bassoon and harpsichord, switching to a full symphony orchestra as the camera moves from face to face, showing the reactions of the courtiers, focusing at greater length upon that of the King, until, with tension rising, the stage music dissolves into the players' theme.

The camera, completing its rotating orbit, returns to the players, while the music reverts to the quiet accompaniment of the play. With the poisoning of the actor-King, the real monarch, convulsed by violent emotions, cries out 'Give me some light', and the sudden swell of the full orchestra, deluging the sweeter sounds of cello, oboe and harpsichord, ends in a gigantic chord. Walton uses two important leitmotivs: one for an early flashback showing the murder of Hamlet's father and for pin-pointing the correlating 'murder' in the players' performance; the other for Ophelia. He does not, however, resort to the overture or introductory music for the usual thematic exposition, as a means of preparing the listener and viewer for what is to come (nothing so hackneyed for the composer of *Façade*!) but restricts himself to anticipating the dark E minor tragedy of the funeral march, made more potent by the sporadic sound of the distant cannon fire of Fortinbras's army.

Other examples of Walton's uncanny flair for creating exactly the right kind of music for particular situations are, firstly, the gripping fugal passage which deepens the anguish of Hamlet's 'O that this too too solid flesh . . .' and, secondly, Ophelia's poignant motiv and the manner in which, after her death, it is converted into the second part of the music following the Hamlet-Laertes duel, of which, incidentally, she was the unwitting cause. Also impressive is the introduction of a sinister theme at the moment when the poisoner enters and then while the camera tracks around the spectators, the subtle infusion into the music of twentieth-century harmony and sonority, with *sul ponticello* strings emphasizing the change. As to why this is done, it must be recognized that the 'play within the play', a dumb-show accompanied by only seven instruments and enacting the base treachery of the King and Queen, is complemented by 'realistic' music (i.e., forming part of the action) with a predominantly seventeenth-century flavour; but, since not only Hamlet but also the composer—and the camera—has to watch the reactions of the guilty couple, the production needs, as a corollary, what might be loosely called 'background' or 'incidental' music. In order to fuse and correlate the realistic and the reflective, the action and the commentary upon the action, Walton effected a brilliant transition in the manner described. This, in every respect, is one of the finest of British film-scores, vividly evoking the atmosphere and feel of a towering Shakespearean masterpiece.

Muir Mathieson, with Walton's authority, adapted the Funeral March for concert-hall use in 1963 and five years later was responsible for *Hamlet and Ophelia*, a poem for orchestra arranged and adapted from the film music.

*The First of the Few*

Walton also wrote some fine music for the patriotic film *The First of the Few*, which dealt with the closing years in the life of R. J. Mitchell, designer of the Spitfire fighter plane. Leslie Howard, who appeared with David Niven in the film, had been greatly moved by the inventive genius and indomitable spirit of Mitchell, and the project derived from his enthusiasm. The picture, spanning twenty glorious years of aeronautical progress, contained scenes of the Battle of Britain shot at an RAF station, with real Service pilots, not actors, in the cockpits of history. Walton's music, especially his picturesque fugal writing, which in one place soars inspirationally like a plane, highlighted the emotional peak of the film, a scene showing the almost frenetic bustle of the aircraft factory, the gleam and bee-like hum of fast-spinning machinery, the deft assembly of parts and the challenging roar of the fighter-plane engines. The music which accompanies the opening titles, a broad, solemn *Crown Imperial* type of march, with an Elgarian flavour and prefaced by fanfares, formed a noble prelude whose final apotheosis, swelling from a bright, optimistic C to a blazing affirmation in G, was, indeed, spellbinding. As for the fugue, Walton, with a sure instinct, substituted for the predictable middle section and development a sad, gentle, exquisitely beautiful violin solo which served as a reminder of Mitchell, who, suffering from a fatal disease and with only a year to live, had unselfishly burned himself out in designing and perfecting the Spitfire. So successful was this music that, a few months later, Walton rescored it for concert-hall use under the title *Prelude and Fugue* (The Spitfire). Arrangements of the 'Spitfire' music include the *Spitfire Prelude* for military band (1966) by Rodney Bashford, for organ in a shortened version (1966) by Dennis Morrell, and for military band (1970) by J. L. Wallace.

*Escape Me Never*

The first film for which Walton wrote music was *Escape Me Never*, an assignment from Paul Czinner which, in the composer's own words, 'nearly drove me into a lunatic asylum'.[1] He was chosen to produce a score for the all-important ballet, and soon found that he could profitably spend from five to ten minutes a day on the task. The music for the opening titles derives from the second part of the ballet music, which is pleasant enough but not particularly notable. It is the Dolomites music, with its Delian atmospherics, its Alpine horns and cowbells, made evocative by colouristic splashes from the vibraphone, that demonstrates Walton's natural and developing flair in the genre. The ballet music has survived in a reduction for piano solo made in 1935.

*As You Like It*

Following this modest but encouraging start, Walton, appointed musical director for a new Paul Czinner production of *As You Like It* (1936), was commissioned to write a considerable amount of music for it.

The film, which starred Elisabeth Bergner and Laurence Olivier, is rarely seen nowadays, but, with its brilliant fanfares and rousing processional marches, reveals the growing confidence and originality of a musical genius exploring what for him was still a comparatively new genre. The blithe, rustic dance quality of the music for the opening title, the clever use of *tremolo* strings and oboe to suggest the gentleness of Rosalind, and the haunting sweetness of the sunrise episode, are particularly memorable. As regards the song 'Tell me where is fancy bred', which comes from the second act of *The Merchant of Venice* and is heard in the finale of the film, Walton took it, in Olivier's words, 'from a score he managed to scrape out of himself for the production of the school play at Christ Church Choir School'.[1] The manuscript of another song, 'Under the Greenwood Tree', a charming pastiche of the Jacobean period which proved surplus to the requirements of the film, is held by Oxford University Press, who published it separately.

*Dreaming Lips*

Walton's third film for Paul Czinner was *Dreaming Lips* (1937), whose cast included Elisabeth Bergner, Raymond Massey and Rosemary Brent. The opening music collates movements from the Beethoven and Tchaikovsky Violin Concertos and adroitly connects them to the waltz from Tchaikovsky's *Serenade in C* (played by Antonio Brosa). The manuscript of the score cannot be traced, and the music is not generally included in his list of credits. There were romantic hints of the *Escape Me Never* ballet music in the taxi scene, but the ravishing violin solo used in the dream, the rumba, foxtrot and tango played in the ballroom scene, and the sad, dark music that permeated the closing sequence, had a fresh, unfamiliar impact.

*Stolen Life*

Walton's fourth film score, commissioned by Czinner for *Stolen Life* (1939), with Elisabeth Bergner and Michael Redgrave heading the cast, was on a higher level. This was a beautifully reflective piece of screen entertainment, with sea and mountain scenes (filmed respectively in Brittany and the French Alps), and must have greatly appealed to the romantic poet in the composer, who created some lovely impressionistic touches. He used a 'love' leitmotiv—rather like a ghostly Alpine call—in the opening and closing scenes, repeating it, in different forms and with an almost Wagnerian mastery, in the hotel, picnic and glacier sequences. Accordions are heard in the quayside scene, a splendid bit of French or cosmopolitan tone-painting that conjures up the market-square or pavement café, with street musicians in the background. Harp and string *glissandi* imitate the swirls and shudders, the howling and roaring, of the wind and waves in the storm sequence. For the scene where Karol is met in the wood, Walton provided music that conveyed all the peace and rusticity of his surroundings.

*Major Barbara*

The score which he wrote for Gabriel Pascal's production of Bernard Shaw's play *Major Barbara* (1941) cannot be traced and may have gone up in smoke when his London home was blitzed in May of that year, or, alternatively, may have been lost by Pascal during his visit to the USA in 1942. Walton set the opening titles to the kind of music which, in a propaganda film intended for the nation as a whole, serves as a rousing clarion-call to battle, but he also introduced a beautifully seductive diatonic tune, written in a pseudo-French impressionistic style and reappearing, suitably re-apparelled, throughout the film. Since the score has disappeared, no further comment is possible.

*Next of Kin*

Although the composer had been called up for war service late in 1940, the War Office had granted him exemption so long as he continued to write music for films of national importance. One of these was a thirty-two-minute instructional documentary entitled *The Next of Kin* (1942), dealing with counter-espionage and security, for which Walton delivered a fine, dignified, if hardly inspired score. A reverberating gong stroke, redolent with menace, riveted the attention of the audience; then followed his familiar rouse-the-people recipe of trumpets, horns and a stirringly Elgarian march tune. An almost *Macbeth*-like atmosphere of tragedy and danger impregnated his music for the more sinister elements of the plot, including the activities of the spy and the build-up to the battle scenes. There was, however, a contrastingly sweet and gentle leitmotiv, with a plaintive oboe set against the strings, which he used for the clifftop love episode and, briefly, elsewhere. Since the people directly associated with *The Next of Kin* were controlled by the Official Secrets Act, with scripts burned immediately they were no longer required, and only those involved in making the picture allowed on the set, no documentation relating to the film now exists. The picture, whose cast was headed by Mervyn Johns and Stephen Murray, was made at Ealing Studios and on location at Mevagissey and the surrounding countryside in Cornwall, where the director, Thorold Dickinsen, had the loan of five hundred troops from the Worcester Regiment for five weeks, some Naval landing craft for several days and a few aircraft for two or three hours. According to him, 'Walton never concealed his distaste for the film and regarded his work on it as a necessary chore that kept him out of uniform. He was professional enough to write music suitable for a film that had to be explicable to the simplest mind. He never appreciated how hard it was to make so complex a subject palatable to the widest range of tastes and reactions.'[1]

*The Foreman Went to France*

Walton joined the Films Division of the Ministry of Information in 1941, and towards the end of that year he received his first official assignment, being asked to provide a score for the propaganda film *The Foreman Went to France*, based on a J. B. Priestley story describing a real incident that followed the collapse of France. An indomitable foreman persuades his manager to let him cross the Channel so that he can recover some vital machines which his firm has just delivered in that country and which otherwise will be seized by the invading Germans. Walton, in a highly imaginative score, used the leitmotiv principle more adventurously and again wrote some exquisite music flavoured by French impressionism. Two instrumental sections are, in fact, sub-titled 'La Ravelse' and 'Moto Poulencuo'; they are quite deliberately and charmingly written and orchestrated in the styles of Ravel and Poulenc respectively. Gordon Jackson, the actor who played with such distinction in the TV series *Upstairs, Downstairs* and *The Professionals*, had a part in *The Foreman Went to France*; he loved the score and praised the big opening tune, so reminiscent of the principal theme of Vaughan Williams's overture *The Wasps*, and also extolled the music for the refugee sequence, which hints at the sombre overtones of Walton's First Symphony.

*Richard III*

The announcement in 1954 that Walton had been invited by Alexander Korda to write the music for a film of *Richard III* must have delighted a host of admirers already captivated by his *Henry V* and other scores in the genre. Laurence Olivier spent some hours discussing musical requirements with Walton, but, in the end, the composer had to produce the score in some haste, and for this reason, perhaps, the quality proved to be variable.

Of the music written, Muir Mathieson, on Walton's authority, subsequently prepared a Suite (published in 1964) which opened with the prelude depicting the Coronation of Edward IV and contained a fine Shakespearean sequence. As happened more than once in the composer's film scores, the suite started with a rousing fanfare and, passing through a brilliant section entitled 'With Drums and Colours' to the stirring conclusion 'Trumpets Sound', presented a good deal of military and ceremonial music. Both the resplendent marching-tune, an Elgarian pomp-and-circumstance concoction, and other motivs in the prelude were sounded briefly by solo trumpets answering each other antiphonally on opposite sides of Bosworth Field the night before the battle. Walton used sparse colouring, but expressive mastery, to highlight Clarence's death in the malmsey-butt, Richard's explosive reaction to the little Duke of York's joke about his deformity, and other key incidents. He softened the rather strident effect of so much martial exuberance in the score with 'Music Plays' No 2, in which a charming, eight-bar Elizabethan type of tune ending in a bright semiquaver cadence is repeated; with a short string and harp *Andante doloroso* piece called 'The Princes in the Tower'; and with a quasi-pastiche of Tudor harmony, 'I would I knew thy heart'. The same Tudor-period flavour, suggested rather than deliberately contrived by imitative devices, also characterized three brief and intimate organ pieces which, published in 1963, derived from the same film music. Apart from the Suite, there is a separate score, *Prelude* 'Richard III', published in 1964 and containing music adapted from the film by Muir Mathieson. An arrangement for military band was made by N. Richardson in 1973.

*Went the Day Well?*

Shortly after completing a really magnificent score for the radio entertainment *Christopher Columbus*, which is dealt with in a subsequent chapter, Walton wrote the music for *Went the Day Well?* (1942), a propaganda film. Based on a Graham Greene story, it relates how, in 1942, lorry loads of German invasion troops, masquerading as Royal Engineers, occupy an English village, Bramley Green. Small discrepancies of speech and uniform expose the deception, and the Germans fortify the village. The Home Guard and the Army are summoned, battle ensues, the enemy are defeated and their dead are buried in Bramley churchyard. Roy Douglas, who assisted Walton with *Major Barbara, Next of Kin, The First of the Few, The Foreman Went to France* and *Christopher Columbus*, gave valuable advice over the orchestration of the new score. For this film Walton wrote a satisfying, workmanlike score of no great distinction. It opens with a simple diatonic tune, presents a gripping 'battle' sequence for the attack on the Home Guard and, for the radio music, resuscitates the waltz from the composer's ballet *The First Shoot*.

*The Battle of Britain*

As mentioned in a previous chapter, Walton suffered a traumatic experience when he fulfilled his commission to write the music for the film *The Battle of Britain* (1969), in that Spitfire Productions rejected the score simply because it would not fit conveniently into an LP recording planned by United Artists, the distributors, and they commissioned Ron Goodwin to provide one instead. Walton had been compelled to work at great speed, having only ten days to create the dogfight sequence, a daunting task for a composer who always worked with painstaking slowness. At least, the portion of his music entitled 'Battle in the Air' was retained—thanks to the persistence and obduracy of the highly indignant Laurence Olivier—and the music added sharp excitement to a Goodwin score which the critic of *The Times* described as 'platitudinous'.[1] It is clear from the fizzing vitality of Walton's music, impregnated with the fresh, youthful ebullience of the First Symphony, that he approached his own task with dedication.

Opening with a sinister *tremolo*, set against the agitated pacing of Air

Vice-Marshal Park (Trevor Howard) in the operations control room, with subsequent atmosphere-evoking vapour trails in the sky, it includes a nerve-stretching passage where jagged syncopations follow the frenetic crossfire and dizzying orbits of a dogfight, and, prefaced by a flamboyant whooping on the horns, one of those grand, patriotic and blood-stirring tunes that lie at the very heart of Walton's music. Some praise is due to his fellow composer Malcolm Arnold, who orchestrated the accompaniment to the Blitz sequences.

*Three Sisters*

Infuriated by the seemingly contemptible treatment meted out to him by United Artists, Walton vowed that he would never write another bar of film music, but in 1969, when his animosity had cooled a little, he did, in fact, produce a score for Laurence Olivier's film version of the National Theatre's production of Chekhov's play *Three Sisters*. It comprises music set against the opening and closing titles, with a lengthier middle section involving the Dream episode.

# 16

# Stage Music

*Troilus and Cressida*

Tchaikovsky, whose own *Eugene Onegin* has gained some popularity, once told his patroness, Madame von Meck, that, 'To refrain from writing operas is the act of a hero, and we have only one such hero in our time—Brahms; heroism of that kind is not for me.' Nor for many other composers, including Sir William Walton, who, in 1954, presented devotees of this most exciting and spectacular of the arts with his three-act opera *Troilus and Cressida*, which radiated a vocal and orchestral rapture that should have made the tops of their heads tingle. Hearing this work, with its delightful, free-flowing melody, makes one realize why he once said, 'I prefer any Verdi to any Wagner,' because the music, a deliberate attempt at neo-Puccini, is heavily steeped in the blatant romanticism of Italian opera. Walton had closely examined the length and style of such great arias as '*Celeste Aïda*' and '*Vissi d'arte*', and his feeling for Italianate vocal writing is manifest in the glorious Act II love-duet 'New life, new love', in which Cressida voices her rediscovered ecstasy. Although much of the score reflects the richly ornate, smoothly expressive style of Verdi and Puccini (which is probably why the avant-garde critics of the day regarded it as old-fashioned), the music at times echoes Strauss, with some of Mussorgsky's darker tone-colours. The orchestration is full of fascinating complexities and very subtle harmonic changes.

Christopher Hassall's libretto has been denigrated as being too flowery and obscure, but his language is nicely balanced between straightforward communication and poetic utterance, with brief flights of lyricism at certain dramatic peaks. One minor fault in the music relates to the red scarf which Cressida takes from her Temple vestments and gives to Troilus as a token of encouragement, as he prepares for battle against the Greeks. The composer, inspired perhaps by *Tristan and Isolde*, attempts to make a leitmotiv out of the scarf, but although it remains a recognizable symbol in the libretto, the music never really serves as a powerful guiding theme, bringing readily to mind the object with which it is associated. If the leitmotiv principle is adopted, surely it must be applied and developed throughout with a painstaking thoroughness and finesse. One notable example occurs in the last act of *Götterdammerung*, where practically every leitmotiv connected with Siegfried is woven into the sombre tapestry of the death march. Yet this is how Walton dealt with the matter, and no sensitive listener could fail to notice how the musical idiom, seductively appealing in its rhythmic inflections and bitter-sweet harmonic flavouring, admirably serves the ruminative, the comic and the martial aspects of the plot.

It has also been said that the heroine is a timid, vacillating character, afraid of life, hovering disconsolately between apprehension and a longing for the Prince's manly protection and reassurance. I can only reply that Hassall would have been wrong to make his Cressida, who, after all, is a Chaucerian girl, into the shallow, fickle creature of Shakespeare's play. A tragic figure, surrounded by falsehood and treachery, she has every reason to be afraid and wins our sympathy by her frail femininity, her defencelessness in a world of cruelty, oppression and deceit. 'Of her lyf she was ful sore in drede,' wrote Chaucer, and he followed this by depicting Cressida as 'Wel nigh out of her wit for sorwe and fere'. Hassall conformed to this concept, but he also, to use Hazlitt's description, presented his heroine as 'a grave, sober, considerate personage . . . who has an alternate eye to her character, her interest, and her pleasure'.

The story of the opera concerns the love of the Trojan Prince Troilus for Cressida, the daughter of Calkas, the Priest of Pallas Athene in Troy, at a time when the Greeks are besieging the city. Act I shows Calkas, who subsequently proves to be a traitor, trying to persuade the starving Trojans to surrender to the enemy. Against this background Prince Troilus, a staunchly loyal Trojan, meets Cressida and falls in love. Pandarus, the brother of Calkas and Cressida's uncle, plays the exact part indicated by his name. In Act II he unites the lovers, but the sudden arrival of the Greek commander Diomede disturbs their new-found happiness; he has come to take Cressida to her father, who has deserted to the Greeks, in exchange for Antenor, the Trojan Captain of the Spears and Troilus's friend, whom the Greeks have captured. In Act III we see Cressida in the Greek camp, anxiously awaiting news of Troilus but unaware that Calkas has arranged for all his messages to be intercepted. Believing herself to be abandoned, she submits to the advances of Diomede. At the climax of the opera Troilus and Pandarus have stolen furtively into the Greek camp. When the Prince reclaims his beloved, Diomede commands her to renounce him, but she refuses. Troilus fights with Diomede, only to be stabbed in the back by Calkas. The sad, disillusioned Diomede orders Calkas to be returned to Troy but keeps Cressida for the use of his soldiers. She escapes this ignominious fate by committing suicide.

An orchestral prelude opens the opera with a long-drawn *adagio* pedal E, and the curtain rises in the tenth bar to reveal a crowd of worshippers and bystanders outside the Temple of Pallas, who is deaf to their entreaties that the war, which has lasted for a whole decade, shall be terminated. Walton establishes the principal characters with a deft sureness of touch, and Calkas, the lugubrious bass, has, for example, a stirring hexameter passage, set largely to repeated notes, in which he informs the crowd that a messenger has brought back a prophecy from Delphi—a false proclamation that angers the long-suffering people. The character of the more impulsive and robust baritone, Antenor, the passionate lyric tenor of the hero, and the sweetly expressive soprano of Cressida are also pinpointed. Pandarus, the *buffo* tenor, has a vocal line glittering with arpeggios and roulades, with short note-values, and the delicacy of the instrumental playing, whenever he makes an appearance, clearly identifies his personality.

Walton's mastery in writing for massed voices makes itself felt not only in the opening scene but in the events that follow, when Antenor's soldiers return without their Captain, whom the Greeks have captured, and when the people cry out after Calkas, who has deserted. In this act the two motives of the opera are heard: the first, preceded by a rising seventh, naming Cressida and appearing at the sound of her name; the second, accompanied by the leitmotiv of the crimson scarf, representing her love and the free giving of it.

In Act II, set in a room of Pandarus's pleasant house, insidious music of remarkable subtlety and refinement reminds us that the old schemer is spinning a web of intrigue, putting on his most suave and cajoling manner in a sequence of modulatory harmonies. The lovers are united in romantic music of ravishing beauty. Walton's flair for spine-chilling dramatic contrasts is demonstrated in the brevity of the little solo for Cressida in the dawn, an episode of haunting loveliness which is interrupted by the harsh menace of Diomede's drum. The two scenes of Act II are divided by an interlude which evokes both the storm outside the house and the surging passion inside as Troilus and Cressida consummate their love. As the new day begins, Diomede, heralded by martial music, arrives with a Greek detachment. He discovers Cressida hiding in an alcove and tells Pandarus to prepare her for the journey. As he leaves, Troilus rushes into the room, swearing to have the infamous 'exchange' revoked. The lovers sing a long duet in which anguished harmonies and throbbing rhythms express the sorrow of parting. Before Cressida is led away, the Prince gives her back her crimson scarf to wear for him.

In Act III, which is set in the Greek camp ten weeks later, distant trumpets and horn fanfares paint the scene. Cressida pines for Troilus in a languishing aria, characterized by Walton's familiar interval of a seventh. Against a flurry of agitated music, Calkas orders her to accept Diomede's love. When her deceitful maid Evadne indicates by a sign that there is no news from Troilus, Cressida gives in. Almost hurling the red scarf at Diomede, she plights her troth in a short agitated duo. A solo by the maid reveals her treachery in destroying Troilus's messages. The voices of the watchmen singing 'All's well!' are heard, and immediately afterwards Troilus and Pandarus creep into the encampment. Troilus sees to his horror the crimson favour on Diomede's helmet. The two men quarrel, but Cressida, asked to decide between them, conquers her fear and walks over to Troilus. The moment of truth for the six principal characters in the opera is expressed through a very beautiful sextet in which the voices build up, stratum by stratum, with Diomede reviling Troy for her falseness; Cressida longing for Troilus, but aware of the fatality of their love; Pandarus reproaching his own unstable philosophy; Calkas remorseful, but dignified; Evadne still nursing a spark of hope for the future. Beneath the great ascending curve of the sextet the chorus murmurs 'False Cressida!' with growing intensity. The climax is reached with the stabbing of Troilus by Calkas, then descends to a quiet, unequivocal C minor ending and the sinister resolution of Cressida's fears as, wrapping the dead Troilus's sword in her red scarf, she stabs herself.

Whatever the faults of the opera—and they have to some extent been exaggerated—the music demonstrates Walton's command of dramatic effect and his ability to create a sense of great emotional tension. Maybe, as some critics have complained, there is nothing strikingly new or innovatory in the music, but why should there be? There is also nothing that could possibly be described as imitation or plagiarism, and a composer must not be expected to invent a new idiom merely because he has taken to opera. Walton uses a large orchestra with a captivating delicacy and refinement in a charmingly Italianate score whose fresh, light Mediterranean atmosphere derives largely from the shimmering filigree string writing and the sweet, buoyant woodwind phrases that comment on much of the recitative. Cressida has some noble monologues, one being the slightly Wagnerian after-love 'From isle to isle chill waters whisper the hour' in Act II, which is one of the opera's most haunting pages. Others are the poignant Act I aria 'Slowly it all comes back—out of my childhood' and, at the tragic close of Act III, the profoundly moving

'Turn, Troilus, turn, on that cold river's brim, beyond the sun's far setting', which she sings as she prepares to take her own life.

The first performance of *Troilus and Cressida* was given, under Sir Malcolm Sargent, at the Royal Opera House on 3 December 1954; then in 1972–6 the composer, making a few pitch adjustments and pruning some of the music, changed the role to that of a mezzo, so that Janet Baker, whom he warmly admired, could sing it in a new Covent Garden production. 'I'm not a natural-born opera composer like Ben Britten, for instance, or maybe Tippett perhaps,' Walton remarked, 'but I think almost every opera could do with cutting. I'm in favour of cutting.'[1]

### *The Bear*

Walton's only other opera, the one-act extravaganza *The Bear*, was commissioned by the Koussevitzky Music Foundation. The librettist was Paul Dehn (also Lennox Berkeley's librettist for *A Dinner Engagement* and *The Castaway*), and, in collaboration with Walton, he adapted Chekhov's original play *The Bear*, sub-titled 'A jest in one act', with a high-spirited enthusiasm.

The story at the centre of this effervescent frolic is threadbare and (literally) farcical. Popova, a pretty widow, has a blind, unreasoning loyalty to the memory of her late and unfaithful husband. She is outraged when Smirnov, one of his more persistent creditors, confronts her. A bitter quarrel ensues, and they point pistols at each other; but they are unable to fire because, quite irrationally, they have fallen in love. The cast is complicated by a third character, Luka, the servant.

This operatic diversion splutters with parodistic wit and a touch of the old *malizia*, rubbing shoulders with Offenbach and Verdi, Tchaikovsky and Poulenc; but, despite its scintillating gaiety, the melodic impetus is never really strong or strikingly effective, and the influence of Stravinsky surfaces too noticeably in the ebullient, syncopated accompaniments. To make sure that the nerves of the listener are constantly stretched, Walton makes his percussion players work like the celebrated Russian kulaks, forcefully and frequently hitting everything within reach, except each other. What humour there is in *The Bear* stems largely from the complete contrast which each character presents to the world and the reality behind it: Popova, outwardly respectable and genteel, is inwardly passionate and volatile; Smirnov, seemingly boorish, is in fact sentimental; while the servility and politeness of Luka hide a nature of sulky, brooding resentment.

### Other Stage Works

Walton did not achieve any great reputation for his incidental music for the theatre, but he composed three scores in the genre which deserve some mention. The first of these, spiced with jazz rather than the flavour of chop suey and incense and written in July 1925, was for Lytton Strachey's tragic melodrama *The Son of Heaven*, which dealt with the Chinese Boxer Rising of 1900—it probably consisted of an overture and interlude (*entr'acte*), but there is no proof of this, as the score has apparently vanished.

Walton also wrote music for J. M. Barrie's play *The Boy David*, in a production staged at the King's Theatre, Edinburgh, on 21 November 1936, with Jean Cadell, Elisabeth Bergner and Leon Quartermaine in the cast; but, again, the manuscript seems to be no longer available.

Finally, there was the music, so far unpublished, for John Gielgud's production of *Macbeth*, premièred at the Opera House, Manchester, on 16 January 1942, with Gielgud in the title-role and Gwen Ffrangcon-Davies as Lady Macbeth. It contained regal fanfares, isolated chordal transitions, a skirling, pseudo-Scottish piece for the banquet scene, crackling thunder-and-rain music for the cackling Witches, and a suitably grim, elegiac 'March of the Eight Kings'.

# 17

# Choral Works

*Belshazzar's Feast*

*Belshazzar's Feast*, a dramatic cantata on texts arranged from Biblical sources by Osbert Sitwell, proved to be one of the corner-stones of modern British music and perhaps, in Britain at least, the finest choral achievement of the twentieth century, Britten's *War Requiem* notwithstanding. Like that deeply compassionate soliloquy of human suffering and nobility, *Belshazzar* exhibits many bold, self-assured points of resistance to new ideas, new techniques; yet, in presenting the splendid barbaric beauty of the Old Testament tale, it also extended the elements of large-scale impressiveness and romantic escape. Indeed, the music so shocked the conventional in 1931 that its performance at a cathedral festival was disallowed.

Walton's continuing awareness of developments in Europe and, in particular, the significance of Igor Stravinsky, is manifest in dissonant harmonies, rhythmic complexity and a style of brilliant orchestration that fuses the old with the new. The elements of progressive experimentalism in *Belshazzar* did not so drastically repudiate the traditional concept of the oratorio or cantata as did *The Dream of Gerontius*, in which Elgar, combining John Henry Newman's Catholicism with a sensuous chromaticism, a mysticism conveyed by marvellously cunning instrumental effects, did for this kind of music what Wagner had done for opera. One thinks of other contemporary choral works of note: Frank Martin's finely sculpted *Golgotha*, full of austere pity; Britten's *Ceremony of Carols* and *St Nicholas*, steeped in the charm, insouciance and ingenuousness of the Middle Ages; Szymanowski's *Stabat Mater*, a devout but coldly atmospheric piece; Janácek's *Festliche Messe*, in which a popularized religious art is denuded of false piety in the medieval manner; Honegger's *King David*, a grand, episodic stage-spectacle; and Tippett's *A Child of Our Time*, that deeply eloquent cry against man's inhumanity to man. These and similar works subordinate the general characteristics of sacred music so that a Biblical subject or doctrinal truth is mirrored 'as it exists' and not as it ought to be on a sublimated level. In so doing, they acquire a universality that transcends narrow indigenous boundaries. Thus it is with *Belshazzar's Feast*, which had such a liberating effect on other British composers, one of whom, George Dyson related the story of another King of Babylon in *Nebuchadnezzar*, performed at the Worcester Festival of 1935.

The unfailing sense of drama running through Walton's score from the first page to the last, the stark, simple imagery and the quality of the music itself make the work mighty and enduring. It expresses in a remarkable degree (especially as Walton was of completely Aryan origins) the fanaticism of the Jewish race and their implacable hatred of the Gentile oppressors. There is not a note too many. Goethe wrote that the first sign of the master was in *Beschränkung* (restriction), which for a creative artist means not merely preferring the small to the large, a sonnet to an epic, but recognizing his own limitations. Walton, a careful, fastidious craftsman, did precisely that.

Despite its Biblical source of inspiration, *Belshazzar's Feast* is not in any sense a 'religious' work but might properly be classified as a Biblical epic, presented with the same kind of musico-dramatic *savoir faire* that Walton was to put into his more imaginative film scores. It breathes the spirit not of Elgar's deeply mystical *Dream of Gerontius*, impregnated with the flavour of death and incense, but of Honegger's *King David*, first performed in 1921, ten years before *Belshazzar*. All three works had this in common: that they dealt a crushing blow to the redoubtable choral traditions of their own countries—a blow from which they never recovered. As regards *Belshazzar* and *King David*, these concise, closely integrated works helped to activate the twentieth-century practice of using the Bible as a source of entertainment, rather than enlightenment—a practice which has a parallel in Strauss's opera *Salome* and his ballet *The Legend of Joseph*. The scenario of Walton's dramatic cantata is phrased in characteristically strong and simple language, and the music itself, a perfect corollary of the text, is refreshingly free from pseudo-Judaisms, anachronistic idioms and facile orientalisms. It exhibits the exotic, nerve-stretching barbarities of the Old Testament without vulgar excesses.

Walton's two brass bands, placed on either side of the conductor, are used antiphonally or stereophonically at strategic points in the score, which provides for baritone solo, double chorus and a large orchestra with organ. The text, selected and arranged by Osbert Sitwell, was taken principally from the narrative of the fall of Babylon in Daniel V, but also incorporates passages from Isaiah, the 137th Psalm ('Sing aloud unto God our strength') and the Revelation of St John ('Babylon the great is fallen'). Irresistibly exciting, with fierce percussion and high dynamics, the music, which runs continuously, fits into three main sections divided by the dramatic recitative of the soloist. The first narrates the prophecy of Isaiah and the lament of the Jews in captivity; the second describes Belshazzar's Feast, interrupted by the pagan hymn praising the idols of Gold, Silver, Iron, etc and culminating in the writing on the wall; the final section is a hymn glorifying the God of Jacob for delivering the Jews from bondage and destroying Babylon.

In the first panel of this musical triptych ('By the waters of Babylon') three trombones playing in unison introduce the prophecy of Israel's subjection, a setting for unaccompanied, four-part men's chorus. Then, preceded by a short orchestral link which contains in the bass one of the cardinal themes of the whole cantata, there follows the moving lament of the Jews in captivity, flowing in long sinuous lines (with a touch of vocal onomatopœia at the phrase 'and hanged our harps upon the willows . . .') and, as it broadens out gradually into eight parts, rising to a passionate climax. Underpinned by an elgiac tread, the baritone soloist enters at the words 'If I forget thee, O Jerusalem' and, with the first section recapitulated, the music fades away into nothingness.

The second section ('Babylon was a great city') blazes with drama and abomination. Belshazzar extols the city of riches and revelry, and his unaccompanied declamation is taken up by the chorus, who describe the joys of the feast. Against rhythmic and harmonic asperities, the sacrilege of drinking from the vessels plundered from the Temple of Jerusalem is highlighted by outbursts of horror. Then follows the most riveting and magnificent episode of the work, marked *a tempo di marcia energica*, where Walton, bringing in the first of his many pomp-and-circumstance marches, uses every choral and instrumental device to give flamboyant effect to the words. It is fascinating to note how great dramatic tension is generated by each of the phrases through which the march passes being prefaced by an *a capella* choral outburst ('Praise ye the god of Gold'). While the chorus sings their praises, the clever use of percussive tone-colours conjures up sonic portraits of the different deities, and the brass bands volley brilliant fanfares back and forth. A long, suspense-creating silence follows the climax, then the music of the first section is resumed at the words 'Thus in Babylon', and the part ends in the recitative 'In that night Belshazzar the King was slain and his Kingdom divided.'

The final section opens with a hymn of praise to the God of Israel. It contains a middle section, developed fugally at the words 'While the kings of the earth lament', with a semi-chorus proclaiming the grief of the kings and merchants on the fall of Babylon, but, against the rapturous Alleluias of the faithful, this resolves into a gloriously triumphant song of adoration for a stately, slow-moving double chorus. A short orchestral postlude concludes a work whose impact on the listener Sir Compton Mackenzie once described as 'like an explosive sunset'.

Throughout the cantata, Walton (for whom exact processes of thematic development were often second nature) relies upon nothing but the music; the phrases grow like branches on a tree, marvellously complementing each other and the symmetry of the whole. There is a bigness, a spaciousness and a depth about the piece, whose glittering splendour will not easily be dimmed by the passing of time.

*Gloria*

To celebrate the 125th anniversary of the Huddersfield Choral Society and the thirtieth year of Sir Malcolm Sargent's conductorship of it, Walton, in 1961, wrote a *Gloria*, his most extended choral work since *Belshazzar's Feast* and one which highlighted the existing pomp and splendour of a notable public event. Covering huge expanses of sound and making fine antiphonal use of two choirs with a characteristic tonality based on an interval of the seventh, the *Gloria* lasts for twenty minutes but has the breadth and substance of a bigger, more imposing piece. It is in many respects a moving and memorable composition, but one which, having no real liturgical function or religious significance, is in a sense polarized and isolated in the Church's musical repertory—a curiosity which is occasionally and perhaps hesitantly brought out of the cupboard by some choral society for an airing. Forcibly propelled and, at times, creating a blazing fresco of sound, it has many parallels with Beethoven's *Missa Solemnis*, summoning in the 'Miserere', with its octave leap to a high B flat, some of the dark, piercing agony of that towering masterpiece and, in the first entry of the voices, volleying impassioned 'Glorias' heavenwards with some of the sacred fire that burns radiantly in its 'Osanna'.

Walton indulges his fondness for ceremonial brass in numerous places, following the first fourteen-bar orchestral summons with an upward-thrusting motto for trumpets and trombones which is echoed, though not actually quoted, at the start of the penultimate section, 'Quoniam', and, in fact, sung unaccompanied to 'Cum sancto spirita', after which—characteristically for a composer who delighted in harsh or pungent contrasts—a massive, plunging chord, containing two shrill dissonances, is heard against a sustained G sharp. The first section, recognizably in D major and ejaculatory in manner, with a final swirling orchestral tutti, is laid out in eight parts.

In the calm, predominantly C major 'in terra pax', whose smoothly flowing consecutive thirds hint at 'goodwill to all mankind', the word 'pax' is shuttled antiphonally between the women's and men's voices, finally settling on a choral, unaccompanied unison. Following a swift change to 'Laudamus te', where the signature changes to five sharps but the actual key-relationship is esoteric, the richly contrapuntal writing makes a fugue seem imminent, but it never arrives. The ejaculatory style returns at 'gratias', with the voices intertwining over an oscillating pedal, and 'Domine Deus' builds up to an impressive climax. At one point, after the altos reiterate 'gloria!' over a fanfare-like motto theme marked '*lento, sotto voce, pianissimo*', the music, introducting the Second Person of the Trinity, the name of Jesus Christ, the Lamb of God, undergoes a very striking change of mood and contrast, with the orchestra at first falling silent, then accompanying the semi-chorus as it sings 'Domine Deus', and echoing, with eight thrillingly agitated chords, the full choir's reverential cry 'Agnus Dei, Filius Patris'.

'Miserere', whose anguish and despair are highlighted by orchestral trills, *tremolandi* and drum rolls, ushers in the solo voices. After the tenor has delivered an unaccompanied melisma, the orchestra replies in a simple, affirmative figure with percussion; then the singer launches the second part of the passage, 'qui tollis peccata mundi', whereupon the alto and bass soloists join him with long-spun phrases, while the choir intones 'miserere nobis' on A flats and B flats. The expression mark '*quasi bisbigliando*' (the Italian for 'almost whispering') reflects the general treatment of a section which, comprising two ideas—'Suscipe deprecationem' and 'Qui sedes ad dexteram'—hinges upon a repeated prayer for mercy, ending on a note of quiet resignation.

Following a trombone introduction not unlike the opening of the work, the chorus sings 'Quoniam tu solus sanctus', beginning with eight-part interjections which, increasing in momentum, gradually coalesce into the blazing, block-chord affirmation 'Tu solus atltissimus Jesu Christe', which rings out unaccompanied. Walton glorifies the concept of the Third Person of the Trinity, first of all by broadening the tempo to *maestoso*, and secondly, starting with a brilliant unison phrase, by constructing a grand, *Belshazzar*-like structure of elaborate figurations, fast *tremolandi* on strings, brightly glinting harp chords, the pounding of the timpani and, underpinning the whole musical edifice, a huge swinging bass like the hieratic tolling of a great bell. Against a tapestry of woodwind chords, the organ joins in.

There is a kind of loosely conceived coda, rooted mostly in D but straying ambivalently around the tonal spectrum, in which the choir not only sings the single word 'Gloria' but adds 'Gloria in excelsis Deo, Amen', to conclude a work which is more notable for its drama, its inventive awareness, than for its religious symbolism.

*Cantico del Sole*

Walton, invited by Lady Dorothy Mayer in 1972 to compose a piece of music for the 1974 Cork International Festival, produced his *Cantico del Sole*, a setting of St Francis of Assisi's poem 'Hymn of the Sun', which extols the beauty of nature. Three other composers, Boris Blacher, Roman Vlad and Brian Boydell, had received similar invitations, calling for an *a capella* part-song with a time-span of three to ten minutes and intended for amateur performance. Dedicated to Lady Dorothy and her husband Sir Robert, the *Cantico del Sole*, a mere seven minutes in length, has a diatonic simplicity mingling rapture and austerity with a Britten-like innocence of spirit. Between the impressively bold, sonorous opening and the radiant climax there is a good deal of thematic legerdemain; the music flows with a certain six-in-a-bar predicatability which sometimes makes for penitential listening but also conjures up much of the childlike joy, the brightly shining pictorialism of a poem steeped in Italian renaissance mysticism. It would have been better if Sir William had not, by compulsion of circumstance, been so devout a Franciscan and had indulged more freely in the sin of musical variety.

*Coronation Te Deum*

1953 was the year of the Coronation of Queen Elizabeth II, which took place in Westminster Abbey on 2 June, and for this great occasion Walton contributed a ceremonial setting of the *Te Deum*, a fittingly majestic work scored for two mixed choruses, two semichoruses, boys' voices, organ, orchestra and military brass. Of the composers commissioned to write music for the Coronation service, Walton was the only one to be born in the twentieth century and, allowing for his known, if harmless asperities and innovations, his Te Deum was a strange but magnificent incursion into an event of traditional splendour and dignity. Yet, such are the rich contrasts of timbres and rhythms, the bold and lordly use of antiphony in a manner faintly reminiscent of the heavenly glories conjured up by the incomparable Giovanni Gabrieli of St Mark's, Venice, and the glowing sound-tapestry of the whole work, that of all the music specially written for the 'Queen's Grace' this was indisputably the finest.

The first antiphony, with the organ solemnly echoing the laudatory praises of the opening section which recurs at 'O Lord save the people', indicated, as did the beginning of Beethoven's 'Choral' Symphony, that something momentous was going to happen. Then followed a superb Berliozian antiphony between Choir 1 and Choir 2, the largest groups of singers, placed respectively in the north and south galleries of the Abbey. Next came antiphony between the full choir and a semichorus, culminating in the sopranos of Cantoris and Decani[1] answering each other, after which a horizontal antiphony channelled doctrinal theses between high and low voices. Orchestra and organ resumed their own antiphonal grandeur, with the different vocal and instrumental segments gradually coalescing into restrained six-part harmony, a coda based on triads for 'Let thy mercy lighten upon us' led to the final, incandescent 'Let me never be confounded'.

The pitch and range of the *Te Deum* admirably suited the high vaulted magnificence of the Abbey, and, since that beloved building is not only a national shrine but also the church of St Peter, so did Walton's quieter choral evensong passages, that could almost have been written by Christopher Le Flemyng, containing fewer 'added' dissonances than Sir William's other vocal compositions. He used quasi-recitative in block harmony, serene melismatic themes, fanfares, full-throated outbursts of jubilation and an easy brilliance of orchestration, with telling interpolations of brass and percussion. The performance in the Abbey was given, under the direction of Sir William McKie, by the Coronation Choir, the Coronation Orchestra, the Trumpeters of the Royal Military School of Music, Kneller Hall (Director, Lt.-Col. Meredith Roberts) and Osborne Peasgood, the organist.

*In Honour of the City of London*

Walton's cantata *In Honour of the City of London*, a setting of the poem of that name by William Dunbar (1465–1520) proclaiming the splendours of the city in the time of Henry VIII, is a short, rather laboured piece. In depicting old London as a place of riotous grandeur and jollity, the music, concentrating on the tumultuousness implicit in the Scottish bard's praise, not infrequently swamps his noble and stately vision. Dunbar wrote in Chaucerian English, and Walton set the existing words, unmodernized, as exemplified in the following lines:

London, thou art of townes A per se.
  Soveraigne of cities, seemliest in sight,
Of high renown, riches and royaltie;
  Of lordis, barons, and many a goodly knyght;
Of most delectable lusty ladies bright;
  Of famous prelatis in habitis clericall;
Of merchauntis full of substaunce and of myght:
  London, thou art the flour of Cities all.

There are five other verses, glorifying the beauty and the bounteous riches of the 'City of cities'. Focused broadly upon a predominantly E tonality, they are set for chorus in four parts but expanding to five, six, seven or eight as required, with a large orchestra which includes piccolo and harp but excludes the double bassoon or bass clarinet. No soloists are used.

The composer George Dyson had already set Dunbar's poem to music but had done so with a fresh melodic sweetness and restraint, spicing his harmonies with a simple flattened seventh, forming a G major triad within his basic E major. Walton, however, regarded Dunbar's vision of a picturesque, diverse London as an opportunity to write virile and compelling music. After the 'famous prelatis' have been given a plainsong greeting, against a curious *pizzicato* counterpoint faintly reminiscent of old instruments, and the merchants rich in 'substaunce' and 'myght' have been suitably highlighted by the strings, a crisp, energetic interlude plunges us into the second verse, in which the accompaniment is elaborated by a new figure based on oscillating semiquavers and a rippling arpeggio, while the chorus varies its four-part formula with a two-by-two alternation. An influx of homophonic, often exultant singing dominates the third verse, while in the fourth, 'Above all rivers thy river hath renown', we hear the gentle lapping of triplets in the orchestra as the female voices, joining again in bright, four-part harmony, sing the praises of the Thames in smooth-flowing melodic lines, after which the men salute the 'towne of townes', and the stanza ends in *a capella* eight-part harmony. Another interlude (*brioso*) prefaces a verse describing London Bridge and the Tower, which opens with the male voices and in which the music, undergoing some of Walton's 'quirky' theme transformations, bubbles with high spirits. The final stanza, 'Strong be they walls', crowns the cantata with a *Belshazzar*-like grandeur created partly by the underpinning of those massive ramparts with a sturdy ground bass, reinforced by choral unison octaves and partly by flashes of typical Waltonian inspiration, such as the heavy rhythmic deployment of brass chords in reference to 'artillery', the onomatopœic device of triplets playing on the surface of the river, and the clever suggestion of bells in the part writing, with, at the very end, an E major carillon of jubilation.

The cantata is much too strenuous for Dunbar's often reflective poem, which calls for a nobler, more spacious setting as well as for greater variety in the musical imagery, but it does provide a glowingly colourful example of Walton's remarkable flair for celebratory works of this kind.

Finally, there is the very simple, but beautiful *Antiphon*, a festive seven-minute anthem with organ accompaniment, which uses the text 'Let all the World in Every Corner Sing' and was composed for the choir of St Paul's Church, New York.

# 18

# Choral Songs

*Where Does the Uttered Music Go?*

This short, meditative, but highly elaborate piece was composed for the unveiling, by the Lord Mayor of London, on 26 April 1946, of a stained-glass window dedicated to Sir Henry Wood, in the Church of St Sepulchre's, London. With its complicated, slightly dissonant harmonies and complex scoring, the music, which expands into parts for six sopranos, six altos, two tenors and two basses, is difficult to sing, although it has a touch of nobility and the final pianissimo phrases produce a thrilling effect. Suffice it to say that the archaically bright vision suggested by Masefield's poem 'Sir Henry Wood', from which the title of the work derives and which deals refulgently, but somewhat ineffectually, with the Miltonian concept of a 'sun-directed influence', inspired Walton to create what is perhaps a clever, rather than a really memorable tribute to the great conductor.

Carols

Mild progressive dissonance also ruffles the texture of two Christmas carols for unaccompanied mixed voices, 'Make we Joy now in this Fest' and 'What Cheer?' Both were published by Oxford University Press; the first appeared in 1932, and the second, which takes its text from Richard Hill's Commonplace Book of the sixteenth century, was a contribution to OUP's first collection of *Carols for Choirs* (1961), although it was also published separately in 1962. Despite their gentle asperities, both carols show the loving, homely humanity, the simple communicativeness, that raises such traditional forms of festive song above the humdrum level of the spurious, 'olde-tyme' hybrids often foisted upon gullible listeners. Sir William would, in spirit, have warmly embraced Edmund Walters, the chorus master of Liverpool Philharmonic Choir, whose Christmas carols, full of bright, unpretentious tunes, childlike imagery and atmospheric sweetness, are among the best of their kind. His compositions, vital, sensitive and flexible, represent a living heritage.

Walton wrote another carol for unaccompanied mixed voices entitled 'All This Time', forming part of OUP's second collection of *Carols for Choirs* of 1970 and appearing as a separate publication the same year. Using a text by an anonymous sixteenth-century writer, it lasts, like the other carols, a little over two minutes in performance, and the simplicity of the vocal scoring admirably matches that of the words. Sir William also composed the brief 'King Herod and the Cock', published by OUP in 1978 in *Carols for Choirs, III.*

Put Off the Serpent Girdle

A song for three-part unaccompanied female voices, with words by Christopher Hassall (verse 1) and Paul Dehn (verse 2), this is yet another example of Walton's flair for re-cycling or re-constituting material intended for, or already used in, his own works, since the music and words of the first verse were taken from 'sketches' for *Troilus and Cressida* subsequently discarded. The song was published by OUP in 1967.

Tell Me Where is Fancy Bred

This is one of Walton's childhood compositions, a four-part song, forty-seven bars long, which he wrote in the summer of 1916, when he was only thirteen and when, to use his own self-denigrating reminiscence, he 'produced about 30 very bad works of various species, songs, motets, Magnificats, etc'. The words are by Shakespeare, and the manuscript is held by the Department of Manuscripts in the British Library (Reference Division).

Under The Greenwood Tree

A syllabic setting in three-part harmony and faintly redolent of the sound of the lute, this pastiche song for solo voice and piano is a little derivative, though charming enough with its captivating Elizabethan period flavour. Walton wrote it for a film in 1936, and OUP published it the following year. There are two separate versions: one for solo voice and orchestra, arranged by Roy Douglas, and one for unison voices published by OUP in 1964.

A Litany

Composed in 1917 as a setting of Phineas Fletcher's poem 'Drop, drop, slow tears', this was another piece of Walton juvenilia. It shows a fluency in choral part-writing that was quite remarkable for a boy of fifteen and foreshadowed the greatness of the man to be. OUP published it in 1930.

# 19

# Church Music

*Jubilate Deo*

Written for the 1972 English Bach Festival at the invitation of Lina Lalandi, the 'Jubilate Deo', a brief, impersonal work scored for double mixed chorus and organ, successfully combines the contemporary and the conventional in music, with the former surfacing immediately in the initial word-setting, which begins with an exhilarating flurried organ solo and reminds one, harmonically and melodically, of the late Herbert Howells. There are two enchanting quiet sections which contrast vividly with the more exalted passages. Towards the close of the work a little treble solo, only four bars long, soars up to a high A, and its touching tranquillity, as conveyed in the beautiful simplicity of a boy's voice, demonstrates the feeling and sincerity which Sir William brought to the piece.

Magnificat and Nunc Dimittis

Scored for mixed chorus and organ, Walton's evening canticles lie firmly within the Anglican tradition, but incorporate some of his characteristic ebullience and, with their rather marked episodic construction, spread over a total span of only seven minutes, have no recognizable idiomatic consistency or thematic development. They serve to remind us that, notwithstanding the subtle, precise and Ravel-like effects which he sometimes achieved (for example, in the *Jubilate Deo*), small-scale choral music (unaccompanied or with organ) was not really Walton's medium. The artistic impact of such pieces is generally related to the passing moment, rather than to the whole sensitory experience.

Set Me as a Seal upon Thine Heart

Walton composed a four-part anthem, 'Set Me as a Seal upon Thine Heart', to celebrate the wedding of the Hon. Ivor Guest and Lady Mabel Fox-Strangways on 22 November 1938, but, containing as it does those devious enharmonic permutations and switches which, at times, threaten his precarious hold on tonality, it is not a work suitable for detailed analysis here, although, like most of his 'difficult' music, it has endearing qualities. When Sir William uses unstable themes and a profusion of 'added' notes that make identification of either the key, or the root or the tonic, almost impossible, one feels that the inspired simplicity which was his brightest facet has been replaced by a sober, calculating efficiency of dubious profitability. The music is set to words taken from *The Song of Solomon*.

The Twelve

The first performance of Walton's noble and elaborate anthem 'The Twelve', scored for mixed voices and organ, took place in Westminster Abbey on 2 January 1966 in a concert celebrating the 900th anniversary of the founding of that great architectural glory. Intended, as the title page proclaims, 'for the feast of any Apostle', this mini-cantata, a setting of words by W. H. Auden, was commissioned by Christ Church, Oxford, because Dr Cuthbert Simpson, the then Dean, considered there was a pressing need for good anthems for such occasions. It has an introductory recitative of moving dignity, short, equally simple solo passages and a big fugal chorus which radiates a *Belshazzar*-like jubilation in the closing bars. There are intriguing hints of Britten and Tippett in the music, the middle section of which has a mystical beauty which is almost unique. The organ part was subsequently orchestrated.

Missa Brevis

Another commission, this time from the Friends of Coventry Cathedral for the Cathedral Choir, resulted in a seven-minute 'Missa Brevis', the first performance of which, scheduled for Easter Day 1966, never took place—for what reason I have been unable to ascertain. The work is scored for double mixed chorus and (in the 'Gloria' only) organ.

# 20

# Solo Songs and Song Cycles

*Anon in Love*

Unlike Robert Schumann, that master of the German *Lied* who, in 1840, his *annus mirabilis*, composed 132 songs, Walton was extremely sparing in the composition of works for voice and solo instrument; but in 1960 he set to music, under the title *Anon in Love*, a selection by Chrisopher Hassall of anonymous sixteenth- and seventeenth-century lyrics on the subject of 'Man in Love' and taken from *The English Galaxy of Shorter Poems* (edited by Gerald Bullett). Scored for tenor voice and guitar, the six songs are by no means easy for the singer: the tonality is a little unusual, and he needs a micrometric sense of pitch, especially in the highly expressive 'Fain I would change that note' and the rollicking 'I gave her cakes and I gave her ale', which has a graceful English flavour.

The words of the first three songs, conjuring decorously with pretty similes, nimble word-play and rhythmic pointing, look back to the robust Elizabethan age, when in great and noble houses madrigal-singing was a regular after-dinner amusement, like bridge today. In the other six, naïve and childlike conceits are replaced by the richer, earthier, more lustful appetites that prevailed a century later when the Italian influence had crept more boldly into the music and drama of Purcell's day.

Throughout 'Fain would I change that note', a lutenist's 'ayre' from Hume's *Musicall Humors* of 1605, the vocal compass is large, ranging over an octave and a half from D to high A, and is matched by that of the guitar, which indulges in bright harmonics. In Song No 2, 'O stay, sweet love', a recurring group of four semiquavers, framed by chords and downward arpeggios from the guitar, with various tunings of the sixth string from D to E, shape a pleasantly melodic but compact musical texture. The words are taken from John Farmer's first set of madrigals of 1599. A concise vocal tune opens Song No 3, 'Lady, when I behold the roses sprouting', and expands, through progressively wider leaps and pinpointed by a repeated semiquaver *gruppetto*, until it spans the compass of a twelfth. In the accompaniment, which hinges upon a rocking arpeggio figure, the guitar exploits a wide range of sonority. The words come from Wilbye's first book of madrigals of 1598. Casting aside the courtly graces and playful dalliance of the madrigal age, Song No 4, 'My love in her attire', a syllabic quasi-patter piece of appropriate brevity, introduces a saucier note, with the guitar flitting capriciously through a predominantly C tonal spectrum. In Song No 5, 'I gave her cakes and I gave her ale', a strophic setting of erotic revelry which prances along on a lilting 6/8 basic rhythm and in which at one point (verse 3) the voice reaches a high B flat, the guitar part preens itself like a gaudy peacock with brilliant chords, arpeggios, grace notes, tapping on the wood, and a profusion of notes. Song No 6, 'To couple is a custom', bedded largely in a sweetly diatonic A minor, is the most seductive of the set and echoes the sentiments of Shelley's 'Love's Philosophy', with the chromatic shifts so characteristic of Walton appearing in the last verse, 'Come fiddler scrape thy crowd', where, in the final climax, the voice soars a full octave. The word 'crowd' is a synonym for 'crwyth', a bowed lyre which preceded the viol. Throughout the song the guitar paces the voice with what one critic fittingly described as 'an oom-pah rhythm'.

In 1971 Walton rescored *Anon in Love* for tenor and small orchestra.

*A Song for the Lord Mayor's Table*

A pearl, an olive and a rose—small things delight us, as Paul Heyes declared, and Walton's *A Song for the Lord Mayor's Table* is also small, but none the less captivating. It lasts a mere fifteen minutes.

He had originally conceived the part of Cressida in his opera *Troilus and Cressida* for Elisabeth Schwarzkopf but (for reasons mentioned on p. 133) she felt unable to accept the part, so it was fortuitous that the Worshipful Company of Goldsmiths should have commissioned Sir William to compose this song-cycle, which he immediately recognized as a perfect setting for her beautifully expressive voice.

It is probable that the term 'song-cycle' is a misnomer: the poems, in fact, deal with different aspects of London, highlighting the appeal which the city has always had for those who were born there. The six songs, with the poetic source of the texts—chosen by Christopher Hassall—are listed below:

1. 'The Lord Mayor's Table' (Thomas Jordan, 1674)
2. 'Glide gently' (William Wordsworth, exact date unknown)
3. 'Wapping Old Stairs' (Anon., 1790)
4. 'Holy Thursday' (William Blake, 1789)
5. 'The Contrast' (Charles Morris, 1798)
6. 'Rhyme' (Anon., eighteenth century)

Walton never mastered the piano, but he used it doggedly and resourcefully throughout his life, and the keyboard accompaniment in the songs is remarkably fine, though his inspiration fails to reach a consistently high level. Song No 1, a ceremonial, pomp-and-circumstance setting of Jordan's rumbustious poem, which gives its own title to the entire work, has four verses, the second of which deploys a figure of repeated piano notes to suggest the bottles of Claret, Canary and Rhenish being uncorked—a figure which, suitably reattired, with seconds instead of thirds, reappears in the next verse. In Song No 2 the fluid music, its flow steadied by a rock-bed bass in the bottom octave (and a clearly defined sustaining pedal), does, indeed, 'glide gently'. Song No 3, 'Wapping Old Stairs', has a curious time signature of one minim per bar and a rich strumming of piano chords, against which the singer, buoyantly riding a *mezza voce* part alternating between two and three crotchets to the bar, conjures up the amorous seafarer with 'a girl in every port'. Song No 4, 'Holy Thursday', in which the interval of the major second is paramount, evokes the picture in Blake's poem of a Charity Children's Service at St Paul's Cathedral, with each of the three stanzas using a different figuration. The disadvantages of country life as compared with those of London are described in Song No 5, 'The Contrast', Walton, as a rhetorical device, frequently gives striking effect to his flighty *scherzando* rhythm by introducing short rests either in the middle of a phrase or between two apposite, linked words. Playing mostly staccato, sometimes in octaves, the piano graphically highlights the noise and bustle of the city, while sustained chords and gentle, bell-like reverberations on an E flat bring reminiscences of rural peace and serenity. Song No 6, 'Rhyme', places its opening verse over a bell *ostinato*, and the reason for this tintinnabulation, coupled with the superimposed tinkling of small bells, becomes obvious with recognition of the old nursery rhyme 'Oranges and Lemons', which comes to us in the longer version from *Gammer Gurton's Garland* (1810). The belfries heard in this musical reliquary are those of St Clement's, St Margaret's, St Giles's, St Martin's, St Peter's, Whitechapel, St John's, St Ann's, Aldgate, St Helen's, Old Bailey, Shoreditch, Stepney and Bow. The singer repeats the tune more frequently and in diverse keys, thus providing a final, happy and smile-inducing course at the Lord Mayor's Table.

The songs were subsequently rescored for soprano and orchestra.

Beatriz's Song

As mentioned in 'Radio Incidental Music', Beatriz's lovely *siciliano*-like song in Walton's score for the radio drama *Christopher Columbus* was published separately by Oxford University Press in 1974, the adaptation for guitar being by Hector Quine.

*Three Songs*

The three songs to words by Edith Sitwell which originally formed part of a set of five for voice and orchestra (*Bucolic Comedies*, 1924, withdrawn) became the *Three Songs* of 1932, written for Dora Stevens (Mrs Hubert Foss) and scored for voice and piano. Deployed initially for the speaking voice or '*parlando*' style in the *Façade* entertainment, the second and third, 'Through Gilded Trellises' and 'Old Sir Faulk', were closely adapted for a singer in the new work; but the first song, 'Daphne', which Walton thought had never been satisfactory when merely declaimed, received a completely fresh and original setting.

Three Solo Songs from *Troilus and Cressida*

The songs listed below are simply three of Cressida's arias from the opera *Troilus and Cressida* prepared for concert performance. The instrumental scoring is for triple woodwind, strings, brass and percussion.

A. 'Slowly it all comes back' (Act I)
B. 'How can I sleep?' (Act II)
C. 'Diomede!' (Act III)

The Passionate Shepherd

Several pieces which Walton composed after his early Piano Quartet have disappeared, and one of these was 'The Passionate Shepherd', scored for tenor voice and ten solo instruments and set to a poem by Christopher Marlowe (1564–93). It was never performed, and I have no knowledge as to whether the score still exists.

Other Songs

One of these, entitled 'Tritons' and published in 1921 by J. Curwen & Sons Ltd, is a setting of a poem by William Drummond (1585–1649), and the first known performance was given in a Gordon Bryan Chamber Concert at the Aeolian Hall, London, on 30 October 1929 by Odette de Foras (soprano) and Gordon Bryan (piano). The manuscript, held by OUP, bears the signature 'W. T. Walton (1920)'. As for the remaining song, 'The Winds', set to a poem by Swinburne, this was sung and played in the same concert by the same artistes, although, as Stephen Tennant (the dedicatee of Walton's *Siesta*) told Dr Craggs, it was probably performed also on 11 December 1921 at 34 Queen Anne's Gate, London, the home of his mother, Lady Glenconner. It has not been possible to trace the manuscript. Both songs are very brief—of little more than a minute in duration.

# 21

# Chamber Music

*String Quartet in A Minor*

A full-blooded composition, distinguished by Walton's characteristic nostalgia and pugnacity, as well as by some of the mellowest music he had ever written, the String Quartet creates a feeling of tension and purpose. The first movement, *Allegro*, which is the longest and most elaborate of the four, opens quietly with a flowing theme for viola, set against an important counter-subject for the second violin. With the two themes inducing a somewhat acid contrast in a slightly dissonant musical texture resulting from the use of 'wrong notes' as harmonic elements, the tempo quickens and after a change of key reaches what might be loosely called the development. After the opening theme has been rhythmically sectionalized and made the subject of a fugue, *con brio*, rising to a *fortissimo* climax in the original key of A minor, the movement ends with a gentle coda (*poco meno mosso*) over a syncopated dominant pedal.

Short and brilliantly witty, virile and alert, the second movement, a simple *scherzo* in 3/8 marked '*Presto*', which conjures up a fairy-dance atmosphere, recalls the Walton of the First Symphony but without the scorpionic sting of that towering masterpiece. In the slow movement ('*Lento*'), which falls into three main sections and is mostly muted, Walton indulges his love of the viola at some length, using it in a freely rhythmic sixteen-bar solo set against quiet accompanying chords to introduce the romantic theme. A beautifully fluid and discursive dialogue between all the instruments, with the strings revealing intimate and tender thoughts, leads to a brief, unmuted climax.

The short finale, '*Allegro molto*', illustrates Walton's rhythmic verve, deploying powerful unisons against passages of 'block' harmony and shattering the spell of sad reverie with outbursts of passion and turbulence, though relaxing the tension in a contrasting lyrical episode. A frenetic coda of bare fifths and open strings brings the work to an exciting conclusion.

In 1971–2, at Neville Marriner's suggestion, Walton adapted the piece for string orchestra, renaming it 'Sonata'. He introduced slight modifications, making direct transcriptions of three of the four movements but partly reappraising and restructuring the first movement with cuts, compressions, key changes and some minor revisions.

Quartet for Piano and Strings

An early Piano Quartet, completed when Walton was only seventeen, revised in 1921, played at the ISCM Festival in 1923 and published in 1924 at the expense of the Carnegie Trust, survived (even after being lost for two years in the post between Italy and Britain) and, although understandably a little immature in places, showed finesse, a frank, though restrained romanticism and heart-warming touches of beauty. Following a performance in Italy and one at the Aldeburgh Festival on 30 June 1973, the composer made up his mind to revise the work. It was Robert Kinloch Anderson, for many years the pianist of the Robert Masters Quartet, who implemented this decision.[1] While the piece was being prepared for an Argo recording (about 1950), he found, when tackling the keyboard part, that, because of Walton's inexperience when he wrote the music, some passages were virtually unplayable. He asked Sir William for advice and tactfully suggested some alterations of a purely practical nature. Then followed what Anderson called 'a grand singing session on the telephone',[2] in which the composer astonished the other man by recalling with great accuracy a work he had created more than thirty years before. Walton agreed to numerous small changes, all of which concerned the keyboard instrument (e.g., figurations, doublings, dynamics between piano and strings, and simplification), leaving Anderson to prepare the new version. By 1973 the original publishers of the score, Stainer & Bell, had relinquished their copyright, and Alan Frank, former Head of the Music Department of Oxford University Press, knowing of Anderson's earlier involvement with the Piano Quartet, invited him to edit a new edition of the work (incorporating the alterations) which his firm hoped to bring out. As the composer himself seemed to have lost some interest in the project, and Kinloch Anderson was, at that time, carrying heavy responsibilities as Chief Producer of EMI's International Classical Division, the revised version was not published until 1976.

The quartet, dedicated to the Right Rev. Thomas Banks Strong, Bishop of Ripon (formerly Dean of Christ Church when Walton was there), is derivative but reveals surprisingly polished, confident scoring, and, although not often played, it has a certain historical interest as the first large-scale manifestation of Walton's romanticism.

Sonata for Violin and Piano

Walton's Sonata for Violin and Piano, a work of great executive difficulty with passages involving octaves, harmonics and double stops that sweep majestically through the whole compass of the violin, has only two movements: 1. *Allegro tranquillo*, 2. *Variazioni*. He composed it in 1949 for Yehudi Menuhin and Louis Kentner; then a year later, feeling the need for revision, he wrote a final and definitive version for a performance given by these artists at the Drury Lane Theatre, London, on 5 February 1950. There are pot-boiling sequential transitions which make for dull listening, but these are partly redeemed by some ravishingly beautiful passages. The first movement, in sonata form, has a very appealing first subject, delivered initially by the violin and expanding rhetorically into a fifteen-bar paragraph against rich chords from the piano, which then plays a reflective melody of its own. Both the development, which begins with sonorous chords at the extremes of the keyboard, and the concluding coda are concerned solely with the first subject. The recapitulation is a fairly brief version of the exposition.

The second movement, full of improvisatory tunefulness and ingenious harmony, is a set of variations on a two-part expressive theme on the violin, characterized partly by dotted note figures and an ambiguous seventh in the key of E flat minor. Variation 1, *Poco più mosso*, presents the melody in 6/8 time, highlighting it with a single chromatic counterpoint. Variation 2, marked *quasi improvisando*, serves up a decorated version on the theme, with bright, sonorous chords in the piano's higher register. The spirited and march-like Variation 3, *Alla marcia molto vivace*, has the character of a scherzo. The violin gives a display of sprightly double-stopping, which is complemented by C major keyboard chords with a dissonant 'drum tap' on the second beat of each bar. In Variation 4, *Allegro molto strepitoso* where the theme is so hazy that the listener may have difficulty in recognizing it, the violin and piano play together in unison and octaves. Variation 5, *Allegro con moto*, is a brilliant *pizzicato* piece for the violin, which, rather capriciously exploring the key of A minor, pours out a continuous stream of quaver arpeggios, while the piano chatters happily away in arabesques. In this variation, which ends with a short violin cadenza, the theme can be identified more easily. Variation 6, *scherzando*, has a firmer, more definable outline and is set in the key of an Aeolian A flat, changing at the B section to E minor. Here the violin arrogates to itself the solo previously allotted to the piano. Variation 7, an *andante tranquillo*, has a 9/8 rhythm, alternating with 6/8, and is the longest section of the sonata. The muted violin plays an elaborate, wide-ranging version of the theme, highlighted by keyboard writing full of semitonal clashes and sharp resolutions which invite imitative repartee from the other instrument. When the coda is reached, the music, bustling along *molto vivace*, seems about to launch itself into a *presto* fugue but receives no real encouragement, and the two instruments conclude the piece with a B flat passage of scintillating fireworks.

Two Pieces for Violin and Piano

Dedicated to 'Vivien and Larry [Olivier]', the two pieces, *Canzonetta* and *Scherzetto*, published in 1951, last only five minutes in performance. The first is based on an old troubadour melody ('A song of Thibault, King of Navarre' from the *MS Chansonnier* Cangé 2nd Piece); the other was originally intended for, but omitted from, the Violin Sonata. In the *Canzonetta* the violin has a smooth-flowing tune, while the dotted-note rhythms of the piano, with grace notes that glitter and catch the attention, convey a charming hint of Slavic rusticity. Walton infuses plenty of light and air into the *Scherzetto*, where, against a sprightly accompaniment, characterized by open fifths, the violin sings a fetching little tune in various forms, with the piano repeating six bars of it. I have no details of a first performance.

Theme (for Variations) for Solo Cello

Since the manuscript is held by the royal dedicatee, nothing can be said about this work except that it formed part of *Music for a Prince*, dedicated to the Prince of Wales by the contributors who, besides Walton, were Lennox Berkeley, Ronald Binge, Arthur Bliss, Vivian Ellis, John Gardner, Joseph Horovitz, Mitch Murray, Steve Race, Ernest Tomlinson, Guy Warrack, Brian Willey, Grace Williams and David Wynne. It was commissioned by the Performing Right Society Ltd.

Toccata for Violin and Piano

This ten-minute work was first performed by Miss K. Goldsmith (violin) and Angus Morrison (piano) at 6 Queen Square, Bloomsbury, London, on 12 May 1925, but the publication was subsequently withdrawn. Oxford University Press hold the manuscript.

String Quartet

Walton's other String Quartet, a product of his crucial, exploratory Sitwellian period, greatly impressed Alban Berg when it was played at the first festival of the ISCM at Salzburg in 1923, but, understandably, the works was immature, and the composer soon withdrew it, although parts of the score still exist. He wrote two of the movements, *Moderato* and *Fuga*, in 1919 for his Exhibition at Christ Church.

*Five Bagatelles for Guitar*

Written for Julian Bream, the *Bagatelles* are not very substantial pieces but have plenty of charm and wit. The first reveals nimble, wayward rhythms and a flavour of acrid harmony; the second, moving along at a slumbrous pace, is both quietly romantic and seductive in the Italian style; the third is a rather sad little study in Cuban rhythm; the fourth flirts capriciously with rapid thrumming effects; and the fifth is full of darting, impetuous music. Walton embroiders the pieces with a simple, if at times elusive, tunefulness, and at the end of the voluptuous slow waltz, as if to emphasize that the sentiment is merely fun-making, the player gives a playful knock on his instrument.

*Passacaglia for Solo Cello*

Mstislav Rostropovich has inspired many composers to write music for him, and one of these was his friend Sir William Walton, who contributed a *Passacaglia for Solo Cello* and heard the great man play it at the Royal Festival Hall on 16 March 1982 for the first time in public, before a delighted audience. Although lasting only seven minutes, this expertly crafted D minor 'conversation piece' has a long, rhapsodic slow section in Walton's familiar vein of elegiac romanticism, whose shapeliness and clarity are free of any tonal acerbities. After several variations, the music plunges into a brief *Scherzo* which, alas, ends all too abruptly.

# 22

# Radio Incidental Music

*Christopher Columbus*

What is to be done with the splendidly picturesque and evocative music which Sir William wrote for the radio drama *Christopher Columbus*, so that it reaches as many people as possible and is always readily available as a complete and separate entity? Commissioned by the BBC to celebrate the 450th anniversary of the discovery of America, it was heard publicly for the first time on 12 October 1942 in a BBC Home Service broadcast. Walton's music is the stuff of which great visions and dreams are made: music impregnated with the beauty as well as the awe-inspiring mystery and terror of the sea; music burning with high adventure or seething with Court intrigue; music throbbing with heartbreak and passion; music that spreads a blazing fresco of sound across a huge visual panorama.

Walton composed the music at the request of Dallas Bower, who had chosen Louis MacNeice's *Christopher Columbus*, one of his most memorable works, as the basis for the BBC's large-scale programme, and the poet facilitated the task with a marvellously gripping and detailed synopsis. Scored for a large orchestra, a chorus and three soloists, with a guitarist, the music reveals many flashes of inspiration, and although the 'cues' are mostly brief—at times scarcely doing more than whet the appetite—they are fashioned superbly. One notes in the valedictory music that fondness for the 6/8 rhythm which came to be associated in Sir William's mind, as in Delius's, with love and the sorrow of parting. He indulges his delight in choral antiphony with dazzling brilliance, converting the simple antithesis between the 'Voice of Doubt' and the 'Voice of Certainty' into a kind of leitmotiv, creating subtle and musically valid contrasts by setting gloomy augmented triad harmony for the tenors and basses against bright, fanfare-like figures for the contraltos and sopranos.

As regards the text, MacNeice said: 'I used for the dialogue an irregular blank verse based upon the rhythms of ordinary speech but capable of being heightened or tightened, flattened or bepurpled to requirements. The lyrics on the other hand I wrote in a regular form and made very simple in sentence and imagery because they were designed to be sung.'[1] Dallas Bower, the producer, imposed no restrictions on Walton, whose orchestral and choral requirements were comparable to those which he used for *Belshazzar's Feast*. The script involved thirty-two speaking parts, and the cast, orchestra and chorus were deployed, under the direction of Boult, in the huge 'open' studio represented by the Corn Exchange at Bedford, where the first performance took place, with Laurence Olivier in the title role. The production, recorded by the Phillips-Hill process, was heard again on 8 April 1973 in the joint celebration of the BBC's fiftieth anniversary and Walton's seventieth birthday.

It is important to realize that the music is not, as in some films, a kind of off-stage Greek chorus, illustrating and commenting upon the action, but a vitalizing force that grows compulsively out of the drama and is an integral part of it. Thus, when the Royal Commission peremptorily refuse Columbus's request for sanction, the repeated shouts of 'No!', first seized upon by the chorus, gradually pervade the augmented-triad despondency of the tenors and basses, so that, as happens when land is sighted, choral speech and choral singing are properly equated. Walton negotiates the transitions between the scenes most effectively. When, for example, the drama switches from Columbus's final meeting with his lady to his farewell visit to the Prior of La Rabida, a plainsong 'Kyrie', built into Beatriz's gentle, *siciliano*-like song 'When will he return?', prepares the listener for what is to follow. Other memorable facets of the music include a lovely fragment for unaccompanied contralto, 'Three lovely ships will leave this shore', two salty choruses or shanties for Columbus's crew, full of the flapping of huge sails and the bustle of men hauling on ropes, and some glorious processional music for Columbus's triumphant cavalcade from Seville to Barcelona. According to MacNeice, the running commentaries in verse during the processional sequence were delivered with much the same tempo and punch that characterize a real running commentary spoken over the noise of a crowd on a sportsground. 'William Walton's music,' he remarked, 'served its purpose admirably i.e., it was structural.'[2] The finale of the score, an extended episode for tenor, chorus and orchestra, shows Walton the sound-painter of huge dramatic landscapes at his most inspired, using added-note harmony, trills, tremolos, bold percussive outbursts and vibrant strings to convey a sense of regal magnificence.

Oxford University Press published an arrangement of 'Beatriz's Song', with guitar accompaniment, in July 1974, but Walton rejected Christopher Palmer's suggestion that a symphonic poem might be constructed from some of the score. Now that, sadly, he is no longer with us, my fervent hope is that, as happened with the riveting music that Prokofiev wrote for Sergei Eisenstein's film *Ivan the Terrible* in 1942, the admittedly fragmented score of *Christopher Columbus* can be 'cobbled together', with skilful use of the vocal parts, to become a cogently dramatic entertainment and an exotic, as well as popular, addition to the concert-hall repertoire.

# 23

# Ballet Music

*The Wise Virgins*

Walton had a number of adventures in the butterfly world of ballet, none of them likely to conjure up a smiling, adulatory Petipa from the choreographic shades. One of his more appealing scores in the genre was composed for the one-act ballet *The Wise Virgins*, based on the parable of the Wise and Foolish Virgins (Matthew XXV), in which he orchestrated music from the religious cantatas of Bach, chosen and arranged by Constant Lambert. Not only the choreography of this enchanting ballet but also the exquisitely simple, yet highly effective sets proved spellbinding, as did Walton's very sensitive adaptation of Bach's music.

The prelude introduces a predominantly pink scene in which a beautifully decorative lamp, from which smoke drifts lazily upwards, provides an ornate frame for a large scroll, supported by angels and showing the Biblical parable. Two golden doors open to admit the Wise Virgins, followed by the bride and her parents; then come the Foolish Virgins, carrying lighted lamps. Heralded by a burst of music, the bridegroom arrives, whereupon the Foolish Virgins, who have only just lit their lamps move in procession with the Bride and Bridegroom through the celestial doors, which close behind them. A few minutes later the Foolish Virgins return and beat upon the doors for admission—suddenly they open, the latecomers are pushed back by the angels and, surrounded by the Wise Virgins and the Heavenly Host, prostrate themselves in abject penitence before the Bride and Bridegroom.

The orchestral suite taken from the music of *The Wise Virgins* was used for the ballet *Cantus Firmus*, given its first performance by the Ballet van Vlaanderen in Antwerp on 15 May 1970. And Walter Goehr, in 1950, made a clever arrangement for two pianos of the gay and exhilarating 'Ah! how ephemeral' which is part of the suite.

*The Quest*

There was also the music Walton wrote for *The Quest*, which, directed by Ninette de Valois for the Sadler's Wells Ballet, received its first performance at the New Theatre, London, on 6 April 1943, with Robert Helpmann as St George, Margot Fonteyn as Una, and Leslie Edwards as Archimago. Details of the music and plot are given in the section of this book entitled 'Other Orchestral Music', but it must be mentioned in passing that the suite, minus a couple of bars, was used, together with the Viola Concerto, for Joe Layton's ballet *O.W.*, premièred by the Royal Ballet on 22 February 1972 at the Sadler's Wells Theatre, London.

*Façade*

The German producer Günter Hess made a ballet adaptation of *Façade* in 1929, but it seems to have been not wholly successful, and little was heard of it after that. A more popular adaptation was the one choreographed by Frederick Ashton and performed in London in 1931, with Alicia Markova, Lydia Lopokova and Ashton as principal dancers. It became a much admired 'novelty' in the Sadler's Wells repertory and drew rave-notices in the United States on 13 October 1949, when the company presented it there with Ashton and Moira Shearer. The choreography consisted of nine comic episodes in front of the façade of a Victorian house.

*Siesta*

From Walton's charmingly wistful *Siesta*, scored with a sunny Italian insouciance and described under 'Other Orchestral Music', came two balletic progeny: a *pas de deux*, premièred at the Sadler's Wells Theatre by the Vic-Wells Ballet on 24 January 1936, and a second *pas de deux*, specially commissioned for his seventieth birthday celebrations and given its first performance at the Maltings, Snape, Aldeburgh, Suffolk, on 28 July 1972.

*The First Shoot*

This very short ballet was used in Part 2 (Scene 19) of C. B. Cochran's revue *Follow the Sun*, staged for the first time in public at the Opera House, Manchester, on 23 December 1935. Osbert Sitwell wrote the scenario, and Frederick Ashton created the choreography, but seemingly the score of Walton's music cannot be traced. Frank Collinson, the conductor for Cochran's production, told Dr Craggs that the music 'was of the same general character and genre as *Façade*'.

The story focuses upon a fashionable Edwardian shooting party, the first given by Lord de Fontenoy since his marriage to the beautiful

Musical Comedy actress Connie Winsome. Following a 'dance of the pheasants', Lady de Fontenoy's admirer Lord Charles Canterbury executes a dance of his own to amuse her, but they are interrupted by the rest of the party, who march around, firing into the air, then dance off to luncheon. Lord Charles stays behind, shoots at another bird and accidentally hits Lady de Fontenoy, who, dragging herself onto the stage, dies in his arms. The other guests enter and stare, wide-eyed, at the couple.

*The Triumph of Neptune*

Walton orchestrated four numbers from the Berners/Sitwell ballet *The Triumph of Neptune*, which was performed for the first time on 3 December 1926 during a season of Russian ballet at the Lyceum Theatre, London. It has not been possible to trace the manuscript or to list the numbers used.

Other Ballet Music

Offshoots from the slender ballet tree planted by Sir William include a 'Galop Final' for piano, intended, but never used, as a finale for a ballet *Devoir de Vacances*, danced to a version of *Music for Children* and staged at the Théâtre des Champs-Elysees, Paris, on 8 November 1949. It lasted a mere three minutes, was marked '*Tempo di galopio (Presto)/Prestissimo/ Presto che possible*' and was in the key of A major.

There was also the early pedagogic overture *Dr Syntax*, a highly elaborate score, according to Angus Morrison, which resulted in a title page, now held by Oxford University Press and reading: 'Dr Syntax—a ballet in one act by Sacheverell Sitwell and P. Wyndham Lewis, with music by W. T. Walton and scenario by P. Wyndham Lewis'. Morrison informed Dr Craggs that, although he could remember little about the music, he had the impression that the texture contained some passages of real Elizabethan counterpoint.

Sir William made an orchestral arrangement of the ballet music which he wrote for the Paul Czinner film *Escape me Never* and which lasted three minutes. As for that towering, high-powered and aggressive masterpiece the First Symphony, it surprised me to learn that the music was used for the ballet *Salome* by André Leclair, given its première at the Royal Flemish Opera House, Antwerp, on 18 December 1971.

# 24

# Music for Brass

It is natural that a composer born in Oldham should have perpetuated the hallowed Lancastrian tradition of the brass band (whether in large of small ensembles), and Walton contributed some interesting pieces in the genre. His flair for, and delight in, music for ceremonial occasions found suitable, though brief, fulfilment in 1959 when he wrote *A Queen's Fanfare* for Her Majesty's entrance at the NATO Parliamentary Conference, and a March for the BBC's TV series based on Churchill's *History of the English Speaking Peoples*, produced by Harry Alan Towers. Both have that feeling of 'rightness' for a special occasion, that air of celebratory brightness, which Walton conjured up with panache and not a note too many. The fanfare falls into two parts: one creates a fittingly solemn, but laudatory atmosphere; the other—an *Allegro* into which it leads directly—has an air of jubilation and sparkling vitality.

One of Sir William's earliest works for this kind of instrumentation was the *Six Pieces for Brass Ensemble*, which Noel de Jongh arranged, grouping the music into two sets, with the first containing Nos 6, 8 and 10, and the second Nos 2, 3 and 4 of the original score of *Music for Children*. Walton also composed his *Fanfares for the Red Army*, designed to celebrate the twenty-fifth anniversary of the decree setting up a Red Army of 'workers and peasants' on 23 February 1918—a commission he might have subsequently regretted in view of Russia's brutal military aggression in the so-called Iron Curtain countries. An even shorter work, spanning only one minute, was *Fanfare for a Great Occasion*, consisting of a number of isolated fanfares from the film *Hamlet* grouped by Sargent into a single piece.

To commemorate the seventy-fifth anniversary of EMI, the famous gramophone record company, Walton wrote a fifty-five-second *Anniversary Fanfare*, which, notwithstanding its miniature proportions, conveys a remarkable sense of spaciousness and dignity. With a sharp ear for programme balance and effect, he stipulated on the manuscript that the fanfare is 'to be *immediately* followed by the Coronation March "Orb and Sceptre" (1953)'. There is also the one-minute *Fanfare for the National*, commissioned by London Weekend Television, written for a programme to mark the opening of the National Theatre and with a suitable hint of the dramatic in its brief flight of rhetoric. In his *March for Concert Band* the composer used not only brass but also wind, string bass and percussion. Arranged by Gilbert Vintner from television station music written in 1962 and lasting about five minutes, this work was subsequently withdrawn. Finally there is the *Roaring Fanfare*, a short, rather jolly peroration which sounded a welcome at London Zoo on 3 June 1976, when HM the Queen arrived to open the new Lion Terraces.

# 25

# Arrangements of Music by other Composers

Walton made five arrangements of music by other composers, the earliest of which was the orchestration in the early 1920s of four numbers from the Berners/Sitwell ballet *The Triumph of Neptune*, whose delightful score, with its piquant flavour of pastiche and comedy, must have been very much to his taste. He also wrote an orchestral arrangement of the National Anthem, heard in a Royal Opera House gala programme on 8 June 1953 and, according to report (no published score is available), as moving and stately a version as one could wish for an event honouring the Coronation of HM Queen Elizabeth II. Another unpublished arrangement, once again for orchestra, was of 'The Star-Spangled Banner', and Walton prepared not only this but also one of 'God Save the Queen' for use by Herbert von Karajan and the Philharmonia Orchestra during their US tour in October and November 1955.

Published scores in the genre include an arrangement for pianoforte of Bach's Choral Prelude '*Herzlich Thut Mich Verlangen*', a one-minute-twenty-second contribution to *A Bach Book for Harriet Cohen*, which the great pianist herself performed. Other contributors were Granville Bantock, Arnold Bax, Lord Berners, Arthur Bliss, Frank Bridge, Eugene Goossens, Herbert Howells, John Ireland, Constant Lambert, Ralph Vaughan Williams and W. Gillies Whittaker.

# Postscript

It is clear from the stark, direct utterance, the heart-warming splendour and the towering, irresistible drama of *Belshazzar's Feast* and the First Symphony, that Sir William Walton acknowledged and steadfastly upheld the profound truths embodied in the following quotations:

Jazz musician Charles Mingus—

> Creativity is more than just being different. Anybody can play weird; that's easy. What's hard is to be as simple as Bach. Making the simple complicated is commonplace: making the complicated simple, awesomely simple—that's creativity.
>
> Quoted by Franz Lidz in *Sports Illustrated*

Philosopher and poet Rabindranath Tagore—

> . . . that training is the most intricate which leads to the utter simplicity of a tune.
>
> The traveller has to knock at every alien door to come to his own, and one has to wander through all the outer worlds to reach the innermost shrine at the end.
>
> From *Gitanjali* (a collection of prose translations from the original Bengali)

# Select Bibliography


Aberconway, Christabel, *A Wiser Woman* (Hutchinson & Co, Publishers, Ltd), 1966

Beck, R. T., 'England: An Account of Composers' in *A History of Western Music*, edited by F. W. Sternfield (Weidenfeld & Nicolson Ltd), 1973

Blades, James, *Drum Roll* (Faber & Faber Ltd), 1977

Bliss, Sir Arthur, *As I Remember* (Faber & Faber Ltd), 1970

Brook, Donald, *Composers' Gallery* (Barrie & Rockliff), 1946

*Busoni, Ferrucio: Letters to His Wife*, translated by R. Ley (Edward Arnold & Co), 1938

Clarke, Mary, *The Sadler's Wells Ballet* (A. and C. Black Ltd), 1955

Cohen, Harriet, *A Bundle of Time* (Faber & Faber Ltd), 1969

Craggs, Stewart, *William Walton: A Thematic Catalogue* (Oxford University Press), 1977

Cross, B., 'William Walton: The Music of *Hamlet*' in *The Film Hamlet: A Record of its Production* (Saturn Press), 1948

Downes, Irene (ed.), *Olin Downes on Music* (Simon & Schuster Inc., New York), 1957

Ellis, Vivian, *I'm On A See-Saw* (Michael Joseph Ltd), 1953

Ewen, David, *The Complete Book of Twentieth Century Music* (Blond Educational Ltd), 1961

Ewen, David *The World of Twentieth Century Music* (Robert Hale Ltd), 1969

Fonteyn, Margot, *Autobiography* (W. H. Allen & Co Ltd), 1975

Geguld, H. M., *Filmguide to Henry V* (Indiana University Press), 1973

Gray, Cecil, *Musical Chairs, or Between Two Stools, being the life and memories of Cecil Gray* (Home & van Thal), 1948

*Grove's Dictionary of Music and Musicians*, edited by Eric Blom (Macmillan & Co Ltd), 1954

Heath, Edward, *Music: A Joy for Life* (Sidgwick & Jackson Ltd), 1976

Holbrooke, J., *Contemporary British Composers* (Cecil Palmer Ltd), 1925

Howes, Frank, *The English Musical Renaissance* (Secker (Martin) & Warburg Ltd), 1966
Howes, Frank, *The Music of William Walton* (Oxford University Press), 1965
Hughes, Spike, *Opening Bars* (Pilot Press), 1946
Hurd, Michael, *Young Person's Guide to English Music* (Routledge & Keegan Paul Ltd), 1965
Irving, Ernest, 'Music and the Film Script' in *The British Film Year Book 1947–48* (Skelton-Robinson Ltd), 1947
Jackson, Gerald, *First Flute* (J. M. Dent & Sons Ltd), 1968
Kennedy, Michael, *Portrait of Elgar* (Oxford University Press), 1968
Kennedy, Michael, *The Works of Ralph Vaughan Williams* (Oxford University Press), 1964
Lambert, Constant, *Music Ho! A Study of Music in Decline*, 3rd edition (Faber & Faber Ltd), 1966
Lesley, Cole, *The Life of Noel Coward* (Jonathan Cape Ltd), 1976
Lutyens, Elizabeth, *A Goldfish Bowl* (Cassell & Co Ltd), 1972
Machlis, Joseph, *Introduction to Contemporary Music* (J. M. Dent & Sons Ltd), 1963
Maine, Basil, *Twang With Our Music* (The Epworth Press), 1957
Menuhin, Yehudi, *Unfinished Journey* (Macdonald & Jane's, Publishers, Ltd), 1976
Mitchell, Donald, *The Language of Modern Music* (Faber & Faber Ltd), 1963
Nevinson, Henry W., *John Masefield: An Appreciation* (William Heinemann Ltd), 1933
Newton, Ivor, *At the Piano: The World of an Accompanist* (Hamish Hamilton Ltd), 1966
Pascal, G., *The Disciple and His Devil* (Michael Joseph Ltd), 1970
Pearson, John, *Façades: Edith, Osbert and Sacheverell Sitwell* (Macmillan London Ltd), 1978
Pound, Reginald, *Sir Henry Wood* (Cassell & Co Ltd), 1969
Princess Alice, Countess of Athlone, *For My Grandchildren: Some Reminiscences* (Evans Bros Ltd), 1979
Quennell, Peter, *The Marble Foot* (William Collins Sons & Co Ltd), 1976
Reid, Charles, *Malcolm Sargent* (Hamish Hamilton Ltd), 1968
Salter, Elizabeth, *Helpmann: The Authorised Biography* (Angus & Robertson (UK) Ltd), 1978
Schafer, Murray, *British Composers in Interview* (Faber & Faber Ltd), 1963
Scholes, Percy A., *The Oxford Companion to Music*, 10th Edition (Oxford University Press), 1970
Searle, Humphrey and Robert Layton, *Twentieth Century Composers*, Volume 3 (Weidenfeld & Nicolson Ltd), 1972

Shead, Richard, *Constant Lambert; with a memoir by Anthony Powell* (Simon Publications, Lutterworth Press), 1973
Sitwell, Edith, *Selected Letters* (Macmillan & Co Ltd), 1970
Sitwell, Edith, *Taken Care Of* (Hutchinson & Co, Publishers, Ltd), 1965
Sitwell, Osbert, *Laughter in the Next Room* (Macmillan & Co Ltd), 1949
Skelton, G., *Paul Hindemith: The Man Behind the Music* (Victor Gollancz Ltd), 1975
Slominsky, Nicolas, *Music Since 1900*, 3rd Edition (Cassell & Co Ltd), 1949
Smith, R. D., 'Castle On The Air' in *Time Was Away: The World of Louis MacNeice*, edited by T. Brown and A. Reid (Dolmen Press), 1974
Sternfield, F. W., *Music in the Modern Age* (Weidenfeld & Nicolson Ltd), 1973
Tertis, Lionel, *My Viola and I: A Complete Autobiography* (Paul Elek Ltd), 1974
*The New Oxford History of Music*, Volume 10, edited by Martin Cooper (Oxford University Press), 1974
*The Music Masters*, Volume IV, edited by A. L. Bacharach (Cassell & Co Ltd), 1952
Thomas, Tony, *Music for the Movies* (A. S. Barnes & Co Tantivy Press), 1973
Tillis, Malcolm, *Chords and Discords: The Life of an Orchestral Musician* (Phoenix House), 1960
Vaughan, David, *Frederick Ashton and His Ballets* (A. and C. Black Ltd), 1977
Vinton, John, *Dictionary of Twentieth Century Music* (Thames & Hudson Ltd), 1974
Westerman, Gerhart von, *Opera* (Thames & Hudson Ltd), 1964
Whistler, Laurence and Ronald Fuller, *The Work of Rex Whistler* (B. T. Batsford Ltd), 1960
Young, Percy M., *A Critical Dictionary of Composers and Their Music* (Dennis Dobson), 1954
Information has also been obtained from many journals, notably the following: *The Daily Telegraph, The Guardian, The Times, The Sunday Times, The Observer, The Financial Times, The Spectator, The New York Post, The Chicago Daily Tribune, The Boston Evening Transcript, The Rand Daily Mail, The Yorkshire Evening News, The Yorkshire Post, The Liverpool Daily Post and Echo, The Manchester Evening News, The Oldham Chronicle, New Statesman and Nation, The Musical Times, Music and Musicians, The Music Review, Music And Letters, The Gramophone, Tempo, The Stage, The Listener, The Radio Times, The Dancing Times* and *Musical America*

# Reference Notes

## THE LIFE

*In the Beginning*

1. Letter from Noel Walton to Hugh Ottoway dated 11 April 1970.
2. Interview by Bob Keogh in the *Oldham Chronicle* dated 29 March 1972.
3. Ibid.
4. Letter from Noel Walton to Hugh Ottoway dated 16 April 1970.
5. Letter from Sir William Walton to Hugh Foss dated 17 May 1932.
6. Letter from Sir William Walton to Hugh Ottoway dated 16 April 1970.
7. Letter from Dr L. Russell to Dr Stewart Craggs dated 17 February 1976.
8. Ibid.
9. Undated letter, 1916 (Oxford University Press, London).
10. Walton, interviewed by Arthur Jacobs in BBC World Service broadcast, 9 December 1977.
11. *The Listener*, 8 August 1968, p. 177.
12. In conversation with Stephen Williams, *Evening Standard*, 5 November 1935, p. 7.
13. Letter dated 27 November 1918.
14. H. Anson, *T. B. Strong—Bishop, Musician, Dean, Vice-Chancellor* (SPCK, 1949), p. 117.
15. Letter dated 12 February 1919.
16. Osbert Sitwell *Laughter in the Next Room* (Macmillan, 1949), p. 170.
17. Murray Schafer, *British Composers in Interview* (Faber & Faber).
18. Letter dated 29 June 1919.
19. Letter dated 17 November 1919.
20. John Pearson, *Façades* (Macmillan, 1978), p. 181.
21. Peter Quennell in London Weekend Television's *South Bank Show*, 15 May 1982.
22. Osbert Sitwell, *Laughter in the Next Room* (Macmillan, 1949), pp. 176–7.

23. *Ferruccio Busoni: Letters to His Wife*, translated by R. Ley (Edward Arnold & Co, 1938), p. 295.
24. Elizabeth Salter, *Helpmann* (Angus & Robertson, 1978), pp. 77–8.
25. John Pearson, 'Behind the Façade' in *The Sunday Times Weekly Review*, 23 July 1978, p. 33.

*2. The Man on Horseback*

1. Sacheverell Sitwell, *Façade—An Entertainment* (OUP, 1972), pp. xiii–xiv.
2. Osbert Sitwell, *Laughter in the Next Room* (Macmillan, 1949), p. 186.
3. Ibid., pp. 188–9.
4. Ibid., p. 188.
5. Ibid., pp. 188–9.
6. Ibid., p. 191
7. John Pearson, *Façades* (Macmillan, 1978), p. 183.
8. *Vogue*, early July 1923, pp. 36, 70.
9. Cole Lesley, *The Life of Noel Coward* (Cape, 1976), pp. 77–8.
10. John Pearson, *Façades* (Macmillan 1978), p. 185.
11. Ibid. p. 187
12. John Pearson, *Façades* (Macmillan, 1978), p. 187.
13. *The Sunday Times*, 2 May 1926, p. 7.

*3. A Different Path*

1. Letter dated 21 November 1942 (the estate of the late Mr F. S. Howes).
2. Herbert Ancliffe, 'The Congress' in *The Music Bulletin*, July 1923, p. 214.
3. Walton, in the BBC's *Desert Island Discs*, 2 April 1982.
4. *The Music Bulletin*, July 1923, p. 225.
5. *The Times*, 14 August 1923, p. 11.
6. Letter from Walton to G. R. Barnes, Head of the Third Programme, the BBC, dated 31 January 1947 (BBC Written Archives, Caversham).
7. Walton in London Week-end Television's *South Bank Show*, 15th May 1982.
8. Peter Quennell. Ibid.
9. Walton. Ibid.
10. Peter Quennell.Ibid.
11. *Boston Evening Transcript*, 27 November 1926, p. 5.
12. *The Unknown Country*, by the present writer (Robert Hale, 1977), p. 150.
13. John Pearson, *Façades* (Macmillan, 1978), p. 202.

14. Ibid.
15. Ibid.
16. *The Curtain*, July 1925, p. 113.
17. *The Stage*, 16 July 1925, p. 16.
18. *Boston Evening Transcript*, 27 November 1926, p. 5.
19. *A Portrait of Sir William Walton*, broadcast by BBC Radio 3 on 4 June 1977.
20. Christabel Aberconway, *A Wiser Woman* (Hutchinson, 1966), pp. 90–2.
21. Ibid.
22. Peter Quennell, *The Marble Foot* (Collins, 1976), pp. 141–2.
23. Ibid.
24. Letter dated 12 September 1928.
25. Letter from Stephen Tennant to Dr Stewart Craggs dated 10 June 1975.
26. Ibid.
27. Osbert Sitwell, *Laughter in the Next Room* (Macmillan, 1949), pp. 194–5.

*4. Belshazzar the King*

1. Letter from Amalfi dated 2 February 1929.
2. Included in a BBC Radio 3 broadcast, *Walton in the Twenties*, on 26 March 1972.
3. Lionel Tertis, *My Viola and I: a complete autobiography* (Elek, 1974), pp. 36–7.
4. *The Times*, 4 October 1929, p. 12.
5. G. Skelton, *Paul Hindemith—The Man Behind the Music* (Victor Gollancz, 1975), pp. 97–8.
6. Ibid.
7. Reprinted in *The Oldham Chronicle*, 12 October 1929.
8. In London Weekend Television's *South Bank Show*, 15 May 1982.
9. Ibid.
10. Ibid.
11. *Daily Express*, 17 December 1929.
12. Ibid.
13. Letter from Amalfi dated 17 January 1930 (Washington State University Library, Pullman).
14. Letter from Amalfi dated 22 January 1930 (Washington State University Library, Pullman).
15. Memorandum dated 30 May 1930 (BBC Written Archives, Caversham).
16. Letter dated 4 September 1930 (BBC Written Archives, Caversham).

17. Undated letter.
18. Charles Reid, *Malcolm Sargent, a Biography* (Hamish Hamilton, 1968), p. 201.
19. *Yorkshire Post*, 14 September 1931, p. 4.
20. Letter dated 18 October 1981 (Humanities Research Centre, University of Texas at Austin).
21. *Yorkshire Evening News*, 7 October 1931, p. 6.
22. Article by Edward Greenfield in *The Guardian*, 29 February 1972.
23. Yehudi Menuhin, *Unfinished Journey* (Macdonald & Jane's, 1976), p. 122.
24. Letter dated 28 January 1932.
25. *Daily Dispatch*, 24 December 1931, pp. 1 and 5.
26. Letter dated 6 February 1932.
27. Harriet Cohen, *A Bundle of Time: Memoirs* (Faber & Faber, 1969), p. 183.
28. Letter from W. Thompson dated 3 June 1932 (BBC Written Archives, Caversham).

*5. Death and Transfiguration*

1. Letter dated 28 January 1932.
2. Undated letter.
3. Undated letter (Mrs Dora Foss).
4. Letter dated 13 September 1934 (Mrs Dora Foss).
5. Letter dated 16 February 1934 (BBC Written Archives, Caversham).
6. *Evening News*, 7 November 1935, p. 1.
7. *The Guardian*, 29 February 1972, p. 10.
8. Murray Schafer, *British Composers in Interview* (Faber & Faber).
9. Alan Jefferson in *Music and Musicians*, March 1965.
10. *The Guardian*, 29 February 1972, p. 10.
11. Undated letter.
12. John Pearson, *Façades* (Macmillan, 1978), p. 311.
13. Tony Thomas, *Music for the Movies* (A. S. Barnes & Co—Tantivy Press, 1973), p. 16.
14. Ibid.
15. Letter dated 2 March 1930 (Dr Stewart Craggs).
16. *Oldham Standard* dated 16 January 1932.
17. Spike Hughes, *Opening Bars* (Pilot Press, 1946), pp. 348–56.
18. Memorandum dated 27 November 1936 (BBC Written Archives, Caversham).
19. *Yorkshire Post*, 7 October 1937, p. 5.
20. *Musical Times*, December 1937.

*6. A Young Man Named Walton . . .*

1. Spike Hughes, *Opening Bars* (Pilot Press, 1946), p. 315.
2. Yehudi Menuhin, *Unfinished Journey* (Macdonald & Jane's, 1976), p. 158.
3. H. Dawkes and J. Tooze, 'A Conversation with Antonia Brosa' in the *Royal College of Music Magazine*, 65 (1), Easter 1969, p. 10.
4. Letter dated 18 January 1939 (Mrs Dora Foss).
5. Edward Greenfield in *The Guardian*, 29 February 1972.
6. *New York Times*, 4 June 1939, p. 5.
7. Letter dated 15 October 1939 from Ashby St Ledgers (Library of Congress, Washington DC, USA).
8. *New York Herald Tribune*, 8 December 1939.
9. Ibid., 6 February 1941.
10. Letter to Dr Stewart Craggs dated 12 January 1976.
11. Paul Jennings, 'The Music Maker' in *The Radio Times*, 7–13 April 1939, p. 11.
12. Letter to Dr Stewart Craggs dated 19 December 1975.
13. Margot Fonteyn, *Autobiography* (W. H. Allen, 1975), p. 85.
14. Laurence Whistler and Ronald Fuller, *The Work of Rex Whistler* (Batsford, 1960), p. 64.
15. David Vaughan, *Frederick Ashton and His Ballets* (A. and C. Black, 1977), pp. 183–6, 473.
16. V. Pascal, *The Devil and His Disciple* (Michael Joseph, 1970), pp. 94–6.
17. Department of Manuscripts, British Library: Add. MS 50617.
18. Letter to Dr Stewart Craggs dated 25 February 1978.
19. Letter to Walton dated 5 May 1940, sent from Ayot St Lawrence.
20. Arthur Bliss, *As I Remember* (Faber & Faber, 1970).

*7. Music for Films*

1. Hubert Foss, 'The Music of William Walton' in *The Listener*, 17 May 1945.
2. Letter from Professor Thorold Dickinson to Dr Stewart Craggs dated 9 November 1975.
3. Letter dated 27 January 1942 (BBC Written Archives, Caversham).
4. Letter dated 8 May 1941 (Department of Manuscripts, National Library of Scotland, Edinburgh).
5. Letter dated 26 January 1942 (Department of Manuscripts, British Library: Add. MS 57787).
6. Letter dated 14 December 1942 (Department of Manuscripts, British Library: Add. MS 57787).
7. Cecil Gray, *Musical Chairs, or Between Two Stools, being the life and reminiscences of Cecil Gray* (Home & van Thal, 1948), pp. 242–3.

8. Letter to Dr Stewart Craggs dated 20 December 1975.
9. Letter dated 27 February 1942 (BBC Written Archives, Caversham).
10. Ernest Irving, 'Music and the Film Script' in *The British Film Year Book 1947–48* (Skelton-Robinson, 1947), pp. 50–1.
11. *New Statesman and Nation*, 29 August 1942, p. 140.
12. Letter dated 24 March 1942 (BBC Written Archives, Caversham).
13. Letter dated 27 April 1942 (BBC Written Archives, Caversham).
14. Letter dated 26 January 1942.
15. Letter dated 27 January 1942.
16. Letter dated 28 January 1942.
17. Letter dated 30 January 1942.
18. Memorandum dated 16 March 1942.
19. Memorandum dated 13 June 1942.
20. Undated letter (probably written in July 1942).
21. Memorandum dated 19 September 1942.
22. Memorandum dated 19 September 1942.
23. Memorandum dated 13 October 1942.
24. *The Listener*, 15 October 1942, p. 508.
25. Christopher Palmer, 'Walton' in *Musical Times*, June 1973, pp. 631–2.
26. Letter dated 3 December 1973.
27. *New Stateman and Nation*, 31 October 1942, p. 288.
28. Letter from Basil Dean to Dr Stewart Craggs dated 3 October 1974.
29. *The Times*, 22 February 1943, p. 4.
30. Frank Howes, *The Music of William Walton* (Oxford University Press, 1965), p. 126.
31. Mary Clarke, *The Sadler's Wells Ballet* (A. and C. Black), pp. 176–7.
32. Letter from Michael Somes to Dr Stewart Craggs dated 20 December 1975.
33. Letter from Beryl Grey to Dr Stewart Craggs dated 31 March 1976.
34. *The Times*, 7 April 1943, p. 6.
35. Letter dated 27 August 1957.
36. Letter from John Warrack to Dr Stewart Craggs dated 17 December 1975.
37. Letter from Vilem Tausky to Dr Stewart Craggs dated 18 December 1975.
38. *The Times*, 5 June 1961, p. 10.
39. Ibid., 23 July 1962, p. 14.
40. Michael Kennedy, *The Works of Ralph Vaughan Williams* (Oxford University Press, 1964), p. 285.
41. Letter dated 7 November 1943 (Department of Manuscripts, British Library: Add. MS 56422).

42. Letter dated 23 December 1943 (Department of Manuscripts, British Library: Add. MS 56422).
43. Letter dated 22 February 1944 (BBC Written Archives, Caversham).
44. Letter dated 14 March 1944 (BBC Written Archives, Caversham).
45. H. M. Geguld, *Filmguide to Henry V* (Indiana University Press, 1973), p. 23.
46. *The Times*, 15 December 1944, p. 8.
47. *A Portrait of Sir William Walton*, broadcast in a BBC Radio 3 programme on 4 June 1977.
48. Ibid.
49. Ibid.
50. James Blades, *Drum Roll* (Faber & Faber, 1977), p. 188.
51. Arthur Bliss, *As I Remember* (Faber & Faber 1970), p. 106.
52. Letter dated 17 January 1945 (BBC Written Archives, Caversham).
53. Letter dated 26 January 1945 (BBC Written Archives, Caversham).
54. *The Times*, 5 March 1945, p. 8.
55. Translation from *Svenska Dagbladet*, 29 October 1945.
56. Letter dated 29 September 1945 (Humanities Research Center, University of Texas at Austin).
57. Letter dated 5 October 1945 (Humanities Research Center, University of Texas at Austin).
58. Letter dated 8 January 1946 (Department of Manuscripts, British Library: Add. MS 56422).
59. Letter dated 12 January 1946 (Department of Manuscripts, British Library: Add. MS 56422).
60. Letter dated 17 January 1946 (Department of Manuscripts, British Library: Add. MS 56422).
61. *The Times*, 27 April 1946, p. 3.
62. Letter dated 2 May 1946 (Department of Manuscripts, British Library: Add. MS 56422).
63. Letter dated 27 May 1946 (Department of Manuscripts, British Library: Add. MS 56422).
64. Henry W. Nevinson, *John Masefield—An Appreciation* (William Heinemann, 1933), p. 3.

*8. A Girl in Argentina*

1. Letter dated 3 August 1939 (BBC Written Archives, Caversham).
2. Desmond Shawe-Taylor in *New Statesman and Nation*, 10 May 1947, p. 334.
3. Letter to Walton from John Lowe dated 13 February 1947 (BBC Written Archives, Caversham).

4. Princess Alice, Countess of Athlone, *For my Grandchildren—Some Reminiscences* (Evans Bros, 1979), p. 275.
5. Ibid.
6. Letter dated 12 August 1947 (BBC Written Archives, Caversham).
7. William Walton, 'The Music of Hamlet,' in *The Film Hamlet–a record of its production*, edited by B. Cross (Saturn Press, 1948), pp. 61–2.
8. Ibid.
9. James Blades, *Drum Roll* (Faber & Faber, 1977), pp. 200–1.
10. *The Listener*, 8 August 1968, p. 173.
11. In London Weekend Television's *South Bank Show*, 15 May 1982.
12. Edward Greenfield in *The Guardian*, 19 May 1971.
13. Ibid.
14. Ibid.
15. Ibid.
16. Letter dated 24 March 1969 (Angus Morrison, London).
17. *Ballet*, January 1950, p. 20.
18. *The Times*, 1 January 1951, p. 3.
19. Edward Greenfield in *The Guardian*, 19 May 1971.
20. Letter dated 29 October 1952 (Arts Council of Great Britain).
21. Undated postcard (Arts Council of Great Britain).
22. Letter dated 31 October 1952 (Arts Council of Great Britain).
23. Letter dated 16 February 1953 (Arts Council of Great Britain).
24. *The Times*, 8 June 1953, p. 3.
25. Undated letter (December 1970) from Sir William McKie to Dr Stewart Craggs.
26. Letter dated 18 November 1952 (Chapter Library, Westminster Abbey, London).
27. Letter dated 17 March 1952 (Chapter Library, Westminster Abbey, London).
28. Undated letter (December 1970) from Sir William McKie to Dr Stewart Craggs.
29. *The Times*, 3 June 1953, p. 15.
30. Letter dated 12 January 1976 sent to Dr Stewart Craggs by Rosamund Strode, assistant to the late Lord Britten.
31. Ibid.

*9. Operatic Rapture from the Convent*

1. *Music and Musicians*, November 1976, p. 34.
2. Letter dated 7 June 1947 (BBC Written Archives, Caversham).
3. Undated letter (1947) (Department of Manuscripts, British Library: Add. MS 57787).
4. *Music and Musicians*, November 1976, p. 34.

5. *Music and Musicians*, December 1954, p. 12.
6. Ibid.
7. Ibid., November 1976, p. 12.
8. Ibid., November 1976, pp. 34–5.
9. *The Times*, 12 November 1976, p. 9.
10. *Music and Musicians*, November 1976, pp. 34–5.
11. Letter dated 3 March 1947 (BBC Written Archives, Caversham).
12. *The Times*, 29 January 1948, p. 6.
13. Letter from Walton to Stanford Robinson dated 28 March 1949 (BBC Written Archives, Caversham).
14. Letter dated 1 March 1950 (BBC Written Archives, Caversham).
15. *The Times*, August 1951, p. 6.
16. Letter from Henry Moore to Dr Stewart Craggs dated 14 July 1976.
17. Letter dated 24 January 1953 (Angus Morrison, London).
18. Letter from Walter Legge dated 19 October 1974.
19. Letter from Sir Hugh Casson to Dr Stewart Craggs dated 27 April 1976.
20. Charles Reid, *Malcolm Sargent, a Biography* (Hamish Hamilton, 1968), pp. 382–3.
21. *The Times*, 4 December 1954, p. 3.
22. *Manchester Guardian*, 4 December 1954, p. 3.
23. Elisabeth Schwarzkopf, *On and Off the Record: A Memoir of Walter Legge* (Faber & Faber Ltd, 1982), p. 3.
24. *The Sunday Times*, 25 March 1962, p. 39.
25. *The Times*, 14 November 1955, p. 3.
26. Charles Reid, *Malcolm Sargent, a Biography* (Hamish Hamilton, 1968), pp. 352–3.
27. *Forward* (Johannesburg), 5 October 1956.
28. *Rand Daily Mail*, 26 September 1956, p. 11.
29. *British Institute of Recorded Sound Bulletin*, winter 1956, pp. 19–21.
30. David Vaughan, *Frederick Ashton and His Ballets* (A. and C. Black, 1977), pp. 291–2.
31. Margot Fonteyn, *Autobiography* (W. H. Allen, 1975), p. 51.
32. Ivor Newton, *At the Piano—The World of an Accompanist* (Hamish Hamilton, 1966), pp. 128–9.
33. Ibid.
34. *Music and Musicians*, February 1957, p. 9.
35. *Cleveland Plain Dealer*, 31 January 1958, p. 17.
36. Malcolm Tillis, *Chords and Discords—the Life of an Orchestral Musician* (Phoenix House, 1960), pp. 128–34.
37. *The Times*, 22 June 1960, p. 7.
38. Ibid., 3 September 1960, p. 9a.

39. *The Oldham Weekly Chronicle*, 2 April 1961.
40. *The Times*, 25 November 1961, p. 4.

*10. A Song in Praise of the City*

1. Letter to Dr Stewart Craggs dated 25 April 1976.
2. Letter from George Malcolm to Dr Stewart Craggs dated 12 May 1976.
3. *The Times*, 9 March 1963, p. 4.
4. Frank Howes, *The Music of William Walton* (Oxford University Press, 1973), pp. 54–5.
5. *New Statesman and Nation*, 3 May 1963, p. 688.
6. *The Times*, 10 April 1964, p. 10.
7. Letter from W. H. Auden to Dr Stewart Craggs dated 8 December 1972.
8. *Yorkshire Post*, 9 February 1966, p. 1.
9. *Musical Times*, July 1967, p. 632.
10. *Evening Argus* (Brighton), 26 April 1968, p. 20.
11. *New York Post*, 9 December 1968, p. 72.
12. *Houston Chronicle*, 16 January 1969, p. 15.
13. *The Guardian*, 29 April 1969, p. 10.
14. *The Sunday Telegraph*, 22 June 1969, p. 2.
15. Letter to Dr Stewart Craggs dated 18 October 1976.
16. *The Times*, 29 April 1971, p. 3.
17. Letter from Marc Wilkinson to Dr Stewart Craggs dated 26 February 1976.
18. Letter dated 11 January 1976.
19. *San Francisco Examiner*, 15 January 1970, p. 23.
20. Letter from Malcolm Arnold to Dr Stewart Craggs dated 3 December 1975.
21. *Financial Times*, 29 April 1971, p. 3.
22. Article by Christopher Ford in *The Guardian*, 30 July 1976, p. 10.
23. Ibid.
24. Ibid.
25. *The Listener*, 16 June 1977, p. 800.
26. *Bath and Wiltshire Evening Chronicle*, 29 May 1972, p. 6.
27. Letter from Lina Lalandi to Dr Stewart Craggs dated 9 December 1975.
28. Ibid.
29. *The Oldham Chronicle*, 29 March 1972.
30. *The Daily Telegraph*, 14 April 1982.
31. Letter dated 20 May 1973 (BBC Written Archives, Caversham).
32. *Hi-Fi News and Record Review*, February 1978, p. 95.

33. Letter from Peter Andry to Walton dated 22 December 1972.
34. Letter from Walton to Professor Aloys Fleischmann dated 4 June 1973.
35. Letter to Walton from Professor Aloys Fleischmann dated 1 August 1973.
36. *The Daily Telegraph*, 6 March 1975.
37. *The World of Music*, Vol. 2 (The Waverley Book Co Ltd), p. 1,622.
38. Letter from John Sanders to Dr Stewart Craggs dated 29 September 1976.
39. *The Daily Telegraph* 23 March 1977.
40. Letter from Peter Hurford's secretary to Dr Stewart Craggs dated 9 December 1976.

*11. Every Man is an Island . . .*

1. *The Gramophone*, March 1982, p. 1239.
2. In London Weekend Television's *South Bank Show*, 15 May 1982.
3. Edward Greenfield in *The Guardian*, 19 May 1971.
4. *Radio Times*, 27 March-2 April 1982, p. 6.
5. *London Musical Events*, March 1951, pp. 14–15.
6. Gillian Widdicombe in *The Observer*, 13 March 1983, p. 7.
7. Elizabeth Lutyens, *A Goldfish Bowl* (Cassell, 1972), pp. 147–8.
8. Spike Hughes, *Opening Bars* (Pilot Press, 1946), pp. 316–18.
9. *Arts Guardian*, 30 July 1976, p. 10.
10. *Oldham Chronicle*, 25 February 1938.
11. *Music and Musicians*, April 1972, pp. 35–36.
12. *Musical Opinion*, November 1976, p. 59.

THE MUSIC

*14. Other Orchestral Music*

*Façade*

1. John Pearson, *Façades* (Macmillan, 1978), p. 180.
2. *The Observer*, 13 March 1983, p. 7.

*Johannesburg Festival Overture*

1. Decca LF 1170 and LF 1171 (9/54)

*15. Film Music*

*Henry V*

1. In the BBC Radio 3 broadcast *A Portrait of Sir William Walton*, 4 June 1977.
2. Ibid.

*Escape Me Never*

1. *The Sunday Telegraph*, 25 March 1962, p. 8.

*As You Like It*

1. Letter from Lord Olivier to Dr Stewart Craggs dated 23 September 1977.

*The Next of Kin*

1. Letter from Thorold Dickinson to Dr Stewart Craggs dated 9 November 1975.

*The Battle of Britain*

1. *The Times*, 16 September 1969, p. 7.

*16. Stage Music*

*Troilus and Cressida*

1. *The Guardian*, 30 July 1976, p. 10.

*17. Choral Works*

*Coronation Te Deum*

1. In cathedrals where antiphonal singing was practised, the Precentor or Cantor occupied a stall on the north side of the choir facing the altar, and this was called the *Cantoris* side, as opposed to that on the south side where the Dean had his stall, known therefore as the *Decani* side.

*21. Chamber Music*

*Quartet for Piano and Strings*

1. Letter from Robert Kinloch Anderson to Dr Stewart Craggs dated 23 March 1976.
2. Ibid.

*22. Radio Incidental Music*

*Music for 'Christopher Columbus'*

1. R. D. Smith, 'Castles on the Air' in *Time was away: the world of Louis MacNeice*, Edited by T. Brown and A. Reid, (Dolmen Press, 1974), p. 91.
2. Louis MacNeice, *Christopher Columbus: a radio play* (Faber & Faber, 1944), pp. 8–9.

# Classified List of First Performances (Including Film Premières)

*Symphonies*

| | |
|---|---|
| Symphony No 1 *First 3 movements* | 3 December 1934 at the Queen's Hall, London. The London Symphony Orchestra, conducted by Sir Hamilton Harty. Complete: 6 November 1935 at the Queen's Hall, London (BBC Symphony Concerts). The BBC Symphony Orchestra, conducted by Sir Hamilton Harty. |
| Symphony No 2 | 2 September 1960 at the Usher Hall (14th Edinburgh Festival). The Royal Liverpool Philharmonic Orchestra, conducted by John Pritchard. |

*Concertos, etc*

| | |
|---|---|
| Concerto for Cello and Orchestra | 25 January 1957 at the Symphony Hall, Boston, USA. Gregor Piatigorsky (cello) and the Boston Symphony Orchestra, conducted by Charles Münch. First London performance: 13 February 1957 at the Royal Festival Hall, London (Royal Philharmonic Society concert). Gregor Piatigorsky and the BBC Symphony Orchestra, conducted by Sir Malcolm Sargent. |
| Concerto for Viola and Orchestra | 3 October 1929 at the Queen's Hall, London (35th season of Henry Wood Promenade Concerts). Paul Hindemith |

| | |
|---|---|
| | (viola) and the Henry Wood Symphony Orchestra, conducted by William Walton. Revised version (1961): 18 January 1962 at the Royal Festival Hall, London (in a programme of Walton's works). John Coulling (viola) and the London Philharmonic Orchestra, conducted by Sir Malcolm Sargent. |
| Concerto for Violin and Orchestra | 7 December 1939 at the Severance Hall, Cleveland Ohio, USA. Jascha Heifetz (violin) and the Cleveland Orchestra, conducted by Artur Rodzinski. |
| *Façade* Suite for Harmonica and Orchestra | 7 June 1958 (BBC Light Music Festival) at the Royal Festival Hall, London. Larry Adler (harmonica) and the BBC Concert Orchestra conducted by Vilem Tausky. |
| *Fantasia Concertante* for Two Pianos, Jazz Band, and Orchestra | According to Mr Angus Morrison and Dr Stewart Craggs, this work was never completely finished. |
| *Sinfonia Concertante* for Orchestra with Piano | 5 January 1928 at the Queen's Hall, London. York Bowen (piano) and the Royal Philharmonic Society Orchestra, conducted by Ernest Ansermet. Revised version: (1943) 9 February 1944 at the Philharmonic Hall, Liverpool. Cyril Smith (piano) and the Liverpool Philharmonic Orchestra, conducted by Malcolm Sargent. |
| *Other Orchestral Music* | |
| *Capriccio Burlesco* | 7 December 1968 at the Philharmonic Hall (Lincoln Center), New York. The New York Philharmonic Orchestra, conducted by André Kostelanetz. First London Performance: 5 February 1969 at the Royal Festival Hall (Royal Philharmonic Society concert). The BBC Symphony Orchestra, conducted by Colin Davis. |
| *Crown Imperial: Coronation March* | 12 May 1937 during the Coronation Service at Westminster Abbey, London. |

| | |
|---|---|
| | The Coronation Orchestra, conducted by Sir Adrian Boult. |
| *Dr Syntax: A pedagogic overture* | This was never performed, and apart from a single page held by Oxford University Press, the original score seems to have vanished. |
| *Façade*: First Suite for Orchestra | 3 December 1926 at the Lyceum Theatre, London (Season of Russian Ballet). William Walton conducted the resident orchestra. |
| *Façade*: Four Dances for small orchestra, arr. Goehr. | A recording was made by the Raymonde Orchestra under Walter Goehr (Columbia DX 938), but there is no record of a concert-hall first performance. |
| *Façade*: Second Suite for Orchestra | 30 March 1938 at Carnegie Hall, New York. The New York Philharmonic Symphony Orchestra, conducted by John Barbirolli.<br>First London performance: 10 September 1938 (BBC Promenade Concert) at the Queen's Hall, London. The BBC Symphony Orchestra, conducted by Sir Henry Wood. |
| Funeral March (*Hamlet*), arr. Mathieson | Unable to trace. |
| *Hamlet and Ophelia* (*Hamlet*), arr. Mathieson | Unable to trace. |
| *Henry V* Suite, arr. Mathieson | Unable to trace. |
| *Henry V* Suite, arr. Malcolm Sargent | 14 September 1945 (Henry Wood Promenade Concert) at the Royal Albert Hall, London. The BBC Choral Society, the Croydon Philharmonic Society, and the BBC Symphony Orchestra, conducted by William Walton. |
| *Improvisations on an Impromptu* of Benjamin Britten | 14 January 1970 at the War Memorial Opera House, San Francisco, USA. The San Francisco Symphony Orchestra, conducted by Josef Krips.<br>First European performance: 27 June 1970 at the Maltings, Snape, Suffolk |

| | |
|---|---|
| | (23rd Aldeburgh Festival). The Royal Liverpool Philharmonic Orchestra, conducted by Charles Groves. First London performance: 20 October 1970 at the Royal Festival Hall, London. The London Philharmonic Orchestra, conducted by Josef Krips. |
| *Johannesburg Festival Overture* | 25 September 1956 at the City Hall, Johannesburg, South Africa. The South African Broadcasting Corporation Symphony Orchestra, conducted by Sir Malcolm Sargent. First UK performance: 13 November 1956 at the Philharmonic Hall, Liverpool. The Liverpool Philharmonic Orchestra, conducted by Efrem Kurtz. First London performance: 23 January 1957 at the Royal Festival Hall, London. The BBC Symphony Orchestra, conducted by Sir Malcolm Sargent. |
| March: *A History of the English-Speaking Peoples* | Unable to trace. |
| *Memorial Fanfare for Henry Wood* | 4 March 1945 at the Royal Albert Hall, London (Sir Henry Wood Memorial Concert). The BBC Symphony Orchestra, the London Philharmonic Orchestra and the London Symphony Orchestra, conducted by Sir Adrian Boult. |
| *Music for Children* | 16 February 1941 at the Queen's Hall, London. The London Philharmonic Orchestra, conducted by Basil Cameron. |
| *Orb and Sceptre: Coronation March* | 2 June 1953 during the Coronation Service in Westminster Abbey, London. The Coronation Orchestra, conducted by Sir Adrian Boult. First concert performance: 7 June 1953 at the Royal Festival Hall, London (the final concert of the Royal Philharmonic Society's Coronation series). The London Symphony Orchestra, conducted by Sir John Barbirolli. |

| | |
|---|---|
| *Partita for Orchestra* | 30 January 1958 at the Severance Hall, Cleveland, Ohio, USA. The Cleveland Orchestra, conducted by George Szell.<br>First UK performance: 30 April 1958 at the Free Trade Hall, Manchester. The Hallé Orchestra, conducted by Sir William Walton.<br>First London performance: 2 May 1958 at the Royal Festival Hall, London. The Hallé Orchestra, conducted by Sir John Barbirolli. |
| *Portsmouth Point: an Overture* | 22 June 1926 at the Tonhalle, Zürich, Switzerland (4th ISCM Festival). The Tonhalle Orchestra, conducted by Dr Volkmar Andrae.<br>First London performance: 28 June 1926 at His Majesty's Theatre, London,—played as a symphonic interlude. The resident orchestra for Diaghilev's Russian Ballet season, conducted by Eugene Goossens. |
| Prelude (*Richard III*), arr. Mathieson | Unable to trace. |
| Prelude and Fugue ('The Spitfire') | 2 January 1943 at the Philharmonic Hall, Liverpool. The Liverpool Philharmonic Orchestra, conducted by William Walton. |
| *Prologo e Fantasia* | 20 February 1982 at the Royal Festival Hall, London. Mstislav Rostropovich and the National Symphony Orchestra of Washington. |
| *The Quest*: Orchestral Suite, arr. Tausky | 3 June 1961 at the Royal Festival Hall, London. The BBC Concert Orchestra, conducted by Vilem Tausky. |
| *Scapino: an Overture* | 3 April 1941 at the Orchestra Hall, Michigan Avenue, Chicago, USA. The Chicago Symphony Orchestra, conducted by Frederick Stock.<br>First UK performance: 12 November 1941 at the Corn Exchange, Bedford. The BBC Symphony Orchestra, conducted by William Walton. |

| | |
|---|---|
| | First London performance: 13 December 1941 at the Royal Albert Hall, London. The London Philharmonic Orchestra, conducted by William Walton<br>Revised version (1950): 13 November 1950 at the Royal Albert Hall, London. The Philharmonia Orchestra, conducted by Wilhelm Furtwängler. |
| 'A Shakespeare Suite' (*Richard III*), arr. Mathieson | Unable to trace. |
| *Siesta* | 24 November 1926 at the Aeolian Hall, London (Guy Warrack series of Chamber Orchestra, Concerts). The Aeolian Chamber Orchestra conducted by William Walton. |
| Sonata for String Orchestra | 2 March 1972 at the Octagon Theatre, Perth, Western Australia. The Academy of St Martin-in-the-Fields, directed by Neville Marriner.<br>First UK performance: 27 May 1972 at the Assembly Rooms, Bath, during the Bath Festival. The Academy of St Martin-in-the-Fields, directed by Neville Marriner.<br>First London performance: 11 July 1972 at the Mansion House, London during the Festival of the City of London. The Academy of St Martin-in-the-Fields, directed by Neville Marriner. |
| Two Pieces for Strings (*Henry V*) | Unable to trace. |
| *Variations on a Theme of Hindemith* | 8 March 1963 at the Royal Festival Hall, London (150th Anniversary Concert of the Royal Philharmonic Society). The Royal Philharmonic Orchestra, conducted by Sir William Walton. |
| *Variations on an Elizabethan Theme (Sellinger's Round) for* String Orchestra | 20 June 1953 at the Parish Church, Aldeburgh, Suffolk (the 6th Aldeburgh Festival of Music and the Arts). The Aldeburgh Festival Orchestra, conducted by Benjamin Britten. |

| | |
|---|---|
| *Varii Capricci* | 4 May 1976 at the Royal Festival Hall, London (Silver Jubilee Concerts). The London Symphony Orchestra, conducted by André Previn. |
| *The Wise Virgins*: Suite for Orchestra from the Ballet | Unable to trace |
| *Film Music* | |
| *As You Like It* | Film first shown at the Carlton Theatre, Haymarket, London, on 3 September 1936. Music played by the London Philharmonic Orchestra, conducted by Efrem Kurtz. |
| *Battle of Britain* | Film first shown at the Dominion Cinema, London, on 15 September 1969. Music played by an un-named orchestra. William Walton conducted the March and Malcolm Arnold the remainder of the score. |
| *Dreaming Lips* | Film first shown at the London Pavilion, London, on 11 October 1937. Music played by the London Symphony Orchestra (solo violin: Antonio Brosa), conducted by Boyd Neel. |
| *Escape Me Never* | Film first shown at the London Pavilion on 14 October 1935. Music played by the British and Dominions Orchestra, conducted by Max Greenebaum. |
| *The First of the Few* | Film first shown at the Leicester Square Theatre, London on 20 August 1942. Music played by the London Symphony Orchestra, conducted by Muir Mathieson. |
| *The Foreman Went to France* | Film first shown at the London Pavilion on 13 April 1942. Music played by the London Philharmonic Orchestra, conducted by Ernest Irving. |
| *Hamlet* | Film first shown at the Odeon Theatre, Leicester Square, London on 4 May 1948 (as a Press preview) and on 6 May 1948 (as a world première). Music played by the Philharmonia Orchestra, conducted by Muir Mathieson. |

| | |
|---|---|
| *Henry V* | Film first shown at the Carlton (Haymarket), London, on 22 November 1944. Music played by the London Symphony Orchestra, conducted by Muir Mathieson. |
| *Major Barbara* | Film first shown at the Savoy, Nassau, the Bahamas, on 21 March 1941 and was screened for the first time in London at the Odeon, Leicester Square, on 4 August 1941. Music played by the London Symphony Orchestra, conducted by Muir Mathieson. |
| *Next of Kin* | Film first shown at the Curzon Theatre, London (requisitioned by the War Office), in January 1942, with the audience consisting of civilians and members of the armed forces holding special security passes. Music played by the London Philharmonic Orchestra, conducted by Ernest Irving. |
| *Richard III* | Film first shown at the Leicester Square Theatre, London, on 13 December 1955. Music played by the Royal Philharmonic Orchestra, conducted by Muir Mathieson. |
| *Stolen Life* | Film first shown at the Plaza Theatre, London, on 18 January 1939. Music played by the BBC Television Orchestra, conducted by Hyam Greenbaum. |
| *Three Sisters* | Film first shown at the Sala Volpi, Venice (Film Festival), on 26 August 1970.<br>First London showing: At the Cameo-Poly Cimema on 2 November 1970. Music played by the Sessions Musicians, conducted by Marc Wilkinson. |
| *Went the Day Well?* | Film first shown at the London Pavilion, London on 1 November 1942. Music played by the London Philharmonic Orchestra, conducted by Ernest Irving. |

*Stage Music*

| | |
|---|---|
| *The Bear* | At the Jubilee Hall, Aldeburgh, Suffolk (20th Aldeburgh Festival), on 3 June 1967.<br>First London performance: At the Sadler's Wells Theatre, London, on 12 July 1967. |
| *The Boy David* | At the King's Theatre, Edinburgh, on 21 November 1936. The music was pre-recorded, and the unnamed orchestra may have been conducted by Walton.<br>First London performance: At His Majesty's Theatre on 14 December 1936. |
| *Macbeth* | At the Opera House, Manchester on 16 January 1942. The London Philharmonic Orchestra, conducted by Ernest Irving.<br>First London performance: At the Piccadilly Theatre on 8 July 1942 by the same conductor and orchestra. |
| *The Son of Heaven* | At the Scala Theatre, London on 12 July 1925. The unnamed orchestra was conducted by Walton, and the timpanist was Constant Lambert. |
| *Troilus and Cressida* | At the Royal Opera House, Covent Garden, London, on 3 December 1954. The Covent Garden Opera Chorus, the Covent Garden Orchestra, conducted by Sir Malcolm Sargent. The cast included Magda Laszlo (Cressida), Richard Lewis (Troilus), Otakar Kraus (Diomede), Peter Pears (Pandarus), Frederick Dalberg (Calkas), Geraint Evans (Antenor) and Monica Sinclair (Evadne).<br>Revised version: At the Royal Opera House, Covent Garden, London, on 23 April 1963. The Covent Garden Opera Chorus and the Covent Garden Orchestra, conducted by Sir Malcolm Sargent. Included in the cast were Marie Collier (Cressida), Andre Turp (Troilus), |

Otakar Kraus (Diomede), John Lanigan (Pandarus), Forbes Robinson (Calkas), Ronald Lewis (Antenor) and Josephine Veasey (Evadne).

2nd revision (1972–6): At the Royal Opera House, Covent Garden, London, on 12 November 1976. The Royal Opera Chorus and the Orchestra of the Royal Opera House, conducted by Lawrence Foster. The cast included Janet Baker (Cressida), Richard Cassilly (Troilus), Benjamin Luxon (Diomede), Gerald English (Pandarus), Richard van Allan (Calkas), Malcolm Rivers (Antenor), and Elizabeth Bainbridge (Evadne).

*Choral Works*

*Antiphon*

20 November 1977. This festive seven-minute anthem was written for and sung by the resident choir at the church of St Paul's, New York, USA. It has an organ accompaniment.

*Belshazzar's Feast*

8 October 1931 at the Town Hall, Leeds (Leeds Triennial Festival). Dennis Noble (baritone), the Leeds Festival Chorus and the London Symphony Orchestra, conducted by Malcolm Sargent.

First London performance: 25 November 1931 at the Queen's Hall. Stuart Robertson (baritone), the National Chorus and the BBC Symphony Orchestra, conducted by Adrian Boult.

*Cantico del Sole*

25 April 1974 at University College, Cork, Ireland. The BBC Northern Singers, conducted by Stephen Wilkinson.

First UK performance: 14 September 1974 at the BBC Studios, Milton Hall, Deansgate, Manchester.

The BBC Northern Singers, conducted by Stephen Wilkinson.
First London performance: 23 November 1974 at the Queen Elizabeth Hall. The Louis Halsey Singers, conducted by Louis Halsey.

*Coronation Te Deum* — 2 June 1953 at Westminster Abbey, London, during the Coronation Service of HM Queen Elizabeth II. The Coronation Choir, The Coronation Orchestra, Trumpeters of the Royal Military School of Music, Kneller Hall (Director, Lt.-Col. Meredith Roberts) and Osborne Peasgood (organ), conducted by Sir William McKie.
First concert performance: 27 July 1953 at the Royal Albert Hall, London (59th season of Henry Wood Promenade Concerts). The BBC Choral Society, the Goldsmiths' Choral Union, the BBC Symphony Orchestra and Arnold Greir (organ), conducted by Sir Malcolm Sargent.

*Gloria* — 24 November 1961 at the Town Hall, Huddersfield. Marjorie Thomas (contralto), Richard Lewis (tenor), John Cameron (bass), the Huddersfield Choral Society and the Royal Liverpool Philharmonic Orchestra, conducted by Sir Malcolm Sargent.
First London performance: 18 January 1962 at the Royal Festival Hall, London. Marjorie Thomas (contralto), Ronald Dowd (tenor), Owen Brannigan (bass), the London Philharmonic Choir, and the London Philharmonic Orchestra, conducted by Sir Malcolm Sargent.

*In Honour of the City of London* — 6 October 1937 at the Town Hall, Leeds (the Leeds Triennial Festival). The Leeds Festival Chorus and the London Philharmonic Orchestra, conducted by Malcolm Sargent.

| | |
|---|---|
| | First London performance: 1 December 1937 at the Queen's Hall, London. The BBC Choral Society and the BBC Symphony Orchestra, conducted by William Walton. |
| *That we may never fail*—vocal adaptation of Crown Imperial | 25 April 1948 at the Adelphi Theatre. London. Peter Dawson, the Kentucky Minstrels, the augmented BBC Variety Orchestra, the Trumpeters of the Royal Military School of Music and Charles Smart (organ), conducted by Leslie Woodgate. |

*Choral Songs*

| | |
|---|---|
| 'All This Time' | Unable to trace. |
| 'A Litany' | Unable to trace. |
| 'King Herod and the Cock' | 24 December 1977 at King's College Chapel, Cambridge during the Festival of Nine Lessons and Carols. |
| 'Make we Joy now in this Fest' | This was commissioned by the *Daily Dispatch* and first published in that newspaper on 24 December 1931. |
| 'Put off the Serpent Girdle' | The music and words of the first verse were taken from 'sketches' for *Troilus and Cressida* subsequently discarded by Walton, and I do no know of any public performance. |
| 'Tell Me Where is Fancy Bred' | The manuscript of this 47-bar composition, held by the Department of Manuscripts, British Library (Reference Division) is dated 2 July 1916. Walton wrote the piece when he was a choirboy at Christ Church. |
| 'Under the Greenwood Tree' | Unable to trace. |
| 'What Cheer?' | Unable to trace. |
| 'Where Does the Uttered Music Go?' | 26 April 1946 at St Sepulchre's Church, Church, Holborn (Sir Henry Wood Memorial Service). The BBC Chorus and the Theatre Revue Chorus, conducted by Leslie Woodgate. |

*Church Music*

| | |
|---|---|
| 'Jubilate Deo' | 22 April 1972 at Christ Church Cathedral, Oxford (the English Bach Festival). The Choir of Christ Church Cathedral, with Simon Darlington (organ), conducted by Simon Preston. |
| 'Magnificat' and 'Nunc Dimittis' | 14 June 1975 at the Cathedral Church of the Holy Trinity, Chichester. The Choir of Chichester Cathedral with Ian Fox (organ), conducted by John Birch. |
| 'Missa Brevis' | Unable to trace. The performance scheduled for Coventry Cathedral on Easter Day 1966 never took place. |
| 'Set me as a Seal upon Thine Heart' | 22 November 1938 at St Mary Abbots Church, Kensington, London. The resident church choir. Organist and choirmaster: Mr F. G. Shuttleworth. |
| 'The Twelve' | 16 May 1965 at Christ Church Cathedral, Oxford. The Choir of Christ Church Cathedral, with Robert Bottone (organ), conducted by Dr Sydney Watson. With orchestral version of organ part: 2 January 1966 at Westminster Abbey (concert celebrating the 900th anniversary of the founding of the Abbey). Ann Dowdall (soprano), Shirley Minty (contralto), Robert Tear (tenor), M. Wakeham (baritone), the London Philharmonic Choir and the London Philharmonic Orchestra, conducted by Sir William Walton. |

*Solo Songs and Song Cycles*

| | |
|---|---|
| *Anon in Love* | 21 June 1960 at Shrubland Park Hall, Claydon, Ipswich (during the 13th Aldeburgh Festival). Peter Pears (tenor) and Julian Bream (guitar).<br>Orchestral version: 21st June 1971 at the Mansion House, London, during the Festival of the City of London. Robert Tear (tenor) and the London Mozart Players, conducted by Harry Blech. |

| | |
|---|---|
| 'Beatriz's Song' | This is a three-minute piece derived from the *Christopher Columbus* music, and I have no record of any public performance. |
| 'The Passionate Shepherd' | Mr Angus Morrison told Dr Stewart Craggs that he saw the score of this early work very briefly. It was never performed and was probably withdrawn. |
| A Song for the Lord Mayor's Table | 18 July 1962 at the Hall of the Worshipful Company of Goldsmiths, London. Elisabeth Schwarzkopf (soprano) and Gerald Moore (piano). Orchestral version: 7 July 1970 at the Mansion House, London, during the Festival of the City of London. Janet Baker (mezzo-soprano) and the English Chamber Orchestra, conducted by George Malcolm. |
| Three Songs | 10 October 1932 at the Wigmore Hall, London. Dora Stevens (soprano) and Hubert Foss (piano). |
| Three Solo Songs from *Troilus and Cressida* | These songs were taken from the opera *Troilus and Cressida* and prepared for concert performance—I have no record of any being given. |
| 'Tritons' | 30 October 1929 at the Aeolian Hall, London, in a Gordon Bryan Chamber Concert. Odette de Foras (soprano) and Gordon Bryan (piano). |
| 'The Winds' | As for *Tritons*—see above. Mr Angus Morrison and Dr Stewart Craggs believe that there were probably earlier public performances of both songs, but this has not been firmly established. |

*Chamber Music*

| | |
|---|---|
| *Façade* | First private performance: 24 January 1922 at 2 Carlyle Square, London. I have been unable to trace the names or collective title of the players, but Edith Sitwell was the reciter and William Walton the conductor. |

First public performance: 12 June 1923 at the Aeolian Hall, London. Dr Craggs believes that the probable performers were: Edith Sitwell (reciter), Robert Murchie (flute, doubling piccolo), Paul Draper (clarinet, doubling bass clarinet), F. Moss (alto saxophone in E flat), Herbert Barr (trumpet), Charles Bender (percussion) and Ambrose Gauntlett (cello). William Walton conducted.

Revised Version (1926): First public performance: 27 April 1926 at the New Chenil Galleries, Chelsea, London. Neil Porter (reciter), B. Macrae (flute and piccolo), Paul Draper (clarinet and bass cl.), A. Cox (saxophone), Herbert Barr (trumpet), Ambrose Gauntlett (cello) and Charles Bender (percussion). Walton conducted.

Definitive version (1942): Following the official 'birth' of *Façade* on 12 June 1923, the Entertainment appeared, over a period of nearly thirty years, in so many different versions that some confusion has arisen concerning facts and dates. The definitive version is that of the full score published by OUP in 1951. This is based on the performance given in the Aeolian Hall, London, on 29 May 1942, which included (though not in the same order of presentation) all the pieces now used in the Entertainment, consisting of a fanfare and twenty-one poems.

*Five Bagatelles for Guitar*

27 May 1972 at the Assembly Rooms, Bath, as part of a Bath Festival Concert. Julian Bream (guitar). He had previously played No 2 at the Queen Elizabeth Hall, London, on 13 February 1972 and Nos 1–3 at the BBC Television Centre, London, on 29 March 1972, as part of a television programme celebrating Walton's seventieth birthday.

| | |
|---|---|
| | First London performance of the complete work: 21 January 1973 at the Queen Elizabeth Hall, London. Julian Bream (guitar). |
| *Passacaglia* for Solo Cello | 16 March 1982 at the Royal Festival Hall, London. Mstislav Rostropovich (cello). |
| Quartet for Piano and Strings | 30 October 1929 at the Aeolian Hall, London (a Gordon Bryan Chamber Concert). Pierre Tas (violin), James Lockyer (viola), John Gabalfa (cello) and Gordon Bryan (piano). There had probably been a previous public performance, in the early 1920s, but no details are available. |
| 1st Quartet for Strings | 4 March 1921 at 19 Berners Street, London (first concert of the London Contemporary Music Centre). The Pennington String Quartet: John Pennington (1st violin), Kenneth Skeaping (2nd violin), Bernard Shore (viola) and Edward Robinson (cello).<br>Revised version: 5 July 1923 at the Royal College of Music, London (an LCMC Concert). The McCullagh String Quartet: Isobel McCullagh (1st violin, Gertrude Newsham (2nd violin), Helen Rawdon Briggs (viola) and Mary McCullagh (cello). |
| 2nd Quartet for Strings | 4 May 1947 at Broadcasting House, London (a BBC Third Programme broadcast). The Blech String Quartet: Harry Blech (1st violin), Lionel Bentley (2nd violin), Keith Cummings (viola) and Douglas Cameron (cello).<br>First public performance: 5 May 1947 at the Concert Hall, Broadcasting House, London. The Blech String Quartet. |
| Sonata for Violin and Piano | 30 September 1949 at the Tonhalle, Zürich, Switzerland. Yehudi Menuhin (violin) and Louis Kentner (piano).<br>First London performance: 5 February |

| | |
|---|---|
| | 1950 at the Theatre Royal, Drury Lane, London. Yehudi Menuhin (violin) and Louis Kentner (piano). |
| Theme (for Variations) for Cello Solo | This work, not intended for public performance, was a contribution to *Music for a Prince*, dedicated to the Prince of Wales. |
| Three Pieces from *Façade* for Harmonica and Piano | No record of any public performance is available. |
| Toccata for Violin and Piano | 12 May 1925 at 6 Queen Square, Bloomsbury, London (LCMC Spring Concert). Miss K Goldsmith (violin) and Angus Morrison (piano). |
| Two Pieces for Violin and Piano | Unable to trace. |
| *Radio Incidental Music* | |
| *Christopher Columbus* | 12 October 1942 at Bedford, broadcast in the BBC Home Service. The BBC Symphony Orchestra and the BBC Chorus, with solo singers Joan Lennard, Bradbridge White, and Stanley Riley, with guitarist George Elliott. Conductor: Sir Adrian Boult. |
| *Ballet Music* (including music by Walton adapted for ballets) | |
| *Cantus Firmus* | The Ballet van Vlaanderen used *The Wise Virgins: Suite from the Ballet* as the music for a ballet *Cantus Firmus*, given its first performance at Antwerp on 15 May 1970. |
| *Devoirs de Vacances* | OUP hold a Walton manuscript of a 'Galop Final' for piano which was intended, but not used, as a finale for the ballet *Devoirs de Vacances*, staged at the Théâtre des Champs-Elysées, Paris, on 8 November 1949 and danced to a version of *Music for Children*. |
| *Dr Syntax* | OUP hold a handwritten title-page which reads: 'Dr Syntax—a ballet in one act by Sacherevell Sitwell and P. Wyndham Lewis, with music by W. T. |

Walton and scenario by P. Wyndham Lewis.' There appears to be no record of the score being completed or of a performance having taken place.

*Escape Me Never*: ballet from the film

As part of the score which he wrote for the film *Escape Me Never*, Walton composed ballet music (piano) which he subsequently arranged for orchestra. OUP published it in 1935. I have no record of any public performance.

*Façade*: Ballet in One Act (based on the Entertainment)

Choreographed by Frederick Ashton, this ballet was premièred at the Maltings, Snape, Suffolk, on 28 July 1972, as part of a programme of opera and ballet 'in honour of the 70th birthday of Sir William Walton', and among the dancers were distinguished members of the Royal Ballet. David Taylor conducted an ensemble consisting of Bernard Richards (cello), Thea King (clarinet), Christopher Nicholls (flute), Philip Jones (trumpet), Stephen Trier (saxophone) and James Holland (percussion). The narrator was Peter Pears.

First London performance: At the Sadler's Wells Theatre, London on 9 October 1972, with the same performers.

*Façade*: Ballet in One Act (based on the First Orchestral Suite)

Choreographed by Gunter Hess and produced by W. G. von Keller, this was first performed at the Chamber Ballet Dancing Theatre, Hagen, Westphalia, on 22 September 1929. Musical Director: Fritz Volkmann.

British production: The first performance of a similar ballet, but with choreography by Frederick Ashton, took place at the Cambridge Theatre, London (the Camargo Society), on 26 April 1931. Constant Lambert conducted the Cambridge Theatre Orchestra.

*The First Shoot*

This short ballet was premièred at the Opera House, Manchester, on 23 December 1935, when Frank Collinson conducted the resident orchestra. Charles B. Cochran was the producer and director.

First London performance: At the Adelphi Theatre, London, on 4 February 1936, with the same cast.

*O.W.*

The orchestral suite which Vilem Tausky arranged from Walton's ballet *The Quest* (see next item) was used, with the exception of a couple of bars, as the music for Joe Layton's ballet *O.W.*, which also made use of the Viola Concerto. This ballet was first performed by the Royal Ballet at Sadler's Wells Theatre, London, on 22 February 1972.

*The Quest*

Under the direction of Ninette de Valois, the Sadler's Wells Ballet gave the first performance at the New Theatre, London, on 6 April 1943.

*Salome*

The music of Walton's Symphony No 1 was used as the music for André Leclair's ballet *Salome*, performed for the first time at the Royal Flemish Opera House, Antwerp, on 18 December 1971.

*Siesta*

The orchestral piece *Siesta* was used as the music for *Ballet—a Pas de Deux*, premièred at the Sadler's Wells Theatre, London (the Vic-Wells Ballet), on 24 January 1936. Pearl Argyle and Robert Helpmann were the soloists. Frederick Ashton choreographed the *pas de deux*, and William Walton conducted the Sadler's Wells Orchestra.

The orchestral score was also used as the music for *Ballet—a new Pas de Deux*, specially commissioned for 'An evening of opera and ballet in honour of the 70th birthday of Sir William Walton'.

Sponsored jointly by the Aldeburgh Festival and the Royal Opera House, Covent Garden, the first performance took place at the Maltings, Snape, Aldeburgh, Suffolk, on 28 July 1972. The soloists were Vyvyan Lorrayne and Barry McGrath; the choreographer was Frederick Ashton. David Taylor conducted the English Opera Group Orchestra.

*The Wise Virgins* — The première of this one-act ballet was given by the Sadler's Wells Ballet at the Sadler's Wells Theatre on 24 April 1940, when Constant Lambert conducted the Sadler's Wells Touring Orchestra. Choreographer: Frederick Ashton. Director: Ninette de Valois.

*Music for Brass*

*Anniversary Fanfare* — 29 November 1973 at the Royal Festival Hall, London. The Kneller Hall Trumpeters, conducted by Lt.-Col. R. B. Bashford.

*Fanfare for a Great Occasion* — 17 March 1962 at the Centennial Hall, Wayville, Australia. The London Philharmonic Orchestra, conducted by Sir Malcolm Sargent. First UK performance: 8 July 1962 in Ely Cathedral. The London Philharmonic Orchestra, conducted by Sir Adrian Boult.

*Fanfare for the National* — 1 April 1976 at the De Lane Lea Studios, Wembley, London. The Band of the Life Guards, conducted by Harry Rabinowitz.

Fanfares for the Red Army — 21 February 1943 at the Royal Albert Hall, London. Trumpets and drums of the Life Guards, the Royal Horse Guards and the Royal Air Force, conducted by Malcolm Sargent.

*A Queen's Fanfare* — 5 June 1959 at Westminster Hall, London. The State Trumpeters.

*Roaring Fanfare* — 3 June 1976 at London Zoo, where it was

| | |
|---|---|
| | played by the Kneller Hall Trumpeters (Conductor: Lt.-Col. R. B. Bashford) as HM the Queen arrived to open the new Lion Terraces. |
| *Six Pieces for Brass Ensemble*: arr. de Jongh from *Music for Children* | OUP published the score of this arrangement in 1967, but I have no record of any performance. |

*Piano Music*

| | |
|---|---|
| '*Herzlich Thut Mich Verlangen*' arr. from Bach's choral prelude | 17 October 1932 at the Queen's Hall, London. Harriet Cohen (piano). |

*Arrangements of Music by Other Composers*

| | |
|---|---|
| The National Anthem, for orchestra | 8 June 1953 at the Royal Opera House, Covent Garden (at a gala performance in honour of the Coronation of HM Queen Elizabeth II). The Covent Garden Orchestra, conducted by John Pritchard. |
| 'The Star-Spangled Banner' | Walton also made arrangements for full orchestra of both 'God Save the Queen' and 'The Star-Spangled Banner' for use by Herbert von Karajan and the Philharmonia Orchestra on their US tour in October and November 1955. I have no details of any first performances. |
| *The Triumph of Neptune* | Four (unidentified) numbers of this Berners/Sitwell ballet were orchestrated by Walton. The first performance took place on 3 December 1926 at the Lyceum Theatre, London, during a season of Russian Ballet, when Henry Defosse conducted the resident orchestra. |

I have deliberately excluded from this classified list a small number of arrangements for piano, organ and concert band. They are of brief duration and, since no details of first performances are available, their inclusion would serve no useful purpose.

# Index

(Numbers printed in italics refer to pages in the Music section)